Marine Conservation and International Law

This book provides a blueprint for an International Legally Binding Instrument (ILBI) for the conservation and sustainable use of marine biodiversity beyond national jurisdiction (BBNJ). The development of an ILBI could signify a pivotal turning point in the law of the sea by addressing regulatory, governance and institutional gaps and deficiencies in the existing international law framework for BBNJ.

This book analyses the essential components an ILBI will require to effectively conserve and sustainably use BBNJ, focusing on marine genetic resources, area-based management tools, environmental impact assessments, capacity-building and marine technology transfer. It investigates potential areas of compromise, as the success of an ILBI will rely upon the support of a powerful bloc of maritime States, principally the United States, the United Kingdom, Russia, the Netherlands, France and Japan. The participation of major maritime powers will be critical as it is their nationals, corporations and flag vessels that have the financial and technical wherewithal to undertake activities beyond national jurisdiction. This bloc of States has historically been the strongest proponent of the Grotian doctrine of 'freedom of the seas' as it aligns with their predominant interest to preserve navigational freedom for their merchant and military fleets. Accordingly, this book assesses the extent to which the Grotian doctrine continues to exert influence on the development of the law of the sea and the development of an ILBI.

Providing a comprehensive overview of this important development in international law, this book will be of interest to students, lecturers and academics of law of the sea, international environmental law and biodiversity law.

Sarah Louise Lothian is a Lecturer at the Australian National Centre for Ocean Resources and Security (ANCORS), University of Wollongong, Australia and a Barrister at the New South Wales Bar.

Routledge Research in International Environmental Law

Climate Change, Forests and REDD
Lessons for Institutional Design
Edited by Joyeeta Gupta, Nicolien van der Grijp and Onno Kuik

International Environmental Law and the Conservation of Coral Reefs
Edward J. Goodwin

International Environmental Law and the International Court of Justice
Aleksandra Cavoski

Enforcement of International Environmental Law
Challenges and Responses at the International Level
Martin Hedemann-Robinson

Marine Pollution, Shipping Waste and International Law
Gabriela Argüello

Compensation for Environmental Damage Under International Law
Jason Rudall

International Environmental Law Compliance in Context
Mechanisms and Case Studies
Belen Olmos Giupponi

Sustainable Fisheries Management and International Law
Marine Fisheries in Bangladesh and the Bay of Bengal
Abdullah Al Arif]

Marine Conservation and International Law
Legal Instruments for Biodiversity Beyond National Jurisdiction
Sarah Louise Lothian

https://www.routledge.com/Routledge-Research-in-International-Environmental-Law/book-series/INTENVLAW

Marine Conservation and International Law

Legal Instruments for Biodiversity Beyond National Jurisdiction

Sarah Louise Lothian

Routledge
Taylor & Francis Group
LONDON AND NEW YORK

First published 2023
by Routledge
4 Park Square, Milton Park, Abingdon, Oxon OX14 4RN

and by Routledge
605 Third Avenue, New York, NY 10158

Routledge is an imprint of the Taylor & Francis Group, an informa business

British Library Cataloguing-in-Publication Data
A catalogue record for this book is available from the British Library

Library of Congress Cataloging-in-Publication Data
A catalog record has been requested for this book

ISBN: 978-1-032-22890-7 (hbk)
ISBN: 978-1-032-23042-9 (pbk)
ISBN: 978-1-003-27537-4 (ebk)

DOI: 10.4324/b22996

Typeset in Galliard
by Deanta Global Publishing Services, Chennai, India

Contents

Acknowledgements

I am indebted to many individuals for their assistance and support during the writing of this book. Primary thanks are extended to my PhD supervisor, Professor Tim Stephens at the University of Sydney, for affording me the opportunity to undertake my thesis under his expert supervision. I thank him for his constant encouragement, invaluable guidance and insightful and constructive comments.

A special thanks to Emeritus Professor Terry Carney for his detailed comments and feedback.

Professor Sarah Dromgoole first inspired me to embark on this journey whilst I was completing my master's degree in maritime law at the University of Nottingham in 2015. I will be forever grateful to Professor Dromgoole for changing the course of my life and legal career. I am grateful also for the support and encouragement of Professor Howard Bennett (University of Nottingham).

Most importantly I want to thank my immediate and extended family for all their love and support throughout every step of the research and writing process. My parents, Anne and David, have provided me with endless encouragement and have always been my biggest cheerleaders in career pursuits and studies. I thank them for instilling in me a strong work ethic and for fostering my love of learning.

This book is dedicated to my parents.

Abbreviations

ABMT	Area-based management tool
ABNJ	Areas beyond national jurisdiction
APEI	Areas of particular environmental interest
ATCM	Antarctic Treaty Consultative Meeting
BBNJ	Biodiversity beyond national jurisdiction
BBNJ Working Group	Ad hoc Open-ended Informal Working Group to study issues relating to the conservation and sustainable use of marine biological diversity beyond areas of national jurisdiction
CAMLR Convention	1980 Convention on the Conservation of Antarctic Marine Living Resources
CARICOM	The Caribbean community
CB	Capacity-building
CBD	1992 Convention on Biological Diversity
CBTT	Capacity-building and technology transfer
CCAMLR	Commission for the Conservation of Antarctic Marine Living Resources
CCZ	Clarion-Clipperton Zone
CEE	Comprehensive environmental evaluation
CHM	Common heritage of mankind
COP	Conference of the Parties
COVID-19	Coronavirus disease 2019
CTCN	Climate Technology Centre and Network
CWC	Cold-water coral
DEIC	Dutch East India Company
DNA	Deoxyribonucleic acid
DOALAS	Division for Ocean Affairs and the Law of the Sea at the United Nations
DOSI	Deep Ocean Stewardship Initiative
DSF Guidelines	2008 FAO International Guidelines for the Management of Deep-Sea Fisheries in the High Seas
EBSA	Ecologically or biologically significant marine area

EEZ	Exclusive economic zone
EIA	Environmental impact assessment
EIS	Environmental impact statement
EMP	Ecosystem monitoring programme
Espoo Convention	1991 Convention on Environmental Impact Assessment in a Transboundary Context
EU	European Union
FAO	Food and Agriculture Organisation of the United Nations
G77	The Group of 77
IAIA	International Association for Impact Assessment
ICJ	International Court of Justice
IEE	Initial environmental evaluation
IGC	Intergovernmental conference
IGO	Intergovernmental organisation
ILBI	International legally binding instrument
ILC	International Law Commission
IMO	International Maritime Organisation
IOC	Intergovernmental Oceanographic Commission
IOC Guidelines	2003 IOC Criteria and Guidelines on the Transfer of Marine Technology
ISA	International Seabed Authority
ISA Recommendations	2013 Recommendations for the guidance of contractors for the assessment of the possible environmental impacts arising from exploration for marine minerals in the Area
ITLOS	International Tribunal for the Law of the Sea
IUCN	International Union for Conservation of Nature
LDC	Least developed country
London Convention	1972 Convention on the Prevention of Marine Pollution by Dumping of Wastes and Other Matter
LTC	Legal and Technical Commission
Madrid Protocol	1991 Protocol on Environmental Protection to the Antarctic Treaty
MGR	Marine genetic resource
MPA	Marine protected area
MSP	Marine spatial planning
MSR	Marine scientific research
Nagoya Protocol	2010 Nagoya Protocol on Access to Genetic Resources and the Fair and Equitable Sharing of Benefits Arising from their Utilisation to the Convention on Biological Diversity
NGO	Non-governmental organisation
NIEO	New International Economic Order
nm	Nautical mile

OBIS	Ocean Biodiversity Information System
OCS	Outer continental shelf
Part XI Agreement	1994 Agreement relating to the Implementation of Part XI of the United Nations Convention on the Law of the Sea of 10 December 1982
PrepCom	Preparatory Committee
PSSA	Particularly sensitive sea area
R&D	Research and development
RFMO/A	Regional fisheries management organisation/ arrangement
Rio Declaration	1992 Rio Declaration on Environment and Development
RSP	Regional seas programme
SID	Small Island Developing State
Stockholm Declaration	1972 Stockholm Declaration on the Human Environment
TT	Technology transfer
UK	United Kingdom of Great Britain and Northern Ireland
UN	United Nations
UNCLOS	1982 United Nations Convention on the Law of the Sea
UNCLOS III	Third United Nations Law of the Sea Conference
UNEP	United Nations Environment Programme
UNESCO	United Nations Educational, Scientific and Cultural Organisation
UNFCCC	1992 United Nations Framework Convention on Climate Change
UNFSA	1995 Agreement for the Implementation of the Provisions of the United Nations Convention on the Law of the Sea of 10 December 1982 relating to the Conservation and Management of Straddling Fish Stocks and Highly Migratory Fish Stocks
UNGA	United Nations General Assembly
UNICPOLOS	United Nations Open-ended Informal Consultative Process on Oceans and the Law of the Sea
US	United States of America
VME	Vulnerable marine ecosystem
WWF	World Wildlife Fund

Introduction

The law of the sea is one of the oldest sub-disciplines of public international law.[1] With its own distinctive principles, institutions and enforcement mechanisms it addresses a broad range of issues relating to activities in the oceans, including the use and protection of the marine environment.[2] Today, the law of the sea faces multiple and complex new challenges. One of the most pressing issues currently on the agenda is the protection of biodiversity beyond national jurisdiction (BBNJ). BBNJ is under threat from a range of pressures and is being lost at a rate that jeopardises the sustainability of marine ecosystems.[3] This could have irreversible and potentially devastating effects. The international community has recognised the need for a new comprehensive legal framework to protect BBNJ. On 19 June 2015, the United Nations General Assembly (UNGA) decided to develop an International Legally Binding Instrument (ILBI) under the 1982 United Nations Convention on the Law of the Sea (UNCLOS)[4] for the conservation and sustainable use of BBNJ.[5] The ILBI will attempt to address one of the greatest challenges of the 21st century—managing the deep ocean environment (including its ecosystems and resources) in a way that does not lead to its long-term decline and maintains its potential to meet the needs of present

1 For concise histories see Donald R. Rothwell and Tim Stephens, *The International Law of the Sea* (Hart Publishing Ltd, 2nd ed, 2016) 45–79; Tullio Treves, 'Historical Development of the Law of the Sea' in Donald Rothwell et al (eds), *The Oxford Handbook of the Law of the Sea* (Oxford University Press, 2015) 1–23; David Anderson, *The Development of the Modern Law of the Sea: Selected Essays* (Martinus Nijhoff, 2008) vol 59, 3–23; R.R. Churchill and A.V. Lowe, *The Law of the Sea* (Manchester University Press, 3rd ed, 1999) 1–24.

2 Sarah Dromgoole, *Underwater Cultural Heritage and International Law* (Cambridge University Press, 2013) 9.

3 Florian Rabitz, *The Global Governance of Genetic Resources: Institutional Change, Structural Constraints* (Routledge, 2017) 132.

4 United Nations Convention on the Law of the Sea, opened for signature 10 December 1982, 1833 UNTS 397 (entered into force 16 November 1994) (UNCLOS).

5 *Development of an International Legally Binding Instrument under the United Nations Convention on the Law of the Sea on the Conservation and Sustainable Use of Marine Biological Diversity of Areas beyond National Jurisdiction*, GA Res 69/292, UN Doc A/RES/69/292 (6 July 2015, adopted 19 June 2015).

DOI: 10.4324/b22996-1

and future generations.[6] The development of an ILBI could therefore signify the beginning of a new chapter in the modern international law of the sea.

0.1 The development of the law of the sea

The evolutionary development of the law of the sea has taken place, in large part, through the complex interplay of competing principles,[7] be it the celebrated controversy between 'open seas' and 'closed seas' that dominated the pages of 17th-century literature, or the more recent debate that underpinned the Third United Nations Conference on the Law of the Sea (UNCLOS III) concerning the Common Heritage of Mankind (CHM) principle and its application to the Area and its mineral resources. A central and persistent theme in all of these historical contests is the doctrine known as *Mare Liberum* or freedom of the seas.[8] Although this doctrine was conceptually defined over four centuries ago by Dutch jurist Huig de Groot (Hugo Grotius),[9] it is still considered 'the most fundamental doctrine of the law of the sea.'[10] Since its inception, the freedom of the seas principle has dominated humanity's relationship with the oceans and its resources.[11] As an ILBI could mark the dawn of a new era in oceans governance, a critical question that warrants investigation is the extent to which the Grotian doctrine continues to exert influence on the development of the law of the sea.

This book provides a comprehensive assessment of negotiations of an ILBI, situating these negotiations against a broader historical context by examining the BBNJ process through the lens of freedom of the seas. Chapter 2 is concerned with the question of whether Grotius' freedom of the seas doctrine continues to have significant influence in shaping the conceptualisation of contemporary ocean problems and solutions to them. It provides a critique of the freedom of the seas regime in order to demonstrate how this concept could place inherent limitations on the adoption of an ILBI that will effectively address the decline in ocean biodiversity. This book further analyses the influence of the freedom of the seas concept on the proposed content of an ILBI by assessing its particular impact on the development of a principled regime for access to, and the sharing

6 Lisa A. Levin, 'Climate Change Impacts on Marine Biodiversity and Resilience' (Conference Paper, Third International Symposium on Effects of Climate Change on the World's Oceans, 25 March 2015).

7 E.D. Brown, 'Freedom of the High Seas versus the Common Heritage of Mankind: Fundamental Principles in Conflict' (1983) 20 *San Diego Law Review* 521, 521.

8 D.P. O'Connell, *The International Law of the Sea* (Clarendon Press, 1983) vol 1, 1.

9 Garry R. Russ and Dirk C. Zeller, 'From Mare Liberum to Mare Reservarum' (2003) 27 *Marine Policy* 75, 75.

10 Rachel Baird, 'Political and Commercial Interests as Influences in the Development of the Doctrine of the Freedom of the High Seas' (1996) 12 *Queensland University of Technology Law Journal* 274, 274 quoting Thomas A. Clingan, *The Law of the Sea: Ocean Law and Policy* (Austin & Winfield, 1994) 10.

11 Russ and Zeller (n 9) 75.

of, marine genetic resources (Chapter 4) and the establishment of a network of high seas marine protected areas (Chapter 5).

0.2 The Grotian doctrine and maritime (flag) States—past and present

An overarching objective of this book is to formulate a blueprint which maps out the essential components an ILBI will require to effectively protect BBNJ. Part of this process necessarily involves examining the objections that have been raised with respect to components of such a blueprint, particularly the opposition expected from a powerful bloc of maritime actors, principally, the United States (US), the United Kingdom (UK), Russia, the Netherlands, France and Japan. The significant role this bloc has played throughout the historical evolution of the law of the sea will become evident in Chapter 2; however, for present purposes, this group will be referred to interchangeably as 'maritime (flag) States,' 'industrialised States' or 'developed States.' Special attention should be paid to this group as historically they have been the strongest proponents of the Grotian doctrine, as it aligns with their predominant interest to preserve navigational freedom for their merchant and military fleets. Chapter 2 of this book investigates whether this group's support of the Grotian tradition persists in the BBNJ negotiation process and if so, what impact this may have on the development of an ILBI.

Throughout the centuries, the freedom of the seas has generally corresponded with the interests of the dominant maritime actors of the day.[12] From the early 18th century to the end of the 19th century, the Grotian doctrine underscored a laissez-faire approach to ocean use, marked by an absence of regulation.[13] This appealed to a large group of maritime powers, principally, the UK, the US, France and the Netherlands, all of whom desired global exploration during the age of the Industrial Revolution and European expansionism.[14]

For almost three centuries, the law of the sea remained mostly customary in origin,[15] with the Grotian tradition the dominant frame of reference.[16] Grotius' *Mare Liberum* was underpinned by two main assumptions: (1) marine resources are inexhaustible; and (2) it is impossible to damage the seas by using them.[17] Both beliefs were undercut by the revolution in ocean technology, especially in

12 Richard Barnes, David Freestone and David M. Ong, 'The Law of the Sea: Progress and Prospects' in Richard Barnes, David Freestone and David M. Ong (eds), *The Law of the Sea Progress and Prospects* (Oxford University Press, 2006) 1, 12.
13 Churchill and Lowe (n 1) 2.
14 R.P. Anand, '"Tyranny" of the Freedom of the Seas Doctrine' (1973) 12 *International Studies* 416, 418.
15 Treves (n 1) 2.
16 Barnes, Freestone and Ong (n 12) 12.
17 John Logue, 'The Revenge of John Selden: The Draft Convention on the Law of the Sea in the Light of Hugo Grotius' Mare Liberum' (1982) 3 *Grotiana* 27, 38.

the 20th century.[18] As the traditional Grotian paradigm no longer provided an adequate legal order for the seas and oceans, the international community began the process of codifying existing customary norms and to progressively develop the law.[19] The modern international law of the sea is therefore largely the product of the 20th century and the series of conferences and conventions held from the 1930s onwards.[20] Most notable among these were the UN's three diplomatic conferences on the law of the sea. The first two conferences produced mixed outcomes. The first resulted in the four Geneva Conventions of 1958 but no comprehensive order for the oceans,[21] while the second ended with no agreement at all. In contrast the third conference involved a remarkable redemption for the law of the sea, culminating in the adoption of UNCLOS, which remains the pre-eminent framework for the contemporary law of the sea.[22] Significantly, under UNCLOS, the scope of the freedom of the seas concept was limited both geographically and functionally.[23]

While some delegations arrived at UNCLOS III with the explicit intention of burying the Grotian doctrine,[24] maritime States, as a political grouping,[25] 'recounted and reasserted the virtues of the freedom of the seas as a time-honoured principle.'[26] Driven by concerns of creeping jurisdiction and the erosion of high seas freedoms, maritime powers used the Grotian concept to counter

18 Ibid.

19 Barnes, Freestone and Ong (n 12) 13; Hugo Caminos and Michael R. Molitor, 'Progressive Development of International Law and the Package Deal' (1985) 79(4) *American Journal of International Law* 871, 871.

20 Dromgoole (n 2) 9.

21 Convention on the High Seas, opened for signature 29 April 1958, 450 UNTS 82 (entered into force 30 September 1962); Convention on the Territorial Sea and the Contiguous Zone, opened for signature 29 April 1958, 516 UNTS 205 (entered into force 10 September 1964); Convention on the Continental Shelf, opened for signature 29 April 1958, 499 UNTS 311 (entered into force 10 June 1964); Convention on Fishing and Conservation of Living Resources of the High Seas, opened for signature 29 April 1958, 559 UNTS 285 (entered into force 20 March 1966).

22 Dromgoole (n 2) 10.

23 Michaela Young, 'Then and Now: Reappraising Freedom of the Seas in Modern Law of the Sea' (2016) 47(2) *Ocean Development & International Law* 165, 180. See, also, Chapter 2, Section 2.2.3.

24 At UNCLOS III, Ambassador J Alan Beesley from Canada quipped that he comes to bury Grotius, not to praise him—see Bernard H. Oxman, 'The Territorial Temptation: A Siren Song at Sea' (2006) 100(4) *The American Journal of International Law* 830, 832.

25 Maritime states formed a group during the UN Seabed Committee meetings (1971 to 1973) and were active, both prior to and during all three UN conferences on the law of the sea. The members included France, the Federal Republic of Germany, Greece, Japan, Liberia, Norway, Panama, the USSR, the UK and the US. During UNCLOS III, there was also a group of five 'Great Maritime Powers' namely, France, Japan, the UK, the US and the USSR. See, generally, Myron H. Nordquist, *United Nations Convention on the Law of the Sea, 1982: A Commentary* (Martinus Nijhoff, 1985) vol I, 79–80.

26 Ram P. Anand, 'Freedom of the Seas: Past, Present and Future' in Hugo Caminos (ed), *Law of the Sea* (Ashgate, 2001) 261, 273.

attempts to extend coastal State jurisdiction further offshore.[27] For example, Greece and other Mediterranean States proposed that a coastal State's sovereign rights over the continental shelf be extended to include cultural resources.[28] Notably, this proposal was blocked by three maritime powers: the US, the UK and the Netherlands.[29] They opposed this extension on the basis that it could 'pave the way for other exceptions, favouring creeping jurisdiction and, ultimately, lead to a regime of full coastal State sovereignty over the continental shelf,'[30] thereby further eroding the Grotian tradition. Maritime States also advanced the Grotian principle to defend their rights to exploit deep-seabed mineral resources and to oppose them being declared CHM.[31] These examples and others are canvassed in Chapter 2 which traces the historical bond that exists between the Grotian doctrine and maritime States This historical analysis is carried out in order to address a key question, namely, to what extent (if any) does the Grotian legacy remain in the mindset of maritime States and continue to condition their position in multilateral treaty negotiations, including the BBNJ process.

Arguably, to be effective, an ILBI will need to gain the support of maritime States, as it is their nationals, corporations and flag vessels that have the technical and financial resources to undertake activities in areas beyond national jurisdiction (ABNJ). For example, France, the UK, Norway and the Netherlands are among the top ten countries to benefit from access to technologies required to explore the ocean's genetic reservoir.[32] Moreover, the US, Germany and Japan account for 70 per cent of patent claims associated with marine genes, including some from international waters.[33] If this group remains outside the ILBI regime, can it be truly effective? Inevitably, as was the case with UNCLOS, the ultimate success of an ILBI will rely on the participation of this bloc of States. As delegations enter what could be the tail-end of the BBNJ negotiation process, this bloc continues to hold serious concerns about the development of an ILBI. These concerns include the impact an ILBI's regulatory framework might have on general principles of ocean governance and the scope of its relationship with its parent treaty, UNCLOS.

UNCLOS enshrines a delicate balance between the rights and jurisdiction of coastal States and flag States, and this balance is a fundamental element of the

27 Kirsten Selvig, 'Expensive Freedom: Establishing Marine Protected Areas on the Open Ocean Requires an End to the Freedom of the Seas' (2013) 22(3) *Minnesota Journal of International Law* 35, 41.

28 Lucius Caflisch, 'Submarine Antiquities and the International Law of the Sea' (1982) 13 *Netherlands Yearbook of International Law* 3, 16–17.

29 Ibid.

30 Ibid.

31 Brown (n 7) 523.

32 Sophie Arnaud-Haond, Jesus M. Arrieta and Carlos M. Duarte, 'Marine Biodiversity and Gene Patents' (25 March 2011) 331 *Science* 1521, 1521.

33 Ibid.

package deal created at UNCLOS III.[34] That package deal was intended to be one that would endure over time. UNCLOS was also careful to strike a number of checks and balances to maintain an equilibrium between its three core principles: freedom of the seas, sovereignty of coastal States and CHM.[35] Thus, should an ILBI depart significantly from the UNCLOS regime or be seen to modify its balance of rights and obligations, it is unlikely to gain support from maritime States. After all, it was an achievement even to get the BBNJ process off the ground, with some States, including the US, Canada, Japan, Korea, Iceland, Norway and Russia, all reluctant to open negotiations for an ILBI.[36] This group argued that a new global instrument could interfere with existing regional and sectoral arrangements in ABNJ and that better implementation of existing instruments would suffice to address BBNJ issues.[37] The position of maritime States therefore warrants particular consideration in this book, not only because they have shown resistance to the development of an ILBI, but because they have traditionally gravitated towards the Grotian doctrine to support their own interests. In turn, this raises the prospect of the BBNJ process getting bogged down in long-standing historical debates, in particular, the ongoing clash between the competing principles of the freedom of the high seas versus the CHM when it comes to the management of oceanic resources.

0.3 Is the BBNJ process a case of history repeating itself?

The debate at UNCLOS III concerning the legal status of the Area and its mineral resources saw a clash between the competing principles of the freedom of the high seas versus the CHM. This battle is playing out again in real-time in the BBNJ process in respect to marine genetic resources (MGRs) of ABNJ. Chapter 2 undertakes a comparative analysis of the ongoing MGR debate and the contest of principles at UNCLOS III. It is evident from this analysis that the arguments pro and contra the freedom of the seas then and now are strikingly similar.[38] This comparative analysis raises another important question in this book as to whether the BBNJ process is a case of history repeating itself,

34 Sarah Dromgoole, 'Reflections on the Position of the Major Maritime Powers with Respect to the UNESCO Convention on the Protection of the Underwater Cultural Heritage 2001' (2013) 38 *Marine Policy* 116, 119 ('Reflections').

35 Helmut Tuerk, 'The Legal Regime of Maritime Areas and the Waning Freedom of the Seas' (Conference Paper, Maritime Issues and United Nations Convention on the Laws of the Sea: Sharing European and Asia Approaches to Territorial Disputes, 4–5 June 2015).

36 See Karen Alvarenga et al, 'Summary of the Working Group on Marine Biodiversity beyond Areas of National Jurisdiction: 13–17 February 2006' *Earth Negotiations Bulletin* (Online Bulletin, 20 February 2006) 8 <https://enb.iisd.org/download/pdf/enb2525e.pdf>.

37 Tullio Scovazzi, 'The Rights to Genetic Resources beyond National Jurisdiction: Challenges for the Ongoing Negotiations at the United Nations' in Catherine Banet (ed) *The Law of the Seabed* (Brill Nijhoff, 2020) 213, 214; Julien Rochette et al, 'A New Chapter for the High Seas?' (Working Paper, Institute for Advanced Sustainability Studies, April 2015) 5.

38 O'Connell (n 8) 2.

with the ancient Grotian doctrine once again at the centre of a very modern dispute.

If the BBNJ negotiations are a case of history repeating, could this mean that the BBNJ process is on track to mirror the outcome at UNCLOS III and that of other negotiations, including the 2001 UNESCO Convention on the Protection of the Underwater Cultural Heritage?[39] In both of those cases, major maritime States exerted considerable influence during the negotiation process, resulting in concessions being made in their favour and provisions being included or removed to appease their views, yet ultimately, they were still not satisfied with the outcome leading to them either abstaining from the vote, or voting against the adoption of the relevant instrument.[40] Take UNCLOS as an example. UNCLOS had the overriding aim of universal participation. However, when it came time to adopt the UNCLOS text in 1982 a large bloc of developed States held back from signing it, mainly due to issues with the Part XI deep-sea mining regime.[41] The impetus to achieve universal participation was the reason UN Secretary General, Javier Perez de Cuellar, convened a series of informal consultations between 1990 and 1994 to resolve areas of concern.[42] The outcome was the 1994 Agreement relating to the Implementation of Part XI (Part XI Agreement) which effectively rewrote aspects of the deep-seabed mining regime.[43] It became clear that the success of UNCLOS relied on the participation of key maritime States and to enable this participation there would need to be a careful balancing of competing interests. Arguably the same reasoning must now be applied in the BBNJ context. The development of an ILBI will require compromise among different competing interests regarding the protection and use of BBNJ.

0.4 Building bridges between competing positions

A running theme throughout this book is the identification and proposal of potential areas of compromise in a quest to build bridges between the competing positions that have surfaced in the BBNJ negotiation process. This is carried out in an effort to find ways that maritime States may participate fully in an ILBI. The

39 Convention on the Protection of the Underwater Cultural Heritage, opened for signature 2 November 2001, 2562 UNTS 1 (entered into force 2 January 2009).

40 Dromgoole, 'Reflections' (n 34) 116.

41 The US voted against its adoption and 17 states abstained, including the German Democratic Republic, the Federal Republic of Germany, Italy, Belgium, Netherlands, Spain, the USSR and the UK.

42 Division for Ocean Affairs and the Law of the Sea, 'The United Nations Convention on the Law of the Sea: A Historical Perspective' Oceans and Law of the Sea United Nations (Web Page) <https://www.un.org/Depts/los/convention_agreements/convention_historical_perspective.htm>.

43 Agreement relating to the Implementation of Part XI of the United Nations Convention on the Law of the Sea of 10 December 1984, opened for signature 16 November 1994, (1994) 33 ILM 1309 (entered into force 28 July 1996).

analysis undertaken in Chapter 2 reveals that the fear of further erosion of the Grotian doctrine continues to drive and underlie the position of maritime States in the BBNJ negotiations. Accordingly, in order to secure universal acceptance, this book maintains that the ILBI will need to be underpinned by a series of macro and micro compromises, carefully designed to appeal to the interests of maritime States, while at the same time promoting the protection of BBNJ. Given the historical attachment of maritime States with the Grotian doctrine, elements of the freedom of the seas concept will need to be carefully woven through the fabric of the ILBI text. This is achievable as the freedom of the seas concept is neither absolute nor static.[44] As O'Connell observed the freedom of the seas 'embodies the balance of jurisdictional functions among States which at any time best serve the community of nations, and its content is subject to constant modification as that community adjusts itself to the solution of new problems' in the law of the sea.[45]

Chapters 4 to 7 of this book investigate potential compromise solutions for the four thematic topics of the BBNJ package deal consisting of:

1. MGRs including questions on the sharing of benefits;
2. Measures such as area-based management tools (ABMTs), including marine protected areas (MPAs);
3. Environmental impact assessments (EIAs);
4. Capacity-building and the transfer of marine technology (CBTT).

0.5 Understanding the essential components of an ILBI

Aside from investigating areas of compromise, the other overarching objective of this book is to understand and analyse the essential components an ILBI will require to effectively conserve and sustainably use BBNJ. Chapters 3 to 7 adopt a primarily doctrinal and textual approach to examine the existing law and assess the adequacy of emerging frameworks. The following provides a brief overview of the issues addressed in each of these chapters.

0.6 A principled backbone

Chapter 3 concerns an important component of the ILBI, which is often overlooked, and that is the role of modern governance principles and tools. Since the 1970s a suite of general principles and legal concepts directed towards the preservation and enhanced protection of the natural environment have emerged. This is largely due to the development of modern environmental law and a number of key international conferences including the 1972 UN Conference

44 O'Connell (n 8) vol 2, 796.
45 Ibid, 796–797.

on the Human Environment (Stockholm Conference),[46] UNCLOS III and the 1992 Rio Conference.[47] The instruments, declarations and actions plans of these conferences have played a significant role in the introduction of modern governance concepts, many of which have gone on to influence UNCLOS and general international law.

Over the last few decades, modern governance principles and approaches have gradually seeped into the preambles and operative parts of ocean-related treaties and policy initiatives. For example, the ecosystem approach is the 'primary framework of action' for addressing the objectives of the 1992 Convention on Biological Diversity (CBD).[48] Currently, however, no standalone declaration of principles for ABNJ exists.[49] Moreover, under the existing law framework for ABNJ, the responsibility for implementing governance tools is dispersed among global, regional and sectoral organisations with no overarching mechanism to ensure these tools are consistently applied in all regions and across all sectors.[50]

While the development of an ILBI presents an opportunity to consolidate and reaffirm relevant governance tools under the one instrument, this book maintains that the real challenge will be determining how to effectively implement and operationalise these tools under an ILBI. Chapter 3 uses four core concepts as analytical tools to consider the potential role of modern governance concepts in an ILBI and to highlight current implementation gaps. These concepts are (1) the protection and preservation of the marine environment, (2) the ecosystem approach, (3) the precautionary principle and (4) the integration approach. In exploring the benefits to be derived from adopting a principle-based approach to ocean governance in ABNJ, Chapter 3 proposes two critical functions for governance tools under an ILBI and suggests ways the package deal elements could be used to implement and operationalise these tools. Chapter 3 contends that an ILBI will require a strong and principled backbone, one that underpins the interpretation of the instrument as a whole and also the implementation and operationalisation of the four corners of the BBNJ package deal.

46 Declaration of the United Nations Conference on the Human Environment, UN Doc A/CONF.48/14/Rev.1 (1973), (1972) 11 ILM 1416 (Stockholm Declaration).

47 United Nations Declaration on Environment and Development, UN Doc A/CONF.151/5/Rev.1 (1992) (Rio Declaration).

48 Convention on Biological Diversity, opened for signature 5 June 1992, 1760 UNTS 143 (entered into force 29 December 1993) (CBD); Vito De Lucia, 'The Ecosystem Approach for Areas beyond National Jurisdiction: Reflections on the Chair's Non-Paper ahead of PREPCOM III' (Blog Post, 20 March 2017) <https://site.uit.no/jclos/2017/03/20/the-ecosystem-approach-for-areas-beyond-national-jurisdiction-reflections-on-the-chairs-non-paper-ahead-of-prepcom-iii/>.

49 Katherine Houghton, 'Identifying New Pathways for Ocean Governance: The Role of Legal Principles in Areas beyond National Jurisdiction' (2014) 49 Marine Policy 118, 120.

50 Robin Warner, 'Conserving Marine Biodiversity in Areas beyond National Jurisdiction: Co-Evolution and Interaction with the Law of the Sea' in Donald Rothwell et al (eds), *The Oxford Handbook of the Law of the Sea* (Oxford University Press, 2015) 752, 758.

0.7 An access and benefit-sharing (ABS) regime built on planks of compromise

Chapter 4 turns to the first element of the package deal, MGRs and questions on benefit-sharing. The natural environment has been an important source of inspiration for new forms of biotechnology.[51] While terrestrial resources have traditionally been the main focus of research and development,[52] BBNJ represents 'a vast, relatively untapped source of new materials, compounds and organisms.'[53] The bacteria at deep-sea hydrothermal vents, for example, attracts increasing scientific and commercial attention as it is 'likely to possess unique characteristics that may lead to ground-breaking innovations in the pharmaceutical and food industries, among others.'[54]

While MGRs found within national waters are accessed subject to UNCLOS, the CBD and other international provisions, access to MGRs in ABNJ is open and there is currently no formal benefit-sharing mechanism in place. Consequently, there is no limit imposed on the type or volume of genetic resources removed from hydrothermal vents or other deep-seabed environments, nor is there a coherent legal and institutional regime to regulate the environmental impacts of MGR activities.[55] Glowka notably referred to this regulatory gap as 'the deepest of ironies'; the irony being that MGRs may be the Area's 'most immediately exploitable and lucrative resource,' even though there is no mechanism in place to ensure their fair and equitable utilisation.[56] Meanwhile, the Area's mineral resources, regulated under Part XI of UNCLOS, are yet to be commercially exploited, even more than 30 years after the adoption of the Convention. The development of an ILBI presents an opportunity to address this legal lacuna.

During the BBNJ negotiation process, two camps have retreated to historically held positions. A powerful bloc of States, including the US, Japan and Russia, maintain that the freedom of the high seas principle, as set out in Part VII of UNCLOS, is applicable to MGRs in ABNJ.[57] In opposition to this, the G77/

51 David Leary and S. Kim Juniper, 'Addressing the Marine Genetic Resources Issue: Is the Debate Heading in the Wrong Direction?' in Clive Schofield, Seokwoo Lee and Moon-Sang Kwon (eds), *The Limits of Maritime Jurisdiction* (Koninklijke Brill, 2014) 769, 770.

52 Ibid.

53 David Farrier and Linda Tucker, 'Access to Marine Bioresources: Hitching the Conservation Cart to the Bioprospecting Horse' (2001) 32(3) *Ocean Development & International Law* 213, 215.

54 Elisa Morgera, 'Do We Need a New Treaty to Protect Biodiversity in the Deep Seas?', SDG Knowledge Hub (Online Commentary, 20 January 2015) <http://sdg.iisd.org/commentary/policy-briefs/do-we-need-a-new-treaty-to-protect-biodiversity-in-the-deep-seas/>.

55 Robin Warner, *Protecting the Oceans beyond National Jurisdiction: Strengthening the International Law Framework* (Martinus Nijhoff, 2009) 21.

56 Lyle Glowka, 'The Deepest of Ironies: Genetic Resources, Marine Scientific Research, and the Area' (1996) 12 *Ocean Yearbook* 154, 155.

57 See Tallash Kantai et al, 'Summary of the Third Session of the Intergovernmental Conference on the Conservation and Sustainable Use of Marine Biodiversity of Areas beyond National Jurisdiction: 19–30 August 2019' *Earth Negotiations Bulletin* (Online Bulletin, 2 September

China coalition[58] argues that MGRs in the Area should not be subject to free access and private ownership, as this model is not equitable.[59] Instead, this bloc advocates for the application of the CHM principle, and for MGR activities to be carried out for the benefit of mankind. An ILBI will either need to resolve the conflict between these competing principles or, as this book suggests, find a 'golden middle-way' between them.

The polarisation of States on the issue of MGRs is particularly acute and has the potential to derail the whole BBNJ process. States remain divided on key questions including whether an ILBI should regulate access to MGRs, what benefits should be shared (if any) and whether intellectual property rights should be addressed. As was the case with UNCLOS, trade-offs will need to be made in order to devise a practicable and effective approach to MGR management.[60] To gain an understanding of these potential trade-offs, Chapter 4 lays out a series of macro and micro compromise solutions (planks of compromise) for the three pillars of an ABS regime as well as the legal regime and governing principle applicable to deep-sea MGRs. The case is made that any further attempt to reconcile deep-seated ideological differences will prove fruitless and potentially reopen the familiar divisions between North and South that characterised UNCLOS III. As an alternative, Chapter 4 proposes a shift away from traditional theoretical paradigms and encourages a pragmatic approach built on key planks of compromise.

0.8 A modern, flexible and compromise approach to MPAs

In seeking to draw together the protection of BBNJ and ocean governance, the ILBI will attempt to regulate particular activities in ABNJ through the use of ABMTs, including MPAs.[61] As the regulation of activities in the marine

2019) 20 ('Summary of IGC 3') <https://enb.iisd.org/download/pdf/enb25218e.pdf>; Elizabeth M. De Santo et al, 'Stuck in the Middle with You (and Not Much Time Left): The Third Intergovernmental Conference on Biodiversity beyond National Jurisdiction' (2020) 117 *Marine Policy* 103957: 1–9, 3.

58 The G77 has 134 member countries.

59 See State of Palestine, 'State of Palestine on Behalf of G77–China, 19 August: Opening Statement,' Submission to the Third Intergovernmental Conference, 19 August 2019 <http://highseasalliance.org/treatytracker/statements/state-of-palestine-on-behalf-of-g77-china-19-august-opening-statement/>; Elisa Morgera et al, 'PrepCom 4 Highlights: Tuesday 11 July 2017' *Earth Negotiations Bulletin* (Online Bulletin, 12 July 2017) 2 <https://enb.iisd.org/download/pdf/enb25133e.pdf> ('PrepCom 4 Highlights: 11 July 2017').

60 Richard J. McLaughlin, 'Exploiting Marine Genetic Resources beyond National Jurisdiction and the International Protection of Intellectual Property Rights: Can They Coexist?' in Davor Vidas (ed), *Law, Technology and Science for Oceans in Globalisation* (Martinus Nijhoff, 2010) 371, 382.

61 ABMTs, such as MPAs, pollution control zones or fisheries closures, are spatial measures that afford a specified area higher protection due to more stringent regulation of one or more human activities, see, generally, David Johnson, Adelaide Ferreira and Ellen Kenchington, 'Climate Change Is Likely to Severely Limit the Effectiveness of Deep-Sea ABMTs in the North Atlantic' (2018) 87 *Marine Policy* 111–122.

environment is intricately 'bound up with, and impacts upon, matters of enormous strategic, military and economic importance,'[62] Chapter 5 considers whether the protection of BBNJ runs the risk of being sacrificed for the sake of much broader geopolitical imperatives, including the economic and security interests of maritime States. Over 15 years ago, Kaye identified 6 broad geopolitical issues that could impede progress towards the negotiation of high seas biodiversity protection areas, namely (1) the traditional high seas framework, (2) high seas fisheries, (3) geographically disadvantaged States, (4) strategic considerations, (5) deep-seabed issues and (6) marine scientific research.[63] Taking Kaye's assessment of key geopolitical factors of relevance to high seas protection as a starting point, Chapter 5 assesses the extent to which these factors continue to exert influence on the development of an MPA framework under an ILBI.

Since Kaye's work 12 high seas MPAs have been developed: 2 in the Southern Ocean under the 1980 Convention on the Conservation of Antarctic Marine Living Resources (CAMLR Convention)[64] and 10 in the North-East Atlantic region under the OSPAR Convention[65] and the North-East Atlantic Fisheries Commission.[66] Using the CAMLR MPAs as a case study, Chapter 5 analyses how geopolitical considerations influenced, shaped or hindered their development and effectiveness. In an effort to overcome geopolitical issues in the BBNJ context, this book encourages the adoption of a modern, flexible and compromise approach to MPAs, one that is underpinned by an expert-driven systematic conservation planning process and involves the use of dynamic management tools, including a network of mobile MPAs and impact assessments.

0.9 Overarching recipe for environmentally sustainable decision-making in ABNJ

EIA is widely accepted as a valuable ABMT for protecting BBNJ and managing human impacts on marine ecosystems.[67] The assessment of anthropogenic pressures on BBNJ presents unique challenges, many of which 'stem from the

62 Dromgoole, 'Reflections' (n 34) 116.

63 Stuart Kaye, 'Implementing High Seas Biodiversity Conservation: Global Geopolitical Considerations' (2004) 28 *Marine Policy* 221.

64 Convention on the Conservation of Antarctic Marine Living Resources, opened for signature 20 May 1980, 1329 UNTS 48 (entered into force 7 April 1982) (CAMLR Convention).

65 Convention for the Protection of the Marine Environment of the North-East Atlantic, opened for signature 22 September 1992, (1992) 32 ILM 1069 (entered into force 25 March 1998) (OSPAR Convention).

66 Elizabeth M. De Santo, 'Implementation Challenges of Area-Based Management Tools (ABMTs) for Biodiversity beyond National Jurisdiction (BBNJ)' (2018) 97 *Marine Policy* 34, 35.

67 High Seas Alliance, 'Key Components and Best Practices for Environmental Impact Assessments,' Submission to the Preparatory Committee established by General Assembly Resolution 69/292 <http://www.highseasalliance.org/wp-content/uploads/2013/04/HSA-EIA-Brief-for-PrepCom2-FINAL-pdf.pdf>.

three dimensional nature of the marine environment with its great depths, pressure and lack of light beneath the photic zone.'[68] Although Article 206 of UNCLOS imposes a general obligation on States to conduct EIA, there is no overarching structure for the application of this tool in ABNJ.[69] The development of an ILBI presents the opportunity to build on the pre-existing obligation in Article 206 and devise an overarching recipe for environmentally sustainable decision-making in ABNJ.

Chapter 6 lays out key ingredients required for an effective EIA framework. There is an existing and impressive architecture already in place concerning the conduct of EIA in the marine environment, emanating from global instruments (UNCLOS and CBD), regional instruments (Espoo Convention[70] and Madrid Protocol[71]) and sectoral guidelines. This book suggests that internationally accepted standards, processes and protocols found within the existing legal framework could be used to shape and underpin EIA ingredients under an ILBI and adjusted to suit the BBNJ context.

0.10 A sine qua non of the ILBI—capacity-building and technology transfer (CBTT)

Chapter 7 deals with CBTT being the last component of the BBNJ package deal. CBTT is not only important for improving the capacity of developing countries to address BBNJ-related issues, but it is 'indispensable for realising the overall objective of marine environmental protection and sustainable development.'[72] Thus, even though CBTT has been recognised as a critical cross-cutting element in the BBNJ process, this book suggests that it should be afforded a higher status and considered a sine qua non of the ILBI.

68 Robin Warner, 'Environmental Assessment in Marine Areas beyond National Jurisdiction' in Rosemary Rayfuse (ed), *Research Handbook on International Marine Environmental Law* (Edward Elgar Publishing Limited, 2015) 291, 291.

69 European Union, 'Development of an International Legally-Binding Instrument under UNCLOS on the Conservation and Sustainable Use of Marine Biological Diversity of Areas beyond National Jurisdiction (BBNJ Process), Written Submission of the EU and Its Member States: Environmental Impact Assessments' (15 February 2017) 2 [2] <https://www.un.org/depts/los/biodiversity/prepcom_files/rolling_comp/EU_Written_Submission_on_Environmental_Assessments.pdf>.

70 Convention on Environmental Impact Assessment in a Transboundary Context, opened for signature 25 February 1991, (1991) 30 ILM 802 (entered into force 10 September 1997) (Espoo Convention).

71 Protocol on Environmental Protection to the Antarctic Treaty, opened for signature 4 October 1991, (1991) 30 ILM 1461 (entered into force 14 January 1998) (Madrid Protocol).

72 People's Republic of China, 'Written Submission of the Government of the People's Republic of China on Elements of a Draft Text of an International Legally Binding Instrument under the United Nations Convention on the Law of the Sea on the Conservation and Sustainable Use of Marine Biological Diversity of Areas Beyond National Jurisdiction' (20 April 2017) 11 [27] <https://www.un.org/depts/los/biodiversity/prepcom_files/streamlined/China.pdf>.

As significant financial and technical resources are required to conduct and manage activities in ABNJ, capacity limitations could constrain the ability of developing States to effectively participate in an ILBI.[73] Least developed countries have already indicated that they will face capacity challenges in implementing all elements of the BBNJ package deal.[74] In order for an ILBI to be effective, developing States will need to be able to participate in and assume their responsibilities and obligations under the instrument.[75]

The framers of UNCLOS recognised the 'differing ability of States to benefit from the ocean.'[76] This is evident in Part XIV of UNCLOS which contains the Convention's normative framework for CBTT. Part XIV can be described as the 'Sleeping Giant of UNCLOS.' Its provisions have enormous untapped potential but have remained dormant, inactive and underutilised since the adoption of the Convention. The development of an ILBI offers a timely and much-needed wake-up call and provides the opportunity to revitalise and strengthen the existing CBTT formula in UNCLOS. Chapter 7 identifies mechanisms to enhance the implementation of existing UNCLOS requirements in an effort to wake the sleeping giant from its slumber.

As the technological gap between developing States and developed, mainly western capitalist States was seen 'as a major factor in economic and political disparity' during UNCLOS III,[77] CBTT discussions have reignited old debates along a North-South divide. For example, BBNJ delegations remain divided on whether CBTT should be mandatory or voluntary.[78] The case is made for BBNJ negotiators to find a 'sweet-spot' for CBTT, 'one that requires enough effort from states to generate real … benefits but not efforts that are so costly that States choose not to participate in, or implement, the agreement.'[79] Chapter 7 offers a potential way forward to assist BBNJ negotiators in finding this elusive sweet-spot.

73 Harriet Harden-Davies, 'Capacity Building and Technology Transfer for Marine Biodiversity in Areas beyond National Jurisdiction' (2017) 111 *American Society of International Law Proceedings of the Annual Meeting* 243, 243. Developing States does not refer to a clearly identified group of States, but rests on self-election—see, generally, Kristin Bartenstein, 'XIV: Development and Transfer of Marine Technology' in Alexander Proelss (ed), *United Nations Convention on the Law of the Sea A Commentary* (C.H. Beck, 2017) 1764, 1773.

74 UN, 'Adopting Two Texts on Oceans, Seas, General Assembly Also Tackles Sustainable Management, Conservation of Marine Life beyond National Jurisdiction' (Meetings Coverage, GA/11985, 5 December 2017).

75 Biliana Cicin-Sain et al, 'Capacity Development as a Key Aspect of a New International Agreement on Marine Biodiversity beyond National Jurisdiction (BBNJ)' (Policy Brief, August 2018) 1.

76 Cymie Payne, 'Biodiversity in High Seas Areas: An Integrated Legal Approach', *American Society of International Law* (ASIL Insights, 1 September 2017) <https://www.asil.org/insights/volume/21/issue/9/biodiversity-high-seas-areas-integrated-legal-approach>.

77 Douglas Yarn, 'The Transfer of Technology and UNCLOS III' (1984) 14(1) *Georgia Journal of International and Comparative Law* 121, 127.

78 See Kantai et al, 'Summary of IGC 3' (n 57) 1–2, 15–16.

79 E.M. De Santo et al, 'Protecting Biodiversity in Areas beyond National Jurisdiction: An Earth System Governance Perspective' (2019) 2 *Earth System Governance* 100029: 1–7, 2.

This book is not confined solely to an exposition and clarification of the current legal framework for ABNJ. Instead, this book has been researched and written as a comprehensive guide to be of use to BBNJ negotiators as they embark on the next round of negotiations and may also be of assistance to policy makers and their legal advisors within governments who will bear the burden of implementing the provisions of an ILBI in the years to come. This book provides an assessment and critique of suggestions and proposals put forward thus far in the BBNJ negotiation process, up to and including the fourth session of the Intergovernmental Conference, and offers compromise solutions for the formation of an effective, practicable and universally acceptable instrument.

Collectively, the chapters of this book provide a comprehensive blueprint for an ILBI, and lay the foundations for building a bridge of compromise over the troubled waters beyond national jurisdiction.

References

Agreement Relating to the Implementation of Part XI of the United Nations Convention on the Law of the Sea of 10 December 1984, opened for Signature 16 November 1994 (1994) 33 *ILM* 1309 (entered into force 28 July 1996).

Alvarenga, Karen, et al., 'Summary of the Working Group on Marine Biodiversity Beyond Areas of National Jurisdiction: 13–17 February 2006' *Earth Negotiations Bulletin* (Online Bulletin, 20 February 2006) <https://enb.iisd.org/download/pdf/enb2525e.pdf> accessed 31 March 2022.

Anand, Ram P., '"Tyranny" of the Freedom of the Seas Doctrine' (1973) 12 *International Studies* 416–429. DOI:10.1177/002088177301200302.

Anand, Ram P., 'Freedom of the Seas: Past, Present and Future' in Hugo Caminos (ed), *Law of the Sea* (Ashgate, 2001) 261.

Anderson, David, *The Development of the Modern Law of the Sea: Selected Essays* (Martinus Nijhoff, 2008) vol 59.

Arnaud-Haond, Sophie, Jesus M. Arrieta and Carlos M. Duarte, 'Marine Biodiversity and Gene Patents' (25 March 2011) 331 *Science* 1521–1522. DOI: 10.1126/science.1200783.

Baird, Rachel, 'Political and Commercial Interests as Influences in the Development of the Doctrine of the Freedom of the High Seas' (1996) 12 *Queensland University of Technology Law Journal* 274–291. DOI: 10.5204/qutlr.v12i0.425.

Barnes, Richard, David Freestone and David M. Ong, 'The Law of the Sea: Progress and Prospects' in Richard Barnes, David Freestone and David M. Ong (eds), *The Law of the Sea Progress and Prospects* (Oxford University Press, 2006) 1. DOI: 10.1093/acprof:oso/9780199299614.003.0001.

Bartenstein, Kristin, 'XIV: Development and Transfer of Marine Technology' in Alexander Proelss (ed), *United Nations Convention on the Law of the Sea A Commentary* (C.H. Beck, 2017) 1764.

Brown, E.D, 'Freedom of the High Seas Versus the Common Heritage of Mankind: Fundamental Principles in Conflict' (1983) 20 *San Diego Law Review* 521–560.

Caflisch, Lucius, 'Submarine Antiquities and the International Law of the Sea' (1982) 13 *Netherlands Yearbook of International Law* 3–32. DOI: 10.1017/S0167676800002993.

Caminos, Hugo and Michael R. Molitor, 'Progressive Development of International Law and the Package Deal' (1985) 79 *American Journal of International Law* 871–890. DOI: 10.2307/2201830.

Churchill, R.R, and A.V. Lowe, *The Law of the Sea* (Manchester University Press, 3rd ed, 1999).

Cicin-Sain, Biliana, Marjo Vierros, Miriam Balgos, Alexis Maxwell, Meredith Kurz, Tina Farmer, Atsushi Sunami, Miko Maekawa, Iwao Fujii, Awni Benham, Julian Barbiere, Salvatore Aricò, Kirsten Isensee, Ward Appeltans, Harriet Harden-Davies, Aimee Gonzales, Stephen Adrian Ross, Alfonso Ascencio Herrera, Chapi Mwango, Annekah Mason, Ronán Long, Larry Hildebrand, Philippe Vallette, Joseph Appiott, Yugraj Yadava, Kouete Koffi Afachawo, Odanwu Chizoba Margaret, Abdul Rahman Bin Abdul Wahab, Andre Polejack, Lizanne Aching, Jenny Bowie-Wilches, Transform Aqorau, Rudolf Hermes, Dominique Benzaken, Laleta Davis-Mattis, Nguyen Chu Hoi, Abou Bamba, Rose Lesley Kautoke and Bojotlhe Butale, 'Capacity Development as a Key Aspect of a New International Agreement on Marine Biodiversity Beyond National Jurisdiction (BBNJ)' (Policy Brief, August 2018) <http://www.fao.org/fileadmin/user_upload/common_oceans/docs/policy-brief-on-bbnj-capacity-development-aug-2018.pdf> accessed 31 March 2022.

Clingan, Thomas A, *The Law of the Sea: Ocean Law and Policy* (Austin & Winfield, 1994).

The Convention for the Protection of the Marine Environment of the North-East Atlantic, opened for signature 22 September 1992 (1992) 32 *ILM* 1069 (entered into force 25 March 1998) (OSPAR Convention).

Convention on Biological Diversity, opened for signature 5 June 1992 (1992) 1760 *UNTS* 143 (entered into force 29 December 1993) (CBD).

Convention on Environmental Impact Assessment in a Transboundary Context, opened for signature 25 February 1991, (1991) 30 *ILM* 802 (entered into force 10 September 1997) (Espoo Convention).

Convention on Fishing and Conservation of Living Resources of the High Seas, opened for signature 29 April 1958 (1958) 559 *UNTS* 285 (entered into force 20 March 1966).

Convention on the Conservation of Antarctic Marine Living Resources, opened for signature 20 May 1980 (1980) 1329 *UNTS* 48 (entered into force 7 April 1982) (CAMLR Convention).

Convention on the Continental Shelf, opened for signature 29 April 1958 (1958) 499 *UNTS* 311 (entered into force 10 June 1964).

Convention on the High Seas, opened for signature 29 April 1958 (1958) 450 *UNTS* 82 (entered into force 30 September 1962).

Convention on the Protection of the Underwater Cultural Heritage, opened for signature 2 November 2001 (2001) 2562 *UNTS* 1 (entered into force 2 January 2009).

Convention on the Territorial Sea and the Contiguous Zone, opened for signature 29 April 1958 (1958) 516 *UNTS* 205 (entered into force 10 September 1964).

De Lucia, Vito, 'The Ecosystem Approach for Areas Beyond National Jurisdiction: Reflections on the Chair's Non-paper Ahead of PREPCOM III' *The NCLOS Blog* (Blog, 20 March 2017) <https://site.uit.no/nclos/2017/03/20/the-ecosystem-approach-for-areas-beyond-national-jurisdiction-reflections-on-the-chairs-non-paper-ahead-of-prepcom-iii/> accessed 31 March 2022.

De Santo, E.M, 'Implementation Challenges of Area-based Management Tools (ABMTs) for Biodiversity Beyond National Jurisdiction (BBNJ)' (2018) 97 *Marine Policy* 34–43. DOI: 10.1016/j.marpol.2018.08.034.

De Santo, E.M, A. Asgeirsdóttir, A. Barros-Platiau, F. Biermann, J. Dryzek, L.R. Goncalves, R.E. Kim, E. Mendenhall, R. Mitchell, E. Nyman, M. Scobie, K. Sun, R. Tiller, D.G. Webster and O. Young, 'Protecting Biodiversity in Areas Beyond National Jurisdiction: An Earth System Governance Perspective' (2019) 2 *Earth System Governance* 100029: 1–7. DOI: 10.1016/j.esg.2019.100029.

De Santo, Elizabeth M, Elizabeth Mendenhall, Elizabeth Nyman and Rachel Tiller, 'Stuck in the Middle with You (and Not Much Time Left): The Third Intergovernmental Conference on Biodiversity Beyond National Jurisdiction' (2020) 117 *Marine Policy* 103957: 1–9. DOI: 10.1016/j.marpol.2020.103957.

Division for Ocean Affairs and the Law of the Sea, 'The United Nations Convention on the Law of the Sea: A Historical Perspective' *Oceans and Law of the Sea United Nations* (Web Page) <https://www.un.org/Depts/los/convention_agreements/convention_historical_perspective.htm> accessed 31 March 2022.

Dromgoole, Sarah, 'Reflections on the Position of the Major Maritime Powers with Respect to the UNESCO Convention on the Protection of the Underwater Cultural Heritage 2001' (2013a) 38 *Marine Policy* 116–123. DOI: 10.1016/j.marpol.2012.05.027.

Dromgoole, Sarah, *Underwater Cultural Heritage and International Law* (Cambridge University Press, 2013b). DOI: 10.1017/CBO9781139020503.

European Union, 'Development of an International Legally-Binding Instrument under UNCLOS on the Conservation and Sustainable Use of Marine Biological Diversity of Areas Beyond National Jurisdiction (BBNJ Process), Written Submission of the EU and Its Member States: Environmental Impact Assessments' (15 February 2017) <https://www.un.org/depts/los/biodiversity/prepcom_files/rolling_comp/EU_Written_Submission_on_Environmental_Assessments.pdf> accessed 31 March 2022.

Farrier, David and Linda Tucker, 'Access to Marine Bioresources: Hitching the Conservation Cart to the Bioprospecting Horse' (2001) 32(3) *Ocean Development & International Law* 213–239. DOI: 10.1080/009083201750397583.

Glowka, Lyle, 'The Deepest of Ironies: Genetic Resources, Marine Scientific Research, and the Area' (1996) 12 *Ocean Yearbook Online* 154–178. DOI: 10.1163/221160096X00111.

Harden-Davies, Harriet, 'Capacity Building and Technology Transfer for Marine Biodiversity in Areas Beyond National Jurisdiction' (2017) 111 *American Society of International Law* Proceedings of the ASIL Annual Meeting 243–245. DOI: 10.1017/amp.2017.75.

High Seas Alliance, 'Key Components and Best Practices for Environmental Impact Assessments', Submission to the Preparatory Committee established by General Assembly Resolution 69/292 <http://www.highseasalliance.org/wp-content/uploads/2013/04/HSA-EIA-Brief-for-PrepCom2-FINAL-pdf.pdf> accessed 31 March 2022.

Houghton, Katherine, 'Identifying New Pathways for Ocean Governance: The Role of Legal Principles in Areas Beyond National Jurisdiction' (2014) 49 *Marine Policy* 118–126. DOI: 10.1016/j.marpol.2014.04.007.

Johnson, David, Adelaide Ferreira and Ellen Kenchington, 'Climate Change is Likely to Severely Limit the Effectiveness of Deep-sea ABMTs in the North Atlantic' (2018) 87 *Marine Policy* 111–122. DOI: 10.1016/j.marpol.2017.09.034.

Kantai, Tallash, Jennifer Bansard, Tasha Goldberg, Katarina Hovden and Asterios Tsioumanis, 'Summary of the Third Session of the Intergovernmental Conference on the Conservation and Sustainable Use of Marine Biodiversity of Areas Beyond National Jurisdiction: 19–30 August 2019' *Earth Negotiations Bulletin* (Online Bulletin, 2 September 2019) <https://enb.iisd.org/download/pdf/enb25218e.pdf> accessed 31 March 2022.

Kaye, Stuart, 'Implementing High Seas Biodiversity Conservation: Global Geopolitical Considerations' (2004) 28 *Marine Policy* 221–226. DOI: 10.1016/j.marpol.2003.09.001.

Leary, David and S.Kim Juniper, 'Addressing the Marine Genetic Resources Issue: Is the Debate Heading in the Wrong Direction?' in Clive Schofield, Seokwoo Lee and Moon-Sang Kwon (eds), *The Limits of Maritime Jurisdiction* (Koninklijke Brill, 2014) 769.

Levin, Lisa A, 'Climate Change Impacts on Marine Biodiversity and Resilience' (Conference Paper, Third International Symposium on Effects of Climate Change on the World's Oceans, 25 March 2015) http://www.ices.dk/news-and-events/news-archive/news/Pages/Biodiversity-Consequences-of-Climate-Change-in-the-Deep-Ocean-and-Sustainability-in-the-21st-Century.aspx accessed 31 March 2022.

Logue, John, 'The Revenge of John Selden: The Draft Convention on the Law of the Sea in the Light of Hugo Grotius' Mare Liberum' (1982) 3 *Grotiana* 27–56. DOI: 10.1163/187607582X00042.

McLaughlin, Richard J, 'Exploiting Marine Genetic Resources Beyond National Jurisdiction and the International Protection of Intellectual Property Rights: Can They Coexist?' in Davor Vidas (ed), *Law, Technology and Science for Oceans in Globalisation* (Martinus Nijhoff Publishers, 2010) 371. DOI: 10.1163/ej.9789004180406.i-610.119.

Morgera, Elisa, 'Do We Need a New Treaty to Protect Biodiversity in the Deep Seas?' SDG Knowledge Hub (Online Commentary, 20 January 2015) <http://sdg.iisd.org/commentary/policy-briefs/do-we-need-a-new-treaty-to-protect-biodiversity-in-the-deep-seas/> accessed 31 March 2022.

Morgera, Elisa, Asheline Appleton, Tallash Kantai and Asterios Tsioumanis, 'PrepCom 4 Highlights: Tuesday 11 July 2017' *Earth Negotiations Bulletin* (Online Bulletin, 12 July 2017) <https://enb.iisd.org/download/pdf/enb25133e.pdf> accessed 31 March 2022.

Nordquist, Myron H.(ed), *United Nations Convention on the Law of the Sea 1982: A Commentary* (Martinus Nijhoff Publishers, 1985).

O'Connell, D.P, *The International Law of the Sea* (Clarendon Press, 1983). DOI: 10.1093/law/9780198253464.001.0001.

Oxman, Bernard H, 'The Territorial Temptation: A Siren Song at Sea' (2006) 100(4) *The American Journal of International Law* 830–851. DOI: 10.1017/S0002930000031912.

Payne, Cymie, 'Biodiversity in High Seas Areas: An Integrated Legal Approach', American Society of International Law (ASIL Insights, 1 September 2017) <https://www.asil.org/insights/volume/21/issue/9/biodiversity-high-seas-areas-integrated-legal-approach> accessed 31 March 2022.

People's Republic of China, 'Written Submission of the Government of the People's Republic of China on Elements of a Draft Text of an International Legally Binding Instrument under the United Nations Convention on the Law of the Sea on the Conservation and Sustainable Use of Marine Biological Diversity of Areas

Beyond National Jurisdiction' (20 April 2017) <https://www.un.org/depts/los/biodiversity/prepcom_files/streamlined/China.pdf> accessed 31 March 2022.

Protocol on Environmental Protection to the Antarctic Treaty, opened for signature 4 October 1991, (1991) 30 *ILM* 1461 (entered into force 14 January 1998) (The Madrid Protocol).

Rabitz, Florian, *The Global Governance of Genetic Resources Institutional Change, Structural Constraints* (Routledge, 2017). DOI: 10.4324/9781315271316.

Rio Declaration, Report of the United Nations Conference on Environment and Development, UN Doc. A/CONF.151/5/Rev.1 (1992) Annex I Rio Declaration on Environment and Development (Rio Declaration).

Rochette, Julien, Glen Wright, Kristina M. Gjerde, Thomas Greiber, Sebastian Unger and Aurélie Spadone, 'A New Chapter for the High Seas?' (Working Paper, Institute for Advanced Sustainability Studies, April 2015) <https://www.iass-potsdam.de/sites/default/files/files/a_new_chapter_for_high_seas_.pdf> accessed 31 March 2022.

Rothwell, Donald R. and Tim Stephens, *The International Law of the Sea* (Hart Publishing Ltd, 2nd ed, 2016).

Russ, Garry R. and Dirk C. Zeller, 'From Mare Liberum to Mare Reservarum' (2003) 27 *Marine Policy* 75–78. DOI: 10.1016/S0308-597X(02)00054-4.

Scovazzi, Tullio, 'The Rights to Genetic Resources Beyond National Jurisdiction: Challenges for the Ongoing Negotiations at the United Nations' in Catherine Banet (ed), *The Law of the Seabed* (Brill Nijhoff, 2020) 213. DOI: 10.1163/9789004391567_012.

Selvig, Kirsten, 'Expensive Freedom: Establishing Marine Protected Areas on the Open Ocean Requires an End to the Freedom of the Seas' (2013) 22(3) *Minnesota Journal of International Law* 35–68.

State of Palestine, 'State of Palestine on Behalf of G77+China, 19 August: Opening Statement', Submission to the Third Intergovernmental Conference, 19 August 2019 <http://highseasalliance.org/treatytracker/statements/state-of-palestine-on-behalf-of-g77-china-19-august-opening-statement/> accessed 31 March 2022.

Stockholm Declaration (Report of the United Nations Conference on the Human Environment, Stockholm, 5-16 June 1972) UN Doc A/CONF.48/14/Rev.1 (1973), (1972) 11 *ILM* 1416 (Stockholm Declaration).

Treves, Tullio, 'Historical Development of the Law of the Sea' in Donald Rothwell et al. (eds), *The Oxford Handbook of the Law of the Sea* (Oxford University Press, 2015) 1. DOI: 10.1093/law/9780198715481.003.0001.

Tuerk, Helmut, 'The Legal Regime of Maritime Areas and the Waning Freedom of the Seas' (Conference Paper, Maritime Issues and United Nations Convention on the Laws of the Sea: Sharing European and Asia Approaches to Territorial Disputes, 4–5 June 2015). <http://www.maritimeissues.com/working-papers/the-legal-regime-of-maritime-areas-and-the-waning-freedom-of-the-seas.html> accessed 31 March 2022.

United Nations, 'Adopting Two Texts on Oceans, Seas, General Assembly Also Tackles Sustainable Management, Conservation of Marine Life beyond National Jurisdiction' (Meetings Coverage, GA/11985, 5 December 2017) <https://www.un.org/press/en/2017/ga11985.doc.htm> accessed 31 March 2022.

United Nations Convention on the Law of the Sea, Opened for signature 10 December 1982, 1833 UNTS 397 (entered into force 16 November 1994) (UNCLOS).

United Nations General Assembly, *Development of an International Legally Binding Instrument under the United Nations Convention on the Law of the Sea on the Conservation and Sustainable Use of Marine Biological Diversity of Areas Beyond National Jurisdiction*, GA Res 69/292, UN Doc A/RES/69/292 (6 July 2015, adopted 19 June 2015).

United Nations General Assembly, *Revised Draft Text of an Agreement Under the United Nations Convention on the Law of the Sea on the Conservation and Sustainable Use of Marine Biological Diversity of Areas Beyond National Jurisdiction* UN Doc A/CONF.232/2020/3 (18 November 2019) <https://documents-dds-ny.un.org/doc/UNDOC/GEN/N19/372/88/PDF/N1937288.pdf?OpenElement> accessed 31 March 2022.

Warner, Robin, *Protecting the Oceans Beyond National Jurisdiction: Strengthening the International Law Framework* (Martinus Nijhoff, 2009).

Warner, Robin, 'Conserving Marine Biodiversity in Areas Beyond National Jurisdiction: Co-Evolution and Interaction with the Law of the Sea' in Donald Rothwell et al. (eds), *The Oxford Handbook of the Law of the Sea* (Oxford University Press, 2015a) 752. DOI: 10.1093/law/9780198715481.003.0033.

Warner, Robin, 'Environmental Assessment in Marine Areas Beyond National Jurisdiction' in Rosemary Rayfuse (ed), *Research Handbook on International Marine Environmental Law* (Edward Elgar Publishing Limited, 2015b) 291. DOI: 10.4337/9781781004777.00024.

Yarn, Douglas, 'The Transfer of Technology and UNCLOS III' (1984) 14(1) *Georgia Journal of International and Comparative Law* 121–153.

Young, Michaela, 'Then and Now: Reappraising Freedom of the Seas in Modern Law of the Sea' (2016) 47(2) *Ocean Development & International Law* 165–185. DOI: 10.1080/00908320.2016.1159088.

1 The promise and limits of international legal protection of BBNJ

Introduction

to take arms against a sea of troubles[1]

The overriding objective of the ILBI will be to ensure the long-term conservation and sustainable use of BBNJ.[2] As it is beyond the scope of this book to provide an exhaustive study of the characteristics of BBNJ, this chapter uses Vulnerable Marine Ecosystems (VMEs) as a medium for exploring fundamental BBNJ issues and to illustrate the urgent need for an ILBI. VMEs have been selected as a case study for two reasons. First, these deep-sea habitats represent a key component of marine biodiversity and are particularly susceptible to human disturbance.[3] Second, VMEs have become the target of a catalogue of anthropogenic activities and uses.

This chapter is designed primarily to introduce the BBNJ process, provide an overview of the current state of play with ILBI negotiations and consider the promise and limits of international legal protection of BBNJ.

1.1 Areas beyond national jurisdiction

1.1.1 The geographical scope of the ILBI

UNCLOS provides a framework of rules for determining the rights and duties of States in respect to their use of maritime space.[4] A critical component of this framework is the division of the ocean into maritime zones, each with its own specific

1 William Shakespeare, *Hamlet*, Act III, Scene I, 59.

2 *Revised Draft Text of an Agreement under UNCLOS on the Conservation and Sustainable Use of Marine Biological Diversity of Areas beyond National Jurisdiction* UN Doc A/CONF.232/2020/3 (18 November 2019) art 2 ('*Revised Draft Negotiating Text*').

3 *Report on the Work of the United Nations Open-ended Informal Consultative Process on Oceans and the Law of the Sea*, UN Doc A/58/95 (26 June 2003) [80]. While much of the deep-sea lies in ABNJ, to meet the ILBI's geographical scope, reference to the deep-sea in this book is limited to the seafloor, water column and biota that exist at a depth greater than 200 m beyond national jurisdiction.

4 Sarah Dromgoole, *Underwater Cultural Heritage and International Law* (Cambridge University Press, 2013) 9.

DOI: 10.4324/b22996-2

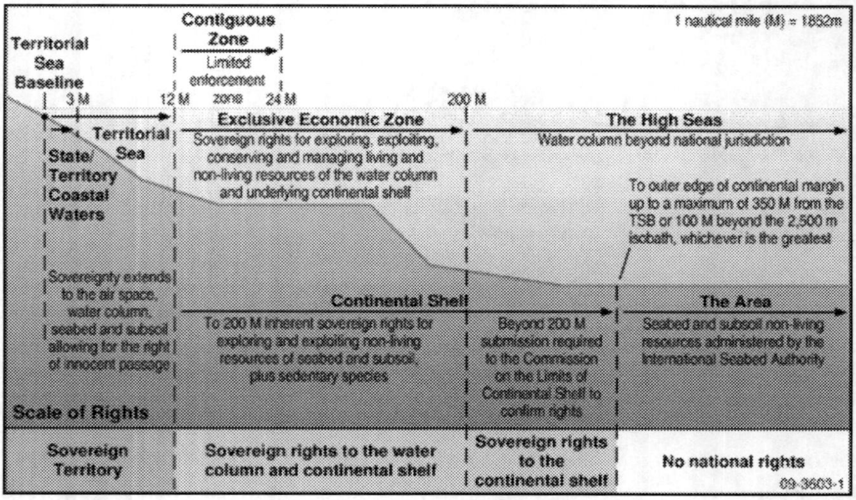

Figure 1.1 Maritime zones under UNCLOS © Commonwealth of Australia (Geoscience Australia) 2021. This image is released under a Creative Commons Attribution 4.0 International Licence. http://creativecommons.org/licenses/by/4.0/legalcode

legal regime[5] (see Figure 1.1). The zones can be divided into two main categories: (1) areas under national jurisdiction; and (2) areas beyond national jurisdiction (ABNJ). Geographically, the ILBI will apply to ABNJ, which comprise two distinct maritime zones, the high seas and the international seabed area (the Area).

1.1.1.1 The high seas

The high seas regime in Part VII of UNCLOS encompasses the water column beyond the 200 nautical miles (nm) exclusive economic zone (EEZ) or the territorial sea where no EEZ has been declared.[6] The high seas are governed by the freedom of the seas principle.[7]

1.1.1.2 The Area

The Area comprises the seabed, ocean floor and subsoil beyond the continental shelves of coastal States (200 nm) or when it exists, beyond their outer continental

5 Ibid.
6 UNCLOS, art 86. This book uses nautical miles (nm), which is 1.15 statute miles or 1852 metres. While M is also an accepted abbreviation for a nautical mile, this book prefers nm to avoid confusion with metres.
7 UNCLOS, art 87.

shelves.[8] Part XI of UNCLOS and the Part XI Agreement establish a regime for the Area, complete with an organisation, the International Seabed Authority (ISA). The Area and its mineral resources are the common heritage of mankind.[9] Activities in the Area, specifically, the exploration and exploitation of mineral resources, are carried out for the benefit of mankind, on whose behalf the ISA acts.[10]

1.2 Marine biological diversity

1.2.1 The material scope of the ILBI

The material scope of the ILBI concerns two important questions: (1) What is marine biodiversity? and (2) Should this term be defined under the new instrument?

1.2.1.1 The concept of biological diversity

Biological diversity (biodiversity) is one of the most cited terms in ecological research, environmental management and conservation.[11] The CBD introduced this concept into international law, almost a decade after the adoption of UNCLOS.[12] Article 2 of CBD defines 'biological diversity' as:

> the variability among living organisms from all sources, including, inter alia, terrestrial, marine and other aquatic ecosystems and the ecological complexes of which they are part; this includes diversity within species, between species and of ecosystems.

This definition recognises three conceptual levels of biodiversity (see Table 1.1).

The CBD's definition applies to biodiversity in all its manifestations in both the marine and terrestrial environment. Marine biodiversity can therefore be understood as encompassing the variability of marine life in all its forms, levels and combinations.[13] In the same way, terrestrial biodiversity can be taken to include all land-based ecosystems (e.g. tropical rainforests, grasslands and deserts) and living organisms found on or underneath the land.

8 UNCLOS, arts 1(1) and 76.
9 UNCLOS, art 133(a).
10 UNCLOS, arts 1(1)(3) and 140.
11 Sabine K.J. Cochrane et al, 'What Is Marine Biodiversity? Towards Common Concepts and Their Implications for Assessing Biodiversity Status' (2016) 3 *Frontiers in Marine Science* 248, 248.
12 Robin Warner, 'Conserving Marine Biodiversity in Areas beyond National Jurisdiction: Co-Evolution and Interaction with the Law of the Sea' in Donald Rothwell et al (eds), *The Oxford Handbook of the Law of the Sea* (Oxford University Press, 2015) 753, 756 ('Conserving Marine Biodiversity').
13 P. Birnie, A. Boyle and C. Redgwell, *International Law and the Environment* (Oxford University Press, 3rd ed, 2009) 588.

Table 1.1 Levels of biodiversity

Level of biodiversity	*Definition*
Ecosystem diversity	The variety and diversity of ecosystems, in terms of species composition, physical structure and ecological processes, within a geographical region or biome.
Species diversity	The abundance and variation of different species found in a biological organisation (i.e. population or ecosystem).
Genetic diversity	The diversity of genetic characteristics within a species (i.e. variation within a population and between populations of the same species).

Like its marine counterpart, terrestrial biodiversity is in a state of decline due to anthropogenic pressures,[14] mainly through the conversion of natural habitats for agricultural and forestry purposes.[15] Worldwide, it is estimated that terrestrial ecological communities have lost more than 20 per cent of their original biodiversity[16] and around 1 million animal and plant species are currently facing extinction.[17] Whilst ambitious biodiversity targets have been proposed over the last 15 years,[18] conservation efforts have not halted the increasing demand for land for the production of food, feed, energy and other materials, putting at risk essential ecosystem services that deliver societal and economic benefits.[19] Clearly, reversing the universal decline in biodiversity will require transformative action.[20] The development and implementation of a strong and effective ILBI could bring about transformative change in the marine environment, particularly in ABNJ. It could also provide invaluable lessons to better support the achievement of future environmental objectives in the terrestrial context.

14 E.S. Brondizio et al (eds), 'Global Assessment Report on Biodiversity and Ecosystem Services of the Intergovernmental Science-Policy Platform on Biodiversity and Ecosystem Services' (IPBES Secretariat, 2019).

15 David Leclère et al, 'Bending the Curve of Terrestrial Biodiversity Needs an Integrated Strategy' (2020) 585 *Nature* 551, 551.

16 Sandra Díaz et al, 'Pervasive Human-Driven Decline of Life on Earth Points to the Need for Transformative Change' (2019) 366 *Science* 1, 3.

17 S. Díaz et al (eds), 'Summary for Policymakers of the Global Assessment Report on Biodiversity and Ecosystem Services of the Intergovernmental Science-Policy Platform on Biodiversity and Ecosystem Services' (IPBES Secretariat, 2019) 12.

18 See, e.g. goals such as those embodied in the CBD, *Strategic Plan 2011–2020, Aichi Biodoversity Targets*, UN Doc COP/10/INF/12/Rev.1 and the Sustainable Development Goals of the UN, *Transforming Our World: 2030 Agenda for Sustainable Development.* Also, the goals specified in the Paris Agreement adopted under the United Nations Framework Convention on Climate Change, opened for signature 9 May 1992, 1771 UNTS 165 (entered into force 21 March 1994) (UNFCCC) and the CBD, *First Draft of the Post-2020 Global Biodiversity Framework*, UN Doc CBD/WG2020/3/3.

19 Leclère et al (n 15) 551.

20 Díaz et al (n 16).

1.2.1.2 Defining marine biodiversity in the ILBI

During the BBNJ process, little time has been devoted to discussing a definition of marine biodiversity. It appears that BBNJ negotiators have taken its meaning and scope for granted. As this term is not referenced in UNCLOS and forms the subject matter of the ILBI, a clear and precise definition should be included in the new instrument. Currently, there is no draft definition in the Revised Draft Negotiating Text. The adoption of a definition in conformity with the CBD is preferable, as it would offer consistency between the two biodiversity-related instruments. Moreover, the definitions in the CBD have received widespread approval.[21]

1.2.2 The significance of BBNJ

ABNJ cover approximately 64 per cent of the ocean by surface area and more than 70 per cent by volume.[22] As one of the largest reservoirs of biodiversity on Earth, ABNJ are home to a rich and diverse web of life, representing nearly 4 billion years of evolution.[23]

Biodiversity is found in the ocean's pelagic and benthic realms. The sun-lit epipelagic zone hosts whales, dolphins, sharks, turtles, fish, rays and seabirds.[24] Many species spend their entire lives in the open ocean or pass through on migratory routes to feeding or breeding grounds. Seaweed, algae and phytoplankton also thrive in this zone due to the availability of sunlight[25] (Figure 1.2).

The mesopelagic and bathypelagic zones (200 m to 4000 m deep) harbour the greatest species diversity, estimated to range from 300,000 to 10 million.[26] This mid-water environment is home to unique marine creatures, from imposing hatchetfish with tortured eyes and sharp pointy teeth to vampire squid that use spiky tentacles to deter predators or capture prey.[27] Bioluminescent organisms

21 As at 1 April 2022, the CBD has reached almost universal acceptance, with 196 Parties.

22 Lisa M. Campbell and Noella J. Gray, 'Area Expansion versus Effective and Equitable Management in International Marine Protected Areas Goals and Targets' (2019) 100 *Marine Policy* 192, 195; A.D. Rogers et al, 'The High Seas and Us: Understanding the Value of High-Seas Ecosystems' (Global Ocean Commission, 2014) 4.

23 A.D. Rogers et al, 'Marine Genetic Resources in Areas beyond National Jurisdiction: Promoting Marine Scientific Research and Enabling Equitable Benefit Sharing' (2021) 8 *Frontiers in Marine Science* 667274, 1–22, 2; The Pew Charitable Trusts, 'Underwater Treasures of the High Seas' (Briefing Booklet, March 2016) 1.

24 Kristina M. Gjerde, 'Ecosystems and Biodiversity in Deep Waters and High Seas' (UNEP Regional Seas Report and Studies No 178, 2006) 11.

25 Brenton Shields, 'Oceanic Zone Plants and Animals' *Sciencing* (Web Page, 22 November 2019) <http://sciencing.com/oceanic-zone-plants-animals-8174254.html>.

26 Ward Appeltans et al, 'The Magnitude of Global Marine Species Diversity' (2012) 22(23) *Current Biology* 2189, 2191.

27 'The Open Ocean' *MarineBio* (Web Page, 16 February 2019) <https://marinebio.org/oceans/open-ocean/>; Bec Crew, 'Deep-sea Hatchetfish' (Web Page, 1 May 2014) *Australian Geographic* <https://www.australiangeographic.com.au/blogs/creatura-blog/2014/05/deep-sea-hatchetfish/>.

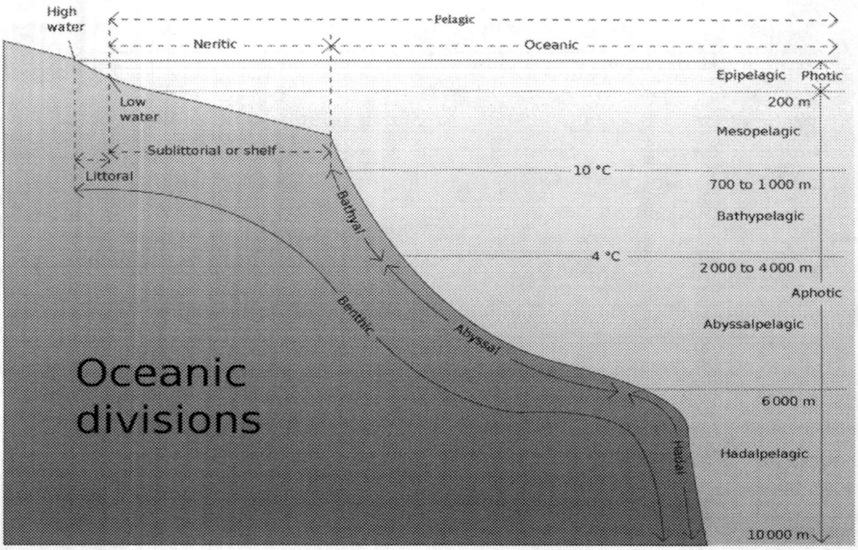

Figure 1.2 The ocean's pelagic and benthic realms. Credit: K. Aainsqatsi at en.wikipedia [Public domain, GFDL (http://www.gnu.org/copyleft/fdl.html) or CC-BY-SA-3.0], via Wikimedia Commons.

also penetrate the pitch-black darkness of the bathypelagic zone, including fire-fly squid and deep-sea comb jelly.

The benthic realm (200 m to almost 11,000 m deep) represents the largest ecosystem on Earth and supports one of the richest sources of biodiversity in a wide array of interconnected habitats.[28] Since 1840, 28 new benthic habitats have been discovered from the continental shelf break to the deep trenches.[29] Three, in particular, are regularly singled out: the geomorphological structure of seamounts, the chemosynthetic ecosystem of hydrothermal vents and the biotic communities of cold-water corals. These biodiversity hotspots are often grouped together under the umbrella term 'Vulnerable Marine Ecosystems' (VMEs).[30]

28 Catherine Banet, 'The Law of the Seabed' in Catherine Banet (ed) *The Law of the Seabed: Access, Uses and Protection of Seabed Resources* (Brill, 2020) 1, 9; Paul Snelgrove et al, 'Global Patterns in Marine Biodiversity' in United Nations, *The First Global Integrated Marine Assessment: World Ocean Assessment I* (Cambridge University Press, 2016) 503, 514.

29 Aline L. Jaeckel, *The International Seabed Authority and the Precautionary Principle* (Brill Nijhoff, 2017) 8.

30 Jake Rice, 'Synthesis of Part VI: Marine Biological Diversity and Habitats' in United Nations, *The First Global Integrated Marine Assessment World Ocean Assessment I* (Cambridge University Press, 2016) 917, 919.

1.2.2.1 Hydrothermal vents—oases of life in a submarine desert

Hydrothermal vents are 'oases of biodiversity on an otherwise sparsely inhabited ocean floor.'[31] They are home to a diverse and highly endemic community of species, including white crabs, ghostly fish and giant red-tipping tubeworms.

The unique physical and functional characteristics of hydrothermal vents stem from their creation. Under enormous pressure, cold seawater seeps through fissures on the ocean floor typically caused by volcanic or tectonic activity.[32] This seawater penetrates down to the Earth's mantle where it is heated by liquid magma.[33] After becoming enriched with metal ions and other substances, the superheated, chemical-rich water (vent fluid) is expelled at high pressure through seafloor vents, resembling a terrestrial geyser.[34] The vent fluid reaches temperatures of 350 to 400°C.[35] When it comes into contact with cold seawater, minerals precipitate out of the solution and deposit on the seafloor.[36] These mineral deposits form chimney-like structures with the largest towering 60 metres.[37] As the vent fluid billows out the chimney top, these geological features are known as 'black smokers' or 'white smokers' depending on their mineral composition.[38]

Without sunlight, hydrothermal vents sustain life through chemosynthesis.[39] Specialised bacteria convert chemicals in the vent fluid into cellular energy and nutrients, which feed the vent's food web.[40] As these specialised bacteria can withstand superheated and oxygen-deprived conditions, they are of great interest to science and industry alike.[41]

31 'Oases on the Ocean Floor,' *WWF* (Web Page, 19 June 2002) <https://wwf.panda.org/wwf_news/?2593/Oases-on-the-ocean-floor>.

32 Ibid.

33 M.K. Tivey, 'Hydrothermal Vent Systems' (1991) 34(4) *Oceanus* 68, 69.

34 Lauren S. Mullineaux et al, 'Exploring the Ecology of Deep-Sea Hydrothermal Vents in a Metacommunity Framework' (2018) 5 *Frontiers in Marine Science* 1–27, 4; 'Hydrothermal Vents,' *Woods Hole Oceanographic Institution* (Web Page) <https://www.whoi.edu/know-your-ocean/ocean-topics/seafloor-below/hydrothermal-vents/>.

35 Robin Warner, *Protecting the Oceans beyond National Jurisdiction: Strengthening the International Law Framework* (Martinus Nijhoff, 2009) 9.

36 Jaeckel (n 29) 9–10.

37 David Edward Johnson, 'Protecting the Lost City Hydrothermal Vent System: All Is Not Lost, or Is It?' (2019) 107 *Marine Policy* 103593, 1–4, 1.

38 Black smokers are composed of iron sulphide giving the chimney a black appearance. White smokers are composed of limestone (calcium carbonate), so the chimneys are ghostly white.

39 Steffen Kiel and Paul A. Tyler, 'Chemosynthetically-Driven Ecosystems in the Deep Sea' in Steffen Kiel (ed), *The Vent and Seep Biota* (Springer, 2010) vol 33, 1, 1.

40 Cindy Lee Van Dover, 'Tighten Regulations on Deep-Sea Mining' (2011) 470 *Nature* 31, 31; David Leary, *International Law and the Genetic Resources of the Deep Sea* (Martinus Nijhoff, 2007) 16.

41 Joanna Mossop, 'Reconciling Activities on the Extended Continental Shelf with Protection of the Marine Environment' in Rosemary Rayfuse (ed), *Research Handbook on International Marine Environmental Law* (Edward Elgar Publishing, 2015) 170, 172; Jaeckel (n 29) 10.

1.2.2.2 Seamounts—majestic mountains in the sea

Seamounts are large submarine mountains that rise up from the seafloor without breaching the ocean surface.[42] The conventional geological definition includes elevations greater than 1000 metres.[43] The first digital Geomorphic Seafloor Features Map identified 9951 seamounts, covering an area of 8,088,550 square kilometres.[44] The North Pacific Ocean boasts the highest concentration and the largest seamount of 15,500 square kilometres.[45] As seamounts are of volcanic origin,[46] they tend to be generated near tectonically active plate boundaries, mid-ocean spreading ridges and subducting zones, and can occur singly, in clusters or in chains.[47] Seamounts generally have a conical form, with steep sides and a hard, basaltic rock surface that provides a stable substratum for species to settle and grow.[48]

Seamounts are hotspots for pelagic and benthic biodiversity.[49] As they rise from the seafloor, they disturb the conditions of an otherwise still ocean bottom, causing an increase in currents.[50] This enhances the delivery of nutrient-rich waters to a community of cold-water corals, molluscs, sponges and other organisms, including the commercially valuable orange roughy.[51] Seamounts also act as rest stops, feeding grounds and reproduction sites for open ocean species.[52]

1.2.2.3 Cold-water corals (CWCs)—lush gardens in the deep-sea

While CWCs are closely associated with seamounts, they are recognised as VMEs in their own right. Lush coral gardens thrive in the icy cold waters (as low as 4°C)

42 P.T. Harris et al, 'Geomorphology of the Oceans' (2014) 352 *Marine Geology* 4, 22.
43 J. Anthony Koslow et al, 'Biological Communities on Seamounts and Other Submarine Features Potentially Threatened by Disturbance' in United Nations, *The First Global Integrated Marine Assessment: World Ocean Assessment I* (Cambridge University Press, 2016) 902, 903. An ecological approach includes knolls and hills below this height, see Snelgrove et al (n 28) 515.
44 The first digital Geomorphic Seafloor Features Map was presented in Harris et al (n 42) 23.
45 Ibid, 20.
46 Markus J. Kachel, *Particularly Sensitive Sea Areas: The IMO's Role in Protecting Vulnerable Marine Areas* (Springer Berlin Heidelberg, 2008) vol 13, 12.
47 Paul Wessel, 'Seamount Characteristics' in Tony Pitcher et al (eds), *Seamounts: Ecology, Fisheries and Conservation* (Blackwell Publishing, 2007) 3, 6; Gregory D. Pendleton, 'State Responsibility and the High Seas Marine Environment: A Legal Theory for the Protection of Seamounts in the Global Commons' (2005) 14(2) *Pacific Rim Law & Policy Journal Association* 485, 488.
48 Harris (n 42) 6; Pendleton (n 47) 488; Snelgrove et al (n 28) 516.
49 Morgan E. Visalli et al, 'Data-Driven Approach for Highlighting Priority Areas for Protection in Marine Areas beyond National Jurisdiction' (2020) 122 *Marine Policy* e103927, 1–14, 3.
50 Snelgrove et al (n 28) 515–516.
51 Ibid.
52 Telmo Morato et al, 'Seamounts are Hotspots of Pelagic Biodiversity in the Open Ocean' (2010) 107(21) *Proceedings of the National Academy of Sciences of the US of America* 9707, 9709.

thousands of metres below the ocean surface,[53] with some estimated to be over 8000 years old.[54]

As filter or suspension feeders, CWCs rely on nutrients and energy they ingest from particulate matter in passing currents.[55] Thus, CWCs tend to be found in locations where current flow is accelerated (i.e. seamounts, continental slopes)[56] and can exist as individual polyps, diversely shaped colonies or reefs made up of one or more species.[57] Their fragile skeletal structure provides a habitat for a highly endemic and thriving community of sea fans, sponges, starfish, crustaceans, fish and other marine life.[58] They also serve as important spawning, nursery, breeding and feeding areas and play a role in carbon cycling.[59]

1.2.3 Ecosystem services

Aside from supporting a wealth of biodiversity, ABNJ are the biophysical 'engines of our planet.'[60] The ocean produces more than half of the world's oxygen and moderates global climate conditions.[61] As the largest carbon reservoir on the planet,[62] the ocean absorbs over one-quarter of the anthropogenic CO_2 emitted into the atmosphere annually and stores 93 per cent of the resultant heat.[63]

53 'Deep-Sea Corals,' *Smithsonian* (Web Page, April 2018) <http://ocean.si.edu/deep-sea-corals>.

54 J.H. Fosså et al, 'Mapping of *Lophelia* Reefs in Norway: Experiences and Survey Methods' in A. Freiwald and J.M. Roberts (eds), *Cold-Water Corals and Ecosystems* (Springer, 2005) 359, 360.

55 Lisa A. Levin et al, 'Defining "Serious Harm" to the Marine Environment in the Context of Deep-Seabed Mining' (2016) 74 *Marine Policy* 245, 254.

56 Erik Cordes et al, 'Cold-Water Corals' in United Nations, *The First Global Integrated Marine Assessment: World Ocean Assessment I* (Cambridge University Press, 2016) 806, 807.

57 Deep-Sea Corals (n 53).

58 Interview with Professor J. Murray Roberts in Joanna Roberts, 'Q&A: To Protect the Atlantic, We First Need to Understand It' *Horizon the EU Research and Innovation Magazine* (Online Magazine, 6 February 2020) <https://horizon-magazine.eu/article/qa-protect-atlantic-we-first-need-understand-it.html>; Cordes et al (n 56) 808.

59 Aaron Lim, Andrew J. Wheeler and Luis Conti, 'Cold-Water Coral Habitat Mapping: Trends and Developments in Acquisition and Processing Methods' (2021) 11(1) *Geosciences* 1, 2; Chiara Paoli et al, 'Ecosystem Functions and Services of the Marine Animal Forests' in Sergio Rossi et al (eds), *Marine Animal Forests the Ecology of Benthic Biodiversity* (Springer Reference, 2019) 1271, 1280.

60 Jeffrey Marlow, 'The High Seas Are Being Exploited. Exploration Must Keep Pace' UNDARK (Web Page, 3 June 2018) <https://undark.org/2018/03/06/high-seas-conservation-exploration/>.

61 R. Blasiak et al, 'The Ocean Genome: Conservation and the Fair, Equitable and Sustainable Use of Marine Genetic Resources' (World Resources Institute, 2020) 7; IUCN, 'Governing Areas beyond National Jurisdiction' (Issues Brief, March 2019) 2.

62 Dr L. Woodall, Dr C. Stewart, Professor A. Rogers, 'Function of the High Seas and Anthropogenic Impacts Science Update 2012–2017' (University of Oxford for High Seas Alliance, July 2017) 7.

63 Kristina M. Gjerde, Nichola A. Clark and Harriet R. Harden-Davies, 'Building a Platform for the Future: The Relationship of the Expected New Agreement for Marine Biodiversity

The economic value of carbon storage by high seas ecosystems is estimated at US $148 billion a year.[64] The ocean also provides food for human consumption, energy resources and biomedical products, as well as cultural services through recreation, tourism and leisure activities.[65] In addition, the world's oceans and seas play a vital role in the traditions, customs and identity of coastal communities.[66] Failure to address threats to BBNJ could therefore compromise the ocean's capacity to provide essential ecosystem services that deliver societal and economic benefits.[67]

1.3 The troubled waters of ABNJ

1.3.1 Increasing threats from anthropogenic activities

One of the most important drivers behind the development of an ILBI has been an awareness of the declining environmental health of the ocean, including in ABNJ. Human activities in ABNJ have grown exponentially since the adoption of UNCLOS.[68] Advancements in science and technology coupled with a growing demand for raw materials and a depletion in terrestrial and coastal resources have increased interest in ABNJ, driving exploration and exploitation.[69] Given their remote nature, ABNJ were long considered protected from anthropogenic impacts.[70] However, the once popular view that the ocean was too big to be affected by human actions 'has been replaced by the reality of the Anthropocene Ocean.'[71] Only 13.2 per cent of the ocean can now be classified as marine

in Areas beyond National Jurisdiction' (2019) 33(1) *Ocean Yearbook Online* 1, 7; *Summary of the First Global Integrated Marine Assessment,* UN Doc A/70/112 (22 July 2015) [12].

64 José María Figueres, Trevor Manuel and David Miliband, 'From Decline to Recovery: A Rescue Package for the Global Economy' (Report, Global Ocean Commission, 2014) 5.

65 Meryl Williams et al, 'Scientific Results to Support the Sustainable Use and Conservation of Marine Life: A Summary of the Census of Marine Life for Decision Makers' (Census of Marine Life International Secretariat Consortium for Ocean Leadership, 2011) 2.

66 Robert Blasiak and Nobuyuki Yagi, 'Governing the High Seas' in Alistair Scrutton (ed), *Our Future on Earth* (Future Earth, 2020) 36, 37.

67 Angel Borja et al, 'Bridging the Gap between Policy and Science in Assessing the Health Status of Marine Ecosystems' (2016) 3 *Frontiers in Marine Science* 271, 271.

68 Glen Wright et al, 'The Long & Winding Road: Negotiating a Treaty for the Conservation and Sustainable Use of Marine Biodiversity in Areas beyond National Jurisdiction' (Study No. 8/2018, IDDRI, August 2018) 16.

69 Eva Ramirez-Llodra, 'Deep-Sea Ecosystems: Biodiversity and Anthropogenic Impacts' in Catherine Banet (ed), *The Law of the Seabed: Access, Uses and Protection of Seabed Resources* (Brill, 2020) 36, 50 ('Deep-Sea Ecosystems'); Glen Wright and Julien Rochette, 'Sea Change: Negotiating a New Agreement on the Conservation and Sustainable Use of Marine Biodiversity in Areas beyond National Jurisdiction' (Issue Brief No. 4/16, IDDRI, March 2016) 1.

70 Elisabeth Druel et al, 'A Long & Winding Road: International Discussions on the Governance of Marine Biodiversity in Areas beyond National Jurisdiction' (Study No. 7/2013, IDDRI, September 2013) 1.

71 Jean-Baptiste Jouffray et al, 'The Blue Acceleration: The Trajectory of Human Expansion into the Ocean' (2020) 2(1) *One Earth* 43, 48.

Table 1.2 Existing and emerging human activities in ABNJ

Status	*Activity*
Existing	Fishing
	Shipping
	Marine scientific research
	Bioprospecting
	Exploration of seabed mineral resources
	Constructing artificial islands and installations
	Pollution and marine litter
	Laying submarine cables
	Military activities
	Overflight
	Archaeological/salvage activities
Emerging	Deep-seabed mining
	Activities proposed to sequester CO_2
	Offshore energy facilities
	Open ocean aquaculture
	Deep-sea tourism
	Ocean fertilisation

wilderness, being biologically and ecologically intact seascapes free of human disturbance.[72]

BBNJ is falling victim to an ever-increasing list of human activities (see Table 1.2). While space limitations prevent an exhaustive examination, the following sections use deep-sea VMEs as a case study to highlight some of the key challenges of BBNJ protection.

1.3.1.1 Fishing

According to the UN Food and Agriculture Organisation 34.2 per cent of all fished species are overfished.[73] As conventional fisheries collapse, deep-sea fish stocks are facing increasing exploitation.[74] Deep-sea fishing is the single greatest risk to VMEs and their associated biodiversity.[75] Seamounts, in particular, have

72 Kendall R. Jones et al, 'The Location and Protection Status of Earth's Diminishing Marine Wilderness' (2018) 28(15) *Current Biology* 2506, 2506. Most of the 13 per cent is located in ABNJ.

73 FAO, *The State of the World Fisheries and Aquaculture 2020: Sustainability in Action* (The States of the World Series, 2020) 54.

74 Mukhisa Kituya and Peter Thomson, '90% of Fish Stocks Are Used Up: Fisheries Subsidies Must Stop Emptying the Ocean,' *World Economic Forum* (Article, 13 July 2018) <http://www.weforum.org/agenda/2018/07/fish-stocks-are-used-up-fisheries-subsidies-must-stop/>.

75 *Oceans and the Law of the Sea: Report of the Secretary-General*, UN Doc A/60/63/Add.1 (15 July 2005) [132].

experienced a steady increase in fishing activities. Fish stocks at seamounts are 'often long lived, with slow growth and delayed maturity making them poorly adapted to sustain heavy fishing pressure.'[76] The removal of a target species can disrupt the seamount's food web, making the ecosystem functionally vulnerable.[77] Destructive fishing gear also poses a threat.[78] Bottom trawlers 'scour the seafloor with steel plates, heavy cables and giant nets, indiscriminately catching everything in their path.'[79] This ground-gear can remove the seamount's benthic fauna converting its forests of corals into rubble.[80] The removal of coral substrate has been documented at heavily fished seamounts, and recovery times are estimated to span centuries to millennia.[81]

1.3.1.2 Deep-seabed mining

There is also growing interest in deep-sea mineral resources.[82] The seafloor massive sulphides at hydrothermal vents, for example, contain high concentrations of copper, zinc, lead, cadmium, gold, silver and nickel and can weigh several thousand to 100 million tonnes.[83] Similarly, the thick ferromanganese crusts of seamounts are high in manganese and iron, and the exploitable minerals of cobalt, copper and platinum.[84] The ISA has entered into 15-year contracts with 22 contractors for the exploration of deep-seabed mineral resources, with over 1 million square kilometres of ABNJ designated as exploratory mining claim areas.[85] As the deep-sea remains the least known ecosystem on Earth,[86] the long-term impacts of seabed mining are difficult to predict.[87]

76 Eva Ramirez-Llodra et al, 'Man and the Last Great Wilderness: Human Impact on the Deep Sea' (2011) 6 *PloS One* 7, 9 ('Man and the Last Great Wilderness').

77 *Impacts of Fishing on Vulnerable Marine Ecosystems: Actions Taken by States and Regional Fisheries Management Organizations and Arrangements to Give Effect to Paragraphs 66 to 69 of General Assembly Resolution 59/25 on Sustainable Fisheries, Regarding the Impacts of Fishing on Vulnerable Marine Ecosystems-Report of the Secretary-General*, UN Doc A/61/154 (14 July 2006) [26].

78 Malcolm R. Clark, 'The Impacts of Deep-Sea Fisheries on Benthic Communities: A Review' (2016) 73 *ICES Journal of Marine Science* Supplement i51, i52.

79 The Pew Environment Group, 'Deep-Sea Fisheries and Vulnerable Ecosystems in the Northeast Atlantic: How the EU Can Reform Its Deep-Sea Management Regime' (Report, July 2012) 2.

80 Koslow et al (n 43) 906–907.

81 Pendleton (n 47) 493.

82 Bethan C. O'Leary et al, 'Options for Managing Human Threats to High Seas Biodiversity' (2020) 187 *Ocean and Coastal Management* 105110, 1–12, 4.

83 Ramirez-Llodra et al, 'Man and the Last Great Wilderness' (n 76) 12.

84 Ibid.

85 ISA, 'Exploration Contracts' (Web Page, 2022) <https://www.isa.org.jm/exploration-contracts>.

86 Jaeckel (n 29) 8.

87 Stefanie Kaiser, Craig R. Smith and Pedro Martinez Arbizu, 'Editorial: Biodiversity of the Clarion-Clipperton Fracture Zone' (2017) 47 *Marine Biodiversity* 259, 259.

The seabed mining process typically consists of a nodule or seafloor collector, a transport system for conveying the material with riser and returner pumps attached to a specially designed production vessel. Seabed mining could also require large, remotely operated machinery to dig into, cut, crush and gather the ore.[88] The sophisticated robotic machines being developed by mining companies, such as Nautilus Minerals, could pose grave environmental threats to VMEs.

Although exploitation activities are yet to commence, simulated mining and test sites indicate that seabed mining could physically damage habitats and fauna, change seafloor topography, increase toxicity levels and create sediment plumes.[89] Toxic sediment plumes could smother and bury species or clog the feeding structures of suspension feeders.[90] The plumes may last weeks or even months and extend miles from their original source.[91] The biota at VMEs are particularly susceptible to these impacts due to slow growth rates and delayed maturity.[92] As these organisms provide important food, habitat and refuge for marine life, their loss could have a dramatic effect on the functioning of deep-sea ecosystems.

1.3.1.3 Marine scientific research (MSR)

MSR is another source of anthropogenic disturbance at VMEs, particularly hydrothermal vents.[93] Scientists may introduce observational equipment (i.e. light and noise) that could detrimentally change the dynamic of the vent environment.[94] Human-operated or remotely operated research vessels can also disturb the vent community, with frequent visits and repeated sampling at the one site.[95] In the past, human-operated vehicles have been used to ram vent chimneys and their tops have been partially or completely removed to collect samples.[96] Competing uses can also arise between researchers requiring physical samples versus those wishing to observe the vent's natural evolution.[97] While international organisations, such as InterRidge, have adopted Codes of Best Practice, stronger

88 Levin et al (n 55) 253.
89 Ramirez-Llodra, 'Deep-Sea Ecosystems' (n 69) 57.
90 Levin et al (n 55) 253.
91 Blasiak and Yagi (n 66) 43.
92 L.M. Wedding et al, 'From Principles to Practice: A Spatial Approach to Systematic Conservation Planning in the Deep Sea' (2013) 280(1773) *Proceedings of the Royal Society of Biological Sciences* 1, 2.
93 Cindy Van Dover, 'Impacts of Anthropogenic Disturbance at Deep-Sea Hydrothermal Vent Ecosystems: A Review' (2014) 102 *Marine Environmental Research* 59, 59 ('Impacts of Anthropogenic Disturbance').
94 Ibid, 64, 66; Joanna Mossop, 'Protecting Marine Biodiversity on the Continental Shelf beyond 200 Nautical Miles' (2007) 38 *Ocean Development and International Law* 283, 286.
95 *Oceans and the Law of the Sea: Report of the Secretary-General*, UN Doc A/60/63/Add.1 (15 July 2005) [174]–[175].
96 Van Dover, 'Impacts of Anthropogenic Disturbance' (n 93) 64.
97 Sophie Arnaud-Haond et al, 'Use of Marine Genetic Resources' in United Nations, *The First Global Integrated Marine Assessment: World Ocean Assessment I* (Cambridge University Press, 2016) 454, 456.

regulatory measures under an ILBI could ensure potential effects are assessed in advance and vent resources are used sustainably.[98]

1.3.1.4 Marine litter

Anthropogenic litter is also an environmental concern for BBNJ.[99] Approximately 6.4 million tonnes of litter enter the oceans annually.[100] Plastics account for 80 per cent of all debris from surface waters to deep-sea sediments.[101] The quantity of plastic litter is expected to rise in coming years as a consequence of the coronavirus disease (COVID-19) pandemic, with plastic linked to personal protective equipment (i.e. face masks, disposable gloves, disinfectant wipes) already being washed up on beaches and coastlines around the world.[102] Scientists have also recently discovered a new species of prawn living 7 kilometres below sea level in the Mariana Trench. This species is known as *Eurythenes plasticus* (the plastic prawn) due to the alarming amount of plastic in its body.[103] Although the impacts of marine litter on benthic habitats have not been studied in detail, known effects in species include suffocation and entanglement as well as physical damage to habitats and chemical pollution from decomposing materials.[104] Marine litter is also a possible vector for the transfer of alien invasive species which can affect the equilibrium among the biotic and abiotic components of deep-sea ecosystems.[105]

1.3.2 Increasing pressure from climate-associated stressors

ABNJ are also facing climate-driven impacts.[106] Climate change is a 'threat magnifier alongside existing conventional threats.'[107] Ocean warming, acidification

98 Ibid; *Oceans and the Law of the Sea: Report of the Secretary-General*, UN Doc A/60/63/Add.1 (15 July 2005) [175].
99 See Pierpaolo Consoli et al, 'The Impact of Marine Litter from Fish Aggregation Devices on Vulnerable Marine Benthic Habitats of the Central Mediterranean Sea' (2020) 152 *Marine Pollution Bulletin* 110928, 1–8, 1.
100 Luisa Galgani et al, 'Impacts of Marine Litter' (Research Paper, Frontiers in Marine Science, July 2019) 2.
101 IUCN, 'Marine Plastics' (Issues Brief, May 2018) 1.
102 Sara Bettencourt, Sonia Costa and Sandra Caeiro, 'Marine Litter: A Review of Educative Interventions' (2021) 168 *Marine Pollution Bulletin* e112446, 1–17, 1.
103 See Johanna N.J. Weston et al, 'New Species of Eurythenes from Hadal Depths of the Mariana Trench, Pacific Ocean (Crustacea: Amphipoda)' (2020) 4748(1) *Zootaxa* 163.
104 Ramirez-Llodra, 'Deep-Sea Ecosystems' (n 69).
105 Wright et al (n 68) 21; Giuseppe Corriero et al, 'Ecosystem Vulnerability to Alien and Invasive Species: A Case Study on Marine Habitats along the Italian Coast' (2016) 26 *Aquatic Conservation Marine and Freshwater Ecosystems* 392, 393.
106 Tim Stephens, 'Warming Waters and Souring Seas: Climate Change and Ocean Acidification' in Donald Rothwell et al (eds), *The Oxford Handbook of the Law of the Sea* (Oxford University Press, 2015) 777, 779.
107 Catherine Redgwell, 'Treaty Evolution, Adaptation and Change: Is the LOSC "Enough" to Address Climate Change Impacts on the Marine Environment' (2019) 34 *The International Journal of Marine and Coastal Law* 440, 443.

and deoxygenation and the changes associated with them (e.g. species migration to cooler waters) pose a threat to the biodiversity, productivity and resilience of the ocean.[108]

While it is beyond the scope of this chapter to examine each anthropogenic stressor, attention is directed to ocean acidification and the risk it poses to scleractinian CWCs. Scleractinia (stony or hard corals) are polyp animals that always possess an external ectodermal, calcareous skeleton.[109]

Since the Industrial Revolution, the ocean has absorbed almost 30 per cent of all anthropogenic CO_2 emissions.[110] The absorption of CO_2 leads to lowered seawater pH and a decrease in carbonate ion concentrations, resulting in a diminished calcium carbonate saturation state.[111] Scleractinian CWCs are particularly susceptible to these changes as they build their skeletons and protective shells from calcium carbonate polymorphs (calcite or aragonite).[112] The global distribution of CWCs is therefore limited, in part, by the depth of the aragonite saturation horizon (the depth below which carbonate minerals dissolve).[113] Below the horizon, seawater is undersaturated with aragonite, which hinders coral growth and is corrosive to their skeletal framework.[114] As ocean acidification intensifies, the saturation horizon will likely become shallower, exposing more corals to undersaturated waters. This could eventually cause their skeletal frameworks to dissolve completely.[115] The weakening of structurally critical parts of the deep-sea CWC reef framework could lead to 'physical habitat collapse on an ecosystem scale, reducing the potential for biodiversity support.'[116] Due to the effects of acidification, the oceans could become uninhabitable for scleractinian CWCs by the end of the century.[117]

108 Siddharth Skekhar Yadav and Kristina Maria Gjerde, 'The Ocean, Climate Change and Resilience: Making Ocean Areas beyond National Jurisdiction More Resilient to Climate Change and Other Anthropogenic Activities' (2020) 122 *Marine Policy* e104184, 1–9, 2.

109 Michael Allaby, *A Dictionary of Zoology* (Oxford University Press, 3rd ed, 2009) (definition of 'Madreporaria, scleractinia; stony corals').

110 Ellycia R. Harrould-Kolieb, 'The United Nations Convention on the Law of the Sea: A Governing Framework for Ocean Acidification?' (2020) 29(2) *Review of European, Comparative and International Environmental Law* 257, 257.

111 Janina V. Büscher, Armin U. Form and Ulf Riebesell, 'Interactive Effects of Ocean Acidification and Warming on Growth, Fitness and Survival of the Cold-Water Coral Lophelia pertusa under Different Food Availabilities' (2017) 4 *Frontiers in Marine Science* 1–14, 2.

112 Ibid.

113 Fiz F. Perez et al, 'Meridional Overturning Circulation Conveys Fast Acidification to the Deep Atlantic Ocean' (2018) 554 *Nature* 515, 515; Cordes et al (n 56) 811.

114 Daisy Dunne, 'Acidification Could Leave Oceans "Uninhabitable" for Cold-Water Corals' Carbon Brief (Web Page, 12 February 2018) <https://www.carbonbrief.org/acidification-could-leave-oceans-uninhabitable-cold-water-corals>.

115 Ibid; Cordes et al (n 56) 811.

116 Uwe Wolfram et al, 'Micromechanical Consequences of Ocean Acidification for Cold-Water Corals' (Conference Paper, 26th Congress of the European Society of Biomechanics, 14 July 2021).

117 Dunne (n 114).

1.3.3 Gaps and limitations in the existing international law framework

Gaps and limitations in the existing international law framework are the other main driver behind the ILBI's development. Rules, regulations and institutional structures have not kept pace with the rapid surge in anthropogenic activities in ABNJ.[118] This is particularly true of UNCLOS, which was hailed as a 'Constitution for the Oceans' upon its adoption.[119] UNCLOS intended to settle 'all issues relating to the law of the sea.'[120] However, UNCLOS drafters could not have foreseen the substantial rise in activity in ABNJ and were unaware of the abundance of life in these maritime zones. While UNCLOS undoubtedly remains the pre-eminent instrument for the contemporary law of the sea, the expansion of the human footprint in ABNJ has exposed gaps and limitations in its framework.[121] Freestone and Mangone offer the following explanation:

> despite the fact that UNCLOS III took nine years to produce the text of the Convention [UNCLOS] … there are still important issues that require future work—either because they were simply unfinished—or because of new expectations and demands. The innovatory 'consensus procedure' and the 'package deal' approach … necessitated a large number of compromises and, as a direct result, a significant number of issues were not fully resolved.[122]

State practice and specialised legal instruments have supplemented UNCLOS, including two Implementation Agreements, one that modified the seabed mining regime in Part XI and the other to address the 'unfinished agenda' of the regulation of high seas fish stocks.[123] The development of an ILBI will attempt to address the 'unanticipated problems' associated with BBNJ.[124]

118 Catherine Blanchard, Carole Durussel and Ben Boteler, 'Socio-Ecological Resilience and the Law: Exploring the Adaptive Capacity of the BBNJ Agreement' (2019) 108 *Marine Policy* e103612, 1–10, 3.

119 T.B. (Tommy) Koh, 'A Constitution for the Oceans' (Statements made on 6 and 11 December 1982 at the Final Session of UNCLOS III at Montego Bay) reprinted in Myron H. Nordquist, *United Nations Convention on the Law of the Sea, 1982: A Commentary* (Martinus Nijhoff, 1995) vol 1, 11.

120 UNCLOS, preamble.

121 A. Eassom et al, 'Horizon Scan of Pressures on Biodiversity beyond National Jurisdiction' (The UN Environment World Conservation Monitoring Centre, 2017) 4.

122 Gerard Mangone and David Freestone, 'The Law of the Sea Convention: Unfinished Agendas and Future Challenges' (1995) 10(2) *The International Journal of Marine and Coastal Law* ix, x.

123 David Freestone, 'A Decade of the Law of the Sea Convention: Is It a Success?' (2007) 39(3) *George Washington International Law Review* 499, 538–539; David Freestone, 'Problems of High Seas Governance' in Davor Vidas and Peter Johan Schei (eds), *The World Ocean in Globalisation: Climate Change, Sustainable Fisheries, Biodiversity, Shipping, Regional Issues* (Brill, 2011) 99, 100.

124 Robin Churchill, 'The LOSC Regime for Protection of the Marine Environment: Fit for the Twenty-First Century?' in Rosemary Rayfuse (ed), *Research Handbook on International Marine Environmental Law* (Edward Elgar Publishing, 2015) 3, 29.

1.3.3.1 General framework nature of UNCLOS

UNCLOS did mark an important turning point in ocean governance being the first international agreement to codify rules and principles for the protection of the entire marine environment.[125] However, UNCLOS provisions relating to environmental protection are only of a framework nature.[126] Take Article 192 as an example. Article 192 requires States to protect and preserve the marine environment. In the *South China Sea Arbitration (Philippines v China)*, a tribunal established under Annex VII of UNCLOS considered the obligation in Article 192 sufficiently broad to include the protection of biodiversity.[127] Yet, Article 192 is only one sentence in length and fails to provide detail or guidance on how this obligation is to be achieved. Freestone laments that 'there are few obligations in international law that are so unqualified' as Article 192.[128]

UNCLOS also lacks modern governance principles and conservation tools. For example, the precautionary principle and ecosystem approach are not explicitly referenced in the Convention, nor are there detailed provisions for the establishment of area-based management tools, which are crucial mechanisms for protecting BBNJ.[129]

1.3.3.2 Patchwork of international, regional and sectoral bodies

Under the UNCLOS umbrella framework, ABNJ are governed, regulated and or managed by a patchwork of governance organisations and bodies, each with their own mandates and priorities. None of these organisations and bodies have a primary focus on BBNJ.[130] While some sectors have taken steps to implement measures to protect BBNJ, their mandates extend to specific regions or activities and often their jurisdictions overlap. For example, to protect ecosystems and their associated biodiversity from deep-sea mining impacts, the ISA has adopted a network of nine Areas of Particular Environmental Interest (APEI) in the Clarion-Clipperton Zone.[131] While VMEs in APEI are protected from mining, they can

125 Alexander Proelss and Katherine Houghton, 'Protecting Marine Species' in Rosemary Rayfuse (ed), *Research Handbook on International Marine Environmental Law* (Edward Elgar Publishing, 2015) 229, 231.

126 Churchill (n 124) 5.

127 *In the Matter of the South China Sea Arbitration (Philippines v. China) (Arbitral Award)* (Permanent Court of Arbitration, Case No 2013-19, 12 July 2016) [941].

128 David Freestone, 'Foreword' in Rosemary Rayfuse (ed), *Research Handbook on International Marine Environmental Law* (Edward Elgar Publishing, 2015) ix, xi.

129 The Pew Charitable Trusts, 'Potential Elements of an UNCLOS Implementing Agreement' (Press Release and Statement, 2012) <http://www.pewtrusts.org/en/about/news-room/press-releases/2012/04/25/potential-elements-of-an-unclos-implementing-agreement>.

130 The Pew Charitable Trusts, 'A Path to Creating the First Generation of High Seas Protected Areas' (Report, 31 March 2020) 5.

131 ISA, *Decision of the Council Relating to an Environmental Management Plan for the Clarion-Clipperton Zone* ISBA/18/C/22 (26 July 2012); Michael Lodge et al, 'Seabed Mining: International Seabed Authority Environmental Management Plan for the Clarion-Clipperton Zone: A Partnership Approach' (2014) 49 *Marine Policy* 66.

nevertheless be adversely impacted by other ocean activities not covered under the ISA mandate.[132]

Existing governance bodies for ABNJ 'bear no real relationship to one another and operate independent of each other without an overarching framework to ensure structure, consistency and coherence.'[133] As highlighted in the first World Ocean Assessment:

> The sustainable use of the ocean cannot be achieved unless the management of all sectors of human activities affecting the ocean is coherent ... This requires taking into account the effects on ecosystems of each of the many pressures, what is being done in other sectors and the way that they interact.[134]

The current law framework provides inadequate protection for BBNJ.[135] There are coverage gaps, weak implementation of and compliance with existing arrangements and cooperation is generally lacking.[136] The BBNJ process was launched to find 'durable solutions' to these issues.[137] As there is no single instrument that deals comprehensively with BBNJ,[138] the development of an ILBI offers the chance 'to write a new chapter for ocean governance,' one that places the conservation and sustainable use of BBNJ at its core.[139]

1.4 A brief historical overview of the BBNJ process

The following sections provide an overview of the BBNJ process to introduce key negotiation documents referenced throughout this book.

132 David Freestone and Viva Harris, 'Particularly Sensitive Sea Areas beyond National Jurisdiction: Time to Chart a New Course?' in Myron H. Nordquist, John Norton Moore and Ronán Long (eds), *International Marine Economy: Law and Policy* (Koninklijke Brill NV, 2017) vol 20, 322, 334–335.

133 Dire Tladi, 'Ocean Governance: A Fragmented Regulatory Framework' in P. Jacquet, R. Pachauri and L. Tubiana (eds), *Oceans: The New Frontier–A Planet for Life* (The Energy and Resources Institute Press, 2011) 99, 101.

134 *Summary of the First Global Integrated Marine Assessment* UN Doc A/70/112 (22 July 2015) [40].

135 Anna-Maria Hubert, 'UN General Assembly Resolution to Develop a New Legally Binding Instrument on the Conservation and Sustainable Use of Marine Biological Diversity of Areas beyond National Jurisdiction' (The NCLOS Blog, 17 August 2015) <https://site.uit.no/nclos/2015/08/17/un-general-assembly-resolution-to-develop-a-new-legally-binding-instrument-on-the-conservation-and-sustainable-use-of-marine-biological-diversity-of-areas-beyond-national-jurisdiction/>.

136 Blanchard, Durussel and Boteler (n 118) 3; Emily Barritt and Jorge E. Viñuales, 'Legal Scan: A Conservation Agenda for Biodiversity beyond National Jurisdiction' (Cambridge Centre for Environment, Energy and Natural Resource Governance, University of Cambridge, May 2016) 7.

137 Blanchard, Durussel and Boteler (n 118) 3.

138 Barritt and Viñuales (n 136) 7.

139 Gillian Anderson, 'This Is Crunch Point for Our Oceans: Let's Do the Right Thing,' *The Guardian* (UK, 19 August 2019).

1.4.1 Early developments

Since the turn of the 21st century, the international community has become increasingly concerned with the challenges facing BBNJ. As early as 2001, Australia and Germany were hosting joint workshops on managing risks to biodiversity in ABNJ.[140] Even though BBNJ-related issues had been raised within various fora,[141] the process to develop the ILBI actually emerged from the UN Open-ended Informal Consultative Process on Oceans and the Law of the Sea (UNICPOLOS).[142] In 2003, UNICPOLOS recommended the UNGA invite relevant international bodies to consider how to better address specific threats to VMEs and to BBNJ more broadly.[143] The UNICPOLOS recommendations prompted the UNGA to take action.[144] On 17 November 2004, the UNGA established an Ad Hoc Open-ended Informal Working Group to study issues relating to the conservation and sustainable use of BBNJ.[145] This event marks the birth of the BBNJ process.

1.4.1.1 Ad hoc Open-ended Informal Working Group (BBNJ Working Group)

The BBNJ Working Group held nine meetings between February 2006 and January 2015. Discussions focused on gaps and limitations in the existing international law framework and whether these necessitated the adoption of a new instrument under UNCLOS.[146] The first few meetings did not achieve any significant outcomes,[147] due largely to the ideological divide between States concerning the legal status of the Area's marine genetic resources.

The fourth meeting marked an important turning point, when delegations agreed for all future discussions to be structured around a package deal of four

140 Druel et al (n 70) 8.

141 Including the UN Secretariat, UNEP, FAO, UNESCO, IMO, CBD Secretariat, IUCN, WWF, Deep-Sea Conservation Coalition and processes including the Joint Group of Experts on the Scientific Aspects of Marine Environmental Protection—see, generally, Julien Rochette and Raphaël Billé, 'Governance of Marine Biodiversity beyond National Jurisdictions: Issues and Perspectives Report of the International Seminar "Towards a New Governance of High Seas Biodiversity"' (Principality of Monaco, 20–21 March 2008)' (2008) 51 *Ocean and Coastal Management* 779, 780.

142 Warner, 'Conserving Marine Biodiversity' (n 12) 765.

143 Alice Bisiaux, Prisna Nuengsigkapian and Charlotte Salpin, 'Summary of the Fourth Meeting of the Open-Ended Informal Consultative Process on Oceans and the Law of the Sea: 2–6 June 2003' *Earth Negotiations Bulletin* (Online Bulletin, 9 June 2003) 7 <https://enb.iisd.org/download/pdf/enb2506e.pdf>.

144 *Report on the Work of the United Nations Open-Ended Informal Consultative Process on Oceans and the Law of the Sea at Its Fifth Meeting*, UN Doc A/59/122 (1 July 2004) [1].

145 *Oceans and the Law of the Sea*, GA Res 59/24, UN Doc A/RES/59/24 (4 February 2005, adopted 17 November 2004) [73].

146 Wright and Rochette (n 69) 2.

147 Druel et al (n 70) 22.

thematic topics, taken together and as a whole. Despite the formulation of the package deal, Working Group discussions became increasingly polarised.[148] Major blocs of countries (EU and G77/China coalition) strongly advocated for a new implementing agreement to UNCLOS.[149] Other States, including the US, Canada, Japan, Iceland and Russia, were reluctant to open negotiations for a new agreement.[150] This debate came to a head at the 2012 UN Conference on Sustainable Development (Rio+20). At Rio+20 many States pushed for an agreement to launch ILBI negotiations. However, due to opposition from a few influential States (i.e. the US and Russia) political consensus was not reached.[151] Instead, world leaders agreed to take a decision on the development of an ILBI by the end of the 69th session of the UNGA (September 2015).[152]

From 2013 to 2015, the BBNJ Working Group continued to engage in substantive debates on the scope, parameters and feasibility of an ILBI.[153] After intense discussions, a consensus was reached at the final meeting and delegations took the historic step of recommending to the UNGA that an ILBI should be developed.[154] The recommendations of the Working Group were approved in UNGA resolution 69/292 of 19 June 2015, which also established a Preparatory Committee to make substantive recommendations on the elements of a draft ILBI text.[155]

1.4.1.2 The Preparatory Committee (PrepCom)

The PrepCom met on four occasions between 2016 and 2017. At PrepCom 1, delegations considered the scope of an ILBI, its relationship with other

148 Ibid, 10.
149 Ibid.
150 Tullio Scovazzi, 'The Rights to Genetic Resources beyond National Jurisdiction: Challenges for the Ongoing Negotiations at the United Nations' in Catherine Banet (ed) *The Law of the Seabed* (Brill Nijhoff, 2020) 213, 214; Julien Rochette et al, 'A New Chapter for the High Seas?' (Working Paper, Institute for Advanced Sustainability Studies, April 2015) 5.
151 Druel et al (n 70) 10.
152 *The Future We Want*, GA Res 66/288, UN Doc A/RES/66/288 (11 September 2012, adopted 27 July 2012) para 162.
153 Elisa Morgera et al, 'Summary of the First Session of the Intergovernmental Conference on an International Legally Binding Instrument under the UN Convention on the Law of the Sea on the Conservation and Sustainable Use of Marine Biodiversity of Areas beyond National Jurisdiction 4–17 September 2018' *Earth Negotiations Bulletin* (Online Bulletin, 20 September 2018) 2 <https://enb.iisd.org/download/pdf/enb25179e.pdf> ('Summary of IGC 1').
154 *Recommendations of the Ad Hoc Open-Ended Informal Working Group to Study Issues Relating to the Conservation and Sustainable Use of Marine Biological Diversity beyond Areas of National Jurisdiction to the Sixty-Ninth Session of the General Assembly* (23 January 2015) [5] <https://www.un.org/Depts/los/biodiversityworkinggroup/documents/AHWG_9_recommendations.pdf>.
155 *Development of an International Legally Binding Instrument under UNCLOS on the Conservation and Sustainable Use of Marine Biological Diversity of Areas beyond National Jurisdiction*, GA Res 69/292, UN Doc A/RES/69/292 (6 July 2015, adopted 19 June 2015) para 1 (a).

instruments and the BBNJ package deal.[156] Initially, the PrepCom process showed promise, 'with delegations prepared to exchange detailed suggestions on "how" to do it, rather than to linger on any remaining ifs.'[157] The aim of PrepCom 2 was to encourage concrete and detailed proposals.[158] The PrepCom Chair, Eden Charles, prepared an indicative list of issues and questions to assist delegations in identifying areas of convergence.[159] Unfortunately, delegations were unable to reach agreement on most substantive issues, and many topics were flagged as requiring further discussion. This continued through PrepCom 3. In an effort to move the process forward, delegations requested the Chair prepare a 'Streamlined non-paper on elements of a draft text,'[160] providing a compilation of ideas and proposals submitted by delegations.

An outcome report (PrepCom Report) was adopted by consensus at PrepCom 4.[161] Section A of the report contains a non-exclusive list of elements that generated convergence among most delegations.[162] Section B includes a list of issues that require the most attention (see Appendix 1) and reveals a high level of divergence on each package deal element.[163] A number of these chasms still exist in the negotiation process today. The PrepCom Report recommended for the UNGA to take a decision on the convening of an Intergovernmental Conference, with a view to developing an ILBI as soon as possible.

1.4.1.3 Intergovernmental Conference (IGC)

On 24 December 2017, the UNGA, in resolution 72/249, decided to convene an IGC to consider PrepCom recommendations.[164] Four meetings of the IGC

156 *Chair's Overview of the First Session of the Preparatory Committee*, [8] <https://www.un.org/Depts/los/biodiversity/prepcom_files/PrepCom_1_Chair's_Overview.pdf>.

157 Elisa Morgera et al, 'Summary of the First Session of the Preparatory Committee on Marine Biodiversity of Areas beyond National Jurisdiction: 28 March–8 April 2016' *Earth Negotiations Bulletin* (Online Bulletin, 11 April 2016) 18 <https://enb.iisd.org/download/pdf/enb25106e.pdf> ('Summary of PrepCom 1').

158 Wright et al (n 68) 44.

159 *Chair's Indicative Suggestions of Clusters of Issues and Questions to Assist Further Discussions in the Informal Working Groups at PrepCom2* <https://www.un.org/Depts/los/biodiversity/prepcom_files/IWGs_Indictive_Issues_and_Questions.pdf>.

160 *Chair's Streamlined Non-Paper on Elements of a Draft Text of an International Legally-Binding Instrument PrepCom 4* (10–21 July 2017) <https://www.un.org/Depts/los/biodiversity/prepcom_files/Chairs_streamlined_nonpaper_to_delegations.pdf>.

161 *Report of the Preparatory Committee: Development of an International Legally Binding Instrument under UNCLOS on the Conservation and Sustainable Use of Marine Biological Diversity of Areas beyond National Jurisdiction*, UN Doc A/AC.287/2017/PC.4/2 (31 July 2017) <https://www.un.org/ga/search/view_doc.asp?symbol=A/AC.287/2017/PC.4/2>.

162 Ibid, 7–8.

163 Ibid, 17–18.

164 *International Legally Binding Instrument under UNCLOS on the Conservation and Sustainable Use of Marine Biological Diversity of Areas beyond National Jurisdiction*, GA Res

were scheduled. At an organisational meeting prior to IGC 1, the President of the deliberations, Rena Lee, was asked to prepare an 'Aid to Discussions' to serve as a starting point for negotiations.[165] This document builds on the PrepCom Report and identifies issues that need further discussion.[166] In opening IGC 1, the President emphasised that the BBNJ process presented a unique opportunity to 'make a difference on how we manage the oceans,' and this appeal appeared to 'breathe new life' into the negotiation process.[167]

During IGC 1, delegations reaffirmed that an ILBI should operationalise and strengthen UNCLOS provisions and should not undermine existing legal instruments, frameworks and bodies. The need to ensure the universality of the ILBI was also emphasised.[168] While informal working groups were established to discuss the package deal, not every delegation was ready to engage in textual negotiations, with some States, including Russia, not entirely convinced of the need for an ILBI.[169]

The expectation at the end of IGC 1 was to 'switch into negotiating mode.'[170] In preparation for IGC 2, the President was requested to prepare a document to facilitate text-based negotiations.[171] This document, known as the 'Aid to Negotiations,' translates ideas and proposals generated during IGC 1 and PrepCom into treaty language.[172] At IGC 2, delegations managed to achieve convergence on a few matters, including the need to promote coherence, complementarity and synergies with other frameworks and bodies. Many delegations called for a streamlined zero draft of an ILBI to be made available in preparation of IGC 3.

The President presented a Draft Text of an ILBI on 17 May 2019.[173] The draft negotiating text features 12 parts and allows delegates to envision the final shape of an ILBI.[174] In spite of this, delegations continue to disagree on a raft of issues.

72/249, UN Doc A/RES/72/249 (19 January 2018, adopted on 24 December 2017) para 1.

165 *President's Aid to Discussions*, UN Doc A/CONF.232/2018/33 (25 June 2018).

166 Ibid, [4].

167 Blanchard, Durussel and Boteler (n 118) 3.

168 *Statement by the President of the Conference at the Closing of IGC 1*, UN Doc A/CONF.232/2018/7 (20 September 2018) 1.

169 Wright et al (n 68) 54.

170 Tallash Kantai et al, 'Summary of the Second Session of the Intergovernmental Conference on the Conservation and Sustainable Use of Marine Biodiversity of Areas beyond National Jurisdiction: 25 March–5 April 2019' Earth Negotiations Bulletin (Online Bulletin, 8 April 2019) 17 <https://enb.iisd.org/download/pdf/enb25195e.pdf>.

171 Morgera et al, 'Summary of IGC 1' (n 153) 3.

172 *President's Aid to Negotiations*, UN Doc A/CONF.232/2019/1 (3 December 2018).

173 *Draft Text of an Agreement under UNCLOS on the Conservation and Sustainable Use of Marine Biological Diversity of Areas beyond National Jurisdiction*, UN Doc A/CONF.232/2019/6 (17 May 2019).

174 Tallash Kantai et al, 'Summary of the Third Session of the Intergovernmental Conference on the Conservation and Sustainable Use of Marine Biodiversity of Areas beyond National Jurisdiction: 19–30 August 2019' *Earth Negotiations Bulletin* (Online Bulletin,

At the conclusion of IGC 3, the President was requested to prepare a Revised Draft Negotiating Text to take into account IGC 3 discussions as well as textual proposals made by delegations. The Revised Draft Negotiating Text was released on 18 November 2019 in preparation for IGC 4.[175]

1.4.1.4 The current state of play

IGC 4 was originally scheduled to begin on 23 March 2020. However, in light of the situation concerning the COVID-19 pandemic, IGC 4 was postponed twice in accordance with UNGA decisions 74/543 and 75/750.[176] In an effort to maintain momentum, BBNJ intersessional work was carried out online in the interim to facilitate dialogue on the package deal and to assist delegations in enhancing their understanding of the issues.[177] After a two-year delay, IGC 4 was held from 7 to 18 March 2022. Despite being lauded 'as the most productive meeting of the IGC process,'[178] delegates were unable to conclude their work at IGC 4 which was the last of the four sessions initially mandated by the UNGA. Many scientists, conservationists and environmentalists were quick to blame UN member States for 'dragging their feet' during the final round of negotiations and for the 'glacial pace' of talks.[179] However, in her closing statement to the Conference, the President expressed optimism that 'with continued

2 September 2019) 21 <https://enb.iisd.org/events/3rd-session-intergovernmental-conference-igc-conservation-and-sustainable-use-marine/summary>.

175 *Revised Draft Negotiating Text* (n 2).

176 *International Legally Binding Instrument under UNCLOS on the Conservation and Sustainable Use of Marine Biological Diversity of Areas beyond National Jurisdiction* (GAOR, 74th sess., Suppl. no. 49, Vol. II) UN Doc A/DEC/74/543 (11 March 2020); *Oceans and the Law of the Sea*, GA Res 75/239, UN Doc A/RES/75/239 (5 January 2021, adopted 31 December 2020); *Oceans and the Law of the Sea: Intergovernmental conference on an International Legally Binding Instrument under the United Nations Convention on the Law of the Sea on the Conservation and Sustainable Use of Marine Biological Diversity of Areas beyond National Jurisdiction*, Singapore: draft decision, UN Doc A/75/L.96 (9 June 2021).

177 See, Division for Oceans Affairs and the Law of the Sea, 'Virtual Intersessional Work of the Intergovernmental Conference on an International Legally Binding Instrument under the United Nations Convention on the Law of the Sea on the Conservation and Sustainable Use of Marine Biological Diversity of Areas beyond National Jurisdiction' *United Nations* (Web Page) <https://www.un.org/bbnj/content/Intersessional-work>.

178 Tallash Kantai and Paola Bettelli, 'Summary of the Fourth Session of the Intergovernmental Conference on an International Legally Binding Instrument under the UN Convention on the Law of the Sea on the Conservation and Sustainable Use of Marine Biodiversity of Areas beyond National Jurisdiction: 7-18 March 2022' *Earth Negotiations Bulletin* (Online Bulletin, 21 March 2022) 1 <https://enb.iisd.org/sites/default/files/2022-03/enb25225e.pdf> ('Summary of IGC 4').

179 Karen McVeigh, 'UN Ocean Treaty Summit Collapses as States Accused of Dragging Out Talks' *The Guardian* (Australia, 22 March 2022) <https://www.theguardian.com/environment/2022/mar/21/un-ocean-treaty-summit-collapses-as-states-accused-of-dragging-out-talks>.

commitment, determination and dedication, we will be able to build bridges and close the remaining gaps.'[180] At the conclusion of IGC 4, delegates requested for the President to take the necessary steps to obtain a UNGA decision to convene a fifth session of the Conference in August 2022.[181]

1.5 Conclusion

This chapter has used deep-sea VMEs as a case study to highlight present challenges confronting BBNJ and to illustrate the urgent need for an ILBI. ABNJ are suffering under the weight of an increasing list of anthropogenic activities. These include traditional maritime uses of fishing and shipping, as well as emerging ocean industries, such as deep-seabed mining, bioprospecting and ocean fertilisation, among others. These activities pose individual, cumulative and synergistic threats to BBNJ and uncertainty surrounds their long-term impact on ABNJ.[182] To compound the situation, the oceans are facing a catalogue of anthropogenic stressors, most notably from the effects of climate change.[183] Ocean warming, acidification and deoxygenation pose significant challenges to the resilience of marine ecosystems and have been associated with the previous five mass extinction events on Earth.[184] The health of the ocean is deteriorating at an unprecedented rate, and unless action is taken to safeguard BBNJ, future generations may witness the next globally significant extinction event. The fate of BBNJ therefore hinges on the development of an 'effective, practicable and future proofed'[185] ILBI. The following chapter considers whether the Grotian tradition could stand in the way of the development of such an instrument.

References

Agreement for the Implementation of the Provisions of the United Nations Convention on the Law of the Sea of 10 December 1982 Relating to the Conservation and Management of Straddling Fish Stocks and Highly Migratory Fish Stocks, Opened for Signature 4 December 1995 (1995) 34 *ILM* 1542 (entered into force 11 December 2001).

Allaby, Michael, *A Dictionary of Zoology* (Oxford University Press, 3rd ed, 2009). DOI: 10.1093/acref/9780199233410.001.0001.

180 Ibid.

181 Kantai and Bettelli, 'Summary of IGC 4' (n 178) 18.

182 Rosemary Rayfuse, 'Climate Change, Marine Biodiversity and International Law' in Michael Bowman et al (eds), *Research Handbook on Biodiversity and Law* (Edward Elgar Publishing Limited, 2016) 123, 124.

183 Stephens (n 106) 779.

184 A.D. Rogers and D. d'A Laffoley, 'International Earth System Expert Workshop on Ocean Stresses and Impacts' (Summary Workshop Report, International Programme on the State of the Ocean, 20 June 2011) 5.

185 *Statement by the President of the Conference at the Closing of IGC 3*, UN Doc A/CONF.232/2019/10 (13 September 2019) 1.

Anderson, Gillian, 'This Is Crunch Point for Our Oceans: Let's Do the Right Thing' *The Guardian* (UK, 19 August 2019).

Appeltans, Ward, Shane T. Ahyong, Gary Anderson, Martin V. Angel, Tom Artois, Nicolas Bailly, Roger Bamber, Anthony Barber, Ilse Bartsch, Annalisa Berta, Magdalena Blazewicz-Paszkowycz, Phil Bock, Geoff Boxshall, Christoper B. Boyko, Simone nunes Brandão, 'The Magnitude of Global Marine Species Diversity' (2012) 22(23) *Current Biology* 2189–2202. DOI: 10.1016/j.cub.2012.09.036.

Ardron, Jeff A, Rosemary Rayfuse, Kristina Gjerde and Robin Warner, 'The Sustainable Use and Conservation of Biodiversity in ABNJ: What Can Be Achieved Using Existing International Agreements?' (2014) 49 *Marine Policy* 98–108. DOI: http://dx.doi.org/10.1016/j.marpol.2014.02.011.

Arnaud-Haond, Sophie, Caroline Bissada, Peyman Eghtesadi Araghi, Elva Escobar-Briones, Francoise Gaill, S. Kim Juniper, Ahmed Kawser, Ellen Kenchington, Nigel Preston, Gabriele Procaccini, Nagappa Ramaiah, Jake Rice, Alex Rogers, Wouter Rommens, Zheng Senlin and Michael Thorndyke, 'Use of Marine Genetic Resources' in United Nations (ed), *The First Global Integrated Marine Assessment: World Ocean Assessment I* (Cambridge University Press, 2016) 454. DOI: https:/doi.org/10.1017/9781108186148.

Banet, Catherine (ed), *The Law of the Seabed: Access, Uses and Protection of Seabed Resources* (Brill, 2020).

Barritt, Emily and Jorge E. Viñuales, *Legal Scan: A Conservation Agenda for Biodiversity Beyond National Jurisdiction* (Cambridge Centre for Environment, Energy and Natural Resource Governance, University of Cambridge, May 2016).

Bettencourt, Sara, Sonia Costa and Sandra Caeiro, 'Marine Litter: A Review of Educative Interventions' (2021) 168 *Marine Pollution Bulletin* e112446: 1–17. DOI: https://doi.org/10.1016/j.marpolbul.2021.112446.

Birnie, P, A. Boyle and C. Redgwell, *International Law and the Environment* (Oxford University Press, 3rd ed, 2009).

Bisiaux, Alice, Prisna Nuengsigkapian and Charlotte Salpin, 'Summary of the Fourth Meeting of the Open-ended Informal Consultative Process on Oceans and the Law of the Sea: 2–6 June 2003' *Earth Negotiations Bulletin* (Online Bulletin, 9 June 2003) <https://enb.iisd.org/download/pdf/enb2506e.pdf> accessed 31 March 2022.

Blanchard, Catherine, Carole Durussel and Ben Boteler, 'Socio-ecological resilience and the law: Exploring the adaptive capacity of the BBNJ Agreement' (2019) 108 *Marine Policy* e103612: 1-10. DOI: 10.1016/j.marpol.2019.103612.

Blasiak, Robert and Nobuyuki Yagi, 'Governing the High Seas' in Alistair Scrutton (ed), *Our Future on Earth* (Future Earth, 2020) 36.

Blasiak, R., R. Wynberg, K. Grorud-Colvert and S. Thambisetty, 'The Ocean Genome: Conservation and the Fair, Equitable and Sustainable Use of Marine Genetic Resources' (World Resources Institute, 2020) <www.oceanpanel.org/blue-papers/ocean-genome-conservation-and- fair-equitable-and-sustainable-use-marine-genetic> accessed 31 March 2022.

Borja, Angel, Michael Elliott, Paul V.R. Snelgrove, Melanie C. Austen, Torsten Berg, Sabine Cochrane, Jacob Carstensen, Roberto Danovaro, Simon Greenstreet, Anna-Stiina Heiskanen, Christopher P. Lynam, Marianna Mea, Alice Newton, Joana Patrício, Laura Uusitalo, María C. Yyarra and Christian Wilson, 'Bridging the Gap between Policy and Science in Assessing the Health Status of Marine Ecosystems' (2016) 3 *Frontiers in Marine Science* 271–293. DOI: 10.3389/fmars.2016.00175.

Brondizio, E.S, J. Settele, S. Díaz and H.T. Ngo, *Global Assessment Report on Biodiversity and Ecosystem Services of the Intergovernmental Science-Policy Platform on Biodiversity and Ecosystem Services* (IPBES Secretariat, 2019). DOI: https://doi.org/10.5281/zenodo.3831673.

Büscher, Janina V, Armin U. Form and Ulf Riebesell, 'Interactive Effects of Ocean Acidification and Warming on Growth, Fitness and Survival of the Cold-Water Coral Lophelia pertusa under Different Food Availabilities' (2017) 4 *Frontiers in Marine Science* 1–14. DOI: 10.3389/fmars.2017.00101.

Campbell, Lisa M. and Noella J. Gray, 'Area Expansion Versus Effective and Equitable Management in International Marine Protected Areas Goals and Targets' (2019) 100 *Marine Policy* 192–199. DOI: 10.1016/j.marpol.2018.11.030.

Convention on Biological Diversity, *First Draft of the Post–2020 Global Biodiversity Framework*, UN Doc CBD/WG2020/3/3 (5 July 2021).

Convention on Biological Diversity, *Strategic Plan 2011–2020, Aichi Biodiversity Targets*, UN Doc COP/10/INF/12/Rev.1 (14 March 2011).

Chair's Indicative Suggestions of Clusters of Issues and Questions to Assist Further Discussions in the Informal Working Groups at the Second Session of the Preparatory Committee <https://www.un.org/Depts/los/biodiversity/prepcom_files/IWGs_Indictive_Issues_and_Questions.pdf> accessed 31 March 2022.

Chair's Overview of the First Session of the Preparatory Committee, <https://www.un.org/Depts/los/biodiversity/prepcom_files/PrepCom_1_Chair's_Overview.pdf> accessed 31 March 2022.

Chair's Streamlined Non-paper on Elements of a Draft Text of an International Legally-binding Instrument under the United Nations Convention on the Law of the Sea on the Conservation and Sustainable Use of Marine Biological Diversity of Areas Beyond National Jurisdiction Fourth Session of the PrepCom (10–21 July 2017) <https://www.un.org/depts/los/biodiversity/prepcom_files/Chairs_streamlined_non-paper_to_delegations.pdf> accessed 31 March 2022.

Churchill, Robin, 'The LOSC Regime for Protection of the Marine Environment: Fit for the Twenty-First Century?,' in Rosemary Rayfuse (ed), *Research Handbook on International Marine Environmental Law* (Edward Elgar Publishing, 2015). DOI: https://doi.org/10.4337/9781781004777.

Clark, Malcolm R, 'The Impacts of Deep-sea Fisheries on Benthic Communities: A Review' (2016) 73 *ICES Journal of Marine Science* Supplement i51–i69. DOI: 10.1093/icesjms/fsv123.

Cochrane, Sabine K.J, Jesper H. Andersen, Tosten Berg, Hugues Blanchet, Angel Borja, Jacob Carstensen, Michael Elliott, Herman Hummel, Nathalie Niquil and Paul E. Renaud, 'What is Marine Biodiversity? Towards Common Concepts and Their Implications for Assessing Biodiversity Status' (2016) 3 *Frontiers in Marine Science* 1–14. DOI: 10.3389/fmars.2016.00248.

Consoli, Pierpaolo, Mauro Sinopoli, Alan Deidun and Franco Andaloro, 'The Impact of Marine Litter from Fish Aggregation Devices on Vulnerable Marine Benthic Habitats of the Central Mediterranean Sea' (2020) 152 *Marine Pollution Bulletin* 110928: 1–8. DOI: 10.1016/j.marpolbul.2020.110928.

Convention on Biological Diversity, opened for signature 5 June 1992 (1992) 1760 *UNTS* 143 (entered into force 29 December 1993) (CBD).

Cordes, Erik, Sophie Arnaud-Haond, Odd-Aksel Bergstad, Patricio Bernal, Ana Paula da Costa Falcão, Andre Freiwald and J Murray Roberts, 'Cold-Water Corals' in United Nations (ed), *The First Global Integrated Marine Assessment: World Ocean*

Assessment I (Cambridge University Press, 2016) 806. DOI: https:/doi.org/10.1017/9781108186148.

Corriero, Giuseppe, Catalso Pierri, Stefano Accoroni, Giorgio Alabiso, Giorgio Bavestrello, Enrico Barbone, Mauro Bastianini, Anna Maria Bazzoni, Fabrizio Bernardi Aubry, Ferdinando Boero, Maria Cristina Buia, Marina Cabrini, Elisa Camatti, Frine Cardone, Bruno Cataletto, Riccardo Cattaneo Vietti, Ester Cecere, Tamara Cibic, Paolo Colangelo, Alessandra De Olazabel, Gianfranco D'Onghia, Stefania Finotto, Nicola Fiore, Daniela Fornasaro, Simonetta Frascheti, Maria Cristina Gambi, Adriana Giangrande, Cinzia Gravili, Rosanna Guglielmo, Caterina Longo, Maurizio Lorenti, Antonella Lugliè, Porzia Maiorano, Maria Grazia Mazzochhi, Maria Mercurio, Francesco Mastrototaro, Michele Mistri, Marina Monti, Cristina Munari, Luigi Musco, Carlotta Nonnis-Marzano, Bachisio Mario Padedda, Francesco Paolo Patti, Antonella Petrocelli, Stefano Piraino, Giuseppe Portacci, Alessandra Pugnetti, Silvia Pulina, Tiziana Romagnoli, Ilaria Rosati, Diana Sarno, Cecilia Teodora Satta, Nicola Sechi, Stefano Schiaparelli, Beatrice Scipione, Letizia Sion, Anotnio Terlizzi, Valentina Tirelli, Cecilia Totti, Angelo Tursi, Nicola Ungaro, Adriana Zingone, Valerio Zupo, Alberto Basset, 'Ecosystem Vulnerability to Alien and Invasive Species: A Case Study on Marine Habitats Along the Italian Coast' (2016) 26 *Aquatic Conservation Marine and Freshwater Ecosystems* 392–409. DOI: 10.1002/aqc.2550.

Crew, Bec, 'Deep-sea Hatchetfish' (Web Page, 1 May 2014) *Australian Geographic* <https://www.australiangeographic.com.au/blogs/creatura-blog/2014/05/deep-sea-hatchetfish/> accessed 31 March 2022.

'Deep-Sea Corals,' *Smithsonian* (Web Page, April 2018) <http://ocean.si.edu/deep-sea-corals> accessed 31 March 2022.

Development of an International Legally Binding Instrument under the United Nations Convention on the Law of the Sea on the Conservation and Sustainable Use of Marine Biological Diversity of Areas Beyond National Jurisdiction, GA Res 69/292, UN Doc A/RES/69/292 (6 July 2015, adopted 19 June 2015).

Díaz S, J. Settele, E.S. Brondízio, H.T. Ngo, J. Agard, A. Arneth, P. Balvanera, K.A. Brauman, S.H.M. Butchart, K.M.A Chan, L.A. Garibaldi, K. Ichii, J. Liu, S.M. Subramanian, G.F. Midgley, P. Miloslavich, Z. Molnár, D. Obura, A. Pfaff, S. Polasky, A. Purvis, J. Razzaque, B. Reyers, R.R. Chowdhury, Y.J. Shin, I. Visseren-Hamakers, K.J. Willis and C.N. Zayas, 'Pervasive human-driven decline of life on Earth points to the need for transformative change' (2019) 366(6471) *Science* eaax3100. DOI: 10.1126/science.aax3100.

Díaz, S, J. Settele, E.S. Brondízio, H.T. Ngo, M. Guèze, J. Agard, A. Arneth, P. Balvanera, K.A. Brauman, S.H.M. Butchart, K.M.A. Chan, L.A. Garibaldi, K. Ichii, J. Liu, S. M Subramanian, G.F. Midgley, P. Miloslavich, Z. Molnár, D. Obura, A. Pfaff, S. Polasky, A. Purvis, J. Razzaque, B. Reyers, R. Roy Chowdhury, Y.J. Shin, I.J. Visseren-Hamakers, K.J. Willis and C.N. Zayas (eds.) *Summary for Policymakers of the Global Assessment Report on Biodiversity and Ecosystem Services of the Intergovernmental Science-Policy Platform on Biodiversity and Ecosystem Services* (IPBES Secretariat, 2019). DOI: https://doi.org/10.5281/zenodo.3553579.

Division for Oceans Affairs and the Law of the Sea, 'Virtual Intersessional Work of the Intergovernmental Conference on an International Legally Binding Instrument under the United Nations Convention on the Law of the Sea on the Conservation and Sustainable Use of Marine Biological Diversity of Areas Beyond National

Jurisdiction' United Nations (Web Page) <https://www.un.org/bbnj/content/Intersessional-work> accessed 31 March 2022.

Draft Text of an Agreement under the United Nations Convention on the Law of the Sea on the Conservation and Sustainable Use of Marine Biological Diversity of Areas Beyond National Jurisdiction, UN Doc A/CONF.232/2019/6 (17 May 2019) <https://documents-dds-ny.un.org/doc/UNDOC/GEN/N19/146/28/PDF/N1914628.pdf?OpenElement> accessed 31 March 2022.

Dromgoole, Sarah, *Underwater Cultural Heritage and International Law* (Cambridge University Press, 2013). DOI: https://doi.org/10.1017/CBO9781139020503.

Druel, Elisabeth, Julien Rochette, Raphaël Billé and Claudio Chiarolla, *A Long & Winding Road: International Discussions on the Governance of Marine Biodiversity in Areas Beyond National Jurisdiction* (Study No. 7/2013, IDDRI, September 2013).

Dunne, Daisy, 'Acidification could leave oceans "uninhabitable" for cold-water corals' Carbon Brief (Web Page, 12 February 2018) <https://www.carbonbrief.org/acidification-could-leave-oceans-uninhabitable-cold-water-corals> accessed 31 March 2022.

Eassom, A, S. Chiba, R. Fletcher, R. Scrimgeour and S. Fletcher, 'Horizon scan of pressures on Biodiversity Beyond National Jurisdiction' (The UN Environment World Conservation Monitoring Centre, 2017) <https://www.cambridgeconservation.org/wp-content/uploads/2017/06/Horizon_Scan_v14_Final.pdf> accessed 21 October 2021.

FAO, *The State of the World Fisheries and Aquaculture 2020: Sustainability in Action* (The States of the World Series, 2020).

Figueres, José María, Trevor Manuel and David Miliband, *From Decline to Recovery: A Rescue Package for the Global Economy* (Report, Global Ocean Commission, 2014).

Fosså, Jan Helge, Björn Lindberg, Ole Christensen, Tomas Lundälv, Ingvald Svellingen and Pål B Mortensen, 'Mapping of *Lopehlia* reefs in Norway: experiences and survey methods,' in A Freiwald and J M Roberts (eds), *Cold-Water Corals and Ecosystems* (Springer, 2005) 359. DOI: https://doi.org/10.1007/3-540-27673-4_18.

Freestone, David, 'A decade of the Law of the Sea Convention: Is it a Success?' (2007) 39(3) *George Washington International Law Review* 499–542.

Freestone, David, 'Problems of High Seas Governance' in Davor Vidas and Peter Johan Schei (eds), *The World Ocean in Globalisation: Climate Change, Sustainable Fisheries, Biodiversity, Shipping, Regional Issues* (Brill, 2011) 99. DOI: https://doi.org/10.1163/9789004204225_007.

Freestone, David, 'Foreword,' in Rosemary Rayfuse (ed), *Research Handbook on International Marine Environmental Law* (Edward Elgar Publishing, 2015) ix. DOI: https://doi.org/10.4337/9781781004777.00005.

Freestone, David and Viva Harris, 'Particularly Sensitive Sea Areas Beyond National Jurisdiction: Time to Chart a New Course?' in Myron H. Nordquist, John Norton Moore and Ronán Long (eds), *International Marine Economy: Law and Policy* (Koninklijke Brill NV, 2017) vol 20, 322. DOI: https://doi.org/10.1163/9789004323445_014.

Galgani, Luisa, Ricardo Beiras, Francois Galgani, Cristina Panti and Angel Borja, 'Impacts of Marine Litter' (Research Paper, *Frontiers in Marine Science*, July 2019). DOI: 10.3389/978-2-88945-931-5.

Gjerde, Kristina M, *Ecosystems and Biodiversity in Deep Waters and High Seas* (UNEP Regional Seas Report and Studies No 178, 2006).

Gjerde, Kristina M, Nichola A. Clark and Harriet R. Harden-Davies, 'Building a Platform for the Future: The Relationship of the Expected New Agreement for Marine Biodiversity in Areas Beyond National Jurisdiction' (2019) 33(1) *Ocean Yearbook Online* 1–44. DOI: 10.1163/9789004395633_002.

Harris, P.T, M. Macmillan-Lawler, M. Rupp and E. Baker, 'Geomorphology of the oceans' (2014) 352 *Marine Geology* 4–24. DOI: 10.1016/j.margeo.2014.01.011.

Harrould-Kolieb, Ellycia R, 'The United Nations Convention on the Law of the Sea: A Governing Framework for Ocean Acidification?' (2020) 29(2) *Review of European, Comparative and International Environmental Law* 257–270. DOI: 10.1111/reel.12321.

Hubert, Anna-Maria 'UN General Assembly Resolution to develop a new legally binding instrument on the conservation and sustainable use of marine biological diversity of areas beyond national jurisdiction' (*The NCLOS Blog*, 17 August 2015) <https://site.uit.no/nclos/2015/08/17/un-general-assembly-resolution-to-develop-a-new-legally-binding-instrument-on-the-conservation-and-sustainable-use-of-marine-biological-diversity-of-areas-beyond-national-jurisdiction/> accessed 31 March 2022.

'Hydrothermal Vents,' Woods Hole Oceanographic Institution (Web Page) <https://www.whoi.edu/know-your-ocean/ocean-topics/seafloor-below/hydrothermal-vents/> accessed 31 March 2022.

In the Matter of the South China Sea Arbitration (Philippines v. China) (Arbitral Award) (Permanent Court of Arbitration, Case No 2013–19, 12 July 2016).

International Legally Binding Instrument under the United Nations Convention on the Law of the Sea on the Conservation and Sustainable Use of Marine Biological Diversity of Areas Beyond National Jurisdiction, GA Res 72/249, UN Doc A/RES/72/249 (19 January 2018, adopted on 24 December 2017).

International Legally Binding Instrument under the United Nations Convention on the Law of the Sea on the Conservation and Sustainable Use of Marine Biological Diversity of Areas Beyond National Jurisdiction (GAOR, 74th sess., Suppl. no. 49, Vol. II) UN Doc A/DEC/74/543 (11 March 2020).

International Seabed Authority, *Decision of the Council Relating to an Environmental Management Plan for the Clarion-Clipperton Zone*, ISBA/18/C/22 (26 July 2012).

International Seabed Authority, 'Exploration Contracts' (Web Page, 2022) <https://www.isa.org.jm/exploration-contracts> accessed 21 October 2021.

International Union for Conservation of Nature, 'Marine Plastics' (Issues Brief, May 2018) <https://www.iucn.org/resources/issues-briefs/marine-plastics> accessed 31 March 2022.

International Union for Conservation of Nature, *Governing Areas Beyond National Jurisdiction* (Issues Brief, IUCN, March 2019).

Jaeckel, Aline L, *The International Seabed Authority and the Precautionary Principle* (Brill Nijhoff, 2017).

Johnson, David Edward, 'Protecting the Lost City Hydrothermal Vent System: All Is not Lost, or Is It?' (2019) 107 *Marine Policy* 103593: 1–4. DOI: 10.1016/j.marpol.2019.103593.

Jones, Kendall R, Carissa J. Klein, Benjamin S. Halpern, Oscar Venter, Hedley Grantham, Caitlin D. Kuempel, Nicole Shumway, Alan M. Friedlander, Hugh P. Possingham and James E.M. Watson, 'The Location and Protection Status of

Earth's Diminishing Marine Wilderness' (2018) 28(15) *Current Biology* 2506–2512. DOI: 10.1016/j.cub.2018.07.081.

Jouffray, Jean-Baptiste, Robert Blasiak, Albert V. Norström, Henrik Österblom and Magnus Nyström, 'The Blue Acceleration: The Trajectory of Human Expansion into the Ocean' (2020) 2(1) *One Earth* 43–54. DOI: https://doi.org/10.1016/j.oneear.2019.12.016.

Kachel, Markus J, *Particularly Sensitive Sea Areas: The IMO's Role in Protecting Vulnerable Marine Areas* (Springer, 2008) Vol 13. DOI: https://doi.org/10.1007/978-3-540-78779-2.

Kaiser, Stefanie, Craig R. Smith and Pedro Martinez Arbizu, 'Editorial: Biodiversity of the Clarion-Clipperton Fracture Zone' (2017) 47 *Marine Biodiversity* 259–264. DOI: 10.1007/s12526-017-0733-0.

Kantai, Tallash and Paola Bettelli, 'Summary of the Fourth Session of the Intergovernmental Conference on an International Legally Binding Instrument under the UN Convention on the Law of the Sea on the Conservation and Sustainable Use of Marine Biodiversity of Areas Beyond National Jurisdiction: 7-18 March 2022' *Earth Negotiations Bulletin* (Online Bulletin, 21 March 2022) 1 <https://enb.iisd.org/sites/default/files/2022-03/enb25225e.pdf> accessed 31 March 2022.

Kantai, Tallash, Asheline Appleton, Priscila Pereira de Andrade, Bernard Soubry and Asterios Tsioumanis, 'Summary of the Second Session of the Intergovernmental Conference on the Conservation and Sustainable Use of Marine Biodiversity of Areas Beyond National Jurisdiction: 25 March–5 April 2019' *Earth Negotiations Bulletin* (Online Bulletin, 8 April 2019a) <https://enb.iisd.org/download/pdf/enb25195e.pdf> accessed 31 March 2022.

Kantai, Tallash, Jennifer Bansard, Tasha Goldberg, Katarina Hovden and Asterios Tsioumanis, 'Summary of the Third Session of the Intergovernmental Conference on the Conservation and Sustainable Use of Marine Biodiversity of Areas Beyond National Jurisdiction: 19–30 August 2019' *Earth Negotiations Bulletin* (Online Bulletin, 2 September 2019b) <https://enb.iisd.org/download/pdf/enb25218e.pdf> accessed 31 March 2022.

Kiel, Steffen and Paul A. Tyler, 'Chemosynthetically-Driven Ecosystems in the Deep Sea' in Steffen Kiel (ed), *The Vent and Seep Biota* (Springer, 2010) vol 33, 1. DOI: https://doi.org/10.1007/978-90-481-9572-5.

Kituya, Mukhisa and Peter Thomson, '90% of Fish Stocks Are Used Up-Fisheries Subsidies Must Stop Emptying the Ocean' World Economic Forum (Article, 13 July 2018) <http://www.weforum.org/agenda/2018/07/fish-stocks-are-used-up-fisheries-subsidies-must-stop/> accessed 31 March 2022.

Koh, T.B. (Tommy), 'A Constitution for the Oceans' in *(Statements Made on 6 and 11 December 1982 at the Final Session of UNCLOS III at Montego Bay) reprinted in Myron H. Nordquist, United Nations Convention on the Law of the Sea, 1982: A Commentary* (Martinus Nijhoff, 1995) vol 1.

Koslow, J. Anthony, Peter Auster and Odd Aksel, 'Biological Communities on Seamounts and Other Submarine Features Potentially Threatened by Disturbance' in United Nations (ed), *The First Global Integrated Marine Assessment: World Ocean Assessment I* (Cambridge University Press, 2016) 902. DOI: https:/doi.org/10.1017/9781108186148.

Leary, David, *International Law and the Genetic Resources of the Deep Sea* (Martinus Nijhoff Publishers, 2007).

Leclère, D, M. Obersteiner, M. Barrett, S.H.M. Butchart, A. Chaudhary, Aiana De Palma, F.A.J. DeClerck, M. Di Marco, J.C. Doelman, M. Dürauer, R. Freeman, M. Harfoot, T. Hasegawa, S. Hellweg, J.P. Hilbers, S.L.L. Hill, F. Humpenöder, N. Jennings, T. Krisztin, G. M. Mace, H. Ohashi, Alexander Popp, A. Purvis, A.M. Schipper, A. Tabeau, H. Valin, H. van Meijl, W.J. van Zeist, P. Visconti, R. Alkemade, R. Almond, G. Bunting, N.D. Burgess, S.E. Cornell, F. Di Fulvio, S. Ferrier, S. Fritz, S. Fujimori, M. Grooten, T. Harwood, P. Havlík, M. Herrero, A.J. Hoskins, M. Jung, T. Kram, H. Lotze-Campen, T. Matsui, C. Meyer, D. Nel, T. Newbold, G. Schmidt-Traub, E. Stehfest, B.B.N. Strassburg, D.P. van Vuuren, C. Ware, J.E.M. Watson, W. Wu and L. Young, 'Bending the Curve of Terrestrial Biodiversity Needs an Integrated Strategy' (2020) 585(7826) *Nature* 551–556. DOI: 10.1038/s41586-020-2705-y.

Letter dated 7 July 2015 from the Co-Chairs of the Ad Hoc Working Group of the Whole on the Regular Process for Global Reporting and Assessment of the State of the Marine Environment, Including Socioeconomic Aspects Addressed to the President of the General Assembly, UN Doc A/70/112 (22 July 2015) annex ('Summary of the First Global Integrated Marine Assessment').

Levin, Lisa A, Kathryn Mengerink, Kristina M. Gjerde, Ashely A. Rowden, Cindy Lee Van Dover, Malcolm R. Clark, Eva Ramirez-Llodra, Bronwen Currie, Craig R. Smith, Kirk N. Sato, Natalya Gallo, Andrew K. Sweetman, Hannah Lily, Claire W. Armstrong and Joseph Brider, 'Defining "Serious Harm" to the Marine Environment in the Context of Deep-Seabed Mining' (2016) 74 *Marine Policy* 245–259. DOI: 10.1016/j.marpol.2016.09.032.

Lim, Aaron, Andrew J. Wheeler and Luis Conti, 'Cold-Water Coral Habitat Mapping: Trends and Developments in Acquisition and Processing Methods' (2021) 11(1) *Geosciences* 1–20. DOI: https://doi.org/10.3390/geosciences11010009.

Lodge, Michael, David Johnson, Gwenaëlle Le Gurun, Markus Wengler, Phil Weaver and Vikki Gunn, 'Seabed Mining: International Seabed Authority Environmental Management Plan for the Clarion-Clipperton Zone: A Partnership Approach' (2014) 49 *Marine Policy* 66–72. DOI: 10.1016/j.marpol.2014.04.006.

Mangone, Gerard and David Freestone, 'The Law of the Sea Convention: Unfinished Agendas and Future Challenges' (1995) 10(2) *The International Journal of Marine and Coastal Law* 151–155. DOI: https://doi.org/10.1163/157180895X00015.

Marlow, Jeffrey, 'The High Seas Are Being Exploited. Exploration Must Keep Pace' *UNDARK* (Web Page, 3 June 2018) <https://undark.org/2018/03/06/high-seas-conservation-exploration/> accessed 31 March 2022.

McVeigh, Karen, 'UN Ocean Treaty Summit Collapses as States Accused of Dragging Out Talks' *The Guardian* (Australia, 22 March 2022) <https://www.theguardian.com/environment/2022/mar/21/un-ocean-treaty-summit-collapses-as-states-accused-of-dragging-out-talks> accessed 31 March 2022.

Morato, Telmo, Simon D. Hoyle, Valerie Allain and Simon J. Nicol, 'Seamounts Are Hotspots of Pelagic Biodiversity in the Open Ocean' (2010) 107(21) *Proceedings of the National Academy of Sciences of the US of America* 9707–9711. DOI: 10.1073/pnas.0910290107.

Morgera, Elisa, Daniela Diz, Tallash Kantai and Asterious Tsioumanis, 'Summary of the First Session of the Preparatory Committee on Marine Biodiversity of Areas Beyond National Jurisdiction: 28 March–8 April 2016' *Earth Negotiations*

Bulletin (Online Bulletin, 11 April 2016) <https://enb.iisd.org/download/pdf/enb25106e.pdf> accessed 31 March 2022.

Morgera, Elisa, Asheline Appleton, Daniela Diz and Asterios Tsioumanis, 'Summary of the First Session of the Intergovernmental Conference on an International Legally Binding Instrument under the UN Convention on the Law of the Sea on the Conservation and Sustainable Use of Marine Biodiversity of Areas Beyond National Jurisdiction 4–17 September 2018' *Earth Negotiations Bulletin* (Online Bulletin, 20 September 2018) <https://enb.iisd.org/download/pdf/enb25179e.pdf> accessed 31 March 2022.

Mossop, Joanna, 'Protecting Marine Biodiversity on the Continental Shelf Beyond 200 Nautical Miles' (2007) 38 *Ocean Development and International Law* 283–304. DOI: 10.1080/00908320701530474.

Mossop, Joanna, 'Reconciling Activities on the Extended Continental Shelf with Protection of the Marine Environment' in Rosemary Rayfuse (ed), *Research Handbook on International Marine Environmental Law* (Edward Elgar Publishing, 2015) 170. DOI: https://doi.org/10.4337/9781781004777.00017.

Mullineaux, Lauren S, Anna Metaxas, Stace E. Beaulieu, Monika Bright, Sabine Gollner, Benjamin M. Grupe, Santiago Herrera, Julie B. Kellner, Lisa A. Levin, Satoshi Mitarai, Michael G. Neubert, Andreas M. Thurnherr, Verena Tunnicliffe, Hiromi K. Watanabe and Yong-Jin Won, 'Exploring the Ecology of Deep-Sea Hydrothermal Vents in a Metacommunity Framework' (2018) 5 *Frontiers in Marine Science* 1–27. DOI: 10.3389/fmars.2018.00049.

'Oases on the Ocean Floor,' *WWF* (Web Page, 19 June 2002) <https://wwf.panda.org/wwf_news/?2593/Oases-on-the-ocean-floor> accessed 31 March 2022.

O'Leary, Bethan C, George Hoppit, Adam Townley, Harriet L. Allen, Christina J. McIntyre and Callum M. Roberts, 'Options for Managing Human Threats to High Seas Biodiversity' (2020) 187 *Ocean and Coastal Management* 105110: 1–12. DOI: 10.1016/j.ocecoaman.2020.105110.

Paoli, Chiara, Monica Montefalcone, Carla Morri, Paolo Vassallo, Carlo Nike Bianchi, 'Ecosystem Functions and Services of the Marine Animal Forests' in Sergio Rossi et al (eds), *Marine Animal Forests the Ecology of Benthic Biodiversity* (Springer Reference, 2019) 1271. DOI: 10.1007/978-3-319-17001-5_38-1.

Pendleton, Gregory D, 'State Responsibility and the High Seas Marine Environment: A Legal Theory for the Protection of Seamounts in the Global Commons' (2005) 14(2) *Pacific Rim Law & Policy Journal Association* 485–514.

Perez, Fiz F, Marcos Fontela, Maribel L. García-Ibáñez, Herlé Mercier, Anton Velo, Pascale Lherminier, Patricia Zunino, Mercedes De La Paz, Fernando Alonso-Pérez, Elisa F. Guallart and Xose A. Padin, 'Meridional Overturning Circulation Conveys Fast Acidification to the Deep Atlantic Ocean' (2018) 554 *Nature* 515–520. DOI: 10.1038/nature25493.

President's Aid to Discussions, UN Doc A/CONF.232/2018/33 (25 June 2018a) <https://documents-dds-ny.un.org/doc/UNDOC/GEN/N18/197/15/PDF/N1819715.pdf?OpenElement> accessed 31 March 2022.

President's Aid to Negotiations, UN Doc A/CONF.232/2019/1 (3 December 2018) <https://documents-dds-ny.un.org/doc/UNDOC/GEN/N18/413/20/PDF/N1841320.pdf?OpenElement> accessed 31 March 2022.

Proelss, Alexander and Katherine Houghton, 'Protecting Marine Species,' in Rosemary Rayfuse (ed), *Research Handbook on International Marine Environmental*

Law (Edward Elgar Publishing, 2015) 229. DOI: https://doi.org/10.4337/9781781004777.00021.

Ramirez-Llodra, Eva, 'Deep-sea Ecosystems: Biodiversity and Anthropogenic Impacts' in Catherine Banet (ed), *The Law of the Seabed: Access, Uses and Protection of Seabed Resources* (Brill, 2020) 36.

Ramirez-Llodra, Eva, Paul A. Tyler, Maria C. Baker, Odd Aksel Bergstad, Malcolm R. Clark, Elva Escobar, Lisa A. Levin, Lenaick Menot, Ashley A. Rowden, Craig R. Smith, Cindy L. Van Dover, 'Man and the Last Great Wilderness: Human Impact on the Deep Sea' (2011) 6 *PloS One* e22588: 1-25. DOI: 10.1371/journal.pone.0022588.

Rayfuse, Rosemary, 'Climate Change, Marine Biodiversity and International Law' in Michael Bowman et al (eds), *Research Handbook on Biodiversity and Law* (Edward Elgar Publishing Limited, 2016) 123.

Recommendations of the Ad Hoc Open-ended Informal Working Group to Study Issues Relating to the Conservation and Sustainable Use of Marine Biological Diversity Beyond Areas of National Jurisdiction to the Sixty-ninth Session of the General Assembly (23 January 2015). <https://www.un.org/Depts/los/biodiversityworkinggroup/documents/AHWG_9_recommendations.pdf> accessed 31 March 2022.

Redgwell, Catherine, 'Treaty Evolution, Adaptation and Change: Is the LOSC 'Enough' to Address Climate Change Impacts on the Marine Environment' (2019) 34 *The International Journal of Marine and Coastal Law* 440–457. DOI: 10.1163/15718085-13431096.

Report of the Preparatory Committee Established by General Assembly Resolution 69/292: Development of an International Legally Binding Instrument under the United Nations Convention on the Law of the Sea on the Conservation and Sustainable Use of Marine Biological Diversity of Areas Beyond National Jurisdiction, UN Doc A/AC.287/2017/PC.4/2 (31 July 2017) <https://www.un.org/ga/search/view_doc.asp?symbol=A/AC.287/2017/PC.4/2> accessed 31 March 2022.

Report on the Work of the United Nations Open-ended Informal Consultative Process on Oceans and the Law of the Sea, UN Doc A/58/95 (26 June 2003).

Report on the Work of the United Nations Open-ended Informal Consultative Process on Oceans and the Law of the Sea at Its Fifth Meeting, UN Doc A/59/122 (1 July 2004).

Revised Draft Text of an Agreement Under the United Nations Convention on the Law of the Sea on the Conservation and Sustainable Use of Marine Biological Diversity of Areas Beyond National Jurisdiction, UN Doc A/CONF.232/2020/3 (18 November 2019) <https://documents-dds-ny.un.org/doc/UNDOC/GEN/N19/372/88/PDF/N1937288.pdf?OpenElement> accessed 31 March 2022.

Rice, Jake, 'Synthesis of Part VI: Marine Biological Diversity and Habitats' in United Nations (ed), *The First Global Integrated Marine Assessment World Ocean Assessment I* (Cambridge University Press, 2016) 917. DOI: https:/doi.org/10.1017/9781108186148.

Roberts, Joanna, 'Q&A: To Protect the Atlantic, We First Need to Understand It' (6 February 2020) *Horizon the EU Research and Innovation Magazine* (Online Magazine) <https://horizon-magazine.eu/article/qa-protect-atlantic-we-first-need-understand-it.html> accessed 31 March 2022.

Rochette, Julien and Raphaël Billé, 'Governance of Marine Biodiversity Beyond National Jurisdictions: Issues and Perspectives Report of the International Seminar

"Towards a New Governance of High Seas Biodiversity" (Principality of Monaco, March 20–21, 2008)' (2008) 51 *Ocean and Coastal Management* 779–781. DOI: 10.1016/j.ocecoaman.2008.10.001.

Rochette, Julien, Glen Wright, Kristina M. Gjerde, Thomas Greiber and Sebastian Unger, *A New Chapter for the High Seas?* (Working Paper, Institute for Advanced Sustainability Studies, April 2015).

Rogers, A.D. and D.d'A. Laffoley, *International Earth System Expert Workshop on Ocean Stresses and Impacts* (Summary Workshop Report, International Programme on the State of the Ocean, 20 June 2011).

Rogers, A.D, U.R. Sumaila, S.C. Hussain, C. Baulcomb, *The High Seas and Us: Understanding the Value of High-Seas Ecosystems* (Global Ocean Commission, 2014).

Rogers, Alex D., Amy Baco, Elva Escobar-Briones, Duncan Currie, Kristina Gjerde, Judith Gobin, Marcel Jaspars, Lisa Levin, Katrin Linse, Muriel Rabone, Eva Ramirez-Llodra, Javier Sellanes, Timothy M. Shank, Kerry Sink, Paul V. R. Snelgrove, Michelle L. Taylor, Daniel Wagner, Harriet Harden-Davies, 'Marine Genetic Resources in Areas Beyond National Jurisdiction: Promoting Marine Scientific Research and Enabling Equitable Benefit Sharing' (2021) 8 *Frontiers in Marine Science* 667274, 1–22.

Scovazzi, Tullio, 'The Rights to Genetic Resources beyond National Jurisdiction: Challenges for the Ongoing Negotiations at the United Nations' in Catherine Banet (ed) *The Law of the Seabed: Access, Uses and Protection of Seabed Resources* (Brill Nijhoff, 2020) 213.

Shakespeare, William, *Hamlet, Act III, Scene I* (1603).

Shields, Brenton, 'Oceanic Zone Plants and Animals' *Sciencing* (Web Page, 22 November 2019) <http://sciencing.com/oceanic-zone-plants-animals-8174254.html> accessed 31 March 2022.

Snelgrove, Paul, Edward Vanden Berghe, Patricia Miloslavich, Phil Archambault, Nicolas Bailly, Angelika Brandt, Ann Bucklin, Malcolm Clark, Farid Dahdouh-Gueba, Pat Halpin, Russell Hopcroft, Kristin Kaschner, Ben Lascelles, Lisa A. Levin, Susanne Menden-Deuer, Anna Metaxas, David Obura, Randall R. Reeves, Tatiana Rynearson, Mayumi Sato, Karen Stocks, Marguerite Tarzia, Derek Tittensor, Verena Tunnicliffe, Bryan Wallace, Ross Wanless, Tom Webb, Patricio Bernal, Jake Rice and Andrew Rosenberg, 'Global Patterns in Marine Biodiversity' in United Nations (ed), *The First Global Integrated Marine Assessment: World Ocean Assessment I* (Cambridge University Press, 2016) 503. DOI: https:/doi.org/10.1017/9781108186148.

Statement by the President of the Conference at the Closing of the First Session of the Intergovernmental Conference on an International Legally Binding Instrument under the United Nations Convention on the Law of the Sea on the Conservation and Sustainable Use of Marine Biological Diversity of Areas Beyond National Jurisdiction, UN Doc A/CONF.232/2018/7 (20 September 2018) <https://documents-dds-ny.un.org/doc/UNDOC/GEN/N18/294/09/PDF/N1829409.pdf?OpenElement> accessed 31 March 2022.

Statement by the President of the Conference at the Closing of the Third Session of the Intergovernmental Conference on an International Legally Binding Instrument under the United Nations Convention on the Law of the Sea on the Conservation and Sustainable Use of Marine Biological Diversity of Areas Beyond National Jurisdiction, UN Doc A/CONF.232/2019/10 (13 September 2019) <https://documents

-dds-ny.un.org/doc/UNDOC/GEN/N19/281/55/PDF/N1928155.pdf ?OpenElement> accessed 31 March 2022.

Stephens, Tim, 'Warming Waters and Souring Seas: Climate Change and Ocean Acidification' in Donald Rothwell et al. (eds), *The Oxford Handbook of the Law of the Sea* (Oxford University Press, 2015) 777. DOI: 10.1093/law/9780198715481.003.0034.

'The Open Ocean' *MarineBio* (Web Page, 16 February 2019) <https://marinebio.org/oceans/open-ocean/> accessed 31 March 2022.

The Pew Charitable Trusts, 'Potential Elements of an UNCLOS Implementing Agreement' (Press Release and Statement, 2012) <http://www.pewtrusts.org/en/about/news-room/press-releases/2012/04/25/potential-elements-of-an-unclos-implementing-agreement> accessed 31 March 2022.

The Pew Charitable Trusts, 'Underwater Treasures of the High Seas' (Briefing Booklet, March 2016).

The Pew Charitable Trusts, 'A Path to Creating the First Generation of High Seas Protected Areas' (Report, 31 March 2020) <https://www.pewtrusts.org/-/media/assets/2020/04/highseas_mpa_report.pdf> accessed 31 March 2022.

The Pew Environment Group, 'Deep-sea Fisheries and Vulnerable Ecosystems in the Northeast Atlantic: How the EU Can Reform its Deep-Sea Management Regime' (Report, July 2012).

Tivey, M.K, 'Hydrothermal Vent Systems' (1991) 34(4) *Oceanus* 68–74.

Tladi, Dire, 'Ocean Governance: A Fragmented Regulatory Framework' in P. Jacquet, R. Pachauri and L. Tubiana (eds) *Oceans: The New Frontier: A Planet for Life* (The Energy and Resources Institute Press, 2011) 99.

United Nations Convention on the Law of the Sea, opened for signature 10 December 1982 (1982) 1833 *UNTS* 397 (entered into force 16 November 1994) (UNCLOS).

United Nations Framework Convention on Climate Change, opened for signature 9 May 1992 (1992) 1771 *UNTS* 165 (entered into force 21 March 1994) (UNFCCC).

United Nations General Assembly, *Oceans and the Law of the Sea:Report of the Secretary-General*, UN Doc A/58/65 (3 March 2003).

United Nations General Assembly, *Oceans and the Law of the Sea*, UN Doc. A/RES/59/24 (4 February 2005, adopted 17 November 2004).

United Nations General Assembly, *Oceans and the Law of the Sea:Report of the Secretary-General,* UN Doc A/60/63/Add.1 (15 July 2005).

United Nations General Assembly, *The Future We Want*, GA Res 66/288, UN Doc A/RES/66/288 (11 September 2012, adopted 27 July 2012).

United Nations General Assembly, *Transforming our World: The 2030 Agenda for Sustainable Development,* UN Doc. A/RES/70/1 (25 September 2015).

United Nations General Assembly, *Oceans and the Law of the Sea*, GA Res 75/239, UN Doc A/RES/75/239 (5 January 2021, adopted 31 December 2020).

United Nations General Assembly, *Oceans and the Law of the Sea, Singapore: Draft Decision Submitted by the President of the General Assembly*, UN Doc A/75/L.96 (9 June 2021).

United Nations Secretary-General, *Impacts of Fishing on Vulnerable Marine Ecosystems: Actions Taken by States and Regional Fisheries Management Organizations and Arrangements to Give Effect to Paragraphs 66 to 69 of General Assembly Resolution*

59/25 on Sustainable Fisheries, Regarding the Impacts of Fishing on Vulnerable Marine Ecosystems-Report of the Secretary-General, UN Doc A/61/154 (14 July 2006).

Van Dover, Cindy Lee, 'Tighten Regulations on Deep-Sea Mining' (2011) 470 *Nature* 31. DOI: 10.1038/470031a.

Van Dover, Cindy Lee, 'Impacts of Anthropogenic Disturbance at Deep-Sea Hydrothermal Vent Ecosystems: A Review' (2014) 102 *Marine Environmental Research* 59–72. DOI: 10.1016/j.marenvres.2014.03.008.

Visalli, Morgan E, Benjamin D. Best, Reniel B. Cabral, William W.L. Cheung, Nichola A. Clark, Cristina Garilao, Kristin Kaschner, Kathleen Kesner-Reyes, Vicky W.Y. Lam, Sara M. Maxwell, Juan Mayorga, Holly V. Moeller, Lance Morgan, Guillermo Ortuño Crespo, Malin L. Pinsky, Timothy D. White, Douglas J. McCauley, 'Data-driven Approach for Highlighting Priority Areas for Protection in Marine Areas Beyond National Jurisdiction' (2020) 112 *Marine Policy* e 103927, 1–14. DOI: 10.1016/j.marpol.2020.103927.

Warner, Robin, *Protecting the Oceans Beyond National Jurisdiction: Strengthening the International Law Framework* (Martinus Nijhoff, 2009).

Warner, Robin, 'Conserving Marine Biodiversity in Areas Beyond National Jurisdiction: Co-Evolution and Interaction with the Law of the Sea' in Donald Rothwell et al. (eds), *The Oxford Handbook of the Law of the Sea* (Oxford University Press, 2015) 752. DOI: 10.1093/law/9780198715481.003.0033.

Warner, Robin, 'Strengthening Governance Frameworks for Conservation and Sustainable Use of Marine Biodiversity in Areas Beyond National Jurisdiction: Southern Hemisphere Perspectives,' (2017) 32(4) *The International Journal of Marine and Coastal Law* 607–634. DOI: http://dx.doi.org/10.1163/15718085-13204064.

Wedding, L.M, A.M. Friedlander, J.N. Kittinger, L. Watling, S.D. Gaines, M. Bennett, S.M. Hardy and C.R. Smith, 'From Principles to Practice: A Spatial Approach to Systematic Conservation Planning in the Deep Sea' (2013) 280(1773) *Proceedings of the Royal Society of Biological Sciences* 20131684: 1–10. DOI: 10.1098/rspb.2013.1684.

Wessel, Paul, 'Seamount Characteristics' in Tony Pitcher et al. (eds), *Seamounts: Ecology, Fisheries and Conservation* (Blackwell Publishing, 2007) 3. DOI: 10.1002/9780470691953.

Weston, Johanna J, Priscilla Carrillo-Barragán, Thomas D. Linley, William D.K. Reid, Alan J. Jamieson, 'New Species of Eurythenes from Hadal Depths of the Mariana Trench, Pacific Ocean (Crustacea: Amphipoda)' (2020) 4748(1) *Zootaxa* 163–181. DOI: https://doi.org/10.11646/zootaxa.4748.1.9.

Williams, Meryl, Heather Mannix, Kristen Yaincik, Patricia Miloslavich and Darlene Trew, *Scientific Results to Support the Sustainable Use and Conservation of Marine Life: A Summary of the Census of Marine Life for Decision Makers* (Census of Marine Life International Secretariat Consortium for Ocean Leadership, 2011).

Wolfram, Uwe, Ali Ozel, Marta Peña-Fernández, Ewan Smith and Sebastian Hennige, 'Micromechanical Consequences of Ocean Acidification for Cold-Water Corals' (Conference Paper, 26th Congress of the European Society of Biomechanics, 14 July 2021) <https://esbiomech.org/conference/esb2021/wp-content/uploads/sites/3/2021/07/Detailed_Program-13-7.pdf> accessed 31 March 2022.

Woodall, L, C. Stewart and A. Rogers, 'Function of the High Seas and Anthropogenic Impacts Science Update 2012–2017' (University of Oxford for High Seas Alliance,

July 2017) <http://www.savethehighseas.org/wp-content/uploads/2017/07/HS-Synthesis-Oxford-f1-1.pdf> accessed 31 March 2022.

Wright, Glen and Julien Rochette, 'Sea Change: Negotiating a New Agreement on the Conservation and Sustainable Use of Marine Biodiversity in Areas Beyond National Jurisdiction' (Issue Brief No. 4/16, IDDRI, March 2016).

Wright, Glen, Julien Rochette, Kristina Gjerde, Isabel Seeger, 'The Long & Winding Road: Negotiating a Treaty for the Conservation and Sustainable Use of Marine Biodiversity in Areas Beyond National Jurisdiction' (Study No. 8/2018, IDDRI, August 2018).

Yadav, Siddharth Skekhar and Kristina Maria Gjerde, 'The Ocean, Climate Change and Resilience: Making Ocean Areas Beyond National Jurisdiction More Resilient to Climate Change and Other Anthropogenic Activities' (2020) 122 *Marine Policy* e104184, 1–9. DOI: 10.1016/j.marpol.2020.104184.

2 The Grotian tradition and its place in the BBNJ negotiations

Is it a case of history repeating itself?

Introduction

For centuries, the law of the sea has been dominated by an ideological battle between two fundamentally divergent doctrines—Mare Liberum versus Mare Clausum.[1] Although the potency of Grotius' Mare Liberum has waxed and waned throughout history, the doctrine has generally aligned with the interests of the most powerful States, including the traditional maritime powers of the US, the UK, France, the Netherlands, Japan and Russia.[2] As this group have historically been the strongest proponents of the Grotian tradition and are critical to the overall success of an ILBI, it is important to assess whether Grotius' freedom of the seas doctrine continues to influence the way governments approach law of the sea issues, including the BBNJ process.[3]

This chapter argues that a historical devotion to the Grotian tradition underlies the position of maritime States in the BBNJ negotiations and this is 'based on an unwavering belief in the principle of freedom of the seas as the governing paradigm.'[4] An understanding of the important role the Grotian doctrine has played and continues to play in the mindset of maritime States is therefore crucial to forming an understanding of their position on key BBNJ issues.

Section 2.1 of this chapter undertakes a historical analysis of the Grotian doctrine and its role in the development of the law of the sea. Section 2.2 provides insight into the special relationship maritime States share with the Grotian tradition, particularly the way it has been adapted throughout the centuries to support their interests. Tying this back to the BBNJ negotiations, it is contended that,

1 Helmut Tuerk, 'The Legal Regime of Maritime Areas and the Waning Freedom of the Seas' (Conference Paper, Maritime Issues and United Nations Convention on the Laws of the Sea: Sharing European and Asia Approaches to Territorial Disputes, 4–5 June 2015).

2 James Kraska, *Maritime Power and the Law of the Sea: Expeditionary Operations in World Politics* (Oxford University Press, 2011) 3.

3 John S. Dryzek, 'Paradigms and Discourses' in Daniel Bodansky, Jutta Brunnée and Ellen Hey (eds), *The Oxford Handbook of International Environmental Law* (Oxford University Press, 2008) 44, 45.

4 Michaela Young, 'Then and Now: Reappraising Freedom of the Seas in Modern Law of the Sea' (2016) 47(2) *Ocean Development & International Law* 165, 179.

DOI: 10.4324/b22996-3

in seeking to preserve their tight grip on Grotius' freedom of the seas principle,[5] maritime States will be driven by two motivations. First, these States will look to ensure that the delicate balance of interests, rights and obligations enshrined in UNCLOS is maintained, including the preservation of high seas freedoms. Second, there will be a strong desire to prevent any further in-roads or erosion of the Grotian principle. Section 2.3 of this chapter reflects upon the role the Grotian doctrine played during UNCLOS III in the debate concerning the legal status of the Area and its mineral resources. This debate saw a clash between the freedom of the high seas versus the common heritage of mankind (CHM). The international community is likely to experience a sense of déjà vu, as these competing principles go head-to-head again in respect to marine genetic resources (MGRs) of ABNJ. Section 2.4 assesses the on-going MGR debate, as their legal status will form an integral component of the ILBI.

Overall, this chapter argues that the role of the Grotian doctrine in the BBNJ negotiations is a case of history repeating itself. While the doctrine has been an important building block in the law of the sea, it has the potential to be used as a roadblock for conservation measures required for BBNJ. Hence, compromise is the only way forward for the development of an ILBI.

2.1 The history and formulation of the Grotian doctrine

2.1.1 The dawn of Mare Liberum

While an exhaustive historical analysis of Grotius' treatise *Mare Liberum* is beyond the scope of this chapter and has in any case been extensively treated elsewhere, it is important to provide a brief account of its origins to assess how the Grotian legacy continues to exert influence in 21st-century debates.

2.1.1.1 Ancient origins

As one of the fathers of modern international law, Hugo Grotius is credited with giving the most impassioned appeal for the freedom of the seas.[6] However, the roots of this principle can be traced back to long before the publication of *Mare Liberum* in 1609. Elements of Grotius' vision were expressed in ancient Greek and Roman times.[7] The 2nd century AD Greek philosopher, Celsus, wrote that the sea is 'common to all men, like the air,'[8] and at the same time, Roman jurist,

5 Ibid, 171.

6 Martine Julia van Ittersum, 'Mare Liberum Versus the Propriety of the Seas? The Debate between Hugo Grotius (1583–1645) and William Welwood (1552–1624) and Its Impact on Anglo-Scotto-Dutch Fishery Disputes in the Second Decade of the Seventeenth Century' (2006) 10 *Edinburgh Law Review* 239, 240.

7 Efthymios Papastavridis, 'The Right of Visit on the High Seas in a Theoretical Perspective: Mare Liberum versus Mare Clausum Revisited' (2011) 24 *Leiden Journal of International Law* 45, 48.

8 Charles Sumner Lobingier, 'The Maritime Law of Rome' (1935) 47 *Juridical Review* 1, 18 discussing Digests XXXIX, quoted in Justinians Digest XLIII, viii. 3.

Ulpian, declared the sea could 'not be subjected to private servitude.'[9] Under Roman Law the sea was open and free for all,[10] on the understanding that it was 'unlimited in both size and resources.'[11] In formulating his own concept, Grotius was able to draw upon these classical themes and appeal to the works of ancient philosophers and writers.[12]

2.1.1.2 Dividing the oceans in half—the catalyst for Mare Liberum

After the fall of the Roman Empire, the notion that the seas were open to all came under attack.[13] The Middle Ages witnessed a trend of formal claims of dominion over vast swathes of the ocean.[14] The most famous example is the Papal Bulls of Pope Alexander VI in 1493 (*Inter Caetera* edict) and the *Treaty of Tordesillas* in 1494. The pontiff sketched a line of longitude in the Atlantic Ocean from pole to pole allocating to Spain all territories to the west of the meridian, and to Portugal all those to the east[15] (Figure 2.1).

While mainly concerned with settling Iberian disputes over colonial expansion, *Inter Caetera* possessed an obvious maritime dimension, symbolising the ambition of some powers to sovereignty not only to land but also to seas in the New World. Such exorbitant claims were 'met with opposition by other seafaring nations that realised both the potential of overseas trade and the effect of the dominance of the ocean by one or two powers.'[16] The main rival against the Spanish claims was England. Queen Elizabeth I took a leading role in the struggle for freedom of the seas,[17] telling the Spanish Ambassador in 1580 that:

> the use of the sea and air is common to all; neither can any title to the ocean belong to any people or private man, forasmuch as neither nature nor regard of the public use permitteth any possession thereof.[18]

9 Ibid, discussing Opiniones, VI, quoted in Justinians Digest VIII iv 13.
10 R.P. Anand, '"Tyranny" of the Freedom of the Seas Doctrine' (1973) 12 *International Studies* 416, 417 ('Tyranny').
11 Kirsten Selvig, 'Expensive Freedom: Establishing Marine Protected Areas on the Open Ocean Requires an End to the Freedom of the Seas' (2013) 22(3) *Minnesota Journal of International Law* 35, 37.
12 David Kenneth Leary, *International Law and the Genetic Resources of the Deep Sea* (Martinus Nijhoff Publishers, 2007) 81; John Logue, 'The Revenge of John Selden: The Draft Convention on the Law of the Sea in the Light of Hugo Grotius' Mare Liberum' (1982) 3 *Grotiana* 27, 51. Grotius referred to other sources including the law of nature, the law of nations and the Bible.
13 Anand, 'Tyranny' (n 10) 417.
14 Young (n 4) 180, Fn 1.
15 Anand, 'Tyranny' (n 10) 417.
16 Wolfgang Graf Vitzthum, 'From the Rhodian Sea Law to UNCLOS III' (2003) 17 *Ocean Yearbook* 56, 57.
17 Papastavridis (n 7) 49.
18 David Anderson, 'The Development of the Modern Law of the Sea' in David Anderson (ed), *Modern Law of the Sea: Selected Essays* (Martinus Nijhoff Publishers, 2008) 5.

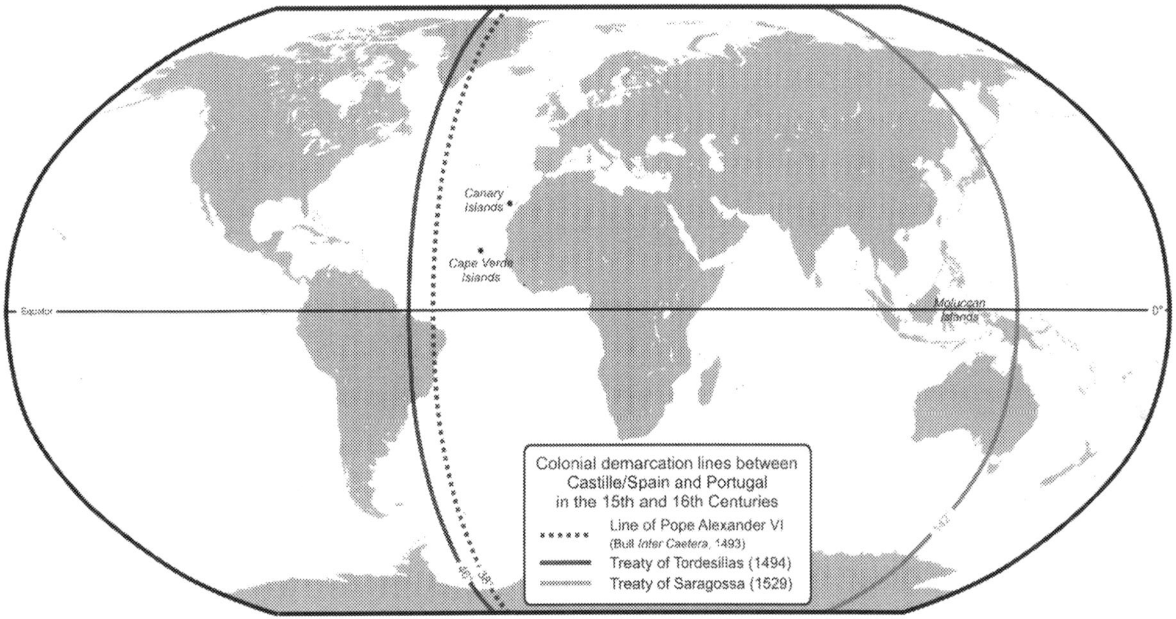

Figure 2.1 Map showing the lines of demarcation between Spanish and Portuguese territory. Credit: Lencer at en.wikipedia [Public domain, GFDL (http://www.gnu.org/copyleft/fdl.html) or CC-BY-SA-3.0], via Wikimedia Commons.

While the 'extravagant pretensions of Spain and Portugal'[19] lay the groundwork for *Mare Liberum*, the events of February 1603 were the main catalyst for the development of the Grotian doctrine.[20]

Seeking Dutch expansion overseas, the Dutch East India Company (DEIC) commenced naval campaigns in the Far East to break the monopoly of trade by the Portuguese.[21] On 25 February 1603, the DEIC captured a 1500-ton Portuguese galleon, the *Santa Catarina*, in the Straits of Malacca.[22] The DEIC sold the ship and cargo and distributed the proceeds between the company and crew.[23] The Portuguese demanded the return of its property leading to a public judicial hearing. It is at this point that Hugo Grotius takes centre-stage. Grotius was engaged by the DEIC to defend the capture of the Portuguese vessel and to refute the extensive claims of sovereignty made by Spain and Portugal.[24] Grotius' defence took the form of a detailed manuscript, *De Jure Praedae Commentarius (Commentary on the Law of Prize and Booty)*,[25] with Chapter XII published separately and anonymously years later as *Mare Liberum*.[26]

2.1.1.3 Open seas versus closed seas—the battle of the books

Mare Liberum made an impassioned appeal for freedom of the seas and commerce.[27] It was 'published primarily to support the economic and political interests'[28] of the Dutch, and the bond between Grotius' work and the Netherlands has remained strong ever since. Maarevold contends that 'the legacy of Hugo Grotius and his *Mare Liberum* of 1609 has been absorbed in Dutch thinking' and 'conditions the orientation and action of its maritime industry.'[29] Thus, *Mare Liberum* had already found favour with one maritime State. Many other nations would follow in embracing the Grotian doctrine, but not before it was met with a particularly spirited response from the British Isles.[30]

19 Anand, 'Tyranny' (n 10) 417.

20 Helen Thornton, 'Hugo Grotius and the Freedom of the Seas' (2004) 16 *International Journal of Maritime History* 17, 17–18.

21 van Ittersum (n 6) 240; Anand, 'Tyranny' (n 10) 417.

22 Young (n 4) 172; Thornton (n 20) 18.

23 Young (n 4) 172.

24 Hugo Grotius et al, *The Freedom of the Seas: Or, the Right which Belongs to the Dutch to Take Part in the East Indian Trade* (Oxford University Press American Branch, 1916) viii; Papastavridis (n 7) 50.

25 Thornton (n 20) 17.

26 W.E. Butler, 'Grotius and the Law of the Sea' in Hedley Bull, Benedict Kingsbury and Adam Roberts (eds), *Hugo Grotius and International Relations* (Clarendon, 1992) 209. The full text of *De Jure Praedae Commentarus* was discovered in 1864 and published four years later.

27 Anand, 'Tyranny' (n 10) 417.

28 Young (n 4) 172.

29 Thijs J. Maarleveld, 'The Netherlands' in Sarah Dromgoole (ed), *The Protection of the Underwater Cultural Heritage* (Martinus Nijhoff Publishers, 2nd ed, 2006) 161, 161.

30 R.R. Churchill and A.V. Lowe, *The Law of the Sea* (Manchester University Press, 3rd ed, 1999) 4.

When *Mare Liberum* was published, King James I had ascended to the English throne. Unlike his predecessor, James I did not endorse open seas. Instead, he declared that Britain had the right to control the seas around its island nation and had maritime jurisdiction extending to the coasts of European neighbours and to North America.[31] British writers saw Grotius' work as a direct threat to the claims of their monarch and rushed to rebut the ideas underpinning *Mare Liberum*. Scottish law professor William Welwood launched an attack in his *Abridgment of all Sea Lawes* (1613) and distinguished English lawyer John Selden responded with a rival treatise entitled 'Mare Clausum, seu de dominio maris libri duo' (1635) roughly translated to 'closed seas.'[32] The dedication of Selden's work to King Charles I takes an obvious swipe at Grotius, stating:

> There are among foreign writers … a few who following chiefly some of the ancient Caesarean lawyers, endeavour to affirm, or beyond reason to easily admit, that all seas are common to the universality of mankind.[33]

The 17th century quickly transcended into a 'battle of the books,'[34] and Grotius and Selden are considered the high point of this 'celebrated doctrinal controversy.'[35]

2.1.1.4 The main components of Mare Liberum

Spatial constraints prevent a detailed textual analysis of *Mare Liberum*; however its main elements are essential to understanding its enduring legacy. Grotius' main objective was to demonstrate that the Dutch had the right to sail to the East Indies.[36] Grotius relied on what he called 'the most specific and unimpeachable axiom of the Law of Nations,' being that 'every nation is free to travel to every other nation and to trade with it' because the sea is common to all.[37] Grotius argued that the sea is 'so limitless that it cannot become the possession of any one and because it is adapted for the use of all,'[38] every nation has the right to 'ply the seven seas and harvest its seafood bounty.'[39] Moreover, Grotius declared that no nation has the right to deny access to any part of the ocean. Things that could not be 'seized nor enclosed'[40] (i.e. the sea and the air) could

31 Ibid, 5; Logue (n 12) 35.

32 Tullio Treves, 'Historical Development of the Law of the Sea' in Donald Rothwell et al (eds), *The Oxford Handbook of the Law of the Sea* (Oxford University Press, 2015) 4.

33 Grotius et al (n 24) ix.

34 Treves (n 32) 4.

35 Papastavridis (n 7) 51.

36 Grotius et al (n 24) 7.

37 Ibid.

38 Ibid, 28.

39 Alex Oude Elferink, 'De Groot–A Founding Father of the Law of the Sea, Not the Law of the Sea Convention' (2009) 30 *Grotiana* 152, 154 ('De Groot').

40 Anand, 'Tyranny' (n 10) 418.

in no way become private property, 'because nature not only allows but enjoins its common use.'[41]

Under the Grotian doctrine, the seas and oceans are a global or common space available to use on the basis of equality.[42] *Mare Liberum* therefore championed the idea of shared opportunities.[43] Yet, even in Grotius' time, 'how much of the common resource each nation wound up with depended … on how much technology it had, and how effectively it competed with others.'[44]

Grotius' doctrine was not met with overwhelming approval during his lifetime. In fact, 'the odds were heavily against him.'[45] Three maritime powers, the British, the Spanish and the Portuguese, all supported Selden's 'closed seas.'[46] Selden's argument was two-fold. First, in opposition to Grotius, Selden argued that 'the sea, by the law of nature or nations, is not common to all men, but capable of private dominion or property.'[47] Nations could therefore 'control as much sea territory as they could dominate militarily.'[48] Second, the king of Great Britain was 'the lord of the sea,'[49] thereby entitling him 'to claim and exercise authority over a defined area' including powers to exclude foreign ships.[50]

Selden also rejected Grotius' argument that the oceans had an 'inexhaustible abundance' of resources.[51] This is an element of Grotius' work that is outdated from a modern-day perspective and is one of the weaknesses of the freedom of the seas concept. As Anderson explains the Grotian doctrine is:

> essentially negative—the prohibition of national claims to sovereignty or some other authority over the open sea. This prohibition, by itself, does not provide a substantive regulatory regime: some regulation is required as soon as the level of activity in a particular area of the high seas … increases to the point where one group of users comes into competition with another.[52]

Thus, the freedom of the seas is not satisfactory for the regulation and management of common-pool resources.[53]

A common-pool resource is one in which (1) exclusion of users through physical and institutional means is difficult and costly, and (2) exploitation by one user

41 Grotius et al (n 24) 29.
42 Anderson (n 18) 5.
43 Jon Van Dyke, 'Sharing Ocean Resources: In a Time of Scarcity and Selfishness' in Harry N. Scheiber (ed), *The Law of the Sea: The Common Heritage and Emerging Challenges* (Martinus Nijhoff Publishers, 2000) vol 34, 3, 35.
44 Ibid.
45 Logue (n 12) 50.
46 Ibid, 50–51.
47 Grotius et al (n 24) ix.
48 Leary (n 12) 81.
49 Grotius et al (n 24) ix.
50 Anderson (n 18) 3.
51 Oude Elferink, 'De Groot' (n 39) 156.
52 Anderson (n 18) 19.
53 Ibid.

reduces availability of the resource for others.[54] These characteristics make management particularly challenging.[55] As Ostrom explains, when resource units (i.e. fish) produced by a common-pool resource are highly valued and access is not restricted or limited, 'individuals face strong incentives to appropriate more and more resource units leading eventually to congestion, overuse, and even the destruction of the resource itself.'[56] Using fish as an example, Anderson contends that the Grotian doctrine 'does not provide sufficient assurance that particular fish stocks on the high seas will not be fished to the point of extinction,'[57] inevitably leading to a tragedy of the commons scenario.[58] The freedom of the seas concept thereby poses a substantial risk in the contemporary era where collective oceans management is essential to confront major shared challenges, including the conservation and sustainable use of BBNJ. Selden recognised early on that marine resources are not limitless and promoted 'surveillance and control' by coastal States.[59]

The tension between *Mare Liberum* and *Mare Clausum* has continued to play out through the evolutionary development of the law of the sea.[60] Reeves contends that Grotius and Selden were 'installed as the apostles, the one of the freedom of the seas, the other of the extravagant and arrogant claims of sea power.'[61] The debate between these concepts continues in the international arena today and is carried out by two opposing political groupings or blocs.[62] Coastal States turn to Selden's 'closed seas' to argue for their rights over national waters and at times, in extending those rights.[63] Maritime States gravitate towards Grotius' vision to 'preserve their predominant interest of freedom of navigation.'[64] A number of States fall into both groups. For example, as the US and the UK are maritime States and large coastal States their interests cut across both categories.

2.1.1.5 Maritime States and Mare Liberum*—a special relationship begins*

During the 18th and 19th centuries the Grotian doctrine became the 'accepted regime of the sea.'[65] Although *Mare Liberum* had not been warmly embraced

54 Elinor Ostrom et al, 'Revisiting the Commons: Local Lessons, Global Challenges' (9 April 1999) 284 *Science* 278, 279.
55 Ibid, 279.
56 Elinor Ostrom, 'The Challenge of Crafting Rules to Change Open-Access Resources into Managed Resources' in G.M Heal (ed), *Is Economic Growth Sustainable?* (Palgrave Macmillan, 2010) 172.
57 Anderson (n 18) 19.
58 Garrett Hardin, 'The Tragedy of the Common' (1968) 162 (3859) *Science* 1243.
59 Papastavridis (n 7) 61.
60 Sarah Dromgoole, *Underwater Cultural Heritage and International Law* (Cambridge University Press, 2013) 9.
61 J.S. Reeves, 'Two Conceptions of the Freedom of the Seas' (1917) 22(3) *The American Historical Review* 535, 536.
62 Dromgoole (n 60) 9.
63 Ibid.
64 Ibid.
65 Treves (n 32) 4

during Grotius' lifetime, two centuries later, he won the 'battle of the books.'[66] Grotius' vision was particularly attractive to a group of powerful maritime States, principally, the UK, the US, France and the Netherlands.[67] This bloc had a vested interest in maintaining freedom of the seas as it ensured 'unimpeded movement of their mercantile and military vessels for the building of empires and for the expansion of trade from far away territories.'[68]

The Grotian doctrine underscored a *laissez-faire* approach to ocean use.[69] Ships of all nations could traverse the open ocean with the only limitation being a customary 3 nm strip off the coast of States.[70] This *laissez-faire* regime was accepted as 'the norm'[71] and became firmly entrenched in the mindset of maritime States. Even Great Britain turned its back on Selden during this time.[72] This is evident in the 1817 case of *The Louis*.[73] Sir William Scott, later Lord Stowell,[74] outlined a fundamental principle 'that all nations being equal, all have an equal right to the uninterrupted use of the unappropriated parts of the ocean for their navigation.'[75] As a result of these developments Britain 'became the strongest champion of the freedom of the seas'[76] and took on the important role of international maritime police.[77] The commercial shipping interests of both European nations and the US ensured continued support for the Grotian doctrine.[78] During the 19th century, the US, as a major naval power, increasingly came to see itself as the custodian of the Grotian tradition. Arguably, the US continues in this role today by carrying out freedom of navigation operations through contested waters, including the South China Sea.

2.1.1.6 The modern codification of the Grotian doctrine

The 20th century witnessed the codification of the freedom of the seas principle. This coincided with the emergence, after World War II, of naval superpowers, the US and the Soviet Union (USSR), both of which shared a common interest in maximising freedom of navigation and maritime communication.[79] The 1958 Convention on the High Seas (1958 Convention) was the first multilateral

66 Anand, 'Tyranny' (n 10) 418.
67 Treves (n 32) 5.
68 Ibid.
69 Churchill and Lowe (n 30) 2 (emphasis included).
70 Leland Holbrook Smith, 'To Accede or Not to Accede: An Analysis of the Current US Position Related to the United Nations Law of the Sea' (2017) 83 *Marine Policy* 184, 185. In 1702, Dutch scholar, Cornelius van Bynkershoek, proposed 'the three-mile rule' which defined a country's territorial waters as extending as far as the range of its coastal cannons.
71 Ibid.
72 Anand, 'Tyranny' (n 10) 419.
73 *The Le Louis* (1817) 2 Dods 210; 165 ER 1464 [234]–[244].
74 Grotius et al (n 24) ix.
75 Ibid, x.
76 Anand, 'Tyranny' (n 10) 419.
77 Papastavridis (n 7) 51.
78 Butler (n 26) 212.
79 Churchill and Lowe (n 30) 2.

treaty to endorse the freedom of the seas principle.[80] It preserved the fundamental freedoms expressed by Grotius in *Mare Liberum*, namely the right to fish and navigate the high seas, and extended the doctrine to other freedoms, including overflight and the laying of submarine cables and pipelines.[81] However, Baird argues that 'the simplicity of Grotius' absolute freedom,' was lost in the 1958 Convention and points to Article 1 which defines 'high seas' as *all parts of the seas that are not included in the territorial sea or in the internal waters of a State*.[82] Baird contends that this definition is a limitation on Grotius' vision which had insisted that 'all the oceans were open seas, where every man was free to travel, navigate and fish.'[83] In this way, the 1958 Convention marks the beginning of a process of continual erosion of the Grotian doctrine, a process that became particularly evident during UNCLOS III.

2.2 The Grotian doctrine and the Constitution for the Oceans

2.2.1 How Mare Liberum *fits within the UNCLOS framework*

Legal commentators hold mixed views regarding the treatment the Grotian doctrine received during UNCLOS III. Allott suggests that under UNCLOS the high seas transitioned from an area of legal freedoms to one of legal powers.[84] Logue argues that ocean nationalism triumphed during UNCLOS III and defeated the free seas principle.[85] In contrast, Tladi contends that the Grotian principle is 'not only confirmed but entrenched' in the UNCLOS text.[86] The following sections examine the impact of the Grotian doctrine on the development of UNCLOS. This will also expose the two motivations that underpin the position of maritime States in the BBNJ negotiations, both of which stem from a deep-seated desire to keep the Grotian tradition alive.

2.2.1.1 Freedom of the high seas

The high seas regime in Part VII of UNCLOS is the obvious place to start this examination. Under Article 86 the high seas comprise *all parts of the sea that are*

80 Elisabeth Druel et al, 'A Long and Winding Road: International Discussions on the Governance of Marine Biodiversity in Areas beyond National Jurisdiction' (Study No. 7/2013, IDDRI, September 2013) 6.

81 Rachel Baird, 'Political and Commercial Interests as Influences in the Development of the Doctrine of the Freedom of the High Seas' (1996) 12 *Queensland University of Technology Law Journal* 274, 289.

82 Ibid.

83 Ibid.

84 Philip Allott, 'Power Sharing in the Law of the Sea' (1983) 77(1) *The American Journal of International Law* 1, 16, 26.

85 Logue (n 12) 53.

86 Dire Tladi, 'Conservation and Sustainable Use of Marine Biodiversity in Areas beyond National Jurisdiction: Towards an Implementing Agreement' in Rosemary Rayfuse (ed), *Research Handbook on International Marine Environmental Law* (Edward Elgar Publishing, 2015) 264.

not included in the exclusive economic zone, in the territorial sea or in the internal waters of a State, or in the archipelagic waters of an archipelagic State. Although this area is 'spatially more limited'[87] than Grotius' vision, the legal status afforded to the high seas under Article 87 'is characterised by the total prevalence of the principle of freedom.'[88] Article 87 declares the high seas 'open to all States' which is a 'deeply rooted reflection of *Mare Liberum*.'[89] It guarantees right of access to and enjoyment of the high seas free from interference, provided due regard is given to the interests of other States.[90] The 'due regard' proviso may be perceived as a limitation on Grotius' absolute freedom;[91] however, it can also be seen as promoting Grotius' idea of 'shared opportunities.'[92] Every state should enjoy and allow others to equally enjoy high seas freedoms.

Part VII of UNCLOS also sets forth a non-exhaustive list of six high seas freedoms.[93] These freedoms are not absolute. A number are subject to other parts of UNCLOS, and all of them must be exercised in accordance with the provisions on the conservation and management of living resources (Part VII, Section 2), the general obligations to protect and preserve the marine environment (Part XII) and any other relevant rules of international law.[94]

Other provisions of Part VII echo the Grotian doctrine. For example, in keeping with the spirit of Grotius' support of shared opportunities, Article 90 provides that every State 'has the right to sail ships flying its flag on the high seas.' Furthermore, Article 89 provides that the high seas is 'a zone of no sovereignty, neither territorial nor functional, open to common use by all States.'[95] Based on the above, it is clear that the Grotian principle forms 'the bedrock of all high seas laws' under Part VII of UNCLOS.[96]

2.2.2 *A balancing act—open seas versus closed seas*

The interplay between the competing notions of 'open seas' and 'closed seas' was front and centre during UNCLOS III. Coastal States came to the negotiation table seeking a clear extension of their jurisdictional reach seaward. This deeply concerned maritime States which sought a continuity of the Grotian system, particularly the maintenance of traditional navigational freedoms.

87 Ibid, 218.
88 Tuerk (n 1) 45.
89 Douglas Guilfoyle, 'The High Seas' in Donald Rothwell et al (eds), *The Oxford Handbook of the Law of the Sea* (Oxford University Press, 2015) 203.
90 Young (n 4) 165.
91 Baird (n 81) 289.
92 Van Dyke (n 43) 3.
93 UNCLOS, art 87.
94 *Oceans and the Law of the Sea: Report of the Secretary-General*, UN Doc A/60/63/Add.1 (15 July 2005) [180].
95 Tuerk (n 1) 45.
96 Selvig (n 11) 37. See, also, UNCLOS art 58 which provides for all States to enjoy high seas freedoms in the EEZ.

Smith outlines the main objectives of maritime States during UNCLOS III.[97] The first objective was to combat 'creeping jurisdiction.'[98] Maritime States were concerned that extending the territorial sea from the customary 3 nm to 12 nm would decrease 'the extent of the high seas common to all' and threaten traditional Grotian freedoms.[99] There were also economic concerns that an extension could 'make surface sea voyages or commercial aircraft flights much more lengthy and costly.'[100] Thus, a careful balance had to be struck between the navigational interests of maritime States and the jurisdictional ambitions of coastal States.[101] As a result, Article 17 of UNCLOS provides for all States to enjoy the right of 'innocent passage' through the territorial sea provided the passage is 'continuous and expeditious'[102] and is 'not prejudicial to the peace, good order or security' of the coastal State.[103]

Another objective of maritime States was the ability to conduct naval missions, which require travel through international straits.[104] Extending the territorial sea to 12 nm would place more than one hundred straits under the national sovereignty of coastal States.[105] This would severely curtail navigational freedom. Again, a compromise had to be found. This compromise came in the form of 'the novel concept of transit passage.'[106] Article 38 of UNCLOS maintains 'the right to unimpeded navigation and overflight' by allowing ships, aircraft and submarines to transit through, over and under international straits.[107] Similar passage rights were also created for archipelagic waters.[108]

The above examples exemplify elements of the package deal created by UNCLOS, which delicately balanced the rights and jurisdiction of coastal States with the desires for freedom of navigation of maritime States. UNCLOS was formulated with the intention that these fundamental principles would endure over time. Thus, a critical issue in the BBNJ negotiations is how to articulate the relationship between an ILBI and its parent treaty UNCLOS. For instance, in its PrepCom submission, Iceland warned against the prospect of the BBNJ negotiations being used as a '*de facto*' way of reopening

97 Smith (n 70) 188.
98 Ibid.
99 Arthur H. Dean, 'The Second Geneva Conference on the Law of the Sea: The Fight for Freedom of the Seas' (1960) 54(4) *The American Journal of International Law* 751, 754. The US was particularly concerned.
100 Ibid, 755.
101 Yoshifumi Tanaka, 'Navigational Rights and Freedoms' in Donald Rothwell et al (eds), *The Oxford Handbook of the Law of the Sea* (Oxford University Press, 2015) 557.
102 UNCLOS, art 18(2).
103 UNCLOS, art 19(1).
104 Smith (n 70) 189.
105 Tuerk (n 1) 39.
106 Ibid.
107 Ibid.
108 UNCLOS, arts 52 and 53 provide for the right of innocent passage through archipelagic waters and the right of archipelagic sea lanes passage.

issues already provided for under the mandates of existing instruments and institutions.[109]

BBNJ delegations have consistently emphasised the role of UNCLOS as establishing the legal framework within which all activities in the oceans and seas are to be carried out.[110] Several delegations have stressed that the integrity of UNCLOS must be preserved.[111] The US, Japan and Norway have stipulated that the ILBI should 'be interpreted and applied in the context of and in a manner consistent with UNCLOS.'[112] Australia has suggested including a provision consistent with Article 4 of UNFSA, which provides that 'Nothing in this Agreement should prejudice the rights, jurisdiction and duties of States under the [UNCLOS] Convention.'[113] Alternatively, the central role of UNCLOS and its implementing agreements could be recognised in the ILBI's preamble.[114]

It is evident that a number of States are approaching the BBNJ negotiations motivated to retain the delicate balance of rights and obligations enshrined in UNCLOS. In particular, there is a strong desire on the part of maritime States to retain high seas freedoms, derived from the Grotian doctrine and preserved in Part VII of the Convention. UNCLOS was undoubtedly successful in undertaking a balancing exercise between the interests of different maritime actors. As Smith contends UNCLOS is really the 'net result of a battle between age old ideologies. The desire for an open ocean with free trade [*Mare Liberum*] pitted against the benefits of apportionment and property rights [*Mare Clausum*].'[115] Should an ILBI depart too much from this carefully crafted UNCLOS framework, or be seen to modify its delicately balanced

109 Iceland, 'Written Submission to the Preparatory Committee established by the General Assembly Resolution 69/292: Development of an International Legally Binding Instrument under the United Nations Convention on the Law of the Sea on the Conservation and Sustainable Use of Marine Biological Diversity beyond National Jurisdiction' (December 2016) 1 <https://www.un.org/depts/los/biodiversity/prepcom_files/rolling_comp/Iceland.pdf> ('Iceland's Written Submission to PrepCom').

110 *Report on the Work of the United Nations Open-Ended Informal Consultative Process on Oceans and the Law of the Sea at its Eighth Meeting*, UN Doc A/62/169 (30 July 2007) [51] ('*UNICPOLOS 2007 Report*').

111 See, e.g. European Union, 'Development of an International Legally-Binding Instrument under UNCLOS on the Conservation and Sustainable Use of Marine Biological Diversity of Areas beyond National Jurisdiction (BBNJ Process), Written Submission of the EU and Its Member States' (25 July 2016) 2 [8] <https://www.un.org/depts/los/biodiversity/prepcom_files/EU&MS_Written_Submission_BBNJ.pdf>.

112 Elisa Morgera et al, 'Prepcom 4 Highlights: Friday 14 July 2017' *Earth Negotiations Bulletin* (Online Bulletin, 17 July 2017) 1 <https://enb.iisd.org/download/pdf/enb25136e.pdf> ('PrepCom 4 Highlights: Friday 14 July 2017').

113 Australia, 'Preparatory Committee on Conservation and Sustainable Use of Marine Biological Diversity of Areas beyond National Jurisdiction (BBNJ), Submission by Australia' (6 December 2016) 2 <https://www.un.org/depts/los/biodiversity/prepcom_files/rolling_comp/Australia.pdf>.

114 Morgera et al, 'Prepcom 4 Highlights: Friday 14 July 2017' (n 112) 2.

115 Smith (n 70) 184.

package deal, maritime States may perceive it as a further attempt to erode the Grotian tradition.

2.2.3 Erosion of the Grotian doctrine

Concern about the erosion of the Grotian doctrine is not a recent development. A 1958 newspaper article appearing in what was then the *Manchester Guardian* questioned whether the 1958 Geneva Conventions on the Law of the Sea would be the final resting place for the Grotian tradition and asked whether the freedom of the seas principle was an 'international lost cause.'[116] In 1975, during UNCLOS III, Conforti warned that the freedom of the seas was facing an unprecedented crisis.[117] Concern over the weakening of the Grotian tradition had also clearly weighed heavily on the minds of members of the International Law Commission (ILC) in their work on the Articles Concerning the Law of the Sea. In considering whether sovereign rights over the continental shelf should be extended to include sedentary fisheries, one member of the ILC, Mr Scelle, expressed a prophetic reservation on the future of the Grotian doctrine:

> What would be left of the principle of the freedom of the high seas at the end of that process of extension? He feared that so little would be left of the high seas as would not suffice to drown a celebrated little book, the author of which was one named Grotius.[118]

Leary notes that 'in the end that little book did not drown, although it was to become decidedly soggy'[119] by the conclusion of UNCLOS III. Arguably, the prospect of an ILBI will stir up this fear once again, particularly as the erosion of the freedom of the seas has 'accelerated in recent years.'[120]

Until the mid-20th century the Grotian doctrine 'remained the major ordering principle of the oceans.'[121] However during UNCLOS III, this principle came under attack on two fronts.[122] The first threat was posed by the principle of sovereignty and what has been characterised as 'a territorial temptation thrust seaward with a speed and geographic scope that would be the envy of the most ambitious conquerors in human history.'[123] Prior to UNCLOS III, the outer limit of the

116 'Freedom of the High Seas: Another International Lost Cause?', *The Manchester Guardian* (4 February 1958) 6.
117 Benedetto Conforti, 'Does Freedom of the Seas Still Exist?' (1975) 1 *Italian Yearbook of International Law* 3, 6.
118 Leary (n 12) 91; 'Summary Record of the 207th Meeting Law of the Sea – Regime of the High Seas' (1953) 1 *Yearbook of the International Law Commission* 144, 146 [26].
119 Leary (n 12) 91.
120 Tuerk (n 1) 35.
121 Oude Elferink, 'De Groot' (n 39) 153.
122 E.D. Brown, 'Freedom of the High Seas versus the Common Heritage of Mankind: Fundamental Principles in Conflict' (1983) 20 *San Diego Law Review* 521, 522.
123 Ibid; Bernard H. Oxman, 'The Territorial Temptation: A Siren Song at Sea' (2006) 100(4) *The American Journal of International Law* 830, 832.

territorial sea was customarily taken to mark the boundary of a coastal state's sovereignty, and everything beyond that boundary fell under Grotius' freedom of the seas doctrine.[124] However, even before UNCLOS III, the pendulum had started to swing in the opposite direction, and ironically, the starting point of this 'immense grab of ocean jurisdiction'[125] came from a major maritime State, the US.

On 28 September 1945, President Harry Truman issued US Presidential Proclamation No. 2667 (Truman Proclamation).[126] By virtue of the proclamation, the US asserted jurisdiction and control over its continental shelf and exclusive rights to its resources. This was 'the first time a coastal state had asserted its right to a specific offshore resources area, distinctive from the idea of a territorial sea.'[127] The Truman Proclamation marked a historical turning point as it was a clear derogation of the principle of *Mare Liberum*.[128] It effectively:

> unleashed a quarter century of territorial and quasi-territorial claims to the high seas so vast that, at the dawn of the Third United Nations Conference on the Law of the Sea, the leader of the Canadian delegation, Ambassador J Alan Beesley, could quip that he comes to bury Grotius, not to praise him.[129]

The claims of sovereignty during this period represented a radical break from the Grotian tradition.[130] Logue even refers to UNCLOS as the 20th-century revenge of John Selden.[131]

UNCLOS effectively subtracted 'from the traditional area of the high seas its richest portion.'[132] This was mainly achieved by granting coastal States sovereign rights over their continental shelf and through the establishment of an EEZ. These maritime zones allowed coastal States to gain a greater portion of resources in and beneath the water column, previously classified as high seas.[133] The EEZ, for example, was one of the most revolutionary features of UNCLOS.[134] Extending to 200 nm, the sui generis legal status of the EEZ grants sovereign rights to coastal States to explore and exploit, conserve and manage the natural resources of the water column, the seabed and subsoil.[135]

124 Brown (n 122) 522.
125 Logue (n 12) 30.
126 Oxman (n 123) 832.
127 Laura Hugh, 'The Truman Proclamation and the Rule of Law' *Australia's Magna Carta Institute* (Blog Post, 28 September 2016) <https://www.ruleoflaw.org.au/truman-proclamation-rule-law/>.
128 Oxman (n 123) 832.
129 Ibid.
130 Logue (n 12) 41.
131 Ibid, 27.
132 Ibid, 40.
133 Oude Elferink, 'De Groot' (n 39) 162.
134 Tuerk (n 1) 41.
135 UNCLOS, arts 56 and 57.

However, for many, the acceptance of the EEZ had caused the pendulum to swing too far in favour of the principle of sovereignty, to the detriment of high seas freedoms.[136] To prevent the Grotian doctrine from disintegrating any further, Franckx argues that one of the fundamental reasons many States chose to ratify UNCLOS was the belief that it would 'stem the tide of increasing national claims in the oceans'[137] and curtail the erosion of the freedom of the seas. Arguably, for this reason, some States, particularly maritime powers, may dig their heels in harder when it comes to placing limitations upon ABNJ in furtherance of the BBNJ agenda, for instance when considering proposals for the establishment of a global network of high seas marine protected areas.

A trend of weakening the Grotian principle is also supported by instruments adopted after UNCLOS.[138] Key provisions in UNFSA, for example, support the contention that the 'high seas are no longer the province of *laissez-faire*.'[139] Article 8(3) of UNFSA provides for 'all States having a real interest in high seas fisheries' the right to become members of a regional fisheries management organisation or arrangement (RFMO/A). However, only those States which are members of an RFMO/A, or which agree to apply relevant conservation and management measures, have access to the applicable fishery resources.[140] Scovazzi argues that UNFSA 'brings an evident "encroachment"' on the traditional freedom of the seas principle.[141] Yet, this encroachment was accepted by a majority of States, including the US, the UK, Russia, the Netherlands, Canada, Norway and Japan.[142] The US was the third State to ratify UNFSA, despite being the only maritime power not to have signed or ratified UNCLOS. The majority of States accepted UNFSA because it 'was considered a necessary tool to promote the conservation and sound management of living marine resources.'[143] This is promising as it suggests that the need for a conservation regime for BBNJ may trump concerns as to the erosion of traditional freedoms. UNFSA could therefore hold the key to understanding a new level of international cooperation when it comes to the conservation of oceanic resources.

The second line of attack on the freedom of the seas principle during UNCLOS III emanated from 'right in the heart' of the Grotian empire, with the declaration that the Area and its mineral resources are the CHM.[144] Before UNCLOS, the

136 The EEZ regime preserves several high seas freedoms, including navigation, overflight and the laying of cables and pipelines—see, UNCLOS, art 58.
137 Erik Franckx, 'The 200-Mile Limit: Between Creeping Jurisdiction and Creeping Common Heritage?' (2007) 39(3) *The George Washington International Law Review* 467, 482.
138 Tullio Scovazzi, 'Marine Protected Areas on the High Seas: Some Legal and Policy Considerations' (2004) 19 *The International Journal of Marine and Coastal Law* 1, 7 ('Marine Protected Areas').
139 Ibid (emphasis included).
140 UNFSA, art 8(4).
141 Scovazzi (n 138) 7.
142 Ibid.
143 Ibid.
144 Brown (n 122) 522 discussing UNCLOS, art 136.

Area was part of the high seas, where all States could enjoy traditional freedoms, including the exploitation of its resources.[145] Under UNCLOS, the Area was internationalised.[146] While the legal status afforded to the Area and its resources could be seen as being reminiscent of Grotius' claim that the seas are 'common to all,' Oude-Elferink warns against confusing the 'idea of common property with the ... notion of common heritage. The latter implies that the use of resources themselves should lead to benefits for all.'[147] Thus, whilst no one State owns the Area's mineral resources, it is not to be equated with the Grotian tradition of absolute freedom.[148] On this basis, Part XI of UNCLOS is also responsible for further erosion of the Grotian doctrine.[149]

2.3 Freedom of the high seas versus CHM

A keen observer of the BBNJ negotiations will be able to spot distinct similarities between the debate concerning MGRs and the problems that plagued UNCLOS III negotiators in developing a regime for the mining of mineral resources in the Area. Reducing these debates down to their fundamental level, they each involve the same maritime actors (developed States versus developing States) and the same issue (the regulation of an ocean resource) and involve a clash between the same principles (freedom of the high seas versus CHM). The following sections examine the history of the interplay between these competing principles to show that the BBNJ negotiations are a little bit of history repeating.

2.3.1 An unequal freedom

In 1873, the Challenger expedition found potato-sized nodules of manganese and other metals on the ocean floor.[150] The commercial exploitation of these nodules was first considered in the late 1960s.[151] From the outset, there was considerable disagreement on the legal status of these mineral resources and the applicable legal regime.[152] Many States argued that the prevailing *laissez-faire* approach, based on the Grotian doctrine, would only serve the needs of developed States as they could muster the necessary finances and mining technology.[153] This would not result in Grotius' vision of shared equal opportunities but

145 Alex Oude Elferink, 'The Regime of the Area: Delineating the Scope of Application of the Common Heritage Principle and Freedom of the High Seas' (2007) 22(1) *The International Journal of Marine and Coastal Law* 143, 144 ('The Regime').
146 Oude Elferink, 'De Groot' (n 39) 163.
147 Ibid, 157.
148 Baird (n 81) 290.
149 Ibid.
150 Churchill and Lowe (n 30) 223.
151 Ibid; Leary (n 12) 44.
152 Churchill and Lowe (n 30) 224.
153 Ibid, 225.

the exact opposite. In 1971, Senator Metcalf echoed this sentiment before the US Congress:

> Those nations which have the capacity to … mine the deep ocean floor benefit from the freedom of the seas doctrine. Those nations without marine technology do not benefit. When one understands that there are dozens of nations which have never benefited from the freedom of the seas doctrine, one can understand the motivation behind their growing demands for greater participation. What is proclaimed by some to be equal freedom for all nations on the high seas has become in fact unequal freedom.[154]

The same argument has been made concerning MGRs of ABNJ. Accessing MGRs requires significant finances, sophisticated technology and advanced laboratory equipment. Currently, a small group of developed countries have the necessary means to explore the ocean's genetic reservoir.[155]

Developing States are concerned that MGR benefits will be unevenly shared causing 'an ever-widening capacity gap between developed and developing countries.'[156] The G77/China bloc, for example, seek an access and benefit-sharing (ABS) scheme based on principles of equity.[157] The position of this bloc is summarised in the 2011 report of the BBNJ Working Group:

> The exclusive exploitation by a few has serious global economic and social implications. We would like to stress how inconsistent this manner of exploitation is with general principles of international law, in particular those on equity; principles that are also enshrined in UNCLOS, as the Area and its resources are to be explored and exploited for the benefit of mankind as a whole.[158]

This is reminiscent of the argument put forward by developing States during UNCLOS III. Conscious of being left behind in MGR activities, developing States once again equate the freedom of the seas principle with 'unequal freedom' or freedom for a few.

154 Gonzalo Biggs, 'Deepsea's Adventures: Grotius Revisited' (1975) 9(2) *The International Lawyer* 271, 277 quoting Senator Lee Metcalf, Report on the Outer Continental Shelf, 117 *Congressional Record* 5758–5759 (10 March 1971).

155 Sophie Arnaud-Haond, Jesus M. Arrieta and Carlos M. Duarte, 'Marine Biodiversity and Gene Patents' (2011) 331 *Science* 1521, 1521.

156 Marjo Vierros et al, 'Who Owns the Ocean? Policy Issues Surrounding Marine Genetic Resources' (2016) 25(2) *Association for the Sciences of Limnology and Oceanography* 29, 30.

157 *Report of the Ad Hoc Open-Ended Informal Working Group to Study Issues Relating to the Conservation and Sustainable Use of Marine Biological Diversity beyond Areas of National Jurisdiction*, UN Doc A/61/65 (20 March 2006) 9 [29] ('*BBNJ Working Group Report*').

158 Vierros et al (n 161) 33 citing statement made on behalf of G77 and China by Minister Diego Limeres, Deputy Permanent Representative of Argentina, to the BBNJ Working Group on 31 May 2011.

2.3.2 *Opposite objectives*

The divergent views on deep-seabed mining posed the greatest challenge at UNCLOS III. The economic and political climate also contributed to the level of discord. At the time, developing States, most of which had gained their independence after World War II, were espousing the idea of a New International Economic Order (NIEO).[159] This had been set in motion in 1967 when Maltese Ambassador, Arvid Pardo, during a UNGA speech,[160] 'enunciated a vision of sharing the bounty of distributive justice, of making the poor richer and equalising the gap between the haves and have-nots.'[161] As the NIEO sought 'to establish more equitable distribution of resources' between States, the potential economic benefits from deep-seabed mineral resources provided the perfect model.[162] Consequently, Pardo called for the international seabed area and its resources to be governed under the CHM principle.[163]

Supported by Pardo's vision, the G77 bloc voiced concerns that the traditional high seas freedoms would be used by developed States to support an open access, freedom of the seas regime for the Area's mineral resources. They feared that Grotius' original idea in *Mare Liberum* of preserving 'the freedom of access for the benefit of all' would digress into a 'first come, first served'[164] approach and be used to further the interests of developed States.

In opposition, the US, along with a powerful bloc of maritime States, argued that there was already 'a right under international law to engage in seabed mining as a high seas freedom.'[165] In denouncing the CHM concept, opposing States relied on the freedom of the high seas (as outlined in the 1958 Convention) as the governing regime.[166] This was evident in the remarks made by Senator Russell Long to the US Congress in 1979. Senator Long argued that a regime, other than the freedom of the high seas, would be an erosion of guaranteed rights:

159 Churchill and Lowe (n 30) 3; Oude Elferink, 'De Groot' (n 39) 163.

160 Arvid Pardo, Address to the 22nd Session of the United Nations General Assembly, UN GAOR, 22nd sess, Agenda Item 92, UN Doc A/6695 (1 November 1967).

161 Van Dyke (n 43) 35.

162 Edward Guntrip, 'The Common Heritage of Mankind: An Adequate Regime for Managing the Deep Seabed?' (2003) 4 *Melbourne Journal of International Law* 376, 380.

163 Smith (n 70) 186.

164 Nico Schrijver and Vid Prislan, 'From Mare Liberum to the Global Commons: Building on the Grotian Heritage' (2009) 30 *Grotiana* 169, 206.

165 Jon Van Dyke and Christopher Yuen, '"Common Heritage" v "Freedom of the High Seas": Which Governs the Seabed?' (1982) 19 *San Diego Law Review* 493, 498; Luke W. Finlay, 'US Policy with Respect to High Seas Fisheries and Deep Seabed Minerals: A Study in Contrasts' (1976) 9(4) *Natural Resources Lawyer* 629, 632.

166 Guntrip (n 162) 381. At the beginning of UNCLOS III, most western States held this view, with States including the US, Canada, the UK, Australia and others repeatedly reaffirming that they regarded deep-seabed mining a permissible exercise of the freedom of the high seas—see, generally, Churchill and Lowe (n 30) 226.

> US citizens are to pay all of these millions of dollars to an international organisation for rights they presently enjoy at no cost under the well-recognised International Law Doctrine of the Freedom of the High Seas.[167]

The above statement could be recycled in the BBNJ negotiations in respect to retaining freedom of access to MGRs in ABNJ.

2.3.3 The leader of the pack—the US

In seeking to protect BBNJ the ILBI will need to regulate MGR activities, such as bioprospecting and biological sampling. To be effective, an ILBI will need to gain the support of a group of developed States, specifically those in Table 2.1 representing the top ten nations that account for 90 per cent of patent claims associated with marine genes, including some from international waters.[168] The US, Germany and Japan together account for 70 per cent.[169] As the US is at the top of the list and remains the only major maritime power not to have signed or ratified UNCLOS,[170] it serves to examine their position during UNCLOS III, as this is likely to project their position on MGR issues.

For a significant portion of UNCLOS III, the US was under the leadership of President Jimmy Carter. Under the Carter administration, a compromise package had initially been agreed to by the US.[171] Under this package, the US 'agreed to help finance the Enterprise (the operating arm of the ISA) and to transfer technology to the developing world as a way of equalising wealth.'[172] However, this agreement was quickly denounced when President Ronald Reagan took office in 1981. Under Reagan's leadership the US had a marked change of attitude towards the compromise package, particularly provisions of the deep-seabed mining regime which were seen as 'repugnant to … fundamental US interests.'[173] Ambassador James L. Malone, who served as the Special Representative of

167 Van Dyke and Yuen (n 165) 495 citing Senator Russell Long, 125 *Congressional Record* S18519 (daily ed. 14 December 1979).

168 Arnaud-Haond, Arrieta and Duarte (n 155) 1521. Of the 30 countries involved in MGR patenting, companies account for 84 per cent of all patents, public and private universities account for 12 per cent, while entities such as governmental bodies, individuals, hospitals and nonprofit research institutes account for 4 per cent—see Robert Blasiak et al, 'Corporate Control and Global Governance of Marine Genetic Resources' (2018) 4 *Science Advances* 5237.

169 Arnaud-Haond, Arrieta and Duarte (n 155) 1521.

170 Notably, the US signed the Part XI Agreement on 29 July 1994 and was the third state to ratify UNFSA on 21 August 1996.

171 A. Rohan Perera, 'A Dawn of a New Era of the Oceans or a Return to the Grotian Ocean? Some Reflections as the Law of the Sea Convention Enters into Force' (1994) 6 *Sri Lanka Journal of International Law* 157, 179.

172 Van Dyke (n 43) 5–6.

173 Perera (n 171) 179.

Table 2.1 Patent claims for a gene of marine origin with source

Country	*Marine organism patent claims*
US	199
Germany	149
Japan	128
France	34
UK	33
Denmark	24
Belgium	17
Netherlands	13
Switzerland	11
Norway	9

the US President for the Law of the Sea Conference,[174] provided evidence to Congress on the main objections to the deep-seabed mining provisions.[175] It is worth examining these objections as they are likely to mirror those the US will adopt in respect to a MGR regime under an ILBI.[176]

The first objection was the 'burdensome international regulation that would restrain private prospecting' for polymetallic nodules.[177] The US rejected Part XI of UNCLOS on the belief that it would deter future development of these resources.[178] The US demanded guaranteed continued access to the Area and was highly suspicious of any decision-making process that had the potential to allow developing countries to block the mining activities of industrialised States and their corporations.[179] The second objection was to 'the creation of a supranational mining company' (The Enterprise) and mandatory technology transfer provisions.[180] The US argued that The Enterprise and developing countries would benefit greatly from mandatory technology transfer, which at the time was largely in US hands.[181] These provisions were also seen to be in violation of US intellectual property laws.[182] The third objection was with the establishment of an international regulatory authority to govern deep-seabed mining.[183] The ISA

174 Ronald Reagan, 'Nomination of James L. Malone to Be the US Ambassador to Belize, 13 December 1985' *The American Presidency Project* (Web Page) <https://www.presidency.ucsb.edu/documents/nomination-james-l-malone-be-united-states-ambassador-belize>.
175 Van Dyke and Yuen (n 165) 497.
176 Although the US is a non-party to UNCLOS, it has actively participated in the BBNJ process, which is open to all States, as it is held under the auspices of the UNGA.
177 Van Dyke and Yuen (n 165) 497.
178 Guntrip (n 162) 384.
179 Perera (n 171) 178.
180 Van Dyke and Yuen (n 165) 497.
181 Ibid.
182 Perera (n 171) 179.
183 Ibid, 177.

would be 'vested with the exclusive power of exploiting mineral resources, for the benefit of mankind as a whole, paying particular attention to the needs of developing countries.'[184] From the US perspective, the ISA would be in a position to limit freedom of access.[185] A number of writers have examined the 'general ideological revulsion'[186] the US has to the ISA. As explained by Ogley:

> Countries (such as the US) that intended or whose companies intended, to invest ... more than a billion dollars a time in nodule mining projects were not prepared to see the risks inherent in such investment compounded by the idiosyncrasies of a possibly capricious Sea-Bed Authority.[187]

One proposal put forward during the BBNJ negotiations is the possible extension to the ISA mandate to encompass the Area's living resources.[188] Based on the above, this proposal is likely to meet strong objections from the US.

2.3.4 Unwanted consequences

Prior to the conclusion of UNCLOS III, many developed States voiced their dissatisfaction with Part XI of UNCLOS. One of the major issues 'was the lack of protection' and recognition for investments already made by States in seabed mining.[189] This appears an appropriate juncture to identify a key difference between the debates concerning mineral resources and MGRs. At UNCLOS III the exploration and exploitation of mineral resources was a pipe dream. Even today, more than three decades after the adoption of UNCLOS, deep-sea mining is still in the exploratory stage. In contrast, it is well documented that the bioprospecting and patenting of MGRs from ABNJ are already under way.[190] As the economic and political interests of States are in play, the debate concerning the legal status of MGRs will have serious consequences.[191] As Heafey explains:

> should MGRs fall under the common heritage of mankind as many developing States maintain, equitable sharing would apply and, consequently,

184 Ibid.
185 Van Dyke and Yuen (n 165) 497.
186 Perera (n 171) 159.
187 Mark W. Zacher and James G. McConnell, 'Down to the Sea with Stakes: The Evolving Law of the Sea and the Future of the Deep Seabed Regime' (1990) 21 *Ocean Development & International Law* 71, 84 quoting R.C. Ogley, *Internationalizing the Seabed* (Gower Publishing Co, 1984) 149.
188 *BBNJ Working Group Report*, UN Doc. A/61/65 (n 157) [71].
189 Churchill and Lowe (n 30) 230.
190 Ascertaining the market value of MGRs is difficult. Some projections indicate that it could run up to €2.8 billion per annum—see Natalie Y. Morris-Sharma, 'Marine Genetic Resources in Areas beyond National Jurisdiction: Issues with, in and outside of UNCLOS' (2017) 20(1) *Max Planck Yearbook of United Nations Law Online* 71, 72–73.
191 Eve Heafey, 'Access and Benefit Sharing of Marine Genetic Resources from Areas beyond National Jurisdiction: Intellectual Property—Friend, Not Foe' (2014) 14(2) *Chicago Journal of International Law* 493, 508.

> products derived from these resources [MGRs] should also be the common heritage of mankind. On the other hand, should MGRs be considered part of the high seas, the obligation of sharing benefits might be eliminated.[192]

Should developed States, which already have a vested interest in MGRs from ABNJ, be given some form of special status in an ILBI to acknowledge their investments? In an attempt to appease the developed States during UNCLOS III, pioneer investor status was provided in a last-minute Resolution II annexed to the Final Act.[193] The pioneer investor States were France, Japan, India and the USSR.[194] In addition, multinational consortia from a number of developed States were also given this status.[195] Despite the special privileges attached to the pioneer status under the Resolution, these still proved unsatisfactory to a large bloc of States. When it came time to adopt the UNCLOS text on 30 April 1982 many developed States held back from signing it. The US voted against its adoption and 17 States abstained.[196] This left the fate of UNCLOS uncertain for quite some time.[197]

The objections to Part XI led to an unwanted consequence in the form of a 'Reciprocating States Regime.' Led by the US, a bloc of 'Like-Minded States' decided to set up an interim measure to permit and regulate deep-seabed mining.[198] BBNJ negotiators will look to avoid any form of history repeating in this respect. Under the Reciprocating States Regime each State adopted similar national legislation, and this was seen as 'an exercise of the undoubted right of States to regulate activities of their nationals on the high seas,'[199] following in the Grotian tradition.

The prospect of UNCLOS entering into force without the participation of the 'Like-Minded States' was deeply unattractive.[200] The UN Secretary-General was forced to take drastic action.[201] As a result of diplomatic efforts carried out during 1990 to 1994, agreement was reached to amend Part XI,[202] including controversial provisions on technology transfer and the ISA.[203] These amend-

192 Ibid, 508–509.
193 Churchill and Lowe (n 30) 20.
194 Ibid, 230.
195 Ibid, including Belgium, Canada, the Federal Republic of Germany, Italy, Japan, the Netherlands, the UK and the US.
196 Ibid, 18.
197 Guntrip (162) 384.
198 Churchill and Lowe (n 30) 232.
199 Ibid, 233. The US enacted the *Deep Seabed Hard Minerals Resources Act* in 1980 and France, Italy, Japan, the USSR, the UK and West Germany followed suit.
200 Ibid, 19–20.
201 R. Churchill, 'The 1982 United Nations Convention on the Law of the Sea' in Donald Rothwell et al (eds), *The Oxford Handbook of the Law of the Sea* (Oxford University Press, 2015) 24, 27.
202 Churchill and Lowe (n 30) 20.
203 Guntrip (n 162) 385.

ments 'were sufficient to overcome the objections of developed States,' most of which ratified UNCLOS within a relatively short time.[204]

In watering down Part XI provisions, Perera asks whether this was an attempt to 'return to a Grotian Ocean'?[205] While this is not strictly true, given the Part XI Agreement did not alter the application of the CHM principle, it did result in the international community acceding 'to the demands of developed States over the management of the deep seabed.'[206] The question is whether this is also on the cards in developing an ABS regime for MGRs under an ILBI.

2.4 The Grotian doctrine's place in the BBNJ negotiations

2.4.1 A feeling of déjà vu?

The development of an ILBI will mark the beginning of the next chapter in the evolution of the law of the sea, and BBNJ negotiations look set to be the battleground for the next great ideological struggle.[207] It is no coincidence that the interplay between two old foes: the freedom of the high seas versus the CHM, has remained at the top of the list of divergent issues in the BBNJ process.[208] The international community is sure to feel a sense of déjà vu as these two principles have a re-match in the BBNJ negotiations in respect to MGRs.

UNCLOS is silent on MGRs, as the concept had not penetrated the international community's awareness at UNCLOS III. The belief, however, that MGRs could be the source of considerable wealth,[209] has resulted in the adoption of contrary positions in the BBNJ negotiations. One of the objectives of an ILBI will be to clarify whether and how MGRs fit into the existing international law framework.[210] So far, the main point of contention has been the legal regime applicable to the Area's MGRs. The discussion below focuses on this issue; however, it should be acknowledged that distinguishing between MGRs in the water column as opposed to those on the seabed is not an easy process.[211]

204 Churchill (n 201) 27.
205 Perera (n 171) 177.
206 Guntrip (n 162) 386.
207 *BBNJ Working Group Report*, UN Doc. A/61/65 (n 157) [28]–[30].
208 See, e.g. *Report of the Preparatory Committee: Development of an International Legally Binding Instrument under UNCLOS on the Conservation and Sustainable Use of Marine Biological Diversity of Areas beyond National Jurisdiction*, UN Doc A/AC.287/2017/PC.4/2 (31 July 2017) Section B ('*PrepCom Report*').
209 Joanna Mossop, 'Marine Bioprospecting' in Donald Rothwell et al (eds), *The Oxford Handbook of the Law of the Sea* (Oxford University Press, 2015) 837.
210 Elisa Morgera, 'Do We Need a New Treaty to Protect Biodiversity in the Deep Seas?', SDG Knowledge Hub (Online Commentary, 20 January 2015) <http://sdg.iisd.org/commentary/policy-briefs/do-we-need-a-new-treaty-to-protect-biodiversity-in-the-deep-seas/>.
211 Tullio Scovazzi, 'The Assumption that UNCLOS is the Legal Framework for All Activities in the Sea' in Salvatore Arico (ed), *Ocean Sustainability in the 21st Century* (Cambridge University Press, 2015) 240. See, also, ch 4, pt 1.5.

2.4.2 Freedom of the high seas versus CHM 2.0

This section outlines the contrary positions of States on the issue of MGRs to show that they mimic the positions taken during UNCLOS III. Druel et al have undertaken an analysis of the position of three major blocs represented in the BBNJ process, the EU and other conservation-minded States such as Australia and New Zealand; the G77/China and Mexico bloc; and the US.[212] Druel et al argue that States such as Canada, Japan, Russia, Iceland, Norway, South Korea and Singapore fall somewhere in between these three main blocs as a 'grey area.'[213] With respect, this work argues that many of the delegations within this grey area will actually fall on the same side as the US as a number of these States have significant biotechnological investments and interests in MGR exploitation. The following examines the issue in line with the political groupings of UNCLOS III, being the G77/China bloc pitted against a powerful group of developed States.

2.4.2.1 Freedom of the high seas and MGRs

The legal regime applicable to MGRs in ABNJ was first considered by the International Community during a 1995 Meeting of the Conference of the Parties to the CBD.[214] At this meeting, the application of the freedom of the high seas principle to MGRs in the Area was perceived to be endorsed in a Note prepared by the CBD Secretariat.[215] The Note read:

> The regime for the Area makes no reference to genetic resources. As a result, it is not clear how [UNCLOS] may apply to the Area's genetic resources. The most plausible interpretation is that, as with all resources of the high seas, other than mineral resources, they are freely accessible, open access resources, appropriable by anyone who collects them. These types of resources are governed by a number of broad principles included under the rubric of the freedom to fish.[216]

References in this note to themes of 'free access' and 'open access to all' clearly hark back to the Grotian doctrine.

A number of BBNJ delegations, most forcefully the US, Japan and Russia, have maintained that the freedom of the seas principle applies to MGRs in ABNJ.[217] These States argue that MGRs are governed under the high seas regime

212 Druel et al (n 80) 31.
213 Ibid.
214 Leary (n 12) 53.
215 Ibid.
216 Subsidiary Body on Scientific, Technical and Technological Advice, *Bioprospecting of Genetic Resources of the Deep-Sea-Bed-Note by the Secretariat*, UN Doc UNEP/CBD/SBTTA/2/15 (24 July 1996) [9].
217 See, e.g. United States of America, 'Views Expressed by the United States Delegation Related to Certain Key Issues under Discussion at the Second Session of the Preparatory

of Part VII of UNCLOS, thereby ensuring open access by all States. Maritime States are reluctant to see the imposition of rules that will hinder MGR access and look to avoid limitations being placed on what they perceive to be guaranteed freedoms.[218] For example, during the eighth meeting of UNICPOLOS, a bloc of maritime States declared that they would oppose an ABS regime 'that might interfere with high seas freedoms' and 'were not convinced of either the need for or desirability of a new international regime to protect MGRs.'[219]

States that maintain that Part VII applies to MGRs in the Area point to Article 133 of UNCLOS.[220] For the purposes of Part XI, Article 133 defines 'resources' as *all solid, liquid or gaseous mineral resources in situ in the Area at or beneath the seabed, including polymetallic nodules.* On its face, Article 133 excludes living resources from the CHM regime in Part XI.[221] Even Article 140 of UNCLOS, which provides that '[a]ctivities in the Area … shall be for the benefit of mankind,' is qualified by including 'as provided for in this Part [Part XI].'[222] Based on a literal interpretation of these provisions, developed States (including Japan, Iceland and South Korea) argue that Part XI only applies to the Area's mineral resources[223] and that Part VII is the default regime 'in the absence of an explicit indication to the contrary in UNCLOS.'[224]

Committee on the Development of an International Legally Binding Instrument under the United Nations Convention on the Law of the Sea on the Conservation and Sustainable Use of Marine Biological Diversity' (9 September 2016) 1 <https://www.un.org/depts/los/biodiversity/prepcom_files/USA_Submission_of_Views_Expressed.pdf>; Elisa Morgera et al, 'Prepcom 4 Highlights: Monday 10 July 2017' *Earth Negotiations Bulletin* (Online Bulletin, 11 July 2017) 2 <https://enb.iisd.org/download/pdf/enb25132e.pdf>; Elisa Morgera et al, 'Summary of the Third Session of the Preparatory Committee on Marine Biodiversity beyond Areas of National Jurisdiction 27 March–7 April 2017' *Earth Negotiations Bulletin* (Online Bulletin, 10 April 2017) 3 <https://enb.iisd.org/download/pdf/enb25129e.pdf>.

218 See, e.g. Iceland's Written Submission to PrepCom (n 113) 1; Tallash Kantai et al, 'Summary of the Second Session of the Intergovernmental Conference on the Conservation and Sustainable Use of Marine Biodiversity of Areas beyond National Jurisdiction: 25 March–5 April 2019' *Earth Negotiations Bulletin* (Online Bulletin, 8 April 2019) 3 citing Japan's submission 'that access to MGRs should not be restricted' <https://enb.iisd.org/download/pdf/enb25195e.pdf>.

219 *UNICPOLOS 2007 Report*, UN Doc A/62/169 (n 110) [79].

220 Tladi (n 86) 261.

221 Craig H. Allen, 'Protecting the Oceanic Gardens of Eden: International Law Issues in Deep-Sea Vent Resource Conservation and Management' (2001) 13 *Georgetown International Environmental Law Review* 563, 630.

222 Tladi (n 86) 261 discussing UNCLOS, art 140(1).

223 Tallash Kantai et al, 'BBNJ IGC-3 Highlights: Wednesday 28 August 2019' *Earth Negotiations Bulletin* (Online Bulletin, 29 August 2019) <https://enb.iisd.org/download/pdf/enb25216e.pdf>; Iceland's Written Submission to PrepCom (n 113); Elisa Morgera et al, 'Summary of the Second Session of the Preparatory Committee on Marine Biodiversity beyond Areas of National Jurisdiction: 26 August–9 September 2016' *Earth Negotiations Bulletin* (Online Bulletin, 12 September 2016) 4 <https://enb.iisd.org/download/pdf/enb25118e.pdf>.

224 Morgera (n 210).

Mimicking its position during UNCLOS III, the US has taken on a leading role in the MGR debate and is the strongest supporter of a freedom of the seas approach. The US appears particularly concerned by the prospect of 'creeping common heritage'[225] and has been vocal in rejecting any increased role for the ISA. The US argues that expansion of the ISA's mandate 'may provide a disincentive for UNCLOS non-parties to participate in a benefit-sharing regime' under an ILBI.[226] Thus, the objections the US had to the ISA during UNCLOS III remain. Arguably, these objections will only heighten given the current populist strain in American politics which is characterised by 'a disdain of perceived limits on sovereignty and a distrust of powerful international institutions.'[227]

In a 2018 article published by the Heritage Foundation, a conservative lobbying organisation, a number of reasons were advanced for the US to stay out of the UNCLOS regime.[228] Several reasons cut to the core of the BBNJ negotiations. One reason is that the ratification of UNCLOS would lead to a redistribution of wealth from the hands of the US to developing States.[229] This concern is evident in the issues the US has raised during MGR discussions, including questions regarding the use of patents, and more generally, of intellectual property rights (IPRs). The US has consistently stressed that 'IPR issues' do not belong in the BBNJ process and that patents should not be used for enforcing benefit-sharing.[230] Japan and the US have also strongly opposed any reference to monetary benefits.[231] Another objection the US has to UNCLOS is the encouragement of technology transfers.[232] The US, Russia, Japan and the EU have repeatedly

225 Franckx (n 137) 467.

226 Elisa Morgera et al, 'PrepCom 1 Highlights: Thursday 7 April 2016' *Earth Negotiations Bulletin* (Online Bulletin, 8 April 2016) 2 <https://enb.iisd.org/download/pdf/enb25105e.pdf>.

227 Roncevert Ganan Almond, 'US Ratification of the Law of the Sea Convention: Measuring the Raison d-Etat in the Trump Era', (24 May 2017) *The Diplomat.*

228 Theodore R. Bromund, James Jay Carafano and Brett D. Schaefer, '7 Reasons U.S. Should Not Ratify UN Convention on the Law of the Sea' *The Heritage Foundation* (Commentary, 4 June 2018) <https://www.heritage.org/global-politics/commentary/7-reasons-us-should-not-ratify-un-convention-the-law-the-sea>. The Heritage Foundation is America's largest conservative research and educational institution. The Trump administration embraced nearly two-thirds of the policy recommendations from the Heritage Foundation's Mandate for Leadership—see 'Trump Administration Embraces Heritage Foundation Policy Recommendations' *The Heritage Foundation* (Web Page, 23 January 2018) <https://www.heritage.org/impact/trump-administration-embraces-heritage-foundation-policy-recommendations>.

229 Ibid.

230 Claudio Chiarolla, Tallash Kantai and Elisa Morgera, 'Summary of the Fifth Meeting of the Working Group on Marine Biodiversity beyond Areas of National Jurisdiction: 7–11 May 2012' *Earth Negotiations Bulletin* (Online Bulletin, 14 May 2012) 3 <http://enb.iisd.org/download/pdf/enb2583e.pdf>.

231 Morgera et al, 'PrepCom 4 Highlights: 10 July 2017' (n 217) 1.

232 Bromund, Carafano and Schaefer (n 228).

asserted that capacity-building and technology transfer should be voluntary in an ILBI.[233]

2.4.2.2 CHM and MGRs

Reminiscent of their position in UNCLOS III, the G77/China bloc has consistently maintained that the Area's MGRs are CHM and rely on a purposive approach to Article 136 of UNCLOS.[234] They contend that Article 136 makes the CHM principle not only applicable to the Area's resources, but to the Area itself.[235] As Article 1 of UNCLOS defines the 'Area' as the *seabed, ocean floor and subsoil*, this bloc argues that these terms should be given their ordinary meaning which would encompass their living and non-living resources.[236] Developing States argue that the freedom of the seas argument is flawed because:

> it ignores the fundamental logic of the Convention [UNCLOS], namely that the regulation of various resources … is dependent on the maritime zone in which the resource is found and not on the nature of the resource … Part VII and the rights contained therein apply only to the high seas and not to the deep seabed.[237]

Flowing on from the argument at UNCLOS III, many delegations argue that MGRs in ABNJ should not be subject to free access as this will lead to an inequitable result. Instead, these States argue for a CHM approach in furtherance of the UNCLOS Preamble which provides for 'equitable and efficient utilisation' of oceanic resources.

2.4.3 Marine protected areas (MPAs)

While the focus of this chapter has been on the contested issue of MGRs, it is important to acknowledge that the Grotian doctrine may have far wider

233 Morgera et al, 'PrepCom 4 Highlights: 10 July 2017' (n 217) 2; Elisa Morgera et al, 'PrepCom 4 Highlights: Wednesday 12 July 2017' *Earth Negotiations Bulletin* (Online Bulletin, 13 July 2017) 2 <https://enb.iisd.org/download/pdf/enb25134e.pdf>.

234 *Letter Dated 5 May 2014 from the Co-Chairs of the Ad Hoc Open-Ended Informal Working Group to the President of the General Assembly*, UN Doc A/69/82 (5 May 2014) annex ('*Co-Chairs' Summary of Discussions*') [50].

235 Oude Elferink, 'The Regime' (n 145) 150.

236 See, e.g. Permanent Mission of Bangladesh to the United Nations New York, 'Written Submission by Bangladesh for the Development of an International Legally Binding Instrument under the United Nations Convention on the Law of the Sea on the Conservation and Sustainable Use of Marine Biological Diversity of Areas beyond National Jurisdiction pursuant to Resolution 69/292: Proposal on the Scope of Marine Genetic Resources' (5 December 2016) <https://www.un.org/depts/los/biodiversity/prepcom_files/rolling_comp/Bangladesh-marine_genetic_resources.pdf>.

237 Tladi (n 86) 262.

implications. ABMTs, including MPAs, are another contentious issue as the effective protection of an area may require significant restrictions on activities. These restrictions may affect the rights of States to use the Area and the superjacent water column. High seas MPAs may not sit comfortably with proponents of the freedom of the seas, as they may perceive this to be a further attempt to erode the Grotian doctrine. This has become evident in the objections made by a number of developed States regarding the establishment of MPAs in Antarctica.[238]

In order to understand how the Grotian doctrine could stand in the way of MPAs, it is important to examine the two main implications of the freedom of the seas principle. First, freedom of the seas means the high seas are free from national jurisdiction.[239] Article 89 of UNCLOS confirms that: '[n]o State may validly purport to subject any part of the high seas to its sovereignty.' Second, freedom of the high seas means freedom of activities there.[240] Taking into account these two implications, the principle implies:

> that no single State, nor group of States, is empowered to lay claim to control over a specific area of the high seas, thus negating the possibility of adopting conservation measures in an area of the high seas that are binding on third States and that might interfere with the free use of the high seas by such third States.[241]

On this basis, the Grotian principle, 'by its very nature, directly undermines conservation on the high seas'[242] and may therefore act as a roadblock to the establishment of essential tools to protect BBNJ.

On the other hand, Scovazzi argues that the dichotomy between the freedom of the seas principle and MPAs may not be as irreconcilable as first appears, due to environmental and conservation obligations in UNCLOS.[243] For example Article 194(5) requires States to adopt measures to protect rare or fragile ecosystems. Arguably, these measures would include MPAs. Also, Articles 117, 118 and 197 of UNCLOS respectively provide that States are obligated to cooperate in the conservation and management of high seas living resources and the protection of the marine environment. These provisions point to an overriding 'obligation to cooperate' particularly in the high seas.[244] This obligation 'implies a duty to act in good faith' which is incumbent upon all States.[245] Thus, the establishment of high seas MPAs should be seen as a fulfilment of this duty to cooperate

238 See Chapter 5, Section 5.3.
239 Yoshifumi Tanaka, *The International Law of the Sea* (Cambridge University Press, 2nd ed, 2015) 155–156.
240 Ibid.
241 Young (n 4) 167.
242 Ibid.
243 Scovazzi, 'Marine Protected Areas' (n 138) 5.
244 Ibid.
245 Ibid.

to abide by obligations already set forth in UNCLOS.[246] Scovazzi argues that the freedom of the seas principle should also be seen in a modern 21st-century context.[247] While acknowledging that freedoms such as navigation and fishing are still important, they should be 'balanced with other interests'[248] including the protection of BBNJ.

2.5 The Grotian doctrine—building block or roadblock?

2.5.1 The only way forward is compromise

For decades, legal commentators have argued that '[t]he time has come to move on from Hugo Grotius' vision and to act on a global scale in the interests of future generations.'[249] In other words, calling for a complete abandonment of the Grotian tradition. Jenks, for example, in 1967, argued that the international community would not be able to meet the 'moral challenges of tomorrow with the intellectual baggage of yesterday.'[250] Sir Hersch Lauterpacht called the conception of freedom of the seas 'rigid and pedantic'[251] and one the international community should discard. More recently, Young has argued that there needs to be an 'emergence of a new ethos that replaces, or at least softens the grip of Grotius' doctrine' on high seas governance.[252] This book argues that this utopian vision, of an abrupt end to the Grotian doctrine, fails to understand that the freedom of the seas principle is far too entrenched in the mindset of particular States and has been intricately woven into the fabric of UNCLOS. A complete dismantling of the Grotian tradition which has served as a building block for the law of the sea is both unrealistic and unfeasible. It is evident from the analysis in this chapter that the freedom of the seas paradigm continues to influence the way governments approach law of the sea issues. Thus, in respect to the BBNJ negotiations, the Grotian tradition 'is bound to remain a powerful legal and ideological tool' in the hands of maritime States 'for rejecting attempts to elaborate stricter regulations to protect the global commons.'[253]

As with UNCLOS, the ultimate success of an ILBI will rely upon the support of a powerful bloc of developed States, particularly those with a vested interest in MGRs. In order for this bloc to agree to essential components of the BBNJ agenda, this work contends that elements of the Grotian doctrine will need to

246 UNFSA also sets out cooperation duties, including obligations relating to the conservation and management of straddling and highly migratory fish stocks—see, e.g. UNFSA, art 8.
247 Scovazzi, 'Marine Protected Areas' (n 138) 5.
248 Ibid, 7.
249 Garry R. Russ and Dirk C. Zeller, 'From Mare Liberum to Mare Reservarum' (2003) 27 *Marine Policy* 75, 76; Young (n 4) 180.
250 C.W. Jenks, *Law in the World Community* (Longmans, 1967) 2.
251 H. Lauterpacht, 'Sovereignty over Submarine Areas' (1950) 27 *British Year Book of International Law* 376, 413.
252 Young (n 4) 167.
253 Oude Elferink, 'De Groot' (n 39) 167.

be carefully woven through the fabric of an ILBI and an effective regime for the conservation and sustainable use of BBNJ. This appears a daunting task; however it is achievable. The freedom of the seas doctrine is not rigid and pedantic. It has been adapted, modified and eroded over the centuries to accommodate the security and other interests of coastal States,[254] and for conservation measures in UNFSA. These various encroachments on the freedom of the seas 'have come to be accepted on the basis of their reasonableness.'[255] For this reason the conservation elements of an ILBI should be 'designed to implement the spirit and intent of Part XII provisions of the LOSC [UNCLOS], rather than radically changing the basic principles and inherent balance of the law of the sea.'[256] After all, a distinctive characteristic of UNCLOS is the accommodation of navigational rights and freedoms with the need to ensure effective marine environmental protection.[257]

In essence, the freedom of the seas principle will act as a counterweight in the BBNJ negotiations. As Butler contends:

> The principle of freedom of the seas expounded by Grotius has served and continues to serve as rhetorical reinforcement for the point of departure when deliberating about matters of maritime jurisdiction. Rather like the presumption of innocence in criminal proceedings, we invoke it constantly to remind ourselves that whatever developments in the law of the sea are to be contemplated, we should measure their validity and impact with reference to the freedom of the seas.[258]

While it is unrealistic to expect agreement to dismantle the freedom of the seas doctrine completely, it is also unrealistic for maritime States not to accept further attenuations of the Grotian principle, in exchange for adequate conservation measures. Ultimately, the ILBI, like its parent treaty UNCLOS, will need to maintain a balance of competing interests.[259]

Arriving at a balanced outcome could be assisted by promoting a renewed sense of, and duty, to cooperate. Schrijver and Prislan argue that the first-come, first-served approach adopted by developed States during UNCLOS III has become 'increasingly qualified and supplemented … by a new law of international cooperation aimed at conservation and sustainable use of natural wealth and resources.'[260] For example, UNFSA embraced this duty to cooperate as its guiding

254 Anand, 'Tyranny' (n 10) 428.
255 Ibid.
256 Robin Warner, 'Conserving Marine Biodiversity in Areas beyond National Jurisdiction: Co-Evolution and Interaction with the Law of the Sea' in Donald Rothwell et al (eds), *The Oxford Handbook of the Law of the Sea* (Oxford University Press, 2015) 752.
257 Oxman (n 123) 843.
258 Butler (n 26) 220.
259 Morris-Sharma (n 190) 71.
260 Schrijver and Prislan (n 164) 168.

principle.[261] As most maritime States have signed or ratified UNFSA, including the US, this may indeed represent a 'new spirit of shared responsibility for the common areas of the planet.'[262]

2.6 Conclusion

> Generations of men have been struggling to agree upon what rights to the resources of the oceans may be claimed by those men who navigate the surface, and who fish the deeps, and who dwell upon the borders of the sea.[263]

In order to assess the impact the freedom of the seas doctrine may have on the outcome of the BBNJ negotiations this chapter has traced the doctrine back to its roots. The historical analysis has shown that the Grotian doctrine has been adapted and moulded throughout the centuries to fit the interests and needs of maritime States, and it is anticipated that these States will once again turn to the Grotian doctrine to support their position on key issues in the BBNJ agenda. While Young argues that 'the freedom principle appears to have morphed into something that was not originally contemplated'[264] by Grotius, this chapter demonstrates that the legacy of *Mare Liberum* has been absorbed into the thinking of many States and continues to condition the position these States take on issues concerning BBNJ.

The analysis in this chapter has shown that while UNCLOS was responsible for making 'considerable in-roads on the scope of the freedom of the seas *ratione materiae*,'[265] it also enshrined the continued relevance of the principle.[266] Unlike Anand, who perceived the freedom of the seas doctrine as having 'lost the breath of life,'[267] this chapter shows that the doctrine is still very much alive and will continue to exert influence on the BBNJ negotiations, particularly on issues concerning MGRs and MPAs. In the face of further erosion of the principle in an ILBI, it is contended that maritime States may take an even harder stance on attempts to limit the Grotian tradition.

The development of an ILBI will require significant compromise and a delicate balance of interests, by both safeguarding elements of the Grotian doctrine, while promoting the protection of BBNJ. This will undoubtedly constitute the next great ideological battle in the law of the sea. The BBNJ negotiations look set to follow in the tradition of attempting to find an equilibrium between competing principles, and in this respect, the development of an ILBI is a case of history repeating itself.

261 Van Dyke (n 43) 11.
262 Ibid, 9.
263 Dean (n 99) 786.
264 Young (n 4) 175.
265 Brown (n 122) 522 (emphasis included).
266 Oude Elferink, 'De Groot' (n 39) 164.
267 Anand, 'Tyranny' (n 10) 429.

References

Agreement for the Implementation of the Provisions of the United Nations Convention on the Law of the Sea of 10 December 1982 Relating to the Conservation and Management of Straddling Fish Stocks and Highly Migratory Fish Stocks, opened for signature 4 December 1995, (1995) 34 ILM 1542 (entered into force 11 December 2001) (UNFSA).

Allen, Craig H, 'Protecting the Oceanic Gardens of Eden: International Law Issues in Deep-Sea Vent Resource Conservation and Management' (2001) 13 *Georgetown International Environmental Law Review* 563–660. DOI: https://digitalcommons.law.uw.edu/faculty-articles/94.

Allott, Philip, 'Power Sharing in the Law of the Sea' (1983) 77(1) *The American Journal of International Law* 1–30. DOI: 10.2307/2201196.

Almond, Roncevert Ganan, 'US Ratification of the Law of the Sea Convention: Measuring the Raison d-Etat in the Trump Era', (24 May 2017) *The Diplomat* <https://thediplomat.com/2017/05/u-s-ratification-of-the-law-of-the-sea-convention/> accessed 31 March 2022.

Anand, R.P, '"Tyranny" of the Freedom of the Seas Doctrine' (1973) 12 *International Studies* 416–429. DOI: 10.1177/002088177301200302.

Anderson, David, *The Development of the Modern Law of the Sea: Selected Essays* (Martinus Nijhoff, 2008) vol 59.

Arnaud-Haond, Sophie, Jesus M. Arrieta and Carlos M. Duarte, 'Marine Biodiversity and Gene Patents' (25 March 2011) 331 *Science* 1521–1522. DOI: 10.1126/science.1200783.

Australia, 'Preparatory Committee on Conservation and Sustainable Use of Marine Biological Diversity of Areas Beyond National Jurisdiction (BBNJ), Submission by Australia' (6 December 2016) <https://www.un.org/depts/los/biodiversity/prepcom_files/rolling_comp/Australia.pdf> accessed 31 March 2022.

Baird, Rachel, 'Political and Commercial Interests as Influences in the Development of the Doctrine of the Freedom of the High Seas' (1996) 12 *Queensland University of Technology Law Journal* 274–291. DOI: 10.5204/qutlr.v12i0.425.

Biggs, Gonzalo, 'Deepsea's Adventures: Grotius Revisited' (1975) 9(2) *The International Lawyer* 271–281.

Blasiak, Robert, Jean-Baptiste Jouffray, Colette C.C. Wabnitz, Emma Sundström, Henrik Österblom, 'Corporate Control and Global Governance of Marine Genetic Resources' (2018) 4 *Sciences Advances* 1–7. DOI: 10.1126/sciadv.aar5237.

Bromund, Theodore R, James Jay Carafano and Brett D. Schaefer, '7 Reasons U.S. Should Not Ratify UN Convention on the Law of the Sea' *The Heritage Foundation* (Commentary, 4 June 2018) <https://www.heritage.org/global-politics/commentary/7-reasons-us-should-not-ratify-un-convention-the-law-the-sea> accessed 31 March 2022.

Brown, E.D, 'Freedom of the High Seas Versus the Common Heritage of Mankind: Fundamental Principles in Conflict' (1983) 20 *San Diego Law Review* 521–560.

Butler, W.E, 'Grotius and the Law of the Sea' in Hedley Bull, Benedict Kingsbury and Adam Roberts (eds), *Hugo Grotius and International Relations* (Clarendon, 1992) 209. DOI: 10.1093/0198277717.003.0006.

Chiarolla, Claudio, Tallash Kantai and Elisa Morgera, 'Summary of the Fifth Meeting of the Working Group on Marine Biodiversity Beyond Areas of National Jurisdiction: 7–11 May 2012' *Earth Negotiations Bulletin* (Online Bulletin, 14

May 2012) <http://enb.iisd.org/download/pdf/enb2583e.pdf> accessed 31 March 2022.

Churchill, Robin, 'The 1982 United Nations Convention on the Law of the Sea' in Donald Rothwell et al (eds), *The Oxford Handbook of the Law of the Sea* (Oxford University Press, 2015) 24. DOI: 10.1093/law/9780198715481.003.0002.

Churchill, R.R. and A.V. Lowe, *The Law of the Sea* (Manchester University Press, 3rd ed, 1999).

Conforti, Benedetto, 'Does Freedom of the Seas Still Exist?' (1975) 1 *Italian Yearbook of International Law* 3–15. DOI: 10.1163/221161375X00011.

Convention on Biological Diversity, Subsidiary Body on Scientific, Technical and Technological Advice, *Bioprospecting of Genetic Resources of the Deep-Seabed-Note by the Secretariat,* UN Doc UNEP/CBD/SBTTA/2/15 (24 July 1996).

Convention on the High Seas, opened for signature 29 April 1958 (1958) 450 *UNTS* 82 (entered into force 30 September 1962).

Dean, Arthur H, 'The Second Geneva Conference on the Law of the Sea: The Fight for Freedom of the Seas' (1960) 54(4) *The American Journal of International Law* 751–789. DOI: 10.2307/2195140.

Dromgoole, Sarah, *Underwater Cultural Heritage and International Law* (Cambridge University Press, 2013). DOI: https://doi.org/10.1017/CBO9781139020503.

Druel, Elisabeth, Julien Rochette, Raphaël Billé, Claudio Chiarolla, 'A Long and Winding Road-International Discussions on the Governance of Marine Biodiversity in Areas Beyond National Jurisdiction' (Study No. 7/2013, IDDRI, September 2013).

Dryzek, John S., 'Paradigms and Discourses' in Daniel Bodansky, Jutta Brunnée and Ellen Hey (eds), *The Oxford Handbook of International Environmental Law* (Oxford University Press, 2008) 44. DOI: 10.1093/oxfordhb/9780199552153.013.0003.

European Union, 'Development of an International Legally-Binding Instrument under UNCLOS on the Conservation and Sustainable Use of Marine Biological Diversity of Areas Beyond National Jurisdiction (BBNJ Process), Written Submission of the EU and Its Member States' (25 July 2016) <https://www.un.org/depts/los/biodiversity/prepcom_files/EU&MS_Written_Submission_BBNJ.pdf> accessed 31 March 2022.

Finlay, Luke W, 'US Policy with Respect to High Seas Fisheries and Deep Seabed Minerals - A Study in Contrasts' (1976) 9(4) *Natural Resources Lawyer* 629–643.

Franckx, Erik, 'The 200-Mile Limit: Between Creeping Jurisdiction and Creeping Common Heritage?' (2007) 39(3) *The George Washington International Law Review* 467–498.

'Freedom of the High Seas: Another International Lost Cause?' *The Manchester Guardian* 4 February 1958.

Grotius, Hugo, Ralph Van Deman Magoffin and James Brown Scott, *The Freedom of the Seas: Or, the Right which Belongs to the Dutch to Take Part in the East Indian Trade* (Oxford University Press American Branch, 1916).

Guilfoyle, Douglas, 'The High Seas' in Donald Rothwell et al (eds), *The Oxford Handbook of the Law of the Sea* (Oxford University Press, 2015) 203. DOI: 10.1093/law/9780198715481.003.0010.

Guntrip, Edward, 'The Common Heritage of Mankind: An Adequate Regime for Managing the Deep Seabed?' (2003) 4 *Melbourne Journal of International Law* 376–405. DOI: https://search.informit.org/doi/10.3316/agispt.20052364.

Hardin, Garrett 'The Tragedy of the Commons' (1968) 162(3859) *Science* 1243–1248.

Heafey, Eve, 'Access and Benefit Sharing of Marine Genetic Resources from Areas Beyond National Jurisdiction: Intellectual Property—Friend, Not Foe' (2014) 14(2) *Chicago Journal of International Law* 493–523.

Hugh, Laura, 'The Truman Proclamation and the Rule of Law' *Australia's Magna Carta Institute* (Blog Post, 28 September 2016) <https://www.ruleoflaw.org.au/truman-proclamation-rule-law/> accessed 22 October 2021.

Iceland, 'Written Submission to the Preparatory Committee established by the General Assembly Resolution 69/292: Development of an International Legally Binding Instrument under the United Nations Convention on the Law of the Sea on the Conservation and Sustainable Use of Marine Biological Diversity Beyond National Jurisdiction' (December 2016) <https://www.un.org/depts/los/biodiversity/prepcom_files/rolling_comp/Iceland.pdf> accessed 31 March 2022.

Jenks, C.W, *Law in the World Community* (Longmans, 1967).

Kantai, Tallash, Asheline Appleton, Priscila Pereira de Andrade, Bernard Soubry and Asterios Tsioumanis, 'Summary of the Second Session of the Intergovernmental Conference on the Conservation and Sustainable Use of Marine Biodiversity of Areas Beyond National Jurisdiction: 25 March–5 April 2019' *Earth Negotiations Bulletin* (Online Bulletin, 8 April 2019a) <https://enb.iisd.org/download/pdf/enb25195e.pdf> accessed 31 March 2022.

Kantai, Tallash, Jennifer Bansard, Tasha Goldberg, Katarina Hovden and Asterios Tsioumanis, 'BBNJ IGC-3 Highlights: Tuesday 27 August 2019' *Earth Negotiations Bulletin* (Online Bulletin, 28 August 2019b) <https://enb.iisd.org/download/pdf/enb25215e.pdf> accessed 31 March 2022.

Kraska, James, *Maritime Power and the Law of the Sea: Expeditionary Operations in World Politics* (Oxford University Press, 2011). DOI: 10.1093/acprof:oso/9780199773381.001.0001.

Lauterpacht, H, 'Sovereignty over Submarine Areas' (1950) 27 *British Year Book of International Law* 376–433.

Leary, David, *International Law and the Genetic Resources of the Deep Sea* (Martinus Nijhoff Publishers, 2007).

Letter Dated 5 May 2014 from the Co-Chairs of the Ad Hoc Open-ended Informal Working Group to the President of the General Assembly, UN Doc A/69/82 (annex 'Co-Chairs' Summary of discussions', 5 May 2014) <https://documents-dds-ny.un.org/doc/UNDOC/GEN/N14/320/48/PDF/N1432048.pdf?OpenElement> accessed 31 March 2022

Lobingier, Charles Sumner, 'The Maritime Law of Rome' (1935) 47 *Juridical Review* 1–32.

Logue, John, 'The Revenge of John Selden: The Draft Convention on the Law of the Sea in the Light of Hugo Grotius' Mare Liberum' (1982) 3 *Grotiana* 27–56. DOI: 10.1163/187607582X00042.

Maarleveld, Thijs J, 'The Netherlands' in Sarah Dromgoole (ed), *The Protection of the Underwater Cultural Heritage* (Martinus Nijhoff Publishers, 2nd ed, 2006). DOI: https://doi.org/10.1163/9789047410454_009.

Morgera, Elisa, 'Do We Need a New Treaty to Protect Biodiversity in the Deep Seas?' *SDG Knowledge Hub* (Online Commentary, 20 January 2015) <http://sdg.iisd.org/commentary/policy-briefs/do-we-need-a-new-treaty-to-protect-biodiversity-in-the-deep-seas/> accessed 31 March 2022.

Morgera, Elisa, Daniela Diz, Tallash Kantai and Asterios Tsioumanis, 'PrepCom 1 Highlights: Thursday 7 April 2016' *Earth Negotiations Bulletin* (Online Bulletin, 8 April 2016a) <https://enb.iisd.org/download/pdf/enb25105e.pdf> accessed 31 March 2022.

Morgera, Elisa, Daniela Diz, Tallash Kantai and Asterios Tsioumanis, 'Summary of the Second Session of the Preparatory Committee on Marine Biodiversity Beyond Areas of National Jurisdiction: 26 August–9 September 2016' *Earth Negotiations Bulletin* (Online Bulletin, 12 September 2016b) <https://enb.iisd.org/download/pdf/enb25118e.pdf> accessed 31 March 2022.

Morgera, Elisa, Asheline Appleton, Tallash Kantai and Asterios Tsioumanis, 'Summary of the Third Session of the Preparatory Committee on Marine Biodiversity Beyond Areas of National Jurisdiction 27 March–7 April 2017' *Earth Negotiations Bulletin* (Online Bulletin, 10 April 2017a) <https://enb.iisd.org/download/pdf/enb25129e.pdf> accessed 31 March 2022.

Morgera, Elisa, Asheline Appleton, Tallash Kantai and Asterios Tsioumanis, 'Prepcom 4 Highlights: Monday 10 July 2017' *Earth Negotiations Bulletin* (Online Bulletin, 11 July 2017b) <https://enb.iisd.org/download/pdf/enb25132e.pdf> accessed 31 March 2022.

Morgera, Elisa, Asheline Appleton, Tallash Kantai and Asterios Tsioumanis, 'PrepCom 4 Highlights: Wednesday 12 July 2017' *Earth Negotiations Bulletin* (Online Bulletin, 13 July 2017c) <https://enb.iisd.org/download/pdf/enb25134e.pdf> accessed 31 March 2022.

Morgera, Elisa, Asheline Appleton, Tallash Kantai and Asterios Tsioumanis, 'Prepcom 4 Highlights: Friday 14 July 2017' *Earth Negotiations Bulletin* (Online Bulletin, 17 July 2017d) <https://enb.iisd.org/download/pdf/enb25136e.pdf> accessed 31 March 2022.

Morris-Sharma, Natalie Y, 'Marine Genetic Resources in Areas Beyond National Jurisdiction: Issues with, in and outside of UNCLOS' (2017) 20(1) *Max Planck Yearbook of United Nations Law Online* 71–97. DOI: 10.1163/13894633_02001004.

Mossop, Joanna, 'Marine Bioprospecting' in Donald Rothwell et al (eds), *The Oxford Handbook of the Law of the Sea* (Oxford University Press, 2015) 837. DOI: 10.1093/law/9780198715481.003.0036.

Ostrom, E, J. Burger, C. Field, R. Norgaard and D. Policansky, 'Revisiting the Commons: Local Lessons, Global Challenges' (9 April 1999) 284 *Science* 278–282. DOI: 10.1126/science.284.5412.278.

Ostrom, Elinor, 'The Challenge of Crafting Rules to Change Open-Access Resources into Managed Resources' in G.M Heal (ed), *Is Economic Growth Sustainable?* (Palgrave Macmillan, 2010) 172. DOI: 10.1057/9780230274280_7.

Oude Elferink, Alex, 'The Regime of the Area: Delineating the Scope of Application of the Common Heritage Principle and Freedom of the High Seas' (2007) 22(1) *The International Journal of Marine and Coastal Law* 143–176. DOI: 10.1163/157180807781475272.

Oude Elferink, Alex, 'De Groot-A Founding Father of the Law of the Sea, Not the Law of the Sea Convention' (2009) 30 *Grotiana* 152–167. DOI: 10.1163/016738309X12537002674448.

Oxman, Bernard H, 'The Territorial Temptation: A Siren Song at Sea' (2006) 100(4) *The American Journal of International Law* 830–851. DOI: 10.1017/S0002930000031912.

Papastavridis, Efthymios, 'The Right of Visit on the High Seas in a Theoretical Perspective: Mare Liberum versus Mare Clausum Revisited' (2011) 24 *Leiden Journal of International Law* 45–69. DOI: 10.1017/S0922156510000580.

Pardo, Arvid, 'Address to the 22nd Session of the United Nations General Assembly' UN GAOR, 22nd sess, Agenda Item 92, UN Doc A/6695 (1 November 1967).

Perera, A. Rohan, 'A Dawn of a New Era of the Oceans or a Return to the Grotian Ocean? Some Reflections as the Law of the Sea Convention Enters into Force' (1994) 6 *Sri Lanka Journal of International Law* 157–184.

Permanent Mission of Bangladesh to the United Nations New York, 'Written Submission by Bangladesh for the Development of an International Legally Binding Instrument under the United Nations Convention on the Law of the Sea on the Conservation and Sustainable Use of Marine Biological Diversity of Areas Beyond National Jurisdiction pursuant to Resolution 69/292: Proposal on the Scope of Marine Genetic Resources' (5 December 2016) <https://www.un.org/depts/los/biodiversity/prepcom_files/rolling_comp/Bangladesh-marine_genetic_resources.pdf> accessed 31 March 2022.

Reagan, Ronald, 'Nomination of James L. Malone to be The US Ambassador to Belize, 13 December 1985' *The American Presidency Project* (Web Page) <https://www.presidency.ucsb.edu/documents/nomination-james-l-malone-be-united-states-ambassador-belize> accessed 31 March 2022.

Reeves, J.S, 'Two Conceptions of the Freedom of the Seas' (1917) 22(3) *The American Historical Review* 535–543. DOI: 10.2307/1842648.

Report of the Ad Hoc Open-ended Informal Working Group to Study Issues Relating to the Conservation and Sustainable Use of Marine Biological Diversity Beyond Areas of National Jurisdiction, UN Doc A/61/65 (20 March 2006) <https://documents-dds-ny.un.org/doc/UNDOC/GEN/N06/277/50/PDF/N0627750.pdf?OpenElement> accessed 31 March 2022.

Report of the Preparatory Committee Established by General Assembly Resolution 69/292: Development of an International Legally Binding Instrument under the United Nations Convention on the Law of the Sea on the Conservation and Sustainable Use of Marine Biological Diversity of Areas Beyond National Jurisdiction, UN Doc A/AC.287/2017/PC.4/2 (31 July 2017) <https://documents-dds-ny.un.org/doc/UNDOC/GEN/N17/237/36/PDF/N1723736.pdf?OpenElement> accessed 31 March 2022

Russ, Garry R. and Dirk C. Zeller, 'From Mare Liberum to Mare Reservarum' (2003) 27 *Marine Policy* 75–78. DOI: 10.1016/S0308-597X(02)00054-4.

Schrijver, Nico and Vid Prislan, 'From Mare Liberum to the Global Commons: Building on the Grotian Heritage' (2009) 30 *Grotiana* 168–206. DOI: 10.1163/016738309X12537002674484.

Scovazzi, Tullio, 'Marine Protected Areas on the High Seas: Some Legal and Policy Considerations' (2004) 19 *The International Journal of Marine and Coastal Law* 1–17. DOI: 10.1163/157180804773788646.

Scovazzi, Tullio, 'The Assumption that UNCLOS is the Legal Framework for All Activities in the Sea' in Salvatore Arico (ed), *Ocean Sustainability in the 21st-Century* (Cambridge University Press, 2015) 240. DOI: https://doi.org/10.1017/CBO9781316164624.013.

Selvig, Kirsten, 'Expensive Freedom: Establishing Marine Protected Areas on the Open Ocean Requires an End to the Freedom of the Seas' (2013) 22(3) *Minnesota Journal of International Law* 35–68.

Smith, Leland Holbrook, 'To Accede or Not to Accede: An Analysis of the Current US Position Related to the United Nations Law of the Sea' (2017) 83 *Marine Policy* 184–193. DOI: 10.1016/j.marpol.2017.06.008.

Tanaka, Yoshifumi, *The International Law of the Sea* (Cambridge University Press, 2nd ed, 2015a). DOI: https://doi.org/10.1017/CBO9781139946261.

Tanaka, Yoshifumi, 'Navigational Rights and Freedoms' in Donald Rothwell et al. (eds), *The Oxford Handbook of the Law of the Sea* (Oxford University Press, 2015b) 557. DOI: 10.1093/law/9780198715481.003.0024.

The Heritage Foundation, 'Trump Administration Embraces Heritage Foundation Policy Recommendations' (Web Page, 23 January 2018) <https://www.heritage.org/impact/trump-administration-embraces-heritage-foundation-policy-recommendations> accessed 31 March 2022.

The Le Louis (1817) 12 Dods 210; 165 ER 1464.

Thornton, Helen, 'Hugo Grotius and the Freedom of the Seas' (2004) 16 *International Journal of Maritime History* 17–38. DOI: 10.1177/084387140401600203.

Tladi, Dire, 'Conservation and Sustainable Use of Marine Biodiversity in Areas Beyond National Jurisdiction: Towards an Implementing Agreement' in Rosemary Rayfuse (ed), *Research Handbook on International Marine Environmental Law* (Edward Elgar Publishing, 2015) 264. DOI: https://doi.org/10.4337/9781781004777.

Treves, Tullio, 'Historical Development of the Law of the Sea' in Donald Rothwell et al (eds), *The Oxford Handbook of the Law of the Sea* (Oxford University Press, 2015) 1. DOI: 10.1093/law/9780198715481.003.0001.

Tuerk, Helmut, The Legal Regime of Maritime Areas and the Waning Freedom of the Seas (Conference Paper, Maritime Issues and United Nations Convention on the Laws of the Sea: Sharing European and Asia Approaches to Territorial Disputes, 4–5 June 2015) <http://www.maritimeissues.com/working-papers/the-legal-regime-of-maritime-areas-and-the-waning-freedom-of-the-seas.html> accessed 31 March 2022.

United Nations, 'Summary Record of the 207th Meeting Law of the Sea-regime of the High Seas' (1953) 1 *Yearbook of the International Law Commission* 144.

United Nations Convention on the Law of the Sea, opened for signature 10 December 1982, 1833 *UNTS* 397 (entered into force 16 November 1994) (UNCLOS).

United Nations General Assembly, *Oceans and the Law of the Sea: Report of the Secretary-General,* UN Doc A/60/63/Add.1 (15 July 2005).

United Nations Open-ended Informal Consultative Process on Oceans and the Law of the Sea, *Report on the Work of the United Nations Open-Ended Informal Consultative Process on Oceans and the Law of the Sea at Its Eighth Meeting*, UN Doc A/62/169 (30 July 2007).

United States of America, 'Views Expressed by the United States Delegation Related to Certain Key Issues under Discussion at the Second Session of the Preparatory Committee on the Development of an International Legally Binding Instrument under the United Nations Convention on the Law of the Sea on the Conservation and Sustainable Use of Marine Biological Diversity' (9 September 2016) <https://www.un.org/depts/los/biodiversity/prepcom_files/USA_Submission_of_Views_Expressed.pdf> accessed 31 March 2022.

Van Dyke, Jon, 'Sharing Ocean Resources-In A Time of Scarcity and Selfishness' in Harry N. Scheiber (ed), *The Law of the Sea: The Common Heritage and Emerging Challenges* (Martinus Nijhoff Publishers, 2000) vol 34, 3. DOI: https://doi.org/10.1163/9789004482586_004.

Van Dyke, Jon and Christopher Yuen, '"Common Heritage" v "Freedom of the High Seas": Which Governs the Seabed?' (1982) 19 *San Diego Law Review* 493–551.

Van Ittersum, Martine Julia, 'Mare Liberum Versus the Propriety of the Seas? The Debate between Hugo Grotius (1583–1645) and William Welwood (1552–1624) and its Impact on Anglo-Scotto-Dutch Fishery Disputes in the Second Decade of the Seventeenth Century' (2006) 10 *Edinburgh Law Review* 239–276. DOI: 10.3366/elr.2006.10.2.239.

Vierros, Marjo, Curtis A. Suttle, Harriet Harden-Davies and Geoff Burton, 'Who Owns the Ocean? Policy Issues Surrounding Marine Genetic Resources' (2016) 25(2) *Association for the Sciences of Limnology and Oceanography* 29–35. DOI: 10.1002/lob.10108.

Vitzthum, Wolfgang Graf, 'From the Rhodian Sea Law to UNCLOS III' (2003) 17 *Ocean Yearbook* 56–59. DOI: 10.1163/221160003X00050.

Warner, Robin, 'Conserving Marine Biodiversity in Areas Beyond National Jurisdiction: Co-Evolution and Interaction with the Law of the Sea' in Donald Rothwell et al. (eds), *The Oxford Handbook of the Law of the Sea* (Oxford University Press, 2015) 752. DOI: 10.1093/law/9780198715481.003.0033.

Young, Michaela, 'Then and Now: Reappraising Freedom of the Seas in Modern Law of the Sea' (2016) 47(2) *Ocean Development & International Law* 165–185. DOI: 10.1080/00908320.2016.1159088.

Zacher, Mark W. and James G. McConnell, 'Down to the Sea with Stakes: The Evolving Law of the Sea and the Future of the Deep Seabed Regime' (1990) 21 *Ocean Development & International Law* 71–103. DOI: 10.1080/00908329009545922.

3 A principled backbone

The potential role of modern governance principles and approaches in an ILBI

Introduction

Developments in modern international environmental law from the 1970s onwards have drawn attention to the important role principles can play in translating broad environmental goals into concrete policies and laws. Stephens notes that, among other things, principles can help to 'explain why and how the natural environment should be valued, how the objectives of resource conservation and ecosystem protection should be achieved, and how environmental values should be balanced against other objectives' of the international community.[1] As these are all relevant questions in the BBNJ negotiation process, the potential contribution of principles to the development of an ILBI warrants particular consideration.

This chapter uses four core concepts as analytical tools to examine the potential role of modern governance principles and approaches in an ILBI. The concepts are (1) the protection and preservation of the marine environment, (2) the ecosystem approach, (3) the precautionary principle and (4) the integration approach. These concepts have been selected because they are widely recognised by governments and commentators as fundamental governance tools for BBNJ.[2] However, the selection of these particular concepts should not be taken to suggest other principles and approaches are not relevant or applicable to ABNJ.

Section 3.1 of this chapter provides an overview of the four concepts and highlights gaps in their implementation under the current legal framework. Section 3.2 explores the benefits to be derived from adopting a principle-based approach to ocean governance in ABNJ and proposes two critical functions for

1 Tim Stephens, *International Courts and Environmental Protection* (Cambridge University Press, 2009) 6.

2 For example, over 30 States have developed or are developing integrated ocean strategies within their national waters—see Karen Scott, 'Integrated Oceans Management: A New Frontier in Marine Environmental Protection' in Donald Rothwell et al (eds), *The Oxford Handbook of the Law of the Sea* (Oxford University Press, 2015) 463, 465. See, also, Arie Trouwborst, 'The Precautionary Principle and the Ecosystem Approach in International Law: Differences, Similarities and Linkages' (2009) 18(1) *Review of European Community & International Environmental Law* 26, 26; *Oceans and the Law of the Sea–Report of the Secretary-General*, UN Doc A/58/65 (3 March 2003) [219].

DOI: 10.4324/b22996-4

governance tools under an ILBI. Lastly, Section 3.3 demonstrates how BBNJ package deal elements could be used to implement and operationalise governance principles and approaches in ABNJ.

This chapter argues that for the ILBI to be effective it will need to have a strong and principled backbone, one that underpins the interpretation of the instrument as a whole and the implementation and operationalisation of the four corners of the package deal.

3.1 Compiling a set of modern governance tools

Due to the development of modern environmental law and a number of key UN conferences, governance principles and approaches have gradually seeped into the preambles and operative parts of ocean-related treaties and policy initiatives. For example, the origins of the four concepts addressed in this chapter can be traced to three of these conferences, namely, the 1972 Stockholm Conference, UNCLOS III and the 1992 Rio Conference. BBNJ negotiators will therefore be dealing with 'generally accepted principles' the content of which has already, to a large extent, been 'hardwired'[3] into UNCLOS and in general international law.[4]

Legal commentators and institutions have put forward proposed lists of principles for inclusion in an ILBI. The lists most often cited include Freestone's 'Principles of Modern Ocean Governance,'[5] the IUCN's related '10 Principles for High Seas Governance'[6] and the list submitted by the Netherlands to the BBNJ Working Group in 2010, based on a comprehensive report by Oude Elferink.[7] Appendix 2 of this book provides a comparison of these lists, which collectively offer a useful starting point for compiling a set of modern ocean governance tools.

3.1.1 Benefits of a single source

As governance tools are currently found in a range of sources, consolidating them within a single instrument could be advantageous. The incorporation of principles in an ILBI will unequivocally confirm their relevance and applicability, and 'provide a sound basis for developing a coherent regime' for ABNJ.[8] A restatement of modern principles could also 'reinforce the collective responsibility'

3 Donald R. Rothwell and Tim Stephens, *The International Law of the Sea* (Hart Publishing Ltd, 2nd ed, 2016) 712.

4 Ibid.

5 David Freestone, 'Modern Principles of High Seas Governance: The Legal Underpinnings' (2009) 39 *Environmental Policy and Law* 44.

6 IUCN, '10 Principles for High Seas Governance' (Web Page) <https://www.iucn.org/downloads/10_principles_for_high_seas_governance___final.pdf>.

7 Alex Oude Elferink, 'Governance Principles for Areas beyond National Jurisdiction' (2012) 27 *The International Journal of Marine and Coastal Law* 205, 206.

8 Ibid.

of all States to protect BBNJ and ensure 'that all activities in ABNJ are held to the same minimum standards.'[9]

A general consensus has emerged that an ILBI should incorporate and 'spell out principles for good oceans governance.'[10] However, there are political and practical issues. Russia questions how governance concepts will work in practice under an ILBI.[11] Will each governance tool be equally applicable to all package deal elements?[12] Delegations disagree on the application of certain principles to package deal issues, and these disagreements tend to fall along political lines. For example, delegations disagree on the governing principle applicable to MGRs, which has reignited the debate between the freedom of the seas versus the CHM.[13]

During PrepCom and the early stages of the IGC process, governance principles were discussed in the context of the package deal.[14] For instance, the President's Aid to Negotiations included an extensive list of principles and approaches, as well as individual lists tailored to each package deal element. These individual lists have been omitted from recent negotiation documents. The Revised Draft Negotiating Text includes only a slimmed down list of 'General Principles and Approaches,' presumably applicable to all package deal topics. This may prove to be a stumbling block in future negotiations, particularly if developing States continue to insist upon the CHM principle.[15] Given the fears and reservations maritime States have concerning further erosion of the Grotian doctrine, these States may be more inclined to support an approach that does not restrict the freedom of the seas more than is necessary to achieve the objectives of the new instrument.[16]

Another risk in attempting to streamline a list of overarching governance principles is that many may be overlooked. Notably, the Revised Draft Negotiating

9 David Freestone, 'Principles Applicable to Modern Ocean Governance' in David Freestone (ed), *Conserving Biodiversity in Areas beyond National Jurisdiction* (Brill Nijhoff, 2019) 49, 55 ('Modern Ocean Governance').

10 *Chair's Overview of the Third Session of the Preparatory Committee*, [13] <https://www.un.org/Depts/los/biodiversity/prepcom_files/Chair_Overview.pdf>.

11 Elisa Morgera, 'Summary of the Seventh Meeting of the Working Group on Marine Biodiversity beyond Areas of National Jurisdiction: 1–4 April 2014' *Earth Negotiations Bulletin* (Online Bulletin, 7 April 2014) 7 <https://enb.iisd.org/oceans/marinebiodiv7/brief/brief_marinebiodiv7e.pdf>.

12 *Chair's Overview of the Second Session of the Preparatory Committee*, 13 <https://www.un.org/Depts/los/biodiversity/prepcom_files/Prep_Com_II_Chair_overview_to_MS.pdf>.

13 See Chapter 2, Section 2.3.

14 *President's Aid to Negotiations*, UN Doc A/CONF.232/2019/1 (3 December 2018) 8–12.

15 See, *Revised Draft Text of an Agreement under UNCLOS on the Conservation and Sustainable Use of Marine Biological Diversity of Areas beyond National Jurisdiction*, UN Doc A/CONF.232/2020/3 (18 November 2019) art 5 ('*Revised Draft Negotiating Text*').

16 *Textual Proposals Submitted by Delegations for Consideration at IGC 4, in Response to the Invitation by the President of the Conference in Her Note of 18 November 2019*, UN Doc A/CONF.232/2020/3 (15 April 2020) International Cable Protection Committee on art 5, 369.

Text is missing key principles, including the protection and preservation of the marine environment of ABNJ.[17]

3.1.2 Implementation gaps

While the development of an ILBI presents an opportunity to consolidate and reaffirm relevant governance tools, the real challenge will be determining how effectively to implement and operationalise these tools under the instrument. Even though the basic principles of the law of the sea are sound, they 'all require a great deal of fleshing out, coordination and much more systematic and rigorous implementation.'[18] Using four core concepts as analytical tools, the following sections demonstrate implementation gaps under the existing international law framework.

3.1.2.1 Protection and preservation of the marine environment

UNCLOS formally introduced one of the most important principles in the law of the sea, namely that States are under an obligation to ensure 'the protection and preservation of the marine environment.' Freestone contends that the codification of this principle in Article 192 signified a 'sea change' as it provided an unprecedented, unqualified and robust obligation on all States to protect the marine environment, including ABNJ.[19]

Since UNCLOS, the principle has been repeatedly reaffirmed and recognised by the international community.[20] For example, the 2009 UNGA resolution on the Oceans and the Law of the Sea emphasised 'the importance of the implementation of Part XII of the Convention in order to protect and preserve the marine environment'[21] and called upon States to take measures either directly or through competent international organisations to fulfil this obligation.[22] The principle has also been enshrined in legal instruments at the global and regional levels, including Agenda 21 and various Regional Seas agreements.[23] The 1989 report

17 Ibid, IUCN Comments on art 5, 299.

18 David Freestone, 'International Governance, Responsibility and Management of Areas beyond National Jurisdiction' (2012) 27 *The International Journal of Marine and Coastal Law* 191, 195.

19 David Freestone, 'Editorial—Principles Applicable to Modern Oceans Governance' (2008) 23(3) *International Journal of Marine and Coastal Law* 385, 387. The ITLOS confirmed the application of Article 192 to ABNJ in *Responsibilities and Obligations of States Sponsoring Persons and Entities with Respect to Activities in the Area* (Advisory Opinion) (Seabed Disputes Chamber, Case No 17, 1 February 2011) [97] and [180] ('*Responsibilities and Obligations of States with Respect to Activities in the Area*').

20 Oude Elferink, (n 7) 215.

21 *Oceans and the Law of the Sea*, GA Res 64/71, UN Doc A/RES/64/71 (4 December 2009 adopted on 12 March 2010) para 112.

22 Ibid.

23 Richard A. Barnes, 'Consolidating Governance Principles for Areas beyond National Jurisdiction' (2012) 27 *The International Journal of Marine and Coastal Law* 261, 276.

of the UN Secretary-General suggested that Article 192 reflects 'a statement of customary international law with regard to the environmental responsibility of States towards the oceans.'[24] This is a view shared by many legal commentators.[25] Czybulka, for example, contends that 'according to a teleological interpretation, Art. 192 forms part of customary law' and is therefore, in principle, binding upon all States.[26]

The binding obligation in Article 192 requires protection *and* preservation. In the *South China Sea Arbitration* (*Philippines v China*), the Tribunal held that the principle extends beyond the avoidance of future damage to the marine environment and includes an obligation to *preserve* in taking active measures to maintain or improve its present condition.[27]

The implementation of Article 192 has been challenging, as it lacks detail and guidance on how the principle is to be implemented or operationalised. To date, no rules, standards or recommended practices have been implemented under this principle to protect BBNJ. Czybulka points to one instance that demonstrates its potential. In 2008 the Council of the European Union adopted Regulation No. 734/2008 to protect deep-sea VMEs from bottom fishing impacts. Recital 2 of the Regulation provides that:

> The absence of a regional fisheries management organization or arrangement does not exempt States from their obligation under the law of the sea to adopt with respect to their nationals such measures as may be necessary for the conservation of the resources of the high seas including the protection of vulnerable ecosystems against the harmful effects of fishing activities.[28]

Although no specific article is relied upon to support this, Czybulka suggests that the Council 'gained its conviction' by a synopsis of Articles 192, 194(5) and 117 of UNCLOS.[29]

24 *Law of the Sea-Report of the Secretary-General*, UN Doc A/44/461 (18 September 1989) para 29.

25 See, e.g. Yoshifumi Tanaka, 'Principles of International Marine Environmental Law' in Rosemary Rayfuse (ed), *Research Handbook on International Marine Environmental Law* (Edward Elgar Publishing, 2015) 31, 34 ('Principles'); Patricia Birnie, Alan Boyle and Catherine Redgwell, *International Law and the Environment* (Oxford University Press, 3rd ed, 2009) 387.

26 Detlef Czybulka, 'Part XII Protection and Preservation of the Marine Environment' in Alexander Proelss (ed), *United Nations Convention on the Law of the Sea: A Commentary* (Hart Publishing, 2017) 1277, 1285.

27 *In the Matter of the South China Sea Arbitration (Philippines v. China) (Arbitral Award)* (Permanent Court of Arbitration, Case No 2013-19, 12 July 2016) [941]. See also, Duncan Currie, 'The Oceans and the Law of the Sea Convention as a Form of Global Governance' (2017) 13(1) *Policy Quarterly* 32, 33.

28 *Regulation (EC) No 734/2008 of the European Parliament and of the Council of 15 July 2008 on the Protection of Vulnerable Marine Ecosystems in the High Seas from the Adverse Impacts of Bottom Fishing Gears* [2008] OJ L 201/8 (Recital 2).

29 Czybulka (n 26) 1281.

Given its lack of implementation, the principle in Article 192 should be reaffirmed under an ILBI. To accord with the objectives of the new instrument, the principle could be reformulated to refer explicitly to BBNJ.[30] Currie and Davis propose re-framing the principle to reflect the commitment made by States at the Rio+20 Conference, namely that:

> States have an obligation to protect, preserve and restore biodiversity and the marine environment and maintain and restore ecosystem integrity in areas beyond national jurisdiction.[31]

An ILBI could thereby 'add a specific layer'[32] to the original formulation of the principle in UNCLOS and reaffirm its applicability to ABNJ.

The principle should also set the framework for the substantive obligations of States under an ILBI.[33] This would resemble its current role under Part XII of UNCLOS. Article 192 establishes the primary obligation of States to protect and preserve the marine environment and also sets out 'the general standards and the framework within which a much more complex and wide ranging structure of powers and duties must operate.'[34] The principle should take on the same role under an ILBI, by providing a primary obligation on States to protect BBNJ while also providing an overarching framework for the implementation and operationalisation of the package deal. After all, ABMTs, including MPAs and EIAs as well as CBTT, have all been identified as ways in which the principle in Article 192 could be given practical effect under an ILBI.[35]

3.1.2.2 The ecosystem approach

Traditional, silo-structured management, focusing on a single species or sector, has proven ineffective in ensuring the health and integrity of marine ecosystems.[36] These conventional approaches pay little attention to cumulative impacts or 'the ecological constraints imposed by individual ecosystems.'[37] In contrast, the ecosystem approach is 'primarily concerned with management at a systems level'[38] and 'aims to conserve ecosystem structure and functioning within ecologically

30 Oude Elferink (n 7) 222.
31 Duncan Currie and Mischa Davis, 'Governance Principles Relevant to Marine Biodiversity in Areas beyond National Jurisdiction' Submission to PrepCom Chair, 25 February 2016, 3.
32 Ibid.
33 Oude Elferink (n 7) 216.
34 Czybulka (n 26) 1279.
35 Currie and Davis (n 31) 10.
36 Rachel D. Long, Anthony Charles and Robert L. Stephenson, 'Key Principles of Marine Ecosystem-Based Management' (2015) 57 *Marine Policy* 53, 53.
37 Scott (n 2) 464.
38 UNEP-WCMC, 'Ecosystem Approach' *Biodiversity A-Z* (Web Page, 17 December 2019) <http://biodiversitya-z.org/content/ecosystem-approach.pdf>.

meaningful boundaries.'[39] This is particularly relevant to deep-sea VMEs, being home to a complex and dynamic mix of biological, genetic and mineral resources 'interacting as a functional unit.'[40] Under the ecosystem approach the species, habitats and genetic diversity at VMEs are considered as one unity. This represents a new paradigm in ocean management as it provides for strategies based on impacts on the entire ecological system rather than component parts.[41]

Currently, there is no universally accepted definition of the ecosystem approach. The Biodiversity Committee of the 1992 Convention for the Protection of the Marine Environment of the North-East Atlantic[42] defines the concept as:

> the comprehensive integrated management of human activities based on the best available scientific knowledge about the ecosystem and its dynamics, in order to identify and take action on influences which are critical to the health of marine ecosystems, thereby achieving sustainable use of ecosystem goods and services and maintenance of ecosystem integrity.[43]

While UNCLOS makes no explicit reference to the ecosystem approach,[44] it has received widespread support.[45] Yet, gaps exist in its implementation in ABNJ.

Firstly, as there is no single way to conceptualise the ecosystem approach, it has been 'developed within several different institutional and legal clusters,' resulting in 'specialised versions.'[46] Vierros, Douvere and Arico point to three:

39 Yoshifumi Tanaka, *The International Law of the Sea* (Cambridge University Press, 2nd ed, 2015) 250 ('*Law of the Sea*').

40 CBD, art 2.

41 Vito De Lucia, 'Competing Narratives and Complex Genealogies: The Ecosystem Approach in International Environmental Law' (2015) 27 *Journal of Environmental Law* 91, 92; Ronán Long, 'Legal Aspects of Ecosystem-Based Marine Management in Europe' (2012) 26 *Ocean Yearbook Online* 417, 425.

42 Convention for the Protection of the Marine Environment of the North-East Atlantic, opened for signature 22 September 1992, (1992) 32 ILM 1069 (entered into force 25 March 1998) (OSPAR Convention).

43 Meeting of the Biodiversity Committee, Draft OSPAR Recommendations on a Network of Marine Protected Areas, BDC 03/10/1-E, annex 13, 1, [6]. This definition has been adopted in the OSPAR Convention, the Helsinki Convention and by the International Council for the Exploration of the Sea (ICES).

44 Rudimentary instances of the concept can be found in UNCLOS, arts 1(4) (definition of 'pollution'), 61(4), 119(1)(b) and 145—see, e.g. Robin Churchill, 'The LOSC Regime for Protection of the Marine Environment: Fit for the Twenty-First Century?' in Rosemary Rayfuse (ed), *Research Handbook on International Marine Environmental Law* (Edward Elgar Publishing, 2015) 3, 11–12; Rosemary Rayfuse, 'Article 119 Conservation and Management of the Living Resources of the High Seas' in Alexander Proelss et al (ed), *United Nations Convention on the Law of the Sea: A Commentary* (Hart Publishing, 2017) 791, 844.

45 The principle has been adopted in the CBD, UNFSA and CAMLR Convention and has been endorsed by the IMO, FAO, UNEP, UNDP and the Global Environmental Facility. The UNGA has endorsed the concept in its resolutions on oceans and the law of the sea over the last decade—see Scott (n 2) 483.

46 Vito De Lucia, 'The Ecosystem Approach for Areas beyond National Jurisdiction: Reflections on the Chair's Non-Paper ahead of PREPCOM III,' The NCLOS Blog (Blog, 20

(1) The ecosystem approach developed in the CBD context;
(2) The ecosystem approach to fisheries;
(3) Integrated marine and coastal area management.[47]

Although there is good consistency between these versions, each one has been tailored to suit the peculiar needs of the relevant institutional and legal cluster and not the specific features of deep-sea environments.[48]

Secondly, ecosystem-based management relies heavily on scientific input. As there is a significant lack of knowledge concerning deep-sea ecosystems and their resilience to human impacts,[49] more research is required to implement the ecosystem approach in ABNJ. This reveals an intersection of the ecosystem approach and precautionary principle. Given the lack of scientific knowledge and the risk of harm, the precautionary principle has obvious applicability. To facilitate the implementation of these governance tools, a Subsidiary Body for Scientific and Technical Advice could be established under an ILBI and tasked with providing scientific and technical assistance in operationalising ecosystem-based management.[50] A clearing-house mechanism could also be created for information-sharing and dissemination. This could assist in implementing the ecosystem approach by providing continuous and updated biological, ecological and oceanographic data on ABNJ.[51]

Lastly, implementation of the ecosystem approach in ABNJ has been hindered by the lack of an overarching institutional structure capable of undertaking the management, monitoring and enforcement tasks required for its effective application. A governing body, such as a Conference of the Parties (COP), could oversee and supervise the operationalisation of ecosystem-based management under an ILBI,[52] in similar fashion to the CBD-COP which has taken an active role and endorsed a set of 12 principles (Malawi Principles) for the application of the ecosystem approach to biodiversity management.[53]

March 2017) <https://site.uit.no/jclos/2017/03/20/the-ecosystem-approach-for-areas-beyond-national-jurisdiction-reflections-on-the-chairs-non-paper-ahead-of-prepcom-iii/>.

47 Marjo Vierros, Fanny Douvere and Salvatore Arico, 'UNU-IAS Report Implementing the Ecosystem Approach in Open Ocean and Deep Sea Environments: An Analysis of Stakeholders, Their Interests and Existing Approaches' (UNU-IAS, 2006) 29, 33 and 34.

48 Ibid 5, 6; De Lucia (n 46).

49 Kathryn J. Mengerink et al, 'A Call for Deep-Ocean Stewardship' (2014) 344(6185) *Science* 696, 698.

50 WWF, 'Proposed Framework and Key Elements of a Third UNCLOS Implementing Agreement' Submission to PrepCom Chair and to DOALOS for PrepCom3, 5 December 2016, 2–7, 10.

51 Ibid.

52 Ibid, 9.

53 Division for Ocean Affairs and the Law of the Sea, Office of Legal Affairs, 'Ecosystem Approaches', *Oceans and Law of the Sea* (Web Page, 21 July 2010) <http://www.un.org/depts/los/ecosystem_approaches/ecosystem_approaches.htm>. The Malawi Principles were presented to the COP-CBD at its fifth meeting—see *Ecosystem Approach: Further Con-*

Unlike many other multilateral treaties, UNCLOS did not provide for the establishment of a standing body or a COP to review its implementation. The UNGA has largely taken on this task, with the Meeting of States Parties to UNCLOS (SPLOS) attributed a limited administrative role.[54] Oude Elferink argues that the absence of a clearly defined review mechanism in UNCLOS 'can be explained by an unwillingness on the part of States to create an institution ... with an explicit competence to deal with all matters arising' under the Convention.[55] Arguably, as the role of a COP would be limited to overseeing and supervising the implementation of the ILBI, it could sit alongside existing institutional structures, like the SPLOS, without undermining or imposing upon their present duties and functions.

While BBNJ delegations recognise the importance of the ecosystem approach, they disagree on its role under an ILBI. Some argue that it should govern the entire instrument,[56] while others insist that it should govern only some thematic areas.[57] This book contends that an ILBI should integrate the ecosystem approach among its governing principles and include an Annex of rules to guide its implementation in ABNJ, similar to Annex II of UNFSA, which guides the precautionary approach to fisheries.[58] This would ensure that the ecosystem approach is used in an operational manner, rather than making generic references to the concept in the preamble or non-operative parts of the instrument.[59] The ecosystem approach should be used to guide the overall interpretation of the ILBI and the implementation of each package deal element. For example, the ecosystem approach could be operationalised through a system of ecologically

ceptual Elaboration, SBSTTA 5 Recommendation V/10, annex 'B. Principles of the Ecosystem Approach.'

54 Alex G. Oude Elferink, 'Reviewing the Implementation of the LOS Convention: The Role of the United Nations General Assembly and the Meeting of State Parties' in Alex G. Oude Elferink and Donald R. Rothwell (eds), *Oceans Management in the 21st Century: Institutional Frameworks and Responses* (Martinus Nijhoff Publishers, 2004) 295, 306. These administrative matters include the election of members of ITLOS and the CLCS and ITLOS financial arrangements—see UNCLOS, Annex II, art 2(3) and Annex VI, arts 4(4), 18 and 19.

55 Ibid, 310.

56 See, e.g Norway, 'Preparatory Committee established by General Assembly Resolution 69/292: Development of an International Legally Binding Instrument under the United Nations Convention on the Law of the Sea on the Conservation and Sustainable Use of Marine Biological Diversity of Areas beyond National Jurisdiction, Comments by Norway' (December 2016) 2 <https://www.un.org/depts/los/biodiversity/prepcom_files/rolling_comp/Norway.pdf>.

57 For example, the EU encourages an ecosystem approach for ABMTs—see, European Union, 'Development of an International Legally-Binding Instrument under UNCLOS on the Conservation and Sustainable Use of Marine Biological Diversity of Areas Beyond National Jurisdiction (BBNJ Process), Written Submission of the EU and Its Member States' (25 July 2016) [14], [18] and [36] <https://www.un.org/depts/los/biodiversity/prepcom_files/EU&MS_Written_Submission_BBNJ.pdf>.

58 WWF (n 50) 2.

59 De Lucia (n 46).

representative and well-connected high seas MPAs.[60] The interlinkage between this concept and MPAs is explored in Section 3.3 of this chapter.

3.1.2.3 The precautionary principle

As anthropogenic impacts in ABNJ have 'substantially outstripped the predictive abilities of scientists,'[61] the precautionary principle has obvious applicability to an ILBI. The precautionary principle exhorts decision-makers 'not to postpone measures to prevent harm where threats of serious or irreversible environmental damage exist simply on the basis of scientific uncertainty.'[62] It thereby signifies 'a departure from the traditional tort-oriented approach which precludes the presumption of harm as a result of an activity of another until a party can show damage and causation.'[63] The precautionary principle inverts the burden of proof by shifting it to the party who wishes to engage in the environmentally risky activity.[64]

There is some disagreement on the meaning and effect of the precautionary concept.[65] It is often bogged down in a terminological debate over its status as a 'principle' or an 'approach.'[66] The International Tribunal on the Law of the Sea (ITLOS) and the International Court of Justice tend to refer to 'the precautionary approach,'[67] while commentators have been more willing to use 'the precautionary principle.' There does not appear to be a significant difference between the legal consequences of either.[68] Peel argues that the interpretation of the concept 'depends on the risk attitude of the interpreter.'[69]

During multilateral negotiations, differences in the appreciation of the 'seriousness' of environmental risks become heightened and oftentimes politically

60 Currie and Davis (n 31) 12.

61 Craig R. Smith et al, 'The Near Future of the Deep-Sea Floor Ecosystems' in Nicholas V.C. Polunin (ed), *Aquatic Ecosystems: Trends and Global Prospects* (Cambridge University Press, 2008) 334, 349.

62 Jacqueline Peel, 'Climate Change Law: The Emergence of a New Legal Discipline' (2008) 32 *Melbourne University Law Review* 922, 962.

63 Simon Marr, *The Precautionary Principle in the Law of the Sea: Modern Decision Making in International Law* (Martinus Nijhoff, 2003) 16.

64 Fernando Gonzalez-Laxe, 'The Precautionary Principle in Fisheries Management' (2005) 29 *Marine Policy* 495, 496.

65 James Crawford, *Brownlie's Principles of Public International Law 8th Edition* (Oxford University Press, 8th ed, 2012) 358.

66 Jacqueline Peel, 'Precaution: A Matter of Principle, Approach or Process?' (2004) 5(2) *Melbourne Journal of International Law* 483, 483 ('Precaution'). ,

67 See, e.g. *Responsibilities and Obligations of States with Respect to Activities in the Area* (n 22); *Southern Bluefin Tuna* (New Zealand v Japan; Australia v Japan) (Provisional Measures) (1999) 117 ILR 148, (1999) 38 ILM 1624, separate opinion of Judge Laing [12]–[21]; *Mox Plant Case* (Ireland v United Kingdom) (provisional measures) (2002) 41 ILM 405, separate opinion of Judge Ad Hoc Székely [24]. See, also, Stephens (n 1) 226.

68 Oude Elferink (n 7) 225. See, also, Katherine Houghton, 'Identifying New Pathways for Ocean Governance: The Role of Legal Principles in Areas beyond National Jurisdiction' (2014) 49 *Marine Policy* 118, 120.

69 Peel, 'Precaution' (n 66) 484.

charged.[70] The BBNJ process is no exception, with delegations divided on the issue. The G77/China bloc, the EU and the African Group prefer the 'principle,' while Japan, Australia, South Korea and the US favour the 'approach.'[71] Maritime (flag) States are likely to opt for the 'approach' as it is perceived to be non-binding in nature, allows for more flexibility and takes into account socio-economic considerations, including the cost-effectiveness of measures.[72]

While the precautionary principle has gradually seeped into the 'lexicon of the law of the sea,'[73] gaps exist in its implementation. Fisher et al argue that the principle has often been 'treated in a "plug & play" manner in that its implementation is characterised as simply requiring the inclusion of the principle in policy or a legislative scheme for it to be effective.'[74] Non-mandatory language is also frequently used to refer to the concept.[75] For example, Article 14(a) of CBD obliges contracting parties to:

> introduce appropriate procedures requiring environmental impact assessment of its *proposed projects that are likely to have significant adverse effects* on biological diversity *with a view to avoiding or minimizing such effects.*[76]

The precautionary principle is 'materialised' through the obligation to undertake EIA; however, this obligation is watered down by the phrase 'as far as possible

70 Ibid.

71 Tallash Kantai et al, 'Summary of the Third Session of the Intergovernmental Conference on the Conservation and Sustainable Use of Marine Biodiversity of Areas beyond National Jurisdiction: 19–30 August 2019' *Earth Negotiations Bulletin* (Online Bulletin, 2 September 2019) 9 <https://enb.iisd.org/events/3rd-session-intergovernmental-conference-igc-conservation-and-sustainable-use-marine/summary>.

72 Aline L. Jaeckel, *The International Seabed Authority and the Precautionary Principle* (Brill Nijhoff, 2017) 21; David L. VanderZwaag, 'The ICJ, ITLOS and the Precautionary Approach: Paltry Progressions, Jurisprudential Jousting' (2013) 35(2) *University of Hawaii Law Review* 617, 618; UN, 'Speakers Consider Criteria for Area-Based Management Tools, as Negotiations on Draft Treaty to Protect Marine Biodiversity Enter Third Day' (Meetings Coverage, SEA/2111, 21 August 2019).

73 Rosemary Rayfuse, 'Precaution and the Protection of Marine Biodiversity in Areas beyond National Jurisdiction' (2012) 27 *The International Journal of Marine and Coastal Law* 773, 774. There is no explicit reference to the precautionary concept in UNCLOS. It has been addressed in UNFSA and in the development of the Mining Code by the ISA. Opinions remain divided on whether it has crystallised into a binding norm of customary international law. Its prevalence in environmental treaties, declarations and resolutions suggests it may have attained this status; however, there has been no authoritative decision on this issue—see, generally, VanderZwaag (n 72) 617.

74 Elizabeth Fisher, Judith Jones and Rene von Schomberg, 'Implementing the Precautionary Principle: Perspectives and Prospects' in Elizabeth Fisher, Judith Jones and Rene von Schomberg (eds), *Implementing the Precautionary Principle: Perspectives and Prospects* (Edward Elgar Publishing, 2006) 1.

75 Rosie Cooney, 'A Long and Winding Road? Precaution from Principle to Practice in Biodiversity Conservation' in Elizabeth Fisher, Judith Jones and Rene von Schomberg (eds), *Implementing the Precautionary Principle: Perspectives and Prospects* (Edward Elgar Publishing, 2006) 223, 223.

76 CBD, art 14(a) (emphasis added).

and as appropriate.' This only pays lip service to the requirements of precaution. As Cooney contends:

> Invocation of the precautionary principle in policy or law will have little substantive or consistent impact on practice if not accompanied by 'materialisation' of the principle into more detailed regulatory or management frameworks and measures that address the threats.[77]

A key challenge for BBNJ negotiators is crafting a governance regime 'genuinely capable of achieving the objectives of precautionary management.'[78] In other words, turning 'the rhetoric of precaution into a reality'[79] for BBNJ. Section 3.3 of this chapter demonstrates how the precautionary principle could be effectively implemented and operationalised through EIA under an ILBI.

3.1.2.4 The integration approach

The integration approach is another key governance tool for the protection and sustainable use of BBNJ.[80] While UNCLOS does not explicitly prescribe the integration approach,[81] it has been adopted by national, regional and global institutions and is a regular feature in UNGA resolutions, UN Secretary-General Reports and the work of UNICPOLOS.[82] Yet, a definition of the concept remains elusive.[83] Rothwell and VanderZwaag suggest that it carries at least nine different connotations.[84] The most common in the oceans context are 'Integrated Ocean Management' (IOM) and 'Integrated Maritime Compliance and Enforcement.'[85] This chapter focuses on IOM.

An IOM approach is holistic in nature and aims to integrate the management of ocean activities 'across sectors, space and time under a unified overarching vision.'[86] Scott identifies four principal components of IOM:

(1) Ecosystem-based management;
(2) The precautionary approach/principle;
(3) EIAs;
(4) Spatial planning, which commonly involves a system of MPAs.[87]

77 Ibid.
78 Rayfuse (n 73) 781.
79 Ibid, 773.
80 Scott (n 2) 465.
81 Oude Elferink (n 7) 230.
82 Scott (n 2) 465.
83 Ibid, 466.
84 Donald Rothwell and David L. VanderZwaag, 'The Sea Change towards Principled Oceans Governance' in *Towards Principled Oceans Governance: Australian and Canadian Approaches and Challenges* (Routledge, 2006) 23–24.
85 Ibid.
86 Scott (n 2) 465.
87 Ibid, 467.

An IOM approach essentially brings together the other governance concepts of this chapter (the ecosystem approach and the precautionary principle) and marries them with elements of the BBNJ package deal (ABMTs including MPAs and EIAs).

While there is little doubt that BBNJ must be governed in an integrated manner, the implementation of the concept in ABNJ is challenging. Currently, a zonal management approach underpins ocean governance,[88] with marine areas 'defined *spatially*, based on distance from the coast.'[89] However, a distance criterion ignores 'the fluid and dynamic nature of the ocean' and the complex relationship that exists between ecosystems and the marine environment that supports them.[90] In contrast, IOM focuses on the unity of marine ecosystems in an ecologically oriented way. This is essential as maritime delimitation lines do not always 'respect the uniqueness of marine ecosystems.'[91] VMEs and their associated biodiversity, for example, do not fit neatly into one maritime zone.[92] Yet, ocean governance in ABNJ remains divided based on the distinction between the high seas water column and the deep-seabed.[93]

ABNJ also remain divided along sectoral lines. Although UNCLOS establishes a general framework for ABNJ, this is implemented at a global and regional level by sectoral regimes. For example, high seas fishing is addressed by the FAO, complemented at a regional level by RFMO/As; the ISA oversees the exploration and exploitation of the Area's mineral resources, and shipping is regulated through international conventions adopted under the IMO. A single-sector approach 'pays scant attention to the coordination between different activities and their cumulative impacts on the marine environment,'[94] with most issues 'dealt with separately within their disciplinary confines and in isolation from one another.'[95] Without coordination among relevant oceans bodies, it is unlikely IOM can be implemented in an effective way.[96] The precautionary principle is also difficult to apply where there is a lack of inter-institutional coordination, as evident from recent reviews of RFMO/A practice.[97] The BBNJ process presents an opportunity to develop a more holistic management approach to ABNJ, by

88 Scott (n 2) 464.
89 Tanaka, '*Law of the Sea*' (n 39) 29–30 (emphasis in original).
90 Ibid.
91 Yoshifumi Tanaka, 'Zonal and Integrated Management Approaches to Ocean Governance: Reflections on a Dual Approach in International Law of the Sea' (2004) 19 *International Journal of Marine and Coastal Law* 483, 486.
92 See Chapter 1, Section 1.2.2.1–1.2.2.3.
93 Scott (n 2) 480–481.
94 Julia A. Ekstrom et al, 'A Tool to Navigate Overlaps in Fragmented Ocean Governance' (2009) 33 *Marine Policy* 532, 532.
95 Georgia Nogueira de Souza Patu, 'Scope and Evolution of Ocean Governance: Improving Cross-Sectoral Management by the Adoption of Principles of International Law' (PhD Thesis, University of Wollongong, 2011) 146.
96 Scott (n 2) 487.
97 Cooney (n 75) 233.

taking into account 'all sectors and uses of the oceans on an equal footing and in an integrated manner,'[98] and recognising the biological interactions between living resources on the deep-seabed and those in the superjacent water column.

3.2 A principle-based approach to the management of ABNJ

3.2.1 Completing the transition to principled ocean governance

The crisis facing BBNJ has called into question the ocean management paradigm under UNCLOS. The Convention embodies a 1970s view of the world and predates legal concepts, such as the precautionary principle and ecosystem approach, now considered essential for good ocean governance.[99] In recent decades, calls have been made for 'principled' ocean governance.[100] To understand what this entails, it is necessary to first examine the ocean governance concept.

The concept of ocean governance emerged in the early 2000s and is considered to represent the most recent phase in the evolution of the international law of the sea.[101] While there is no generally accepted definition of the term,[102] Rothwell and Stephens describe ocean governance as:

> those formal and informal rules, arrangements, institutions and concepts which structure the ways in which sea space is used, how ocean problems are monitored and assessed, what activities are permitted or prohibited, and how sanctions and other responses are applied.[103]

It is understood to reflect 'the need and desire to pursue a holistic, integrated and/or cross-sectoral approach' to oceans management and is therefore a key driver in the on-going BBNJ negotiation process.[104]

The concept of 'principled' ocean governance is founded on the understanding that modern governance tools can (1) provide content to the ocean governance

98 *Report of the Ad Hoc Open-Ended Informal Working Group to Study Issues Relating to the Conservation and Sustainable Use of Marine Biological Diversity beyond Areas of National Jurisdiction*, UN Doc A/61/65 (20 March 2006) [58].

99 Marcus Haward and Joanna Vince, *Oceans Governance in the Twenty-First Century: Managing the Blue Planet* (Edward Elgar, 2008) 26–27.

100 Donald Rothwell and David L. VanderZwaag, *Towards Principled Oceans Governance: Australian and Canadian Approaches and Challenges* (Routledge, 2006) 2.

101 Erik J. Molenaar, 'Ocean Governance beyond Boundaries: Origins, Trends and Current Challenges' in Andres M. Cisneros-Montemayor, William W.L. Cheung and Yoshitaka Ota (eds), *Predicting Future Oceans: Sustainability of Ocean and Human Systems Amidst Global Environmental Change* (Elsevier, 2019) 419, 419.

102 Yoshinobu Takei 'A Sketch of the Concept of Ocean Governance and Its Relationship with the Law of the Sea' in Cedric Ryngaert, Erik J. Molenaar and Sarah M.H. Nouwen (eds), *What's Wrong with International Law?: Liber Amicorum A.H.A. Soons* (Brill Nijhoff, 2015) vol 27, 48, 60.

103 Rothwell and Stephens (n 3) 462.

104 Molenaar (n 101) 419.

concept, (2) improve the management of ocean uses and resources and (3) decrease the negative effects of governance failures,[105] including the fragmentation, overlap and gaps that characterise the existing law framework for ABNJ. It is contended that, to achieve effective or well-functioning ocean governance, an ILBI will require a strong and principled backbone, one that underpins the interpretation of the instrument as a whole and the implementation and operationalisation of its operative parts relating to the four elements of the BBNJ package deal.

The introduction of governance tools into existing ocean-related instruments has already contributed to a partial shift in the governance paradigm towards 'principled' ocean governance. Rothwell and VanderZwaag argue that governance principles have acted 'like engines of change'[106] in spurring this shift. This book maintains that the transition to 'principled' ocean governance is not complete, particularly in ABNJ. While governance concepts have been recognised in ocean-related treaties and policies, and in the practice of some institutions, their implementation in ABNJ has been inconsistent and inadequate, as demonstrated by the four analytical tools used in Section 3.1 of this chapter. BBNJ negotiators will therefore need to find ways and means to give governance tools full practical effect under an ILBI. Only then can it be said that there has been a complete and full transition to 'principled' ocean governance in ABNJ.

To give modern governance principles and approaches full practical effect in ABNJ, governance tools need to play two critical functions under an ILBI.

3.2.2 Function 1—guides for ocean governance in ABNJ

Oude Elferink contends that 'governance principles' provide '*guidance* to States and other actors in adopting and implementing specific rules or approaches.'[107] Terms such as '*guidance*' and '*direction*' have become synonymous with the concept of governance principles, even when the term is split into its separate components. For example, while there are significant differences in opinion as to what the term 'governance' means, most commentators 'agree that it has to do with taking decisions about *direction*.'[108] More specifically, direction on 'how power and responsibilities are exercised, how decisions are taken, and how citizens or other stakeholders have their say.'[109]

Principles, on the other hand, are often defined by way of comparison to rules. Dworkin argues that principles and rules 'differ in the character of the *direction* they give.'[110] According to Dworkin, a rule is 'applicable in an all-or-nothing

105 de Souza Patu (n 95) 35.
106 Rothwell and VanderZwaag (n 84) 23–24.
107 Oude Elferink (n 7) 207.
108 John Graham et al, 'Governance Principles for Protected Areas in the 21st Century: Prepared for the Fifth World Parks Congress Durban, South Africa' (Institut on Governance, 2003) 2.
109 Ibid, 2–3.
110 R. Dworkin, *Taking Rights Seriously* (Duckworth, 1977) 24.

fashion'[111] while a principle 'states a reason that argues in one *direction*, but does not necessitate a particular decision.'[112] Similarly, Paradell-Trius argues that 'principles do not directly prescribe conduct, but act as reasons or considerations inclining decision-makers to choose a particular course of action.'[113] Modern governance principles should therefore be used to 'guide' ocean governance in ABNJ.

Pierre and Peters' four pillars of governance can be used to demonstrate the potential guiding role of modern governance tools in an ILBI.[114] According to Pierre and Peters 'governance' consists of the following elements:

(1) Articulating a common set of priorities;
(2) Coherence (ensuring consistency and coordination);
(3) Steering;
(4) Accountability (and evaluation).[115]

Drawing inspiration from these four pillars, modern governance principles and approaches could be used to guide the articulation 'of a common set of priorities' for ocean management in ABNJ. For example, a main priority of the ILBI should be to protect BBNJ through the establishment of a system of ecologically representative and well-connected high seas MPAs.[116] Secondly, governance principles under an ILBI should assist in ensuring consistency, coordination and coherence in oceans management. One of the elements of ocean governance still lacking in ABNJ are 'mechanisms to ensure coordination and cooperation within and across sectors, States, regions and institutions.'[117] A comprehensive set of guiding principles could provide such a mechanism under an ILBI. As Houghton suggests, principles can be a:

> highly effective means of encouraging coherent, consistent State practice, amplifying ... treaty obligations, and providing a basis for COPs to maximise their mandates in favour of the environment when guiding the implementation of treaties.[118]

111 Ibid.
112 Ibid, 26.
113 Lluis Paradell-Trius, 'Principles of International Environmental Law: An Overview' (2009) 93 *Review of European Community and International Environmental Law (RECIEL)* 95, 96.
114 J. Pierre and B.G. Peters, *Governing Complex Societies: Trajectories and Scenarios* (Palgrave MacMillan, 2005).
115 Ibid, 3–5.
116 Currie and Davis (n 31) 3, 11.
117 Kristina M. Gjerde et al, 'Regulatory and Governance Gaps in the International Regime for the Conservation and Sustainable Use of Marine Biodiversity in Areas beyond National Jurisdiction' (Environmental Policy and Law Papers Online-Marine Series No 1, IUCN, 2008) 4.
118 Houghton (n 68) 120.

Thirdly, a set of modern governance concepts could 'steer' how marine spaces in ABNJ are used, what tools and approaches are deployed and the means by which they are implemented.[119] Lastly, governance principles could assist in holding States accountable for their actions in ABNJ and provide a means of evaluation. Within the existing law framework there is a lack of mechanisms to ensure transparency and accountability.[120] Governance tools under an ILBI should therefore include principles directed at open decision-making processes, public availability of information and stakeholder participation.

3.2.3 Function 2—meat for the bones of the BBNJ package deal

A second function for modern governance principles and approaches is to put meat on the bones of the BBNJ package deal. In its current state, the package deal is little more than a skeletal framework; it simply sets 'out a list of highly complex mechanisms and tools of a procedural nature which still require legal structuring in order to generate substantive obligations.'[121] Governance tools could provide greater substance for the elements of the BBNJ package deal. To achieve this, governance principles should be anchored in the ILBI's preamble to guide in its overall interpretation and also integrated into its operative parts to underpin the mechanisms and tools of the package deal.

3.3 The implementation and operationalisation of governance principles and approaches through the BBNJ package deal

3.3.1 Turning rhetoric into action

Using the core concepts identified in Section 3.1 of this chapter, the following sections examine how governance tools could be implemented and operationalised under an ILBI. The following analysis focuses on the interlinkage between (1) the ecosystem approach and MPAs, (2) the precautionary principle and EIAs and (3) the integration approach and CBTT.

3.3.2 Implementing and operationalising the ecosystem approach through MPAs

An MPA is a clearly defined geographical space, designated, regulated and managed to achieve specific conservation objectives.[122] As MPAs aim to conserve

119 Haward and Vince (n 99) 21–22.

120 IUCN, 'Co-Chair's Report of Workshop on High Seas Governance for the 21st Century' (Workshop Report, IUCN, 17–19 October 2007) 23.

121 Houghton (n 68) 121.

122 Tullio Scovazzi and Ilaria Tani, 'Problems Posed by Marine Protected Areas Having a Transboundary Character' in P. Mackelworth (ed), *Marine Transboundary Conservation and Protected Areas* (Routledge, 2016) 17.

ecosystems, their functions and resources,[123] they are an important tool for implementing an ecosystem approach to ocean management. Accordingly, an ILBI can operationalise the ecosystem approach by establishing a system of ecologically representative and well-connected high seas MPAs.[124]

The establishment of MPAs requires a number of steps and the ecosystem approach should underscore each one, from the identification and designation of priority areas to the management and enforcement of protective measures.[125] Priority protection areas could be selected based on their ecological or biological significance or they could be marine sites at critical risk from a particular sector.[126] Laffoley suggests using five ecological factors to guide in the identification and design of MPA networks:

(i). Include the full range of biodiversity present in the biogeographic region;
(ii). Ensure that ecologically significant areas are incorporated;
(iii). Maintain long-term protection;
(iv). Ensure ecological linkages;
(v). Ensure maximum contributions of individual MPAs to the network.[127]

These factors reinforce an ecosystem approach by focusing on ecological interaction and aiming to conserve ecosystem functioning within ecologically meaningful boundaries.[128] A Subsidiary Body for Scientific and Technical Advice could be tasked with formulating a similar list of ecological factors for inclusion in an ILBI to assist in the identification of priority protection areas.

Once MPA sites are identified, appropriate management tools are required. While the ecosystem approach is the strategic concept, it is ecosystem-based management (EBM) that should be employed as the 'tactical and operational means to implement' it.[129] As EBM is multi-sectoral and aims to bring together the

123 Tundi Agardy et al, 'Dangerous Targets? Unresolved Issues and Ideological Clashes around Marine Protected Areas' (2003) 13 *Aquatic Conservation: Marine and Freshwater Ecosystems* 353, 355.

124 Currie and Davis (n 31) 11.

125 WWF, 'Giving Effect to Holistic Integrated Ocean Management through Regional Delivery of Global Standards, Obligations and Commitments: WWF Second Iteration of Rolling Submission to PrepCom Chair and to DOALOS for PrepCom 3,' 14 March 2017 <http://www.un org/depts/los/biodiversity/prepcom_files/rolling_comp/WWF_BBNJ_Prep_Com3_2017.pdf>.

126 Jeff A. Ardron et al, 'The Sustainable Use and Conservation of Biodiversity in ABNJ: What Can Be Achieved Using Existing International Agreements?' (2014) 49 *Marine Policy* 98, 103.

127 Rafael Sardá et al, 'Ecosystem-Based Management for Marine Protected Areas: A Systematic Approach' in Paul D. Goriup (ed), *Management of Marine Protected Areas* (Wiley Blackwell, 2017) 145, 147.

128 Tanaka, '*Law of the Sea*' (n 39) 250.

129 Sardá et al (n 127) 159.

human, biological and physical components of an ecological system,[130] it could be applied as the framework for managing a network of high seas MPAs to fully incorporate them within a clear ecosystem approach strategy.[131]

However, EBM is notoriously difficult to implement in practice and lacks a universal application framework.[132] Thus, a key challenge for BBNJ negotiators will be devising operational rules and guidance to ensure its effective implementation in ABNJ. BBNJ negotiators could draw upon the experience of the Commission for the Conservation of Antarctic Marine Living Resources (CCAMLR). The CCAMLR is the decision-making body of the CAMLR Convention which governs the use of marine life in the Southern Ocean surrounding Antarctica. These waters are a mix of high seas and coastal State maritime zones, some of which are contested by the original signatories of the 1959 Antarctic Treaty.[133] Since the early 1980s, the CCAMLR has practiced an ecosystem approach to fishery management and continues to be a leader in its implementation.[134] The CCAMLR thereby offers a unique insight into how the ecosystem approach can be applied in practice in ABNJ and could offer 'real world' solutions for overcoming implementation challenges under an ILBI.

Although the CAMLR Convention predates modern definitions of the ecosystem approach, it reflects an 'ecosystemic view of the ocean.'[135] For example, its geographical scope is determined by the natural habitat of Antarctic marine living resources.[136] Instead of abiding by 'the biologically arbitrary limit of the 1959 Antarctic Treaty,'[137] the CAMLR Convention applies to marine living resources south of 60 degrees south latitude as well as those northward of the

130 Ibid, 151.

131 Ibid.

132 See, generally, Wesley S. Patrick and Jason S. Link, 'Myths That Continue to Impede Progress in Ecosystem-Based Fisheries Management' (2015) 40(4) *Fisheries* 155; Long, Charles and Stephenson (n 36) 53–54.

133 The Antarctic Treaty, opened for signature 1 December 1959, 402 UNTS 71 (entered into force 23 June 1961). On jurisdictional issues concerning the CCAMLR area and its interaction with the law of the sea, see generally Tim Stephens, 'An Icy Reception or a Warm Embrace? The Antarctic Treaty System and the International Law of the Sea' in Klaus Dodds, Alan D. Hemmings and Peder Roberts (eds) *Handbook on the Politics of Antarctica* (Edward Elgar Publishing Limited, 2017) 439–452.

134 Denzil G.M. Miller, Eugene N. Sabourenkov and David C. Ramm, 'Managing Antarctic Marine Living Resources' (2004) 19(3) *The International Journal of Marine and Coastal Law* 317, 363.

135 Adriana Fabra and Virginia Gascón, 'The Convention on the Conservation of Antarctic Marine Living Resources (CCAMLR) and the Ecosystem Approach' (2008) 23 *International Journal of Marine and Coastal Law* 567, 574.

136 Catherine Redgwell, 'Protection of Ecosystems under International Law: Lessons from Antarctica' in Alan Boyle and David Freestone (eds) *International Law and Sustainable Development: Past Achievements and Future Challenges* (Oxford University Press, 1999) 205, 211.

137 Ibid.

Antarctic Treaty Area up to the Antarctic Convergence[138] which forms part of the natural boundary of the Antarctic marine ecosystem.[139]

The CAMLR Convention is also considered a pioneer in EBM as it departed from the traditional single-species approach and adopted a broader multispecies ecosystem management strategy.[140] EBM principles are embedded within Article II of the CAMLR Convention.[141] These principles 'map directly onto the concepts of ecosystem productivity, health and resilience'[142] by requiring activities to be conducted in a way that prioritises the maintenance of ecological relationships and prevents irreversible changes to the Antarctic marine environment. The ecosystem approach is implicitly formulated in Article II(3)(b), which imposes an obligation to maintain the ecological relationships between harvested, dependent and related populations of Antarctic marine living resources.[143] Acknowledging the interconnectedness of species at a systems level lies at the heart of an EBM approach.[144] It is contended that, just like the CAMLR Convention, an explicit incorporation of EBM principles into the objectives of an ILBI could be effective in implementing an ecosystem approach in ABNJ and could guide the operationalisation of conservation measures including MPAs.

An ecosystem monitoring programme (EMP), like the one adopted by the CCAMLR, could also prove critical to the implementation of an ecosystem approach under an ILBI.[145] As monitoring all facets of a marine ecosystem is highly impractical, the EMP collects data from a network of designated sites afforded special protection.[146] This data can be used in decision-making processes,

138 The Antarctic Convergence is a boundary between colder, less saline waters closest to Antarctica, and warmer, more saline waters found north of this front, see Marcus Haward, 'Biodiversity in Areas beyond National Jurisdiction (BBNJ): The Commission for the Conservation of Antarctic Marine Living Resources (CCAMLR) and the United Nations BBNJ Agreement' (2021) 11(2) *The Polar Journal* 303-316.

139 CAMLR Convention, art 1(1); Philipp P. Nickels, 'Revisiting Bioprospecting in the Southern Ocean in the Context of the BBNJ Negotiations' (2020) 51(3) *Ocean Development & International Law* 193, 195.

140 Haward (n 138) 1; Redgwell (n 136) 206.

141 Andrew Constable, 'Lessons from CCAMLR on the Implementation of the Ecosystem Approach to Managing Fisheries' (2011) 12(1) *Fish and Fisheries* 138, 138.

142 G.M. Watters et al, 'Decision-Making for Ecosystem-Based Management: Evaluating Options for a Krill Fishery with an Ecosystem Dynamics Model' (2013) 23(4) *Ecological Applications* 710, 710.

143 Fabra and Gascón (n 135) 574–575.

144 Toni Wi, 'The Ecosystem Approach to Fisheries Management in CCAMLR' (Master's thesis, University of Canterbury, 2007) 43.

145 'Ecosystem Monitoring Program (CEMP)' *CCAMLR* (Web Page, 23 October 2013) <https://www.ccamlr.org/en/science/ccamlr-ecosystem-monitoring-program-cemp>; Vito De Lucia, 'The Ecosystem Approach and the Negotiations towards a New Agreement on Marine Biodiversity in Areas beyond National Jurisdiction' (2019) 2 *Nordic Journal of Environmental Law* 7, 24.

146 Monitoring sites have been afforded special protection by CCAMLR conservation measures, see e.g. CCAMLR, 'Procedure for According Protection to CEMP Sites' Conservation Measure 91–01 (2004).

including the designation of spatial management tools. A monitoring programme could fill in knowledge gaps concerning deep-sea ecosystems and assist in identifying priority protection sites in ABNJ.

The institutional framework of the CAMLR Convention has also played a key role in bringing the ecosystem approach into practice. For example, the Scientific Committee is tasked with providing the best available scientific information to the CCAMLR.[147] In turn, the CCAMLR is obligated to take into account the recommendations and advice of the Scientific Committee in decision-making.[148] This committee also sets up working groups to provide advice on the implementation of the ecosystem approach, including contributions by scientists and research institutions.[149] A Scientific and Technical Body under an ILBI could be accorded a similar function. As cooperation with other organisations is best practice in EBM, the ILBI's Scientific and Technical Body could coordinate with a diverse range of multilateral intergovernmental organisations (IGOs), non-governmental organisations (NGOs) and industry associations to align respective efforts in pursuing EBM in ABNJ.[150]

While the CCAMLR has pioneered the development of novel and innovative ways to implement the ecosystem approach, it is not without its flaws.[151] Under the CCAMLR, decision-making is by consensus. However, the need to reconcile the interests of all Member States can slow down progress in the implementation of EBM.[152] For example, persistent clashes between fishing interests and conservation objectives has hindered progress in the designation of high seas MPAs in the Southern Ocean, even though spatial management tools form an essential part of an EBM approach. Consensus decision-making may also result in the adoption of 'decisions that reflect the lowest common denominator,'[153] something BBNJ negotiators should consider when crafting the decision-making process of an ILBI. More work is also required to develop a fully integrated approach to EBM in the Southern Ocean. Katsanevakis et al propose the integration of MPA networks within a broader ecosystem-based spatial management framework.[154] MPA networks are more resilient to pressures than individual MPAs, as they spatially spread potential risks, build redundancies (especially among key species) and allow species to shift in response to large-scale changes, including climate change effects.[155] Thus, while BBNJ negotiators should draw inspiration from the work of the CCAMLR, they should also learn from its mistakes.

147 'Scientific Committee' *CCAMLR* (Web Page, 13 March 2020) <https://www.ccamlr.org/en/science/scientific-committee>.
148 Ibid.
149 Fabra and Gascón (n 135) 582.
150 Wi (n 144) 121.
151 Miller, Sabourenkov and Ramm (n 134) 323.
152 Fabra and Gascón (n 135) 582.
153 Ibid.
154 Stelios Katsanevakis et al, 'Ecosystem-Based Marine Spatial Management: Review of Concepts, Policies, Tools and Critical Issues' (2011) 54 *Ocean & Coastal Management* 807, 817.
155 Ibid.

3.3.3 Implementing and operationalising the precautionary principle through EIA

We now turn to the interlinkage between EIA and the precautionary principle. EIA is used to identify and evaluate activities that may have significant impacts on the environment. The assessment process helps to decide whether activities should proceed and under what circumstances. As EIAs are clearly precautionary in nature, they are a key tool for the implementation of the precautionary principle.[156] Pursuant to Article 206 of UNCLOS, States are obliged to assess the potential effects of activities under their jurisdiction or control that may cause substantial pollution of, or significant and harmful changes to the marine environment. To date, this obligation has been rarely invoked and poorly implemented.[157] Currently there is no overarching international instrument that develops the obligation in Article 206, nor is there any requirement to carry out EIA for a wide range of activities in ABNJ.[158] The development of an ILBI therefore offers the opportunity to build upon the existing UNCLOS obligation by defining general principles for EIA and setting minimum standards to be fulfilled.[159] The precautionary principle should guide and underpin the various stages of EIA under an ILBI. While it is beyond the scope of this chapter to examine each stage of the process, the following focuses on screening and decision-making.

Screening is used to determine whether an activity should be subject to an EIA. An ILBI will need to set out what threshold criteria it will use to trigger an assessment. Taking into account the embryonic state of scientific knowledge that exists concerning BBNJ, Druel suggests an 'explicit operationalisation of the precautionary principle.'[160] On this basis, an ILBI could stipulate:

> that all human activities likely to significantly affect marine biodiversity would be subject to prior assessment and the only activities allowed to proceed would be the ones which could be managed to prevent significant adverse impacts, individually or cumulatively, to ensure that there is no net biodiversity loss in general and a net positive impact in critical habitats.[161]

156 Elisabeth Druel, 'Environmental Impact Assessments in Areas beyond National Jurisdiction: Identification of Gaps and Possible Ways Forward' (Study No. 01/13, IDDRI, January 2013) 10.

157 Elisabeth Druel et al, 'A Long and Winding Road: International Discussions on the Governance of Marine Biodiversity in Areas beyond National Jurisdiction' (Study No. 07/13, IDDRI, September 2013) 18.

158 Ibid.

159 Ibid.

160 Elisabeth Druel et al, 'Sustaining Marine Life beyond Boundaries: Options for an Implementing Agreement for Marine Biodiversity beyond National Jurisdiction under the United Nations Convention on the Law of the Sea' (2014) 49 *Marine Policy* 90, 93.

161 Ibid.

Alternatively, precautionary reference points could be developed under an ILBI and used to trigger EIA and other management tools.[162] Annex II of UNFSA, for example, provides for two types of reference points: (1) conservation reference points to constrain harvesting within safe biological limits, and (2) target reference points to meet management objectives. A Scientific and Technical body could be tasked with designing reference points to suit BBNJ.

Precautionary measures could also be used in the decision-making process in determining whether to approve an activity. Where there is a lack of scientific certainty, an activity should not be allowed to take place until precautionary management measures are implemented. These measures could include an 'obligation to apply the best available technology or best environmental practice,' and an 'obligation to apply environmental quality standards,' such as precautionary buffer limits set at a level below that assumed to be potentially hazardous for BBNJ.[163] Moreover, application of the precautionary principle could mean that a certain activity is entirely prohibited under an ILBI unless the party wishing to carry out the activity can produce evidence to prove that it will not be detrimental to the marine environment of ABNJ.[164]

3.3.4 Implementing and operationalising the integration approach through CBTT

Next is the integration approach. This tool could be implemented and operationalised through an ILBI's provisions concerning CBTT. Currently, few States have the scientific and technical resources required to undertake BBNJ research.[165] Thus, underlying the development of an ILBI is a clear and urgent need to assist developing States to gain the necessary understanding of BBNJ-related issues.[166]

To achieve this, BBNJ negotiators will need to strengthen the current international framework for CBTT. Under Part XIV of UNCLOS, States are required to promote the development of the scientific and technological capacity of developing States with respect to the conservation of marine resources, the protection and preservation of the marine environment, marine scientific research (MSR) and other activities.[167] However, Part XIV has long been recognised as one of

162 Lawrence Juda, 'The 1995 United Nations Agreement on Straddling Fish Stocks and Highly Migratory Fish Stocks: A Critique' (1997) 28 *Ocean Development & International Law* 147, 152–153.

163 Marr (n 63) 15.

164 Ibid.

165 Harriet Harden-Davies, 'Capacity Building and Technology Transfer for Marine Biodiversity in Areas beyond National Jurisdiction' (2017) 111 *American Society of International Law Proceedings of the Annual Meeting* 243, 243.

166 Vladimir Golitsyn, 'Capacity Building: A View from the United Nations' in Myron Nordquist et al (eds), *Law, Science and Ocean Management* (Brill Nijhoff, 2007) 381, 399.

167 UNCLOS, art 266(2).

the most under-implemented parts of UNCLOS.[168] To assist in the effective implementation of existing CBTT provisions, an ILBI could apply an integrated approach to:

(a) The sharing of data, information, knowledge and research;
(b) The development and access to infrastructure and equipment (hardware and software);
(c) The strengthening of human resources and technical expertise through exchange, technical support, education and training;[169]
(d) Cooperation and collaboration in MSR activities including through international, regional and national scientific and technical institutions.

Mechanisms to support the application of an integrated approach to CBTT are lacking under the current law framework. For example, no coherent mechanism exists to assist States to communicate technological need or to request CB.[170] A clearing-house mechanism could assist in this regard. In fostering an integrated approach to CBTT, a clearing-house mechanism could carry out the following functions under an ILBI:

(1) Serve as a central information repository (one-stop hub) where scientific and technical information is stored, processed and disseminated;[171]
(2) Serve as a platform to connect users in a collaborative setting by providing a human and technological network to facilitate scientific and technical cooperation within and between States Parties, non-Parties, IGOs, NGOs, industry associations, research institutions, experts and practitioners in relevant fields and civil society.

An online interactive platform could connect users and stakeholders across different regional and thematic communities to new initiatives, best practices and tools.[172] This could be used as a mechanism for exchanging information on BBNJ and linked to other internationally recognised data portals, such as the Ocean Biogeographic Information System.[173]

168 Robert Blasiak et al, 'Negotiating the Use of Biodiversity in Marine Areas beyond National Jurisdiction' (2016) 3 *Frontiers in Marine Science* 1–10, 6.
169 See '*Revised Draft Negotiating Text*' (n 18) art 46(1).
170 Harriet Harden-Davies and Paul Snelgrove, 'Science Collaboration for Capacity Building: Advancing Technology Transfer through a Treaty for Biodiversity beyond National Jurisdiction' (2020) 7 *Frontiers in Marine Science* 14, 1.
171 See, e.g. The Global Sustainable Consumption and Production (SCP) clearing-house launched by UNEP in 2013.
172 See, e.g. 'The Fiji Clearing House for Risk Transfer' *United Nations Climate Change* (Web Page, 2020) <https://unfccc.int/process-and-meetings/bodies/constituted-bodies/executive-committee-of-the-warsaw-international-mechanism-for-loss-and-damage-wim-excom/fiji-clearing-house-for-risk-transfer>.
173 Harden-Davies and Snelgrove (n 170) 7.

Article 51 of the Revised Draft Negotiating Text provides for the establishment of a clearing-house mechanism. While it remains unclear exactly what form this will take under an ILBI, one of its overriding purposes should be to implement an integrated approach to the protection of BBNJ by promoting cooperation in CBTT and MSR.

3.4 Conclusion

The international law governing the protection of the marine environment 'is not merely a mosaic of specific rules.'[174] Rather, it is a major area of legal specialisation with its own distinct principles, norms and concepts, which together with rules form a system for governing the use of maritime space.[175] This chapter has focused on the important role modern governance principles and approaches play within this system by considering their potential contribution to the conservation and sustainable use of BBNJ.

This chapter has used four core concepts as analytical tools to examine the potential role of governance principles and approaches in an ILBI. These concepts were specifically selected because of their particular relevance and applicability to BBNJ. The analysis undertaken of these concepts has exposed gaps and limitations in their implementation under the current legal framework, particularly in ABNJ. The development of an ILBI presents an opportunity to close these implementation gaps by completing the transition to 'principled' ocean governance.

To achieve 'principled' ocean governance in ABNJ, modern governance tools should perform two critical functions under an ILBI. First, they should be used as guides, not only for the interpretation of the instrument as a whole and its operative provisions, but to direct State parties in the protection of BBNJ and in the responsible management of activities in ABNJ. Second, governance tools should be used to put meat on the bones of the skeletal framework of the BBNJ package deal. In this role, governance principles can set out 'critical ways' to achieve the ILBI's objectives while providing substance for the instrument's rules.[176]

While the protection of BBNJ will not be secured through principles alone, the interlinkage between modern governance tools and elements of the BBNJ package deal will enhance the effectiveness of an ILBI and provide the instrument with a principled backbone, one it requires to be effective in addressing one of the greatest challenges of the 21st century—managing the deep-ocean environment and its ecosystems and resources.[177]

174 Tanaka, 'Principles' (n 25) 31.

175 Ibid; Sarah Dromgoole, *Underwater Cultural Heritage and International Law* (Cambridge University Press, 2013) 9.

176 Currie and Davis (n 31) 1.

177 Lisa A. Levin, 'Climate Change Impacts on Marine Biodiversity and Resilience' (Conference Paper, Third International Symposium on Effects of Climate Change on the World's Oceans, 25 March 2015).

References

Agardy, Tundi, Peter Bridgewater, Michael P. Crosby, Jon Day, Paul K. Dayton, Richard Kenchington, Dan Laffoley, Patrick McConney, Peter A. Murray, John E. Parks and Lelei Peau, 'Dangerous Targets? Unresolved Issues and Ideological Clashes Around Marine Protected Areas' (2003) 13 *Aquatic Conservation: Marine and Freshwater Ecosystems* 353–367. DOI: 10.1002/aqc.583.

Ardron, Jeff A, Rosemary Rayfuse, Kristina Gjerde and Robin Warner, 'The Sustainable Use and Conservation of Biodiversity in ABNJ: What Can Be Achieved Using Existing International Agreements?' (2014) 49 *Marine Policy* 98–108. DOI: 10.1016/j.marpol.2014.02.011.

Barnes, Richard A, 'Consolidating Governance Principles for Areas Beyond National Jurisdiction' (2012) 27 *The International Journal of Marine and Coastal Law* 261–290. DOI: https://doi.org/10.1163/157180812X633627.

Birnie, P, A. Boyle and C. Redgwell, *International Law and the Environment* (Oxford University Press, 3rd ed, 2009).

Blasiak, Robert, Jeremy Pittman, Nobuyuki Yagi and Hiroaki Sugino, 'Negotiating the Use of Biodiversity in Marine Areas Beyond National Jurisdiction' (2016) 3 *Frontiers in Marine Science* 1–10. DOI: 10.3389/fmars.2016.00224.

CBD, *Subsidiary Body on Scientific, Technical and Technological Advice, Ecosystem Approach: Further Conceptual Elaboration, SBSTTA 5 Recommendation V/10, Annex 'B. Principles of the Ecosystem Approach'* <https://www.cbd.int/recommendation/sbstta/?id=7027> accessed 31 March 2022.

CCAMLR, 'Procedure for According Protection to CEMP Sites' (2004) Conservation Measure 91-01 <https://cm.ccamlr.org/en/measure-91-01-2004>.

Chair's Overview of the Second Session of the Preparatory Committee, <https://www.un.org/Depts/los/biodiversity/prepcom_files/Prep_Com_II_Chair_overview_to_MS.pdf> accessed 31 March 2022.

Chair's Overview of the Third Session of the Preparatory Committee, <https://www.un.org/Depts/los/biodiversity/prepcom_files/Chair_Overview.pdf> accessed 31 March 2022.

Churchill, Robin, 'The LOSC Regime for Protection of the Marine Environment: Fit for the Twenty-First Century?' in Rosemary Rayfuse (ed), *Research Handbook on International Marine Environmental Law* (Edward Elgar Publishing, 2015) 3. DOI: https://doi.org/10.4337/9781781004777.

Constable, Andrew, 'Lessons from CCAMLR on the Implementation of the Ecosystem Approach to Managing Fisheries' (2011) 12(1) *Fish and Fisheries* 138–151. DOI: 10.1111/j.1467-2979.2011.00410.x.

Convention for the Protection of the Marine Environment of the North-East Atlantic, opened for signature 22 September 1992 (1992) 32 *ILM* 1069 (entered into force 25 March 1998) (OSPAR Convention).

Convention on Biological Diversity, opened for signature 5 June 1992, 1760 *UNTS* 143 (entered into force 29 December 1993) (CBD).

Convention on the Conservation of Antarctic Marine Living Resources, opened for signature 20 May 1980 (1980) 1329 *UNTS* 48 (entered into force 7 April 1982) (CAMLR Convention).

Cooney, Rosie, 'A Long and Winding Road? Precaution from Principle to Practice in Biodiversity Conservation' in Elizabeth Fisher, Judith Jones and Rene von Schomberg (eds), *Implementing the Precautionary Principle: Perspectives and*

Prospects (Edward Elgar Publishing, 2006) 223. DOI: https://doi.org/10.4337/9781847201676.00022.

Crawford, James, *Brownlie's Principles of Public International Law* (Oxford University Press, 8th ed, 2012). DOI: 10.1093/he/9780199699698.001.0001.

Currie, Duncan, 'The Oceans and the Law of the Sea Convention as a Form of Global Governance' (2017) 13(1) *Policy Quarterly* 32–36. DOI: 10.26686/pq.v13i1.4646.

Currie, Duncan and Mischa Davis, 'Governance Principles Relevant to Marine Biodiversity in Areas Beyond National Jurisdiction Submission to the Chair' (25 February 2016) <https://www.un.org/depts/los/biodiversity/prepcom_files/greenpeace.pdf> accessed 31 March 2022.

Czybulka, 'Detlef, 'Part XII Protection and Preservation of the Marine Environment' in Alexander Proelss (ed) *United Nations Convention on the Law of the Sea: A Commentary* (Hart Publishing, 2017) 1277.

De Lucia, Vito, 'Competing Narratives and Complex Genealogies: The Ecosystem Approach in International Environmental Law' (2015) 27 *Journal of Environmental Law* 91–117. DOI: 10.1093/jel/equ031.

De Lucia, Vito, 'The Ecosystem Approach for Areas Beyond National Jurisdiction: Reflections on the Chair's Non-Paper ahead of PREPCOM III,' *The NCLOS Blog* (Blog, 20 March 2017) <https://site.uit.no/nclos/2017/03/20/the-ecosystem-approach-for-areas-beyond-national-jurisdiction-reflections-on-the-chairs-non-paper-ahead-of-prepcom-iii/> accessed 31 March 2022.

De Lucia, Vito, 'The Ecosystem Approach and the Negotiations Towards a New Agreement on Marine Biodiversity in Areas Beyond National Jurisdiction' (2019) 2 *Nordic Journal of Environmental Law* 7–25. <https://nordiskmiljoratt.se/onewebmedia/NMT2019nr2_deLucia.pdf> accessed 31 March 2022.

Division for Ocean Affairs and the Law of the Sea, Office of Legal Affairs, 'Ecosystem Approaches', *Oceans and Law of the Sea* (Web Page, 21 July 2010) <http://www.un.org/depts/los/ecosystem_approaches/ecosystem_approaches.htm> accessed 31 March 2022.

Dromgoole, Sarah, *Underwater Cultural Heritage and International Law* (Cambridge University Press, 2013). DOI: 10.1017/CBO9781139020503.

Druel, Elisabeth, *Environmental Impact Assessments in Areas Beyond National Jurisdiction* (Study No. 01/13, IDDRI, January 2013).

Druel, Elisabeth and Kristina M. Gjerde, 'Sustaining Marine Life Beyond Boundaries: Options for an Implementing Agreement for Marine Biodiversity Beyond National Jurisdiction under the United Nations Convention on the Law of the Sea' (2014) 49 *Marine Policy* 90–97. DOI: 10.1016/j.marpol.2013.11.023.

Druel, Elisabeth, Julien Rochette, Raphaël Billé and Claudio Chiarolla, *A Long & Winding Road: International Discussions on the Governance of Marine Biodiversity in Areas Beyond National Jurisdiction* (Study No. 7/2013, IDDRI, September 2013).

Dworkin, R, *Taking Rights Seriously* (London: Duckworth, 1977).

Ecosystem Monitoring Program (CEMP), *CCAMLR* (Web Page, 23 October 2013) <https://www.ccamlr.org/en/science/ccamlr-ecosystem-monitoring-program-cemp> accessed 31 March 2022.

Ekstrom, Julia A, Oran R. Young, Steve D. Gaines, Maria Gordon and Bonnie J. Mccay, 'A Tool to Navigate Overlaps in Fragmented Ocean Governance' (2009) 33 *Marine Policy* 532–535. DOI: 10.1016/j.marpol.2008.11.007.

European Union, 'Council Regulation (EC) No. 734/2008 on the Protection of Vulnerable Marine Ecosystems in the High Seas from the Adverse Impacts of Bottom Fishing Gears' (15 July 2008) 201(8) *OJ L* (Recital 2).

European Union, 'Development of an International Legally-Binding Instrument under UNCLOS on the Conservation and Sustainable Use of Marine Biological Diversity of Areas Beyond National Jurisdiction (BBNJ Process), Written Submission of the EU and Its Member States' (25 July 2016) <https://www.un.org/depts/los/biodiversity/prepcom_files/EU&MS_Written_Submission_BBNJ.pdf> accessed 31 March 2022.

Fabra, Adriana and Virginia Gascón, 'The Convention on the Conservation of Antarctic Marine Living Resources (CCAMLR) and the Ecosystem Approach' (2008) 23 *International Journal of Marine and Coastal Law* 567–598. DOI: 10.1163/092735208X331854.

Fisher, Elizabeth, Judith Jones and Rene von Schomberg, 'Implementing the Precautionary Principle: Perspectives and Prospects' in Elizabeth Fisher, Judith Jones and Rene von Schomberg (eds), *Implementing the Precautionary Principle: Perspectives and Prospects* (Edward Elgar Publishing, 2006) 1. DOI: https://doi.org/10.4337/9781847201676.00009.

Freestone, David, 'Editorial: Principles Applicable to Modern Oceans Governance' (2008) 23(3) *International Journal of Marine and Coastal Law* 387–391. DOI: 10.1163/092735208X331827.

Freestone, David, 'Modern Principles of High Seas Governance: The Legal Underpinnings' (2009) 39 *Environmental Policy and Law* 44–49. DOI: https://content.iospress.com/articles/environmental-policy-and-law/epl39-1-03.

Freestone, David, 'International Governance, Responsibility and Management of Areas Beyond National Jurisdiction' (2012) 27 *The International Journal of Marine and Coastal Law* 191–204. DOI: 10.1163/157180812X633609.

Freestone, David, 'Principles Applicable to Modern Ocean Governance' in David Freestone (ed), *Conserving Biodiversity in Areas Beyond National Jurisdiction* (Brill Nijhoff, 2019). DOI: 10.1163/9789004391703_003.

Gjerde, Kristina M, 'Regulatory and Governance Gaps in the International Regime for the Conservation and Sustainable Use of Marine Biodiversity in Areas Beyond National Jurisdiction' (Environmental Policy and Law Papers Online—Marine Series No 1, IUCN, 2008).

Golitsyn, Vladimir, 'Capacity Building: A View from the United Nations' in Myron Nordquist et al (eds), *Law, Science and Ocean Management* (Brill Nijhoff, 2007) 381.

González-Laxe, Fernando, 'The Precautionary Principle in Fisheries Management' (2005) 29 *Marine Policy* 495–505. DOI: 10.1016/j.marpol.2004.09.002.

Graham, John, Bruce Amos and Tim Plumptre, 'Governance Principles for Protected Areas in the 21st Century: Prepared for the Fifth World Parks Congress Durban, South Africa' (Institut on Governance, 2003).

Harden-Davies, Harriet, 'Capacity Building and Technology Transfer for Marine Biodiversity in Areas Beyond National Jurisdiction' (2017) 111 *American Society of International Law* Proceedings of the ASIL Annual Meeting 243–245. DOI: 10.1017/amp.2017.75.

Harden-Davies, Harriet and Paul Snelgrove, 'Science Collaboration for Capacity Building: Advancing Technology Transfer Through a Treaty for Biodiversity Beyond National Jurisdiction' (2020) 7 *Frontiers in Marine Science* 1–14. DOI: 10.3389/fmars.2020.00040.

Haward, Marcus, 'Biodiversity in Areas Beyond National Jurisdiction (BBNJ): The Commission for the Conservation of Antarctic Marine Living Resources (CCAMLR) and the United Nations BBNJ Agreement' (2021) 11(2) *The Polar Journal* 303–316. DOI: 10.1080/2154896X.2021.1984658.

Haward, Marcus and Joanna Vince, *Oceans Governance in the Twenty-First Century: Managing the Blue Planet* (Edward Elgar, 2008).

Houghton, Katherine, 'Identifying New Pathways for Ocean Governance: The Role of Legal Principles in Areas Beyond National Jurisdiction' (2014) 49 *Marine Policy* 118–126. DOI: 10.1016/j.marpol.2014.04.007.

In the Matter of the South China Sea Arbitration (Philippines v. China) (Arbitral Award) (Permanent Court of Arbitration, Case No 2013–19, 12 July 2016).

IUCN, '10 Principles for High Seas Governance' <https://www.iucn.org/sites/dev/files/import/downloads/10_principles_for_high_seas_governance___final.pdf> accessed 31 March 2022.

IUCN, 'Co-Chair's Report of Workshop on High Seas Governance for the 21st Century' (*Workshop Report*, IUCN, 17–19 October 2007) <https://www.iucn.org/sites/dev/files/import/downloads/iucn_workshop_co_chairs_summary_new_iucn_format.pdf> accessed 31 March 2022.

Jaeckel, Aline L., *The International Seabed Authority and the Precautionary Principle* (Brill Nijhoff, 2017).

Juda, Lawrence, 'The 1995 United Nations Agreement on Straddling Fish Stocks and Highly Migratory Fish Stocks: A Critique' (1997) 28 *Ocean Development & International Law* 147–166. DOI: 10.1080/00908329709546100.

Kantai, Tallash, Jennifer Bansard, Tasha Goldberg, Katarina Hovden and Asterios Tsioumanis, 'Summary of the Third Session of the Intergovernmental Conference on the Conservation and Sustainable Use of Marine Biodiversity of Areas Beyond National Jurisdiction: 19–30 August 2019' *Earth Negotiations Bulletin* (Online Bulletin, 2 September 2019) <https://enb.iisd.org/download/pdf/enb25218e.pdf> accessed 31 March 2022.

Katsanevakis, Stelios, Vanessa Stelzenmüller, Andy South, Thomas Kirk Sørensen, Peter J.S. Jones, Sandy Kerr, Fabio Badalamenti, Christos Anagnostou, Patricia Breen, Guillem Chust, Giovanni D'anna, Mike Duijn, Tatiana Filatova, Fabio Fiorentino, Helena Hulsman, Kate Johnson and Aristomenis P. Karageorgis, 'Ecosystem-based Marine Spatial Management: Review of Concepts, Policies, Tools and Critical Issues' (2011) 54 *Ocean & Coastal Management* 807–820. DOI: 10.1016/j.ocecoaman.2011.09.002.

Law of the Sea-Report of the Secretary-General, UN Doc A/44/461 (18 September 1989).

Levin, Lisa A., 'Climate Change Impacts on Marine Biodiversity and Resilience' (Conference Paper, Third International Symposium on Effects of Climate Change on the World's Oceans, 25 March 2015) <http://www.ices.dk/news-and-events/news-archive/news/Pages/Biodiversity-Consequences-of-Climate-Change-in-the-Deep-Ocean-and-Sustainability-in-the-21st-Century.aspx> accessed 31 March 2022.

Long, Rachel D, Anthony Charles and Robert L. Stephenson, 'Key Principles of Marine Ecosystem-based Management' (2015) 57 *Marine Policy* 53–60. DOI: 10.1016/j.marpol.2015.01.013.

Long, Ronán, 'Legal Aspects of Ecosystem-Based Marine Management in Europe' (2012) 26 *Ocean Yearbook Online* 417–484. DOI: 10.1163/22116001-92600083.

Marr, Simon, *The Precautionary Principle in the Law of the Sea: Modern Decision Making in International Law* (Martinus Nijhoff, 2003).

Meeting of the Biodiversity Committee, *Draft OSPAR Recommendations on a Network of Marine Protected Areas*, BDC 03/10/1-E.

Mengerink, Kathryn J, Cindy L. Van Dover, Jeff Ardron, Maria Baker, Elva Escobar-Briones, Kristina Gjerde, J. Anthony Koslow, Eva Ramirez-Llodra, Ana Lara-Lopez, Dale Squires, Tracey Sutton, Andrew K. Sweetman and Lisa A. Levin, 'A Call for Deep-Ocean Stewardship' (2014) 344(6185) *Science* 696–698. DOI: 10.1126/science.1251458.

Miller, Denzil G.M, Eugene N. Sabourenkov and David C. Ramm, 'Managing Antarctic Marine Living Resources' (2004) 19(3) *The International Journal of Marine and Coastal Law* 317–363. DOI: 10.1163/1571808042886075.

Molenaar, Erik J, 'Ocean Governance Beyond Boundaries: Origins, Trends and Current Challenges' in Andres M. Cisneros-Montemayor, William W.L. Cheung and Yoshitaka Ota (eds) *Predicting Future Oceans: Sustainability of Ocean and Human Systems Amidst Global Environmental Change* (Elsevier, 2019) 419. DOI: https://doi.org/10.1016/B978-0-12-817945-1.00040-X.

Morgera, Elisa, 'Summary of the Seventh Meeting of the Working Group on Marine Biodiversity Beyond Areas of National Jurisdiction: 1–4 April 2014' *Earth Negotiations Bulletin* (Online Bulletin, 7 April 2014) <https://enb.iisd.org/oceans/marinebiodiv7/brief/brief_marinebiodiv7e.pdf> accessed 31 March 2022.

MOX Plant (Ireland v United Kingdom) (Provisional Measures) (2002) 41 *ILM* 405.

Nickels, Philipp P., 'Revisiting Bioprospecting in the Southern Ocean in the Context of the BBNJ Negotiations' (2020) 51(3) *Ocean Development & International Law* 193–216. DOI: 10.1080/00908320.2020.1736773.

Norway, 'Preparatory Committee Established by General Assembly Resolution 69/292: Development of an International Legally Binding Instrument under the United Nations Convention on the Law of the Sea on the Conservation and Sustainable Use of Marine Biological Diversity of Areas Beyond National Jurisdiction, Comments by Norway' (December 2016) <https://www.un.org/depts/los/biodiversity/prepcom_files/rolling_comp/Norway.pdf> accessed 31 March 2022.

Oude Elferink, Alex, 'Governance Principles for Areas Beyond National Jurisdiction' (2012) 27(2) *The International Journal of Marine and Coastal Law* 205–259. DOI: 10.1163/157180812X633618.

Oude Elferink, Alex G., 'Reviewing the Implementation of the LOS Convention: The Role of the United Nations General Assembly and the Meeting of State Parties' in Alex G. Oude Elferink and Donald R. Rothwell (eds), *Oceans Management in the 21st Century: Institutional Frameworks and Responses* (Martinus Nijhoff Publishers, 2004) 295.

Paradell-Trius, Lluis, 'Principles of International Environmental Law: An Overview' (2009) 93 *Review of European Community and International Environmental Law* 93–99. DOI: 10.1111/1467-9388.00240.

Patrick, Wesley S. and Jason S. Link, 'Myths That Continue to Impede Progress in Ecosystem-Based Fisheries Management' (2015) 40(4) *Fisheries* 155–160. DOI: 10.1080/03632415.2015.1024308.

Patu, Georgia Nogueira de Souza, '*Scope and Evolution of Ocean Governance: Improving Cross-sectoral Management by the Adoption of Principles of International Law*' (PhD Thesis, University of Wollongong, 2011).

Peel, Jacqueline, 'Precaution: A Matter of Principle, Approach or Process?' (2004) 5(2) *Melbourne Journal of International Law* 483–501.

Peel, Jacqueline, 'Climate Change Law: The Emergence of a New Legal Discipline' (2008) 32 *Melbourne University Law Review* 922–979.

Pierre, J. and B.G. Peters, *Governing Complex Societies: Trajectories and Scenarios* (Palgrave MacMillan, 2005) DOI: https://doi.org/10.1057/9780230512641.

President's Aid to Negotiations, UN Doc A/CONF.232/2019/1 (3 December 2018) <https://documents-dds-ny.un.org/doc/UNDOC/GEN/N18/413/20/PDF/N1841320.pdf?OpenElement> accessed 31 March 2022.

Rayfuse, Rosemary, 'Precaution and the Protection of Marine Biodiversity in Areas Beyond National Jurisdiction' (2012) 27 *The International Journal of Marine and Coastal Law* 773–781. DOI: 10.1163/15718085-12341257.

Rayfuse, Rosemary, 'Article 119 Conservation and Management of the Living Resources of the High Seas' in Alexander Proelss et al. (ed), *United Nations Convention on the Law of the Sea A Commentary* (Hart Publishing, 2017).

Redgwell, Catherine, 'Protection of Ecosystems under International Law: Lessons from Antarctica' in Alan Boyle and David Freestone (eds), *International Law and Sustainable Development: Past Achievements and Future Challenges* (Oxford University Press, 1999) 205. DOI: 10.1093/acprof:oso/9780198298076.001.0001.

Report of the Ad Hoc Open-ended Informal Working Group to Study Issues Relating to the Conservation and Sustainable Use of Marine Biological Diversity Beyond Areas of National Jurisdiction, UN Doc A/61/65 (20 March 2006) <https://documents-dds-ny.un.org/doc/UNDOC/GEN/N06/277/50/PDF/N0627750.pdf?OpenElement> accessed 31 March 2022.

Responsibilities and Obligations of States Sponsoring Persons and Entities with Respect to Activities in the Area (Advisory Opinion) (Seabed Disputes Chamber, Case No. 17, 1 February 2011).

Revised Draft Text of an Agreement Under the United Nations Convention on the Law of the Sea on the Conservation and Sustainable Use of Marine Biological Diversity of Areas Beyond National Jurisdiction, UN Doc A/CONF.232/2020/3 (18 November 2019) <https://documents-dds-ny.un.org/doc/UNDOC/GEN/N19/372/88/PDF/N1937288.pdf?OpenElement> accessed 31 March 2022.

Rothwell, Donald and David L. VanderZwaag, 'The Sea Change towards Principled Oceans Governance' in *Towards Principled Oceans Governance: Australian and Canadian Approaches and Challenges* (Routledge, 2006) 23.

Rothwell, Donald R. and David L. VanderZwaag, *Towards Principled Oceans Governance: Australian and Canadian Approaches and Challenges* (Routledge, 2006).

Rothwell, Donald R. and Tim Stephens, *The International Law of the Sea* (Hart Publishing Ltd, 2nd ed, 2016)

Sardá, Rafael, Susana Requena, Carlos Dominguez-Carrió and Josep Maria Gili, 'Ecosystem-based Management for Marine Protected Areas: A Systematic Approach' in Paul D. Goriup (ed), *Management of Marine Protected Areas: A Network Perspective* (Wiley Blackwell, 2017) 145.

'Scientific Committee' *CCAMLR* (Web Page, 13 March 2020) <https://www.ccamlr.org/en/science/scientific-committee> accessed 31 March 2022.

Scott, Karen, 'Integrated Oceans Management: A New Frontier In Marine Environmental Protection' in Donald Rothwell et al (eds), *The Oxford Handbook of the Law of the Sea* (Oxford University Press, 2015) 463. DOI: 10.1093/law/9780198715481.003.0021.

Scovazzi, Tullio and Ilaria Tani, 'Problems Posed by Marine Protected Areas Having a Transboundary Character' in P. Mackelworth (ed), *Marine Transboundary Conservation and Protected Areas* (Routledge, 2016) 17.

Smith, Craig R, Lisa A. Levin, Anthony Koslow, Paul A. Tyler and Adrian G. Glover, 'The Near Future of the Deep-Sea Floor Ecosystems' in Nicholas V.C. Polunin (ed), *Aquatic Ecosystems: Trends and Global Prospects* (Cambridge University Press, 2008) 334.

Southern Bluefin Tuna (New Zealand v Japan; Australia v Japan) (Provisional Measures) (1999) 117 *ILR* 148, (1999) 38 ILM 1624.

Stephens, Tim, *International Courts and Environmental Protection* (Cambridge University Press, 2009). DOI: https://doi.org/10.1017/CBO9780511576034.

Stephens, Tim, 'An Icy Reception or a Warm Embrace? The Antarctic Treaty System and the International Law of the Sea' in Klaus Dodds, Alan D. Hemmings and Peder Roberts (eds) *Handbook on the Politics of Antarctica* (Edward Elgar Publishing Limited, 2017) 439. DOI: https://doi.org/10.4337/9781784717681.00040

Takei, Yoshinobu, 'A Sketch of the Concept of Ocean Governance and Its Relationship with the Law of the Sea' in Cedric Ryngaert, Erik J. Molenaar and Sarah M.H. Nouwen, *What's Wrong with International Law?: Liber Amicorum A.H.A. Soons* (Brill Nijhoff, 2015) vol 27, 48. DOI: https://doi.org/10.1163/9789004294585_007.

Tanaka, Yoshifumi, 'Zonal and Integrated Management Approaches to Ocean Governance: Reflections on a Dual Approach in International Law of the Sea' (2004) 19 *International Journal of Marine and Coastal Law* 483–514. DOI: 10.1163/1571808053310143.

Tanaka, Yoshifumi, *The International Law of the Sea* (Cambridge University Press, 2nd ed, 2015a).

Tanaka, Yoshifumi, 'Principles of International Marine Environmental Law,' in Rosemary Rayfuse (ed), *Research Handbook on International Marine Environmental Law* (Edward Elgar Publishing, 2015b) 31. DOI: https://doi.org/10.4337/9781781004777.00009.

Textual Proposals Submitted by Delegations for Consideration at the Fourth Session of the Intergovernmental Conference, in Response to the Invitation by the President of the Conference in Her Note of 18 November 2019 (A/CONF/232/2020/3) <https://www.un.org/bbnj/sites/www.un.org.bbnj/files/textual_proposals_compilation_-_15_april_2020.pdf> accessed 31 March 2022.

The Antarctic Treaty, opened for signature 1 December 1959 (1959) 402 *UNTS* 71 (entered into force 23 June 1961).

'The Fiji Clearing House for Risk Transfer' *United Nations Climate Change* (Web Page, 2020) <https://unfccc.int/process-and-meetings/bodies/constituted-bodies/executive-committee-of-the-warsaw-international-mechanism-for-loss-and-damage-wim-excom/fiji-clearing-house-for-risk-transfer> accessed 31 March 2022.

Trouwborst, Arie, 'The Precautionary Principle and the Ecosystem Approach in International Law: Differences, Similarities and Linkages' (2009) 18(1) *Review of European Community & International Environmental Law* 26–37. DOI: 10.1111/j.1467-9388.2009.00622.x.

UNEP-WCMC, *Biodiversity A-Z: Ecosystem Approach* <http://biodiversitya-z.org/content/ecosystem-approach.pdf> accessed 31 March 2022.

United Nations, 'Speakers Consider Criteria for Area-Based Management Tools, as Negotiations on Draft Treaty to Protect Marine Biodiversity Enter Third Day' (Meetings Coverage, SEA/2111, 21 August 2019).

United Nations Convention on the Law of the Sea, opened for signature 10 December 1982 (1982) 1833 *UNTS* 397 (entered into force 16 November 1994) (UNCLOS).

United Nations General Assembly,*Oceans and the Law of the Sea: Report of the Secretary-General,* UN Doc A/58/65 (3 March 2003).

United Nations General Assembly, *Oceans and the Law of the Sea*, GA Res 64/71, UN Doc A/RES/64/71 (4 December 2009 adopted on 12 March 2010).

VanderZwaag, David L, 'The ICJ, ITLOS and the Precautionary Approach: Paltry Progressions, Jurisprudential Jousting' (2013) 35(2) *University of Hawaii Law Review* 617–632.

Vierros, Marjo, Fanny Douvere and Salvatore Arico, *UNU-IAS Report Implementing the Ecosystem Approach in Open Ocean and Deep Sea Environments An Analysis of Stakeholders, Their Interests and Existing Approaches* (UNU-IAS, 2006).

Watters, G.M, S.L. Hill, J.T. Hinke, J. Matthews and K. Reid, 'Decision-making for Ecosystem-based Management: Evaluating Options for a Krill Fishery with an Ecosystem Dynamics Model' (2013) 23(4) *Ecological Applications* 710–725. DOI: 10.1890/12-1371.1.

Wi, Toni, 'The Ecosystem Approach to Fisheries Management in CCAMLR' (Master's thesis, University of Canterbury, 2007).

WWF, 'Proposed Framework and Key Elements of a Third UNCLOS Implementing Agreement WWF Submission to the BBNJ PrepCom Chair and to DOALOS for PrepCom3' (5 December 2016) <https://www.un.org/depts/los/biodiversity/prepcom_files/rolling_comp/World_Wildlife_Fund.pdf> accessed 31 March 2022.

WWF, 'Giving Effect to Holistic Integrated Ocean Management through Regional Delivery of Global Standards, Obligations and Commitments: WWF Second Iteration of Rolling Submission to the BBNJ PrepCom Chair and to DOALOS for PrepCom 3' (14 March 2017) <http://www.un.org/depts/los/biodiversity/prepcom_files/rolling_comp/WWF_BBNJ_Prep_Com3_2017.pdf> accessed 31 March 2022.

4 A blueprint for Blue Gold

The search for planks of compromise in an ILBI

Introduction

When a broad table is to be made, and the edges of planks do not fit,

the artist takes a little from both and makes a good joint.

In like manner, here, both sides must part with some of their demands,

in order that they may join in some accommodating proposition.[1]

In recent decades, marine genetic resources (MGRs) (sometimes referred to as 'Blue Gold') have caught the attention of the research and development (R&D) sector.[2] The marine realm has the 'most phylogenetic and genomic diversity on Earth,'[3] and modern biosciences and analytical technologies have accelerated capacities to utilise MGRs, evidenced by a steady growth in marine patented genes.[4] MGRs found within national waters are accessed subject to UNCLOS, the CBD and other international provisions. By contrast, access to MGRs in ABNJ is open and currently there is no formal benefit-sharing mechanism in place.

The issue of MGRs in ABNJ highlights deep fissures in global debates over distributive justice and sustainable development.[5] A limited number of States

1 Benjamin Franklin, 'Constitutional Convention Debate' (Speech, 30 June 1787) in E.H. Scott, *Journal of the Federal Convention Kept by James Madison; Reprinted from the Edition of 1840* (Albert, Scott & Co, 1893) 278.

2 Thomas Greiber, 'Common Pools for Marine Genetic Resources: A Possible Instrument for a Future Multilateral Agreement Addressing Marine Biodiversity in Areas beyond National Jurisdiction' in Evanson Chege Kamau and Gerd Winter (eds), *Common Pools of Genetic Resources: Equity and Innovation in International Biodiversity Law* (Routledge, 2013) 399, 399–400 ('Common Pools').

3 Sophie Arnaud-Haond, Jesus M. Arrieta and Carlos M. Duarte, 'Marine Biodiversity and Gene Patents' (2011) 331 *Science* 1521, 1521.

4 Increasing at a rate of 12 per cent annually—see, ibid.

5 Charlotte Salpin, 'Marine Genetic Resources of Areas beyond National Jurisdiction: Soul Searching and the Art of Balance' in Elisa Morgera and Kati Kulovesi (eds), *Research Handbook on International Law and Natural Resources* (Edward Elgar Publishing, 2016) 411, 411.

DOI: 10.4324/b22996-5

have the technical and financial wherewithal to access and utilise these resources.[6] This raises the age-old question of whether it is fair to benefit from global commons resources without assuming concomitant benefit-sharing obligations.[7] To complicate matters, there is an increasing trend to privatise innovations derived from MGRs and protect them through intellectual property rights (IPRs). From an environmental perspective, MGRs are a fragile resource that needs to be sustainably used to preserve the genetic resource pool for future generations.[8] Thus, BBNJ negotiators are faced with several complex questions, including (1) how should access to MGRs be managed to minimise environmental impacts and ensure their sustainable use?; and (2) how can benefits be shared in an equitable and economically justifiable manner without hindering R&D?[9] These questions are at the forefront of BBNJ discussions, as delegates attempt to devise a fair and effective access and benefit-sharing (ABS) regime.

The purpose of this chapter is two-fold. First, it examines and explores each of the multiple layers of legal and policy issues relating to MGR exploitation. Leary has compared the MGR issue to the act of slicing into an onion, 'you remove one layer-only to reveal yet another layer of issues for policy-makers to grapple with.'[10] Taking up Leary's metaphor, this chapter seeks to unpeel the onion. The second purpose of this chapter is to investigate potential areas of compromise in regulating access to, and the benefits from, MGRs. We have seen that the legal characterisation of MGRs in ABNJ has 'been marked by a Grotian approach of unrestricted access and use.'[11] Given the reluctance of maritime States to agree to further in-roads on the Grotian principle, an ABS regime will need to be underpinned by a series of sophisticated macro and micro compromises, carefully designed to appeal to the interests of maritime States, while at the same time promoting the conservation and sustainable use of MGRs.

Drawing inspiration from Benjamin Franklin's home-spun analogy which opens this chapter, the development of an ABS regime is analogous to a broad table in need of construction. Currently the planks of this table cannot come together to make a good joint due to the fierce ideological divide between developed (maritime) States and developing States and an unwillingness to compromise or give up some of their demands. Taking on the role of Franklin's artist this chapter identifies potential areas of compromise (Planks of Compromise) for the

6 Arnaud-Haond, Arrieta and Duarte (n 3) 1521.
7 Salpin (n 5) 412.
8 Charles Lawson, *Regulating Genetic Resources: Access and Benefit Sharing in International Law* (Edward Elgar Publishing, 2012) 1.
9 Thomas Greiber, 'Access and Benefit Sharing in Relation to Marine Genetic Resources from Areas beyond National Jurisdiction: A Possible Way Forward' (Research Project, Federal Agency for Nature Conservation, 2011) 8 ('Possible Way Forward').
10 David Leary, 'International Law and the Genetic Resources of the Deep Sea' in Davor Vidas (ed), *Law, Technology and Science for Oceans in Globalisation* (Martinus Nijhoff Publishers, 2010) 353, 369 ('International Law').
11 Salpin (n 5) 413.

three pillars of an ABS regime as well as the legal regime and governing principle applicable to MGRs in ABNJ. Overall, this chapter formulates a course of action the international community could follow to find a pragmatic way forward.

4.1 Unpeeling layers of scope

4.1.1 A common understanding of MGRs

MGRs are not specifically referred to in UNCLOS, nor is there an internationally agreed legal definition.[12] Clearly, an effective ABS regime will require a common understanding of MGRs. Existing international environmental instruments could be used to craft a definition under an ILBI.[13] For example, Article 2 of CBD defines 'genetic resources' as *genetic material of actual or potential value* with 'genetic material' referring to *any material of plant, animal, microbial or other origin containing functional units of heredity*. As a subset of genetic resources, MGRs can be understood as encompassing genetic material from all living marine organisms ranging from mammals, fish, invertebrates and plants to fungi, bacteria, archaea and viruses.[14] The definition of MGRs under an ILBI should be flexible to cope with the discovery of new species, genes and adaptations.

Delegates, including the US, Japan, Canada and Iceland, are concerned about how broadly the term MGRs will be construed and whether it will extend to high seas fisheries.[15] Rabitz warns that any attempt 'to create an obligation to share the benefits from the utilisation of fish' could 'blow the negotiation process right out of the water.'[16] Other delegations, including Switzerland, Bangladesh and Indonesia, have queried the justification for including genetic resources from some organisms and not others.[17] A distinction could therefore be made between

12 Harriet Harden-Davies, 'Deep-Sea Genetic Resources: New Frontiers for Science and Stewardship in Areas beyond National Jurisdiction' (2016) 137 *Deep-Sea Research II* 504, 505.

13 Gaute Voigt-Hanssen, 'Current "Light" and "Heavy" Options for Benefit-Sharing in the Context of the United Nations Convention on the Law of the Sea' (2018) 33(4) *The International Journal of Marine and Coastal Law* 683, 685.

14 Robert Blasiak et al, 'Corporate Control and Global Governance of Marine Genetic Resources' (2018) 4 *Sciences Advances* 1–7, 1; Harlan Cohen, 'Ensuring Conservation and Sustainable Use of Marine Genetic Resources: Current and Future Challenges' (Conference Paper, United Nations Open-ended Informal Consultative Process, Eighth Meeting, 27 June 2007).

15 Jacqueline Joyce Espenilla, 'Access, Conservation and Sustainable Use of Marine Genetic Resources in Areas beyond National Jurisdiction: Emerging Issues of Consensus and Contention' (2016) *Columbia Journal of Environmental Law* [Field Report] 1, 4.

16 Florian Rabitz, *The Global Governance of Genetic Resources Institutional Change, Structural Constraints* (Routledge, 2017) 143.

17 See Elisa Morgera et al, 'Summary of the First Session of the Intergovernmental Conference on an International Legally Binding Instrument under the UN Convention on the Law of the Sea on the Conservation and Sustainable Use of Marine Biodiversity of Areas beyond National Jurisdiction 4–17 September 2018' *Earth Negotiations Bulletin* (Online Bulletin,

fish used as a commodity and fish used for research on their genetic properties.[18] This could be based on a scientifically-informed threshold, whereby, if a particular fish species is extracted for bioprospecting purposes beyond a certain volume (depending on the species and habitat variability), it would be considered a commodity.[19] This would represent a micro plank of compromise.

Another controversial issue is whether MGRs should be differentiated from their derivatives. The CBD defines 'genetic material' as containing *functional units of heredity*;[20] however this phrase is not defined. The wider scientific interpretation targets primary metabolites (i.e. genes, proteins and enzymes) that contain DNA.[21] Others argue the term encompasses secondary metabolites or derivatives, being naturally occurring compounds that do *not* contain DNA.[22] As modern bioscience involves R&D on naturally occurring compounds, failure to include derivatives in an ILBI could significantly narrow the scope for benefit-sharing and discard a large amount of biotechnological applications.[23] This issue was the subject of debate during Nagoya Protocol negotiations.[24] The CBD was criticised for appearing to exclude material obtained from derivatives.[25] The Protocol addresses this gap by defining 'derivatives' as *a naturally occurring biochemical compound resulting from ... genetic resources, even if it does* not *contain functional units of heredity*. Arguably, the adoption of a definition in conformity

---

20 September 2018) 4 ('Summary of IGC 1') <https://enb.iisd.org/events/1st-session-intergovernmental-conference-igc-international-legally-binding-instrument-12>.

18 *Chair's Streamlined Non-Paper on Elements of a Draft Text of an International Legally Binding Instrument under UNCLOS on the Conservation and Sustainable Use of Marine Biological Diversity of Areas beyond National Jurisdiction PrepCom 4* (10–21 July 2017) 14 ('*Chair's Streamlined Non-Paper*').

19 See Eritrea, 'Development of an International Legally Binding Instrument under the United Nations Convention on the Law of the Sea on the Conservation and Sustainable Use of Marine Biological Diversity of Areas beyond National Jurisdiction: Submission Paper from the State of Eritrea' (26 April 2017) <https://www.un.org/depts/los/biodiversity/prepcom_files/streamlined/Eritrea.pdf>. A scientific and technical body under an ILBI could define this threshold.

20 CBD, art 2.

21 Arianna Broggiato et al, 'Fair and Equitable Sharing of Benefits from the Utilisation of Marine Genetic Resources in Areas beyond National Jurisdiction: Bridging the Gaps between Science and Policy' (2014) 49 *Marine Policy* 176, 177.

22 Harden-Davies (n 12) 506.

23 Elisa Morgera, Matthias Buck and Elsa Tsioumani, *Unraveling the Nagoya Protocol: A Commentary on the Nagoya Protocol on Access and Benefit-Sharing to the Convention on Biological Diversity* (Brill, 2014) vol 2, 66.

24 Nagoya Protocol on Access to Genetic Resources and the Fair and Equitable Sharing of Benefits Arising from Their Utilization to the Convention on Biological Diversity, opened for signature 2 February 2011, Doc. UNEP/CBD/COP/DEC/X/1 (entered into force 12 October 2014) (Nagoya Protocol).

25 Carlos M. Correa, 'Access to and Benefit-Sharing of Marine Genetic Resources beyond National Jurisdiction: Developing a New Legally Binding Instrument' in Charles R. McManis and Burton Ong (eds), *Routledge Handbook of Biodiversity and the Law* (2017) 157, 166.

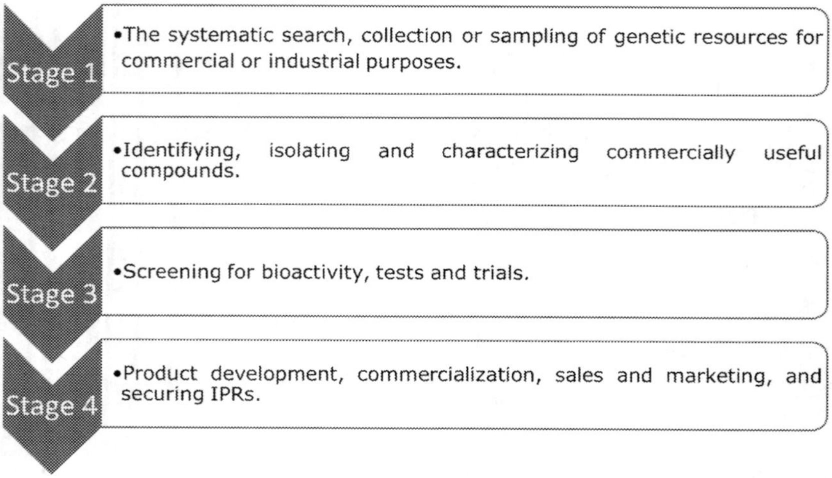

Figure 4.1 Overview of bioprospecting stages.

with the Nagoya Protocol would bring certainty to MGR users both within and beyond national jurisdiction.

4.1.2 Marine scientific research (MSR) versus bioprospecting

MGR collection and analysis essentially involves two activities, bioprospecting and MSR. In general terms, bioprospecting is 'the search for commercially valuable genetic resources'[26] and usually consists of four stages (see Figure 4.1).[27]

There is a long-standing debate around whether bioprospecting amounts to applied MSR and falls under Part XIII of UNCLOS.[28] MSR is not defined in the Convention. In its ordinary sense, it is understood 'as any scientific study or related experimental work having the *marine environment* as *its object* which is designed to increase knowledge of the oceans.'[29] Article 246 of UNCLOS relates to MSR in the EEZ and on the continental shelf and provides for two kinds of MSR projects. Pure MSR is carried out 'to increase scientific knowledge of the marine environment for the benefit of all mankind' (Article 246(3)),

26 Tullio Scovazzi, 'The Rights to Genetic Resources beyond National Jurisdiction: Challenges for the Ongoing Negotiations at the United Nations' in Catherine Banet (ed), *The Law of the Seabed* (Brill Nijhoff, 2020) 213, 223 ('Rights to Genetic Resources').

27 Cf *Oceans and the Law of the Sea – Report of the Secretary-General*, UN Doc A/62/66 (12 March 2007) [150].

28 Ibid.

29 Yoshifumi Tanaka, *The International Law of the Sea* (Cambridge University Press, 2nd ed, 2015) 360.

while applied MSR is 'of direct significance' to the exploration and exploitation of living or non-living resources (Article 246(5)). Mossop argues that Article 246(5) includes bioprospecting as it refers to research activities undertaken with the intention of financial gain.[30] Yet, UN Secretary-General Reports generally differentiate between bioprospecting and MSR.[31] Scovazzi contends that 'it is impossible to establish a clear-cut distinction,'[32] as the activities are essentially indistinguishable at sample collection.[33] Thus, rather than attempting to define or distinguish between them, BBNJ negotiators should ensure that an ILBI effectively captures MGRs derived from both activities, including all stages from sample extraction to commercialisation.[34]

BBNJ negotiators will also need to consider the three main pathways to access MGRs. In-situ access involves the collection of samples within their natural surroundings (i.e. finding and working with the physical raw materials of ecosystems and habitats in ABNJ).[35] The US argues that an ILBI should be limited to in-situ MGRs.[36] This is problematic as most biodiscovery begins with ex-situ or in-silico access.[37] Ex-situ access occurs when the resource is acquired away from its natural habitat, such as from biorepositories, culture collections and research institutions.[38] In-silico refers to direct access to genetic data (i.e. whole genomes and isolated gene sequences).[39] In-silico testing uses information technology to generate value in genetic material without physical access to the original source.[40]

30 Joanna Mossop, 'Protecting Marine Biodiversity on the Continental Shelf beyond 200 Nautical Miles' (2007) 38 *Ocean Development & International Law* 283, 294.

31 See, e.g. *Oceans and the Law of the Sea: Report of the Secretary-General*, UN Doc A/60/63/ADD.1 (15 July 2005) [202]; *Oceans and the Law of the Sea: Report of the Secretary-General*, UN Doc A/59/62 (4 March 2004) [261].

32 Tullio Scovazzi, 'The Concept of Common Heritage of Mankind and the Genetic Resources of the Seabed beyond the Limits of National Jurisdiction' (2007) 25 *Agenda Internacional* 11, 18.

33 Rabitz (n 16) 143.

34 David Kenneth Leary, *International Law and the Genetic Resources of the Deep Sea* (Martinus Nijhoff Publishers, 2007) 157.

35 Marcel Jaspars and Abbe E.L. Brown, 'Benefit Sharing: Combining Intellectual Property, Trade Secrets, Science and an Ecosystem-Focused Approach' in Myron H. Nordquist and Ronán Long (eds), *Marine Biodiversity of Areas beyond National Jurisdiction* (Brill/Nijhoff, 2021) 107; Evanson Chege Kamau, 'Access-Related Issues' (Information Paper 4, IUCN, May 2013) 23.

36 *Chair's Non-Paper on Elements of a Draft Text of an International Legally-Binding Instrument under UNCLOS on the Conservation and Sustainable Use of Marine Biological Diversity of Areas beyond National Jurisdiction* (28 February 2017) 22 ('*Chair's Non-Paper*').

37 Arianna Broggiato et al, 'Mare Geneticum: Balancing Governance of Marine Genetic Resources in International Waters' (2018) 33 *The International Journal of Marine and Coastal Law* 3, 14.

38 Ibid.

39 Ibid.

40 Kamau (n 35) 23.

Opinions remain divided on whether in-silico data, particularly digital sequence information, should fall within the ILBI's scope.[41] Developing States argue that the 'growing trend in bio-based research to rely on digital information may ultimately render physical access' to MGRs unnecessary.[42] Thus, an ABS regime limited to in-situ access would quickly become obsolete.[43] Switzerland, Japan and South Korea oppose the inclusion of digital sequence information in an ILBI, mainly due to challenges in data tracking.[44] In-silico data has been notoriously difficult to track and trace.[45] However, a number of organisations are devising ways to combat this. For example, the Global Catalogue of Microorganisms is working to ensure ABS compliance under the Nagoya Protocol by linking a unique identifier of each strain of microorganism to an Internationally Recognised Certificate of Compliance.[46] This could also be a viable option to track and trace MGRs under an ILBI.[47]

4.1.3 Monetary versus non-monetary benefits

BBNJ delegations also disagree on the benefits to be shared under an ABS regime. The African Group, CARICOM, PSIDS and CLAM prefer both monetary and non-monetary benefits, while the US, the Republic of Korea, Japan, Russia and Switzerland support sharing non-monetary benefits only.[48] Discussions tend to focus on monetary benefits, being financial or economic outcomes (i.e. payments, royalties, IPRs and patents).[49] Leary and Juniper suggest that a 'gold fever' has taken hold of the international community and academia, with many convinced that MGRs are a 'pot of gold' waiting to be discovered at the bottom of the ocean.[50] However, there is minimal evidence of commercial-scale development of

41 Elisa Morgera, 'Fair and Equitable Benefit-Sharing in a New Treaty on Marine Biodiversity: A Principled Approach towards Partnership Building?' (Working Paper No. 16, Benelex, 2018) 16.

42 Ibid.

43 Ibid.

44 Morgera et al, 'Summary of IGC 1' (n 17).

45 Broggiato et al (n 37) 19.

46 Juncai Ma, Linhuan Wu and Ipek Kurtböke, 'Skerman and beyond: 2019 Status of the Global Catalogue of Microorganisms' (2019) 40(3) *Microbiology Australia* 121, 121.

47 See *Revised Draft Text of an Agreement under UNCLOS on the Conservation and Sustainable Use of Marine Biological Diversity of Areas beyond National Jurisdiction*, UN Doc A/CONF.232/2020/3 (18 November 2019) Article 13(3)(a) ('*Revised Draft Negotiating Text*').

48 See, e.g. Tallash Kantai et al, 'Summary of the Second Session of the Intergovernmental Conference on the Conservation and Sustainable Use of Marine Biodiversity of Areas beyond National Jurisdiction: 25 March–5 April 2019' *Earth Negotiations Bulletin* (Online Bulletin, 8 April 2019) 4 ('Summary of IGC 2') <https://enb.iisd.org/events/2nd-session-intergovernmental-conference-igc-conservation-and-sustainable-use-marine/summary>.

49 Jessica Battle and Duncan Currie, 'Some Critical Issues to be Resolved on Marine Genetic Resources in the Context of the Marine Biological Diversity Preparatory Committee Discussions' (Discussion Paper, WWF International, March 2016) 5.

50 David Leary and S. Kim Juniper, 'Addressing the Marine Genetic Resources Issue: Is the Debate Heading in the Wrong Direction?' in Clive Schofield, Seokwoo Lee and Moon-Sang Kwon (eds), *The Limits of Maritime Jurisdiction* (Koninklijke Brill, 2014) 769, 773.

MGRs from ABNJ.[51] While a number of patents and pending applications exist, they do not necessarily equate to marketable products.[52] A lengthy (between 10 and 15 years) and costly R&D process is required before commercialisation, and the chances of success are extremely low.[53] As the prospects of monetary benefits are uncertain,[54] BBNJ negotiators should proceed with caution. As Leary and Juniper contend, 'one only needs to recall the so far unrealised potential of deep-sea manganese nodules to appreciate how gold fever can lead to the creation of marine resource regulatory regimes far ahead of any real-world requirement.'[55] An equal amount of attention should therefore be paid to non-monetary benefits, which may deliver more tangible gains in the long term.

The President's Aid to Negotiations provides a list of non-monetary benefits including MSR cooperation, the exchange of scientific information and CBTT.[56] The annex to the Nagoya Protocol also includes a non-exhaustive list of benefits that could be adapted to suit the BBNJ context (see Appendix 3). CARICOM, the African Group and CLAM, for example, support the development of a non-exhaustive list of benefits under an ILBI, rather than a list of benefits to be reviewed and developed at a later stage.[57] As non-monetary benefits are already shared through gene banks, digital databanks, scientific journals and patent pools, an ILBI could build upon these existing benefit-sharing practices to improve MGR accessibility.

4.1.4 Vertical and horizontal layers of complexity

Vertical and horizontal transboundary situations also pose a challenge to MGR management in ABNJ. For example, Japan and the US argue that an ILBI should only cover MGRs in the Area and not the superjacent water column.[58] However, MGRs do not neatly adhere to the artificial legal boundaries established by UNCLOS.[59] Certain organisms are found at different stages in their life cycle in

51 S. Kim Juniper, 'Technological, Environmental, Social and Economic Aspects' (Information Paper 3, IUCN, May 2013) 20–21.

52 Marjo Vierros et al, 'Emerging and Unresolved Issues: Marine Genetic Resources' in Salvatore Arico (ed), *Ocean Sustainability in the 21st Century* (Cambridge University Press, 2015) 212.

53 David Leary, 'Agreeing to Disagree on What We Have or Have Not Agreed on: The Current State of Play of the BBNJ Negotiations on the Status of Marine Genetic Resources in Areas beyond National Jurisdiction' (2019) 99 *Marine Policy* 21, 27 ('Agreeing to Disagree').

54 Anja Morris, 'Marine Genetic Resources in Areas beyond National Jurisdiction: How Should the Exploitation of the Resources Be Regulated' (2018) 22 *New Zealand Journal of Environmental Law* 57, 61.

55 Leary and Juniper (n 50) 785.

56 *President's Aid to Discussions*, UN Doc A/CONF.232/2018/33 (25 June 2018) para 3.2.2(ii).

57 See, e.g. Kantai et al, 'Summary of IGC 2' (n 48) 4.

58 *Chair's Non-Paper* (n 36) 22.

59 Rabitz (n 16) 135.

the water column or on the deep-seabed,[60] and some move constantly between the maritime zones.[61] It is therefore difficult to see how an ILBI could distinguish between MGRs in the Area and those in the high seas.[62] Accordingly, an ABS regime should be harmonised across both zones.[63]

As MGRs can also move horizontally as a result of ecological processes and transportation pathways,[64] the same MGR could potentially fall under two different regimes, the CBD/Nagoya Protocol and an ILBI.[65] This issue will need to be carefully addressed, to prevent legal loopholes including the falsification of sampling geo-references to avoid ABS obligations.[66]

4.2 A legal regime for MGRs of ABNJ

4.2.1 A compromise for the ideological tug-of-war

A fierce debate has ensued for over two decades concerning the legal status of MGRs in the Area.[67] This debate has 're-opened the familiar divisions between North and South that characterised'[68] UNCLOS III, with two camps retreating to 'traditional trench warfare positions.'[69] A majority of developing States argue that MGRs are Common Heritage of Mankind (CHM) and the regime in Part XI of UNCLOS should apply. Developed (maritime) States maintain that MGRs are governed by the freedom of the seas principle enshrined in Part VII of UNCLOS.

As Chapter 2 outlined the difficulties experienced in trying to fit MGRs under the rubric of Part VII or Part XI of UNCLOS, the purpose of this section is to demonstrate the complex nature of a debate between the principles that lie at their core. The CHM and the freedom of the seas 'are antithetical in nature and fundamentally opposing in a myriad of ways.'[70] They pull in different directions with the Grotian principle allowing States freedom and the CHM restricting

60 Penelope Ridings, 'Redefining Environmental Stewardship to Deliver Governance Frameworks for Marine Biodiversity beyond National Jurisdiction' (2018) 75(1) *ICES Journal of Marine Science* 435, 436.

61 Kamau (n 35) 26. The microbial community at hydrothermal vents serves as an example.

62 Leary, 'International Law' (n 10) 366.

63 Harden-Davies (n 12) 508.

64 *Oceans and the Law of the Sea - Report of the Secretary-General*, UN Doc A/62/66/Add.2 (10 September 2007) [189].

65 Scovazzi, 'Rights to Genetic Resources' (n 26) 237.

66 Thomas Greiber, 'Meaning and Scope' (Information Paper 1, IUCN, May 2013) 5.

67 Lyle Glowka sparked the debate on whether a specific international legal regime was required to regulate ABS of MGRs from ABNJ—see Lyle Glowka, 'The Deepest of Ironies: Genetic Resources, Marine Scientific Research, and the Area' (1996) 12 *Ocean Yearbook* 154, 155.

68 Leary and Juniper (n 50) 785.

69 Ibid.

70 Colm Hastings, 'Time to Set the Record Straight: The Legal Status of Marine Genetic Resources Found within the Deep Seabed Area. The Freedom of the High Seas, the Common Heritage of Mankind – or Neither?' (LLM Thesis, University of Iceland, 2018) 25.

freedom in the interest of the greater good.[71] It is therefore an ideological tug-of-war. Engaging in this debate will only prolong a stalemate and prevent BBNJ discussions from moving forward.[72] Thus, rather than attempting to reconcile these 'radically opposed philosophies,'[73] this book proposes a shift away from this theoretical paradigm to a pragmatic approach built on key planks of compromise.

4.2.2 The CHM principle

There is no concise or fully agreed definition of CHM.[74] It is made up of elements drawn from UNGA Resolution 2749 (17 December 1970)[75] and reflected in Part XI of UNCLOS.[76] The first element is non-appropriation (Article 137); second, international management; third, exclusively peaceful use (Article 141); and fourth, benefit-sharing (Articles 137(2), 140(2)).[77] Equitable benefit-sharing, implying distributive justice, has always been the most controversial feature of CHM, particularly amongst developed States, who stand to lose out under such a system.[78] During BBNJ negotiations, the US, Japan, South Korea and Russia have vehemently opposed the application of CHM to MGRs. Yet, this opposition to CHM is not new nor is it unique to the BBNJ context.

The CHM principle has been a source of controversy for decades.[79] Contrasting ideologies and inconsistent interpretations have hindered the development of the

71 Dire Tladi, 'The Common Heritage of Mankind and the Proposed Treaty on Biodiversity in Areas beyond National Jurisdiction: The Choice between Pragmatism and Sustainability' (2015) 25(1) *Yearbook of International Environmental Law* 113, 119.

72 Eve Heafey, 'Access and Benefit Sharing of Marine Genetic Resources from Areas beyond National Jurisdiction: Intellectual Property—Friend, Not Foe' (2014) 12(2) *Chicago Journal of International Law* 493, 511.

73 Lee Kimball et al, 'Balancing the Interests?' (1978) 4 *Environmental Policy and Law* 69, 69 quoting the chairman of the Seventh Session of UNCLOS III Frank Njenga of Kenya in his report on Special Negotiating Group I.

74 Natalie Y. Morris-Sharma, 'Marine Genetic Resources in Areas beyond National Jurisdiction: Issues with, in and outside of UNCLOS' (2017) 20(1) *Max Planck Yearbook of United Nations Law Online* 71, 81.

75 *Declaration of Principles Governing the Sea-Bed and the Ocean Floor, and the Subsoil Thereof, beyond the Limits of National Jurisdiction*, GA 2749 (XXV) UN Doc A/RES/2749(XXV) (17 December 1970).

76 Ridings (n 60) 436.

77 Jimena Murillo, 'Common Concern of Humankind and its Implications in International Environmental Law' (2008) 5 *Macquarie Journal of International and Comparative Environmental Law* 5(2) 133, 135.

78 John E. Noyes, 'The Common Heritage of Mankind, Past, Present and Future' (2011) 40 *Denver Journal of International Law and Policy* 447, 451; Hastings (n 70) 92.

79 Jennifer Frakes, 'The Common Heritage of Mankind Principle and the Deep Seabed, Outer Space, and Antarctica: Will Developed and Developing Nations Reach a Compromise?' (2003) 21(2) *Wisconsin International Law Journal* 409, 410.

CHM principle, and since the adoption of UNCLOS the concept 'has failed to find traction beyond the seabed.'[80] For example, the CHM regime for 'the moon and other celestial bodies never took full effect, and the initial conceptualisation of plant genetic resources as common heritage was almost immediately retracted.'[81] Moreover, arguments for climate change and biodiversity to be subject to a CHM regime did not find favour.[82] Nor is the CHM principle given effect in the special regime applicable to Antarctica, despite its designation as 'a nature reserve, devoted to peace and science' under the Madrid Protocol.[83] Consequently, some commentators consider the CHM concept 'to be out of fashion due to its lack of use in practice and its subsequent rejection by modern environmental treaty regimes.'[84] Guntrip argues that CHM 'is no more than an inchoate concept, consisting of yet undeveloped standards,'[85] and Leary suggests that it is 'not very useful as a means to achieving practical and just solutions' for political, economic and social problems.[86] Others, however, consider it to be a general principle of international law with enduring significance.[87] It is evident from BBNJ discussions that CHM remains the point of departure for developing States.[88]

80 Edward Guntrip, 'The Common Heritage of Mankind: An Adequate Regime for Managing the Deep Seabed?' (2003) 4 *Melbourne Journal of International Law* 376, 404; Duncan French, 'Common Concern, Common Heritage and Other Global(-ising) Concepts: Rhetorical Devices, Legal Principles or a Fundamental Challenge?' in Michael Bowman, Peter Davies and Edward Goodwin (eds), *Research Handbook on Biodiversity and Law* (Edward Elgar Publishing, 2016) 334, 342.

81 Ibid, 342.

82 Ibid.

83 The Antarctic Treaty does not expressly include CHM language, although elements of the concept appear in the text, and in the other instruments that comprise the Antarctic Treaty System; see generally, Carol R. Buxton, 'Property in Outer Space: The Common Heritage of Mankind Principle vs. the First in Time First in Right, Rule of Property' (2004) 69(4) *Journal of Air Law and Commerce* 689, 696.

84 Prue Taylor, 'The Common Heritage of Mankind: A Bold Doctrine Kept within Strict Boundaries' in David Bollier and Silke Helfrich (eds), *The Wealth of the Commons: A World beyond Market & State* (Levellers Press, 2012) 566, 566.

85 Guntrip (80) 404.

86 Leary, 'International Law' (n 10) 365 quoting Mr Meeker, Legal Advisor to the US State Department, in a speech to the American Foreign Law Association, 9 June 1965, quoted in Wolfgang Friedmann, 'United States Policy and the Crisis of International Law: Some Reflections on the State of International Law' (1965) 59(4) *The American Journal of International Law* 857, 868.

87 Taylor (n 84) 566.

88 See Group of 77, 'Interventions on Behalf of the Group of 77 and China by Mr. Emad Morcos Mattar, Counsellor, Permanent Mission of Egypt to the United Nations, on Agenda Item 7: Marine Genetic Resources, Including Questions on the Sharing of Benefits, at the First Session of the Intergovernmental Conference on an International Legally Binding Instrument under the United Nations Convention on the Law of the Sea on the Conservation and Sustainable Use of Marine Biological Diversity of Areas beyond National Jurisdiction' (New York, 13 September 2018) <https://www.g77.org/statement/getstatement.php?id=180913> ('Interventions of G77/China').

4.2.3 The freedom of the high seas

Maritime States are equally reluctant to move from their position. This bloc argues that MGRs in ABNJ are governed by the freedom of the high seas principle, which is a testament to the enduring bond that exists between this bloc and the Grotian doctrine.[89] These countries are mindful of the fact that UNCLOS 'is a carefully-balanced "package deal" of rights and obligations, and are wary of destabilising UNCLOS by countenancing the possibility that its precepts are in dispute or flawed.'[90] Developed States also have a vested interest in extending the Grotian principle to MGRs, as it would enable them 'to assert a relative monopolisation' over the resource and the international patent market.[91]

In opposition, developing States argue that a freedom of the seas approach would inherently limit the ability of the international community to effectively protect MGRs,[92] as exploitation would be subject to flag State jurisdiction. To date, no State has adopted any specific legislation to regulate bioprospecting in ABNJ.[93]

4.2.4 The golden middle way

Based on the above analysis, it is difficult to see how the two sides of this ideological debate can be reconciled.[94] In an effort to move beyond ideological differences, this book proposes a pragmatic approach built on compromise. BBNJ negotiators need to find what Greek philosophers referred to as 'the Golden Middle Way,'[95] that is, the desirable middle between two extremes. One arrives at this golden mean or mid-point by first perceiving or envisaging the extremes (freedom of the seas versus CHM) and then negotiating a passage between them.[96] This exercise will necessarily involve both camps giving up some of their demands in order to find 'some accommodating proposition.'[97]

89 See Chapter 2.

90 Robynne Boyd et al, 'Summary of the Eighth Meeting of the Open-Ended Informal Consultative Process on Oceans and the Law of the Sea: 25 to 29 June 2007' *Earth Negotiations Bulletin* (Online Bulletin, 2 July 2007) 10 <https://enb.iisd.org/download/pdf/enb2543e.pdf>.

91 Hastings (n 70) 81.

92 Ibid, 31.

93 Robin Warner, *Protecting the Oceans beyond National Jurisdiction: Strengthening the International Law Framework* (Martinus Nifhoff Publishers, 2009) vol 3, 228.

94 Leary, 'Agreeing to Disagree' (n 53) 24.

95 In ancient Greek philosophy, especially that of Aristotle, the golden mean or golden middle way is the desirable middle between two extremes, one of excess and the other of deficiency. See Aristotle, 'Nicomachean Ethics' (Book II) in Aristotle and H. Rackman (eds), *The Nicomachean Ethics* (Harvard University Press, 2nd ed, 1934) vol 73.

96 Stanley B. Cunningham, 'Getting It Right: Aristotle's "Golden Mean" as Theory Deterioration' (1999) 14(1) *Journal of Mass Media Ethics* 5, 7.

97 Benjamin Franklin, 'Constitutional Convention Debate' in Scott (n 1) 278.

During the BBNJ process calls have been made for a sui generis regime to bridge the gap between freedom of the seas and CHM.[98] Delegations, most notably the EU, have suggested pursuing a 'third approach'[99] to avoid 'counterproductive theoretical considerations.'[100] The EU argues that the determination of the legal status of MGRs should not be a precondition for addressing benefit-sharing provisions.[101] As Tladi explains, the EU 'approach purports to give effect to the demands of adherents' of CHM, but relies on benefit-sharing terminology, so as to avoid reference to the controversial CHM phrase.[102] The EU has negotiated on the basis that an ABS regime should be linked to BBNJ protection.[103] This linkage has resulted in the formation of a EU-G77/China coalition.[104] During the last meeting of the BBNJ Working Group, the EU noted areas of commonality with the G77/China bloc's non-paper and expressed confidence that their 'two texts could be merged to represent the views of a larger group of like-minded States.'[105] Consequently, several developing States have signalled a willingness to trade CHM 'in exchange for tangible gains under a pragmatic benefit-sharing' arrangement.[106]

To be clear, developing States continue to promote CHM as their default position. The Draft Text of an ILBI had attempted to avoid direct mention of the CHM principle; however, this elicited particularly strong reactions from developing States at IGC3. The African Group, for example, asserted that adopting an ILBI without this principle 'would be like giving life to a treaty of this importance without a soul, or like putting a ship in the water without a navigational instrument.'[107] It is therefore unsurprising that the CHM principle

98 Ridings (n 60) 437.
99 Tladi (n 71) 117.
100 Elisa Morgera et al, 'Summary of the First Session of the Preparatory Committee on Marine Biodiversity of Areas beyond National Jurisdiction: 28 March–8 April 2016' *Earth Negotiations Bulletin* (Online Bulletin, 11 April 2016) 18 <https://enb.iisd.org/events/1st-session-bbnj-preparatory-committee/summary-report-28-march-8-april-2016>.
101 European Union, 'Development of an International Legally Binding Instrument under UNCLOS on the Conservation and Sustainable Use of Marine Biological Diversity of Areas beyond National Jurisdiction (BBNJ Process), Written Submission of the EU and Its Member States: Marine Genetic Resources, Including Questions on the Sharing of Benefits' (22 February 2017) 2 <https://www.un.org/depts/los/biodiversity/prepcom_files/rolling_comp/EU_Written_Submission_on_Marine_Genetic_Resources.pdf>.
102 Tladi (n 71) 114.
103 Rabitz (n 16) 147.
104 Ibid.
105 Tallash Kantai, Alice Miller and Elisa Morgera, 'Summary of the Ninth Meeting of the Working Group on Marine Biodiversity beyond Areas of National Jurisdiction: 20–23 January 2015' *Earth Negotiations Bulletin* (Online Bulletin, 26 January 2015) 5 <https://enb.iisd.org/download/pdf/enb2594e.pdf>.
106 Rabitz (n 16) 131.
107 Permanent Mission of Algeria to the United Nations New York, 'Statement on Behalf of the African Group by H.E. Ambassador Mohammed Bessedik, Deputy Permanent Representative, Chargé d'affaires a.i., At the Third Session of the Intergovernmental Conference on an International Legally Binding Instrument under the United Nations Convention on

has made its way back into the Revised Draft Negotiating Text.[108] However, for some States CHM 'can be whittled down to benefit-sharing.'[109] This reflects the evolution of the benefit-sharing concept in international law, as it was initially seen 'within the conceptual landscape of the New International Economic Order.'[110] For example, Mexico asserts that MGRs will be CHM provided they are 'regulated under a benefit-sharing approach that adequately incentives their economic exploitation.'[111] Several members of the G77/China bloc have also moved away from strict CHM terminology.[112] During PrepCom, China used 'common well-being of humankind' instead of CHM and Argentina used 'common heritage of humanity.'[113] This is promising, as it suggests that these States may be open to compromise.

In contrast to the EU's third approach, this book suggests that a 'Golden Middle Way' can be pursued. This proposal differs from the EU's approach in two critical respects. First, rather than attempting to satisfy the demands of only one bloc of States (developing States), this proposal attempts to accommodate a number of competing interests, including the scientific community, the R&D sector and a key bloc of powerful maritime States. The effectiveness of an ILBI will be limited if the States with the most significant biotechnology powers do not agree to its terms.[114] Second, the EU has not provided any solid proposals or

---

the Law of the Sea on the Conservation and Sustainable Use of Marine Biological Diversity of Areas beyond National Jurisdiction, General Exchange of Views (Item 5)' (New York, 19 August 2019) <http://statements.unmeetings.org/media2/21996848/algeria-obo-african-group.pdf>.

108 *Revised Draft Negotiating Text* (n 47) art 5(c).

109 Tladi (n 71) 123.

110 Morgera (n 41) 3.

111 *Scope, Parameters and Feasibility of an International Instrument under UNCLOS: Informal Working Document Compiling the Views of Member States, Prepared in Accordance with General Assembly Resolution 68/70 paragraph 201* (4 December 2014) 18.

112 Leary, 'Agreeing to Disagree,' (n 53) 25.

113 People's Republic of China, 'Written Submission of the Chinese Government on Elements of a Draft Text of an International Legally Binding Instrument under the United Nations Convention on the Law of the Sea on the Conservation and Sustainable Use of Marine Biological Diversity of Areas Beyond National Jurisdiction' (7 March 2017) 3 < https://www.un.org/depts/los/biodiversity/prepcom_files/rolling_comp/China.pdf>; People's Republic of China, 'Written Submission of the Government of the People's Republic of China on Elements of a Draft Text of an International Legally Binding Instrument under the United Nations Convention on the Law of the Sea on the Conservation and Sustainable Use of Marine Biological Diversity of Areas Beyond National Jurisdiction' (20 April 2017) 4 <https://www.un.org/depts/los/biodiversity/prepcom_files/streamlined/China.pdf>; Argentina, 'Written Submission to the Preparatory Committee established by the United Nations General Assembly Resolution 69/292' (2017) (Unofficial courtesy translation) <https://www.un.org/depts/los/biodiversity/prepcom_files/streamlined/Argentina_unofficial_courtesy_translation.pdf>.

114 Pamela Schoenberg, 'A Polarizing Dilemma: Assessing Potential Regulatory Gap-Filling Measures for Arctic & Antarctic Marine Genetic Resource Access & Benefit Sharing' (2009) 42 *Cornell International Law Journal* 271.

strategies for how its third approach can be achieved and has focused mainly on non-monetary benefit-sharing. This book proposes a path made up of a series of macro and micro compromises for each pillar of an ABS regime. Before turning to this, the following sections argue that the Common Concern of Humankind (CCH) principle could provide a suitable governance framework for an ILBI and act as a plank of compromise between CHM and freedom of the seas.

4.3 A guiding principle for MGRs

4.3.1 The CCH concept—a potential circuit-breaker?

The CCH concept has not been comprehensively defined.[115] It was introduced during negotiations of the CBD as a viable alternative to CHM[116] and is based on the 'equitable sharing of burdens in the protection of the environment, rather than benefits of exploitation from common resources.'[117] Notably, the concept does not refer to the interests of States.[118] Instead, 'it is humanity as a whole, the multitude of individuals whose concerns are at issue.'[119] This accords with Justice Weeramantry's separate opinion in the *Gabcíkovo/Nagymaros Project* case. Justice Weeramantry speculated that:

> we have entered an era of international law in which international law subserves not only the interests of individual States, but looks beyond them and their parochial concerns to the greater interests of humanity and planetary welfare ... International environmental law will need to proceed beyond weighing the rights and obligations of parties within a closed compartment of individual State self-interest, unrelated to the global concerns of humanity as a whole.[120]

Depicting a problem as a common concern acknowledges the existence of a shared issue that 'transcends the boundaries of a single state' and requires collective action in response.[121]

115 Edith Brown Weiss, 'The Coming Water Crisis: A Common Concern of Humankind' (2012) 1(1) *Transnational Environmental Law* 153, 164.

116 Chelsea Bowling, Elizabeth Pierson and Stephanie Ratte, 'The Common Concern of Humankind: A Potential Framework for a New International Legally Binding Instrument on the Conservation and Sustainable Use of Marine Biological Diversity in the High Seas,' Communication to the Preparatory Committee established by the United Nations General Assembly Resolution 69/292 (2016) 3 <http://www.un.org/depts/los/biodiversity/prepcom_files/BowlingPiersonandRatte_Common_Concern.pdf>.

117 Murillo (n 77) 138.

118 Dinah Shelton, 'Common Concern of Humanity' (2009) 39(2) *Environmental Policy and Law* 83, 83.

119 Ibid.

120 *Gabcíkovo-Nagymaros Project* (Hungary v. Slovakia) [1997] ICJ Rep 7, separate opinion of Vice-President Weeramantry [115].

121 Shelton (n 118) 83.

There are now four references to the CCH concept in international treaties.[122] For example, the CBD Preamble affirms biodiversity conservation as CCH, and the same status is accorded to 'change in the Earth's climate and its adverse effects' under the United Nations Framework Convention on Climate Change (UNFCCC).[123]

The key question is whether the conservation and sustainable use of BBNJ meets the CCH threshold. The following are considered fundamental characteristics of a CCH:

(a) The interests concerned extend beyond individual States and touch on values of global significance;
(b) Threats to the interests concerned are marked by their gravity, long-term implications and potential irreversibility of impacts;
(c) Safeguarding the interests requires cooperation and collective responsibility by all sectors of society.[124]

Arguably, the ecological and genetic significance of BBNJ, along with its importance to evolution and to the maintenance of 'life sustaining systems of the biosphere,' make it a CCH.[125] BBNJ is under threat from anthropogenic pressures and is being lost at a rate that jeopardises the sustainability of marine ecosystems, with potentially irreversible and devastating effects.[126] The protection of BBNJ and its 'genetic heritage'[127] is also a global challenge that requires cooperation and collaboration to prevent long-term harm.[128] The conservation and sustainable use of BBNJ thereby bear all the hallmarks of a CCH and should be affirmed as such under an ILBI.

122 Nadia Sanchez Castillo-Winckels, 'Why "Common Concern of Humankind" Should Return to the Work of the International Law Commission on the Atmosphere' (2016) 29(1) *Georgetown Environmental Law Review* 132, 136. Plant genetic resources and the safeguarding of intangible cultural heritage have also been declared CCH.

123 United Nations Framework Convention on Climate Change, opened for signature 9 May 1992, 1771 UNTS 165 (entered into force 21 March 1994) (UNFCCC).

124 Friedrich Soltau, 'Common Concern of Humankind' in Cinnamon P Carlarne, Kevin R Gray and Richard Tarasofsky (eds), *The Oxford Handbook of International Climate Change Law* (Oxford University Press, 2016) 202, 207–208; Laura Horn, 'Climate Change and the Future Role of the Concept of the Common Concern' (2015) 2(1) *Australian Journal of Environmental Law* 24, 27.

125 French (n 80) 345.

126 Rabitz (n 16) 132.

127 Bleuenn Guilloux, *Marine Genetic Resources, R&D and the Law 1: Complex Objects of Use* (ISTE Ltd, 2018) 128.

128 IUCN, 'Submission by IUCN following the Second Session of the Preparatory Committee on the Development of an International Legally Binding Instrument under the United Nations Convention on the Law of the Sea on the Conservation and Sustainable Use of Marine Biological Diversity of Areas beyond National Jurisdiction' (5 December 2016) 4 ('IUCN Submission') <https://www.un.org/depts/los/biodiversity/prepcom_files/rolling_comp/IUCN.pdf>.

4.3.2 The potential role of CCH in an ILBI

The adoption of CCH could 'forge a meaningful, logical and necessary link' between an ILBI, the CBD and international efforts to combat climate change.[129] Moreover, the CBD was never intended to stand alone in the biodiversity field.[130] It was 'designed to be complemented by a network of ancillary instruments' focusing on other aspects of biodiversity conservation.[131] Thus, it makes sense for BBNJ to be governed by the same guiding principle as biodiversity within national waters.

The CCH concept could also represent a promising middle ground between proponents of freedom of the seas and those defending the CHM.[132] Arriving at this suggested balanced outcome could be assisted by promoting a renewed sense of, and duty, to cooperate. The CCH concept could underpin this duty in an ILBI, as it implies a legal obligation for the whole community to cooperate in a matter of international concern.[133] Applying CCH to the BBNJ context, the international community would essentially have one right and one duty, the former being a legitimate interest in biodiversity and its MGRs and the latter being a common responsibility to assist in their protection.[134] The CCH concept could therefore act as an anchor in BBNJ negotiations to 'foster a sense of stewardship, collaboration and partnership,'[135] without diminishing the importance of or impinging upon other key principles in the international law of the sea.

The following sections of this chapter will identify potential areas of compromise (Planks of Compromise) for the three pillars of an ABS regime in an effort to secure a balance between the competing interests at play.

4.4 Access—the first pillar of an ABS regime

4.4.1 To regulate, or not to regulate, that is the question

Discussions concerning access have been divisive during the BBNJ process. The main point of contention has been whether access should be regulated and conditions imposed on commercial and non-commercial research.[136] The pure scientific sector accesses MGRs to study the marine environment.[137] The majority of

129 Bowling, Pierson and Ratte (n 116) 1.
130 M.J. Bowman, 'Environmental Protection and the Concept of Common Concern of Humankind' in M. Fitzmaurice, D.M. Ong and P. Merkouris (eds), *Research Handbook on International Environmental Law* (Edward Elgar Publishing, 2010) 494, 504.
131 Ibid.
132 Greiber, 'Possible Way Forward' (n 9) 37
133 Murillo (n 77) 143.
134 Ibid, 141.
135 IUCN Submission (n 128) 3.
136 Morgera (n 41) 4.
137 Kamau (n 35) 25.

these studies are put into the public domain.[138] The R&D sector accesses MGRs 'to unlock their commercial potential.'[139] This sector has a greater interest in keeping its research secret and protecting its inventions through IPRs.[140] BBNJ negotiators need to weigh up the potential impact regulation may have on these two sectors. At the same time, consideration needs to be given to the access disparity that exists between developed and developing States. A range of access models have been proposed during the BBNJ process, some stringent and others light in their regulatory approach. This book argues that a golden middle way between these proposals could be an access model built on compromise.

4.4.1.1 A stringent approach to access

Some BBNJ delegates seek a stringent access model akin to the CBD/Nagoya Protocol.[141] The CBD's ABS regime is built on an equity relationship between Provider States and Users.[142] The Provider State is to facilitate access but has the sovereign right to make access subject to prior informed consent, usually by way of a permit.[143] Access is also subject to mutually agreed terms which attempt to balance the bargaining power between the two parties. The Nagoya Protocol takes matters further by requiring an ABS Agreement which stipulates access and benefit-sharing conditions.[144] Applying this model to the BBNJ context, an ILBI could provide that MGR access requires prior informed consent from an authorised body by way of a permit.[145] This body could process applications and negotiate access terms on a case-by-case basis, including an up-front access fee.[146]

Interestingly, Article 10bis of the Revised Draft Negotiating Text appears to adopt the CBD/Nagoya Protocol model in respect to access to traditional knowledge of indigenous peoples and communities associated with MGRs collected in ABNJ.[147] This provision was inserted in response to calls, particularly

138 Ibid.
139 Ibid.
140 Ibid.
141 See, e.g. Jamaica, 'Submission of the Government of Jamaica on Access and Benefit Sharing Regime for Marine Genetic Resources in Areas beyond National Jurisdiction' (2016) 6 <https://www.un.org/depts/los/biodiversity/prepcom_files/rolling_comp/Jamaica-access_and_benefit_sharing.pdf>.
142 Lyle Glowka, 'Evolving Perspectives on the International Seabed Area's Genetic Resources: Fifteen Years after the "Deepest of Ironies"' in David Vivas (ed), *Law, Technology & Science for Oceans in Globalisation IUU Fishing, Oil Pollution, Bioprospecting, Outer Continental Shelf* (Brill Online Books & Journals 2010) 401 ('Evolving Perspectives').
143 CBD, art 15(2) and (5).
144 Marjo Vierros et al, 'Who Owns the Ocean? Policy Issues Surrounding Marine Genetic Resources' (2016) 25(2) *Association for the Sciences of Limnology and Oceanography* 29, 31.
145 Voigt-Hanssen (n 13) 15.
146 Ibid.
147 *Revised Draft Negotiating Text* (n 47) art 10bis.

from the Pacific Small Island Developing States (PSIDS)[148] and the Alliance of Small Island States (AOSIS),[149] that the interests of indigenous peoples and local communities need to be safeguarded when it comes to accessing traditional and indigenous knowledge associated with MGRs. In its current form, Article 10bis would oblige States Parties to adopt legislative, administrative or policy measures, requiring bioprospectors or researchers to obtain the prior informed consent or approval and involvement of relevant indigenous peoples and local communities in order to access traditional knowledge associated with MGRs in ABNJ. In addition, access to such traditional knowledge would be on mutually agreed terms. While the insertion of Article 10bis is 'a small victory in and of itself,' it will be interesting to see whether this provision makes it into the final text.[150] Currently, the provision is fully bracketed which indicates that there is also support for a 'no text' option.

Other States, however, including Norway, argue that an access regime requiring prior informed consent and mutually agreed terms contained within applications, permits and contracts will be costly and cumbersome.[151] The scientific community has also warned that an overly burdensome regulatory regime is likely to create administrative and financial barriers to R&D and cause a 'research chill.'[152] Stringent access regulations could 'impose undue and unnecessary burdens on the research community at the expense of enhancing knowledge' of BBNJ.[153] Biodiversity research has already been curtailed within national waters as a result of extremely prohibitive ABS regimes.[154] The adoption of the Nagoya

148 See *Textual Proposals Submitted by Delegations for Consideration at IGC 4, in Response to the Invitation by the President of the Conference in Her Note of 18 November 2019*, UN Doc A/CONF.232/2020/3 (15 April 2020) joint textual proposal by Australia, Maldives, New Zealand, Norway, and the Pacific Small Island Developing States, 43 ('Textual Proposals Submitted by Delegations'); Clement Yow Mulalap et al, 'Traditional Knowledge and the BBNJ Instrument' (2020) 122 *Marine Policy* 104103.

149 See *Textual Proposals Submitted by Delegations* (n 148) AOSIS, 2.

150 Vito De Lucia, 'A Very Quick Look at the Revised Draft Text of the New Agreement on Marine Biodiversity in Areas beyond National Jurisdiction' EJIL: Talk! (Blog of the European Journal of International Law, 23 January 2020) <https://www.ejiltalk.org/a-very-quick-look-at-the-revised-draft-text-of-the-new-agreement-on-marine-biodiversity-in-areas-beyond-national-jurisdiction/>.

151 Norway, 'Preparatory Committee established by General Assembly Resolution 69/292: Development of an International Legally Binding Instrument under the United Nations Convention on the Law of the Sea on the Conservation and Sustainable Use of Marine Biological Diversity of Areas beyond National Jurisdiction, Comments by Norway' (December 2016) 2<https://www.un.org/depts/los/biodiversity/prepcom_files/rolling_comp/Norway.pdf>.

152 Bevis Fedder, *Marine Genetic Resources, Access and Benefit Sharing Legal and Biological Perspectives* (Routledge, 2013) 26.

153 Paul Oldham et al, *Valuing the Deep: Marine Genetic Resources in Areas beyond National Jurisdiction* (Technical Report, Department for Environment Food and Rural Affairs, 2014) 29.

154 K.D. Prathapan et al, 'When the Cure Kills—CBD Limits Biodiversity Research' (2018) 360 *Science* 1405, 1405.

Protocol has caused a number of countries to 'tighten their control over genetic resources,' and consequently it is now extremely difficult to obtain an access permit for non-commercial research in South Asia, East Africa and South America.[155] A 2016 survey found that very few commercial ABS agreements have been concluded, with restrictive access procedures a contributing factor.[156]

Moreover, a strict approach will fail to recognise the great risks undertaken by commercial bioprospectors, who fund expeditions without guaranteed returns.[157] An overly strict ABS regime with too many constraints might discourage investors.[158] Arguably, a stringent access approach will also deter maritime States as this bloc is likely to perceive this as a further attempt to erode the Grotian principle and an encroachment on traditional high seas freedoms.

4.4.1.2 A light approach to access

The US, Japan and Russia would prefer an ILBI not to address access to MGRs.[159] These States argue that UNCLOS provides for open access and there is no need for additional rules.[160] Other BBNJ delegates would prefer the MSR community to be given an enhanced role to advise on effective but 'light-touch' access measures.[161] A light approach could involve advance notification of access, with specific reporting obligations.[162] However, this approach, on its own, is unlikely to provide adequate protection for target ecosystems or ensure the sustainable use of MGRs in the long term.

4.4.2 An access model built on compromise

In an attempt to balance competing interests, this book proposes an access model built on compromise. The following sets out the elements of compromise that could underpin this access model under an ILBI. These draw upon elements in

155 Ibid, 1406.

156 Nicholas Pauchard, 'Access and Benefit Sharing under the Convention on Biological Diversity and Its Protocol: What Can Some Numbers Tell Us about the Effectiveness of the Regulatory Regime?' (2017) 6(1) *Resources* 11.

157 'International Seminar on Conservation and Sustainable Use of Marine Biodiversity beyond National Jurisdiction' (Summary Report, German Federal Agency for Nature Conservation and IUCN Environmental Law Centre, 2012) 28 <https://www.bfn.de/fileadmin/ABS/IUCN-BfN_BBNJ_Seminar_Report_-_final.pdf>

158 Ibid.

159 Elisa Morgera et al, 'Summary of the Fourth Session of the Preparatory Committee on Marine Biodiversity beyond Areas of National Jurisdiction: 10–21 July 2017' *Earth Negotiations Bulletin* (Online Bulletin, 24 July 2017) 9 <https://enb.iisd.org/download/pdf/enb25141e.pdf>.

160 Ibid.

161 DOSI, 'Deep-Sea Marine Scientific Research and Genetic Resources in Areas beyond National Jurisdiction', Submission to PrepCom 1 (22 March 2016) 2 <https://www.un.org/depts/los/biodiversity/prepcom_files/DOSI.pdf> ('DOSI').

162 Morgera (n 41) 4.

existing ABS regimes as well as ideas developed by Tvedt and Jørem in 2013 and expanded upon more recently by Broggiato et al.[163]

4.4.2.1 An open access approach

In order to appeal to the interests of maritime States, this book proposes an open access approach to MGRs, subject to prior notification.[164] BBNJ negotiators could draw inspiration from the Obligatory Prior Electronic Notification system proposed by Broggiato et al,[165] or the Antarctic Treaty System's Electronic Information Exchange System (EIES). While Article II of the Antarctic Treaty recognises the 'freedom of scientific investigation' this is not unconditional. For example, Article VII of the Treaty requires States to provide advance notice of 'all expeditions to and within Antarctica, on the part of its ships or nationals, and all expeditions to Antarctica organised in or proceeding from its territory.' Moreover, the collection of biological specimens also requires prior notification.[166] This advance notice is made though a web-based EIES which functions as a central repository of information and enables parties to comply with various reporting requirements.

An ILBI could adopt a similar reporting system requiring collectors, whether they be researchers or bioprospectors, to submit advance notification of their intention to access MGRs in-situ. This notice could be lodged with a centralised database publicly available in an online registry.[167] When lodging the notice, the collector could be obliged to provide a minimum dataset of information (see Appendix 4), essentially building upon existing reporting practices within the MSR community.[168]

Weaving an open access approach through the ABS regime of an ILBI could appeal to proponents of the Grotian doctrine. This approach would guarantee right of access to MGRs for all States which is in keeping with the Grotian tradition. Every State should enjoy and allow others to equally enjoy MGRs in ABNJ, which would also reflect Grotius' vision of 'shared opportunities.'[169] While an obligation to provide advance notification may be perceived as a limitation on high seas freedoms, it is only a modest qualification of the Grotian principle in an attempt to provide adequate conservation measures. An open access approach is also likely to draw support from the scientific community. In a 2016 survey

163 Morten Walløe Tvedt and Ane E. Jørem, 'Bioprospecting in the High Seas: Regulatory Options for Benefit-Sharing' (2013) 16(3–4) *The Journal of World Intellectual Property* 150; Broggiato et al (n 37).

164 See, *Revised Draft Negotiating Text* (n 47) art 10(1).

165 Broggiato et al (n 37) 18–21.

166 ATCM, *Biological Prospecting*, Res 7, ATCM XXVII-CEP VIII (adopted 17 June 2005).

167 Broggiato et al (n 37) 18–21.

168 A.D. Rogers et al, 'Marine Genetic Resources in Areas beyond National Jurisdiction: Promoting Marine Scientific Research and Enabling Equitable Benefit Sharing' (2021) 8 *Frontiers in Marine Science* 667274, 1–22, 17; Oldham et al (n 153) 19.

169 See Chapter 2, Section 2.1.1.4.

conducted by the Deep Ocean Stewardship Initiative (DOSI) a majority of the deep-sea MSR community expressed a desire to have an access model based on notification, rather than authorisation.[170]

4.4.2.2 Environmentally sound access—linking ABS with ABMTs

Developing States have voiced environmental concerns regarding an open access or freedom of the seas approach to MGRs in ABNJ. In order to address these concerns and to ensure environmentally sound access conditions, an ABS regime should be linked to other elements of the BBNJ package deal. For example, an EIA should be required if the MGR activity has the potential to cause significant adverse impacts to BBNJ.[171] An ILBI could provide a screening stage to trigger an EIA.[172] Potential triggers could include sampling at VMEs, the use of destructive equipment or the need for large collections of biomass.[173]

The EIA procedure under the Madrid Protocol could serve as a template as it provides a three-tier screening process based on the level of impact of a proposed activity. For example, if an activity is likely to have more than a minor or transitory impact, a Comprehensive Environmental Evaluation (CEE) is required. The CEE considers impacts, alternatives, mitigation measures and gaps in knowledge or uncertainties. After being circulated to all Contracting Parties, the CEE is reviewed by the Committee for Environmental Protection to the Antarctic Treaty which provides advice to the Antarctic Treaty Consultative Meeting to assist in making the final decision on whether the activity should proceed.[174]

An authorised body could be tasked with overseeing similar EIA obligations under an ILBI. Humphries et al suggest the establishment of an ABNJ Activity Notification Monitoring System which could offer researchers 'a one-stop shop' for determining whether their activities trigger EIA and other obligations under an ILBI.[175] For instance, stricter access conditions could be imposed in high seas MPAs designated under the instrument.[176]

To further strengthen an open access approach, a Code of Conduct could be formulated and incorporated into an ILBI for MGR collection and sampling.[177]

170 DOSI (n 161) annex ('*DOSI Deep-Sea Genetic Resources Survey: Summary of Results and Observations*') 4.
171 DOSI, 'Considerations Regarding Deep-Sea Marine Scientific Research in Areas beyond National Jurisdiction: Submission' (1 September 2016) <https://www.un.org/depts/los/biodiversity/prepcom_files/DOSI_2.pdf>.
172 Broggiato et al (n 37) 20–21.
173 Ibid; Kamau (n 35) 26.
174 Elisabeth Druel, 'Environmental Impact Assessments in Areas beyond National Jurisdiction' (Study No. 01/13, IDDRI, January 2013) 22.
175 Fran Humphries et al, 'A Tiered Approach to the Marine Genetic Resource Governance Framework under the Proposed UNCLOS Agreement for Biodiversity beyond National Jurisdiction' (2020) 122 *Marine Policy* 103910, 4.
176 Voigt-Hanssen (n 13) 17.
177 See *Revised Draft Negotiating Text* (n 47) art 13(1).

Such a Code of Conduct should aim to mitigate environmental impacts of MGR activities, set data recording standards and maximise use of samples to avoid unnecessary re-sampling, particularly at VMEs.[178]

4.4.2.3 A common pool approach to ex-situ MGRs

While an open access approach is likely to appeal to maritime States, it will not assist those States that lack the necessary means to undertake MGR activities in-situ. Thus, as a potential trade-off, an ILBI should provide facilitated access to a common pool of ex-situ MGRs. In-situ access could be made conditional on the collector depositing samples, data or a certain quantity of biological material in a common ex-situ collection.[179] This is likely to appeal to developing States and the MSR community as it would ensure equal levels of opportunity.[180] As Jaspars argues:

> if everybody has the ability to exploit equally, then a system based on an open access or common domain approach will lead to greater fairness and also development of those resources in countries that would not normally have access to them.[181]

An obligation to deposit data or samples into the public domain also accords with current practice within the MSR community.[182] Most publicly funded research places obligations on researchers to deposit taxonomic and genetic discoveries in open access bioinformatic databases,[183] thereby enabling further engagement by scientists in developing countries.

In adopting a common domain approach, an ILBI could follow the model in the International Treaty on Plant Genetic Resources for Food and Agriculture (ITPGRFA).[184] The ITPGRFA employs a multilateral system (MLS) of ABS that

178 DOSI (n 161) annex (‘*DOSI Deep-Sea Genetic Resources Survey: Summary of Results and Observations*’) 4. See, e.g. InterRidge Statement of Commitment to Responsible Research Practices at Deep-Sea Hydrothermal Vents.

179 Tvedt and Jørem (n 163) 153.

180 Broggiato et al (n 37) 21.

181 Centre for International Law, University of Singapore, ‘Conservation and Sustainable Use of Marine Biological Diversity of Areas beyond National Jurisdiction: Preparing for the PrepCom’ (Report of the BBNJ Workshop of the Centre for International Law, National University of Singapore, February 2016) 50 <https://cil.nus.edu.sg/publication/workshop-report-conservation-and-sustainable-use-of-marine-biological-diversity-of-areas-beyond-national-jurisdiction-preparing-for-the-prepcom/> (‘Centre for International Law’).

182 Broggiato et al (n 37) 21.

183 Key databases include the World Register of Marine Species, OBIS, International Nucleotide Sequence Database Collaboration Group, Encyclopaedia of Life and GenBank.

184 International Treaty on Plant Genetic Resources for Food and Agriculture, opened for signature on 3 November 2001, 2400 UNTS 303 (entered into force on 29 June 2004) (ITPGRFA).

ensures facilitated access to a common pool of germplasm from 64 designated food and forage crops for research, breeding, conservation and training.[185] Access is conditional on signing a Standard Material Transfer Agreement (SMTA) which sets out fixed terms and conditions on access and utilisation. The SMTA enables the legal obligations of the ITPGRFA to be passed on to subsequent recipients of the MLS resource, by way of a contractual nexus.[186] To facilitate ex-situ access under an ILBI, a user could be required to sign an SMTA with fixed terms and conditions regarding access and utilisation of the MGR, including benefit-sharing obligations.

4.5 Benefit-sharing—the second pillar of an ABS regime

4.5.1 A stringent approach to benefit-sharing

Conscious of missing out on potential benefits, developing States would prefer a stringent approach to benefit-sharing. This could entail mandatory monetary benefit-sharing in the form of access fees, milestone payments and royalties linked to commercialisation.[187] However, developed States caution against such an interventionist approach and are particularly reluctant to see the imposition of monetary benefit-sharing obligations, particularly ones that target R&D.[188] Greiber argues that some payment types are also not practical in the BBNJ context, as they will require a complex and potentially costly institutional and administrative structure.[189]

Arguably, too much emphasis has been placed on potential monetary benefits from MGRs. BBNJ negotiators need to consider that only seven commercial products derived from MGRs are currently on the market, including one from a species found both within and beyond national jurisdiction.[190] Moreover, no single authoritative valuation of MGRs has been undertaken.[191] Thus, there is

> little evidence of the proverbial pot of gold said to be waiting to be discovered in the biodiversity of the deep sea. There may well be a few specks of gold, but as yet no hard or substantiated evidence of great riches.[192]

185 ITPGRFA, annex I.

186 Petra Drankier et al, 'Marine Genetic Resources in Areas beyond National Jurisdiction: Access and Benefit-Sharing' (2012) 27 *The International Journal of Marine and Coastal Law* 375, 381.

187 *Chair's Non-Paper* (n 36) 28–29.

188 See, e.g. Kantai et al, 'Summary of IGC 2' (n 48) 4.

189 Thomas Greiber, 'Types of Benefits and Benefit-Sharing' (Information Paper 1, IUCN, May 2013) 31–32 ('Types of Benefits').

190 Voigt-Hanssen (n 13) 13.

191 Oldham et al (n 153) 197.

192 Leary and Juniper (n 50) 773–774.

Leary has compared the situation to the phenomena of fake news in the era of the Trump Presidency.[193] Leary explains:

> Certain 'alternate facts' relating to the level and extent of commercial interest in MGRs in ABNJ have repeatedly been asserted loud enough and often enough that they have now come to be accepted as fact, even though the supporting evidence for these claims is woefully lacking. The alternate facts are the repeated assertions that there is huge industry interest in the commercialisation of MGR from ABNJ; that numerous products are already on the market ... and that massive profits are already being reaped by developed State companies.[194]

That said, this situation could change in the future. BBNJ negotiators should therefore devise a modern and flexible benefit-sharing model which works practically today and paves the way for a future increase in monetary benefits.[195]

4.5.2 A light approach to benefit-sharing

A light approach to benefit-sharing would focus solely on non-monetary benefits, like Part XIII of UNCLOS. Pursuant to Part XIII, States and competent international organisations are required to:

- Promote MSR cooperation (Article 242(1));
- Publicise and disseminate information on proposed major research programmes and knowledge resulting from MSR (Article 244(1));
- Actively promote the flow of scientific data and strengthen the MSR capabilities of developing States through educational programmes and training of their technical and scientific personnel (Article 244(2)).

While a light approach is likely to appeal to a key bloc of developed (maritime) States, developing States seek rules that will ensure they share in any and all types of benefits. On this basis, Part XIII is deficient in several respects.

First, it lacks the necessary implementing regulations to 'concretise the broad benefit-sharing obligations and support their operationalisation.'[196] Second, MSR and bioprospecting are usually not considered to be the same activity (even if both are difficult to distinguish in practice). Third, Part XIII is limited to non-monetary benefits and distinguishes between MSR conducted in the Area and that undertaken on the high seas.[197] Lastly, Part XIII has been criticised for not providing legal certainty in respect to IPRs.[198] There is broad acceptance that an

193 Leary, 'Agreeing to Disagree' (n 53) 22.
194 Ibid.
195 Voigt-Hanssen (n 13) 23.
196 Greiber, 'Types of Benefits' (n 189) 35.
197 UNCLOS, arts 87, 256 and 257.
198 Greiber, 'Types of Benefits' (n 189) 35.

ABS regime should work within the existing IP framework.[199] A controversial question is whether an ILBI should allow for the appropriation of innovations developed from MGRs via patents or other IPRs.[200] Some BBNJ delegates suggest that an ILBI should prohibit the exercise of IPRs where this would limit MGR access.[201] Article 241 of UNCLOS is used to support this argument.

Article 241 provides that MSR 'activities shall not constitute the legal basis for any claim' to the marine environment or its resources. As patents offer exclusive rights of use and exploitation for the period of protection, some commentators argue that IPRs are contrary to Article 241.[202] However, a patent is granted for new and useful inventions.[203] As naturally occurring elements, MGRs are not invented but discovered.[204] A patent does not grant any right to the natural resource on which an invention is based, nor does it grant any kind of ownership right to the patent holder.[205] MGRs should therefore not be considered IP. To be covered by a patent, an MGR would need to be artificially modified and meet the 'patentability requirements of novelty, inventive step and industrial application.'[206] On this basis, IPRs are not necessarily contrary to Article 241 or to the act of benefit-sharing. Patents actually promote disclosure as they are published, which accords with UNCLOS objectives of dissemination of knowledge and access to information.[207] They also constitute a key incentive behind R&D. Thus, rather than attempting to prohibit IPRs, BBNJ negotiators should seek 'to maintain the incentives created by the patent system while balancing global interests in benefit-sharing.'[208] The following planks of compromise may assist in striking the right balance and could underpin a benefit-sharing model under an ILBI.

4.5.3 A benefit-sharing model built on compromise

To secure the support of both maritime States and the R&D sector, monetary benefits should be shared in the event of commercial utilisation, like the ITPGRFA. When a product is developed using an MLS resource under the

199 Australia, 'Preparatory Committee on Conservation and Sustainable Use of Marine Biological Diversity of Areas beyond National Jurisdiction (BBNJ): Submission by Australia' (6 December 2016) 4<https://www.un.org/depts/los/biodiversity/prepcom_files/rolling_comp/Australia.pdf>. At the international level, two fora are relevant, the World Intellectual Property Organization and the World Trade Organization.

200 Fran Humphries, Muriel Rabone and Marcel Jaspars, 'Traceability Approaches for Marine Genetic Resources under the Proposed Ocean (BBNJ) Treaty' (2021) *Frontiers in Marine Science* 661313, 1–21, 5 ('Traceability Approaches'); Correa (n 25) 167.

201 *Chair's Streamlined Non-Paper* (n 18) 19.

202 Drankier et al (n 186) 396.

203 Heafey (n 72) 510.

204 Ibid.

205 Ibid.

206 Centre for International Law (n 181) 52.

207 Heafey (n 72) 509–510.

208 Ibid, 512.

ITPGRFA, an equitable share of the resulting monetary benefits (1.1 per cent of product sales) is paid into an International Benefit-sharing Fund.[209] An ILBI could adopt a similar approach and provide for a royalty payment to be made to a BBNJ Contribution Fund. Tvedt and Jørem suggest 'a trigger point closer to actual commercialisation to encourage innovation.'[210] This could be when product revenues exceed a particular sum or when the product has been on the market for a certain period.[211] In terms of the royalty payment, a predetermined and fixed percentage would be preferable to give investors a solid basis for making investment decisions on MGR exploitation.[212] A lower percentage rate may be appropriate due to the expense and difficulties of travelling to and operating in ABNJ.[213]

While a common domain approach to ex-situ MGRs could provide an important source of non-monetary benefit-sharing under an ILBI, it may not appeal to the commercial sector as they consider this information to be business-sensitive.[214] A way to circumvent this issue could be via an embargo period.[215] An embargo option would enable a collector to keep material and data private for a certain period to enable them to:

(i) Publish research results confidentially;
(ii) Advance their research;
(iii) Apply for IPRs.[216]

Broggiato et al suggest the embargo period should be reasonable to 'secure biodiscovery investments' but not free the collector from their benefit-sharing obligations.[217] A collector could also be provided with the option to extend the embargo period via an exclusivity fee payable to a BBNJ Contribution Fund.[218]

To further safeguard the interests of the R&D sector, an ILBI could provide for a commercial developer to retain the bulk of the profits made on a product based on resources derived from the common pool; however, the developer could also be required to pay royalties to the collector who originally extracted the relevant MGR.[219] This would reward the collector and provide an important incentive to exchange information under the ABS regime.[220]

209 ITPGRFA, art 13(2)(d) and Standard Material Transfer Agreement, art 6.7 and annex 2(1).
210 Tvedt and Jørem (n 163) 153.
211 Ibid, 154.
212 Ibid, 153; Broggiato et al (n 37) 10.
213 Humphries et al (n 175) 4.
214 Voigt-Hanssen (n 13) 17. See, also, *Revised Draft Negotiating Text* (n 47) art 11(3)(a).
215 Broggiato et al (n 37) 8.
216 Ibid.
217 Ibid, 22.
218 Ibid, 28; Battle and Currie (n 49) 8.
219 Greiber, 'Possible Way Forward' (n 9) 39–40.
220 Ibid.

In an attempt to address the uneven research capabilities between States and foster MSR cooperation, an ABS regime could incorporate CBTT initiatives based on Part XIV of UNCLOS. For example, Article 269 calls for the exchange of scientists. Taxonomy is one key area that would benefit from the exchange of specialist knowledge. Moreover, new approaches such as microbial metagenomics require sophisticated bioinformatics tools and training that are generally not accessible to developing States.[221] Taxonomic and biological research would therefore benefit from the streamlining of access to a common pool of MGRs under an ILBI. This research could open up new discoveries of species and ecosystem services and also shed light on new conservation measures for BBNJ.[222]

4.6 Monitoring and compliance—the third pillar of an ABS regime

4.6.1 A choice of institutions

Monitoring and compliance concern two key issues. First, what body should oversee potential breaches of ABS provisions under an ILBI? And, second, how should MGR use be monitored to ensure compliance? In other words, what is the best method to track and trace? A genetic resource can be passed on to multiple users and change its nature along the R&D chain.[223] This can complicate tracking and monitoring and hence compliance and enforcement.

4.6.1.1 Extending an existing mandate

The growing interest in MGRs warrants the establishment of an institutional mechanism to manage ABS under an ILBI.[224] While there is general consensus on this point, there is considerable disagreement on the form, scope and mandate of this institution.[225] Rather than creating a new bureaucracy, some delegates suggest taking a pragmatic approach by simply expanding the mandate of an existing international structure.[226]

The ISA is therefore seen as a viable option. The ISA is already tasked with the management and control of the Area, including handling access applications for exploration of mineral resources; the adoption of rules, regulations and procedures to protect and preserve the marine environment; the

221 Juniper (n 51) 17.

222 Adrian G. Glover et al, 'Managing a Sustainable Deep-Sea "Blue Economy" Requires Knowledge of What Actually Lives There' (2018) 7 *eLife* 1–7, 4.

223 Kamau (n 35) 27.

224 Espenilla (n 15) 6.

225 Ibid.

226 Fernanda Millicay, 'A Legal Regime for the Biodiversity of the Area' in Myron H. Nordquist (ed), *Law, Science and Ocean Management* (Martinus Nijhoff Publishers, 2007) 739, 819–820.

promotion of MSR and the collection and dissemination of research results.[227] The ISA has also incorporated modern governance principles and approaches in its mining regime, including the ecosystem approach. Arguably, a truly integrated ecosystem approach to the seabed requires one institution to oversee the protection of BBNJ from all activities. As mineral resources and MGRs are often intrinsically linked at deep-sea ecosystems, there should be some coherence between the ISA's mining regime and an ABS scheme to avoid regulatory conflicts.[228]

However, the ISA's structure may not be suitable for MGRs, as it was tailored to suit the regulation of non-renewable bulk commodities.[229] Although the ISA has the mandate to distribute wealth generated from mineral resources, it is unclear whether it would be able to manage an MGR benefit-sharing mechanism.[230] Regulating both activities might quickly outrun the ISA's capacities,[231] particularly as it has not yet developed rules or procedures for equitable benefit-sharing and its ability to distribute wealth remains untested.[232] Expanding the ISA's mandate might also be interpreted as bringing MGR regulation too close to the CHM concept and provoke strong objections from developed (maritime) States.[233]

4.6.2 A new body

As the ISA comes with 'ideologically controversial baggage'[234] it does not represent 'a real compromise solution.'[235] Accordingly, a new body or organisation should be established under an ILBI to undertake monitoring and compliance functions.

4.6.2.1 A compliance system built on notification and traceability

A new body could establish a centralised compliance system to oversee ABS obligations. This could provide a cost-effective way to track and trace, as trust will be placed in collectors to report certain milestones.[236] States would be responsible for ensuring that persons/companies/vessels under their jurisdiction comply with the ILBI's ABS provisions. Failure to abide by such conditions should be reported to the relevant State to impose penalties.[237]

227 Espenilla (n 15) 6.
228 Voigt-Hanssen (n 13) 16.
229 Ibid, 7.
230 Heafey (n 72) 519
231 Fedder (n 152) 153–154.
232 Heafey (n 72) 519.
233 See Chapter 2, Section 2.3.3.
234 Tvedt and Jørem (n 163) 161.
235 Greiber, 'Possible Way Forward' (n 9) 30.
236 Broggiato et al (n 37) 30.
237 Ibid, 31.

The Group of Pacific Small Island States has stressed the importance of the traceability of MGRs and has called for a universal tracking system.[238] One option is for MGRs to be uniquely identified using an alphanumeric identifier or electronic tag.[239] This could remain with the MGR for life, offering a method to track and trace its subsequent use(s) and location(s).[240] As samples taken from ABNJ may contain millions of organisms and could take weeks to years to analyse, Humphries et al suggest that it may be more appropriate to initially use 'bulk collection identifiers.'[241] This could store provenance information for the MGR until such time as a unique identifier could be allocated.[242]

Setting up a tracking system under an ILBI should not be difficult with tools now available through advanced computer programmes and the internet. Jaspars and Brown note that there is already 'existing technology through Global Positioning System data and use of digital object identifiers that would render tracing the journey of MGR along the scientific and commercial supply chain as both possible and best practice.'[243] Inspiration could also be drawn from national models,[244] or the Pandemic Influenza Preparedness Framework's Influenza Virus Traceability Mechanism that records the movement of H5N1 and other influenza viruses between laboratories that conduct virus surveillance and assess pandemic risks and measures.[245]

4.6.2.2 Management of contribution fund and other relevant tasks

A new body could also oversee an ABS clearing-house modelled on the Nagoya Protocol, which enhances legal certainty on ABS procedures and monitors the utilisation of genetic resources along the R&D chain.[246] Under an ILBI, a clearing-house mechanism could act as a central repository for MGR samples and tasked with holding BBNJ-related data.[247] A clearing-house website could also facilitate the exchange of information on access to samples, data and CBTT.[248]

238 Permanent Mission of the Republic of Nauru to the United Nations, 'PSIDS Submission to the Second Meeting of the Preparatory Committee for the Development of an International Legally Binding Instrument under the United Nations Convention on the Law of the Sea on the Conservation and Sustainable Use of Marine Biological Diversity of Areas beyond National Jurisdiction (BBNJ PrepCom)' (29 August 2016) <https://www.un.org/depts/los/biodiversity/prepcom_files/PSIDS_Submission_BBNJ.pdf>.
239 *President's Aid to Discussions* (n 56) art 13.3(b); Rogers et al (n 168) 17.
240 Broggiato et al (n 37) 19.
241 Humphries et al (n 175) 5.
242 Ibid.
243 Jaspars and Brown (n 35) 124.
244 See, e.g. Brazil's online electronic registration system 'SisGen' <https://sisgen.gov.br/paginas/login.aspx>.
245 Humphries et al (n 175) 4; Humphries et al, 'Traceability Approaches' (n 200) 10.
246 CBD Secretariat, 'The ABS Clearing-House', Convention on Biological Diversity (Website, 7 June 2020) <https://www.cbd.int/abs/theabsch.shtml>.
247 Espenilla (n 15) 7.
248 *Chair's Streamlined Non-Paper* (n 18) 49.

4.7 Conclusion

As only a small portion of ABNJ have been investigated in any great detail,[249] the potential discovery of new species, genes and adaptations will continue to fuel interest in MGRs in the coming decades. For this reason, it is imperative that BBNJ negotiators formulate a flexible, efficient and effective ABS regime. This ABS regime will need to balance a number of competing interests. First, it will need to contribute to the realisation of a just and equitable international economic order by taking into account the needs of developing States. Second, it will need to protect rather than hinder MSR. Third, it will need to offer potential benefits to those players who currently lead the R&D sector in MGRs.[250]

This chapter has exposed the layers of complex legal and policy issues facing BBNJ negotiators and the highly entrenched positions that have been adopted during the BBNJ process. If delegations continue to retreat to 'traditional trench warfare positions,'[251] little or no progress can be expected. It would be unfortunate if differing ideological commitments prevented the conclusion of an ILBI.[252] In an attempt to move MGR discussions forward, this chapter has argued that an ABS regime will need to be underpinned by a set of micro and macro compromises.

The CCH concept could provide a rationale legal foundation for the conservation and sustainable use of BBNJ including MGRs, by bridging the gap between freedom of the seas and CHM. Such a golden middle way needs to be found for the three pillars of an ABS regime. In respect to access, an open access approach could appeal to maritime States and overcome fears of further erosion of the Grotian doctrine. This could be underpinned by key compromises, including the provision of advance notice and benefit-sharing obligations. Maritime States, the R&D sector and the deep-sea MSR community are unlikely to agree to a stringent approach to benefit-sharing and a light approach will not address the equity concerns of developing States. Between these two extremes, a benefit-sharing model could be built on compromise. Access could trigger certain benefit-sharing obligations including the sharing of MGRs to a common domain. Accessible collections can promote sustainable use and encourage research and innovation.[253] A common domain approach could be coupled with an embargo option to sustain the biodiscovery pipeline. In respect to monitoring and compliance, this chapter argues for the establishment of a new body to oversee a compliance system centred around reporting obligations. Maritime States are unlikely to agree to an extension to the ISA's mandate given its close affiliation with the CHM principle.[254]

249 E. Ramirez-Llodra et al, 'Deep, Diverse and Definitely Different: Unique Attributes of the World's Largest Ecosystem' (2010) 7 *Biogeosciences* 2851, 2852.
250 Greiber, 'Common Pools' (n 2) 408.
251 Leary and Juniper (n 50) 785.
252 Leary, 'Agreeing to Disagree' (n 53) 24.
253 Tvedt and Jørem (n 163) 160.
254 See Chapter 2, Section 2.3.3.

The elements of compromise identified in this chapter represent potential trade-offs that could be made in an attempt to balance the competing interests at play. These elements could hold the key to building a bridge between these competing positions and at the same time serve as a way to weave elements of the Grotian tradition through an ILBI text to secure the support of a key bloc of developed (maritime) States. Overall, the planks of compromise identified in this chapter could assist in developing an effective ABS regime that achieves the equitable and efficient utilisation of an ocean resource while also attempting to secure universal acceptance of the ILBI.

References

Argentina, 'Written Submission to the Preparatory Committee established by the United Nations General Assembly Resolution 69/292' (2017) (Unofficial courtesy translation) <https://www.un.org/depts/los/biodiversity/prepcom_files/streamlined/Argentina_unofficial_courtesy_translation.pdf>.

Aristotle and H. Rackman (eds), *The Nicomachean Ethics* (Harvard University Press, 2nd ed, 1934) vol 73.

Arnaud-Haond, Sophie, Jesus M. Arrieta and Carlos M. Duarte, 'Marine Biodiversity and Gene Patents' (25 March 2011) 331 *Science* 1521–1522. DOI: 10.1126/science.1200783.

ATCM, *Biological Prospecting, Res 7*, ATCM XXVII-CEP VIII (adopted 17 June 2005).

Australia, 'Preparatory Committee on Conservation and Sustainable Use of Marine Biological Diversity of Areas beyond National Jurisdiction (BBNJ): Submission by Australia' (6 December 2016) ('Written submission of Australia to PrepCom', 6 December 2016) <https://www.un.org/depts/los/biodiversity/prepcom_files/rolling_comp/Australia.pdf> accessed 31 March 2022.

Battle, Jessica and Duncan Currie, 'Some Critical Issues to be Resolved on Marine Genetic Resources in the Context of the Marine Biological Diversity Preparatory Committee Discussions' (Discussion Paper, WWF International, March 2016).

Blasiak, Robert, Jean-Baptiste Jouffray, Colette C.C. Wabnitz, Emma Sundström, Henrik Österblom, 'Corporate Control and Global Governance of Marine Genetic Resources' (2018) 4 *Sciences Advances* 1–7. DOI: 10.1126/sciadv.aar5237.

Bowling, Chelsea, Elizabeth Pierson and Stephanie Ratte, 'The Common Concern of Humankind: A Potential Framework for a New International Legally Binding Instrument on the Conservation and Sustainable Use of Marine Biological Diversity in the High Seas' Communication to the Preparatory Committee established by the United Nations General Assembly Resolution 69/292 (2016) <http://www.un.org/depts/los/biodiversity/prepcom_files/BowlingPiersonandRatte_Common_Concern.pdf> accessed 31 March 2022.

Bowman, M. J, 'Environmental Protection and the Concept of Common Concern of Humankind' in M Fitzmaurice, D M Ong and P Merkouris (eds), *Research Handbook on International Environmental Law* (Edward Elgar Publishing, 2010) 494. DOI: https://doi.org/10.4337/9781849807265.00036.

Boyd, Robynne, et al, 'Summary of the Eighth Meeting of the Open-ended Informal Consultative Process on Oceans and the Law of the Sea: 25 to 29 June 2007' *Earth Negotiations Bulletin* (Online Bulletin, 2 July 2007) <https://enb.iisd.org/download/pdf/enb2543e.pdf> accessed 31 March 2022.

Broggiato, Arianna, Sophie Arnaud-Haond, Caludio Chiarolla, Thomas Greiber, 'Fair and Equitable Sharing of Benefits from the Utilization of Marine Genetic Resources in Areas Beyond National Jurisdiction: Bridging the Gaps between Science and Policy' (2014) 49 *Marine Policy* 176–185. DOI: 10.1016/j.marpol.2014.02.012.

Broggiato, Arianna, Thomas Vanagt, Laura E. Lallier, Marcel Jaspars, Geoff Burton and Dominic Muyldermans, 'Mare Geneticum: Balancing Governance of Marine Genetic Resources in International Waters' (2018) 33 *The International Journal of Marine and Coastal Law* 3–33. DOI: 10.1163/15718085-13310030.

Buxton, Carol R, 'Property in Outer Space: The Common Heritage of Mankind Principle vs. the First in Time First in Right, Rule of Property' (2004) 69(4) *Journal of Air Law and Commerce* 689–707.

Castillo-Winckels, Nadia Sanchez, 'Why "Common Concern of Humankind" Should Return to the Work of the International Law Commission on the Atmosphere' (2016) 29(1) *Georgetown Environmental Law Review* 131–151.

CBD, 'The ABS Clearing-House', Convention on Biological Diversity (Website, 7 June 2020) <https://www.cbd.int/abs/theabsch.shtml> accessed 31 March 2022.

Centre for International Law, University of Singapore, 'Conservation and Sustainable Use of Marine Biological Diversity of Areas Beyond National Jurisdiction: Preparing for the PrepCom' (*Report of the BBNJ Workshop of the Centre for International Law, National University of Singapore*, February 2016) <https://cil.nus.edu.sg/wp-content/uploads/2015/10/CIL-report-of-BBNJ-workshop-21-March-2016-final-2.pdf> accessed 31 March 2022.

Chair's non-paper on Elements of a Draft Text of an International Legally-binding Instrument under the United Nations Convention on the Law of the Sea on the Conservation and Sustainable Use of Marine Biological Diversity of Areas Beyond National Jurisdiction Third Session of the PrepCom (27 March–7 April 2017) (28 February 2017) <https://www.un.org/Depts/los/biodiversity/prepcom_files/Chair_non_paper.pdf> accessed 31 March 2022.

Chair's Streamlined non-paper on Elements of a Draft Text of an International Legally-binding Instrument under the United Nations Convention on the Law of the Sea on the Conservation and Sustainable Use of Marine Biological Diversity of Areas Beyond National Jurisdiction Fourth Session of the PrepCom (10–21 July 2017) <https://www.un.org/depts/los/biodiversity/prepcom_files/Chairs_streamlined_non-paper_to_delegations.pdf> accessed 31 March 2022.

Cohen, Harlan, 'Ensuring Conservation and Sustainable Use of Marine Genetic Resources: Current and Future Challenges' (Conference Paper, United Nations Open-ended Informal Consultative Process, Eighth Meeting, 27 June 2007) <https://www.un.org/depts/los/consultative_process/documents/8_cohen.pdf> accessed 31 March 2022.

Convention on Biological Diversity, opened for signature 5 June 1992 (1992) 1760 *UNTS* 143 (entered into force 29 December 1993) (CBD).

Correa, Carlos M, 'Access to and Benefit-Sharing of Marine Genetic Resources Beyond National Jurisdiction: Developing a New Legally Binding Instrument' in Charles R. McManis and Burton Ong (eds), *Routledge Handbook of Biodiversity and the Law* (Routledge, 2017) 157. DOI: 10.4324/9781315530857-11.

Cunningham, Stanley B, 'Getting It Right: Aristotle's "Golden Mean" as Theory Deterioration' (1999) 14(1) *Journal of Mass Media Ethics* 5–15. DOI: 10.1207/S15327728JM140101.

Declaration of Principles Governing the Sea-Bed and the Ocean Floor, and the Subsoil Thereof, beyond the Limits of National Jurisdiction, GA 2749 (XXV) UN Doc A/RES/2749(XXV) (17 December 1970).

De Lucia, Vito, 'A Very Quick Look at the Revised Draft Text of the New Agreement on Marine Biodiversity in Areas Beyond National Jurisdiction' *EJIL: Talk! Blog* (Blog of the European Journal of International Law, 23 January 2020) <https://www.ejiltalk.org/a-very-quick-look-at-the-revised-draft-text-of-the-new-agreement-on-marine-biodiversity-in-areas-beyond-national-jurisdiction/> accessed 31 March 2022.

DOSI, 'Deep-Sea Marine Scientific Research and Genetic Resources in Areas Beyond National Jurisdiction: Submission by the Deep Ocean Stewardship Initiative Working Group on Deep-Sea Genetic Resources, to the first Preparatory Committee Meeting for the Development of an International Legally-binding Instrument on the Conservation and Sustainable Use of Marine Biological Diversity in Areas Beyond National Jurisdiction, under the United Nations Convention on the Law of the Sea' (22 March 2016a) <https://www.un.org/depts/los/biodiversity/prepcom_files/DOSI.pdf> accessed 31 March 2022

DOSI, 'Considerations regarding Deep-Sea Marine Scientific Research in Areas Beyond National Jurisdiction: Submission' (1 September 2016b) <https://www.un.org/depts/los/biodiversity/prepcom_files/DOSI_2.pdf> accessed 31 March 2022.

Drankier, Petra, Alex G. Oude Elferink, Bert Visser and Tamara Takács, 'Marine Genetic Resources in Areas Beyond National Jurisdiction: Access and Benefit-Sharing' (2012) 27 *The International Journal of Marine and Coastal Law* 375–433. DOI: 10.1163/157180812X637984.

Druel, Elisabeth, 'Environmental Impact Assessments in Areas Beyond National Jurisdiction' (Study No. 01/13, IDDRI, January 2013).

Eritrea, 'Development of an International Legally Binding Instrument under the United Nations Convention on the Law of the Sea on the Conservation and Sustainable Use of Marine Biological Diversity of Areas beyond National Jurisdiction: Submission Paper from the State of Eritrea' (26 April 2017) (Written submission of Eritrea to PrepCom', 26 April 2017) <https://www.un.org/depts/los/biodiversity/prepcom_files/streamlined/Eritrea.pdf> accessed 31 March 2022.

Espenilla, Jacqueline Joyce, 'Access, Conservation and Sustainable Use of Marine Genetic Resources in Areas Beyond National Jurisdiction: Emerging Issues of Consensus and Contention' (2016) *Columbia Journal of Environmental Law* [Field Report] 1–7.

European Union, 'Development of an International Legally Binding Instrument under UNCLOS on the Conservation and Sustainable Use of Marine Biological Diversity of Areas beyond National Jurisdiction (BBNJ Process), Written Submission of the EU and Its Member States: Marine Genetic Resources, Including Questions on the Sharing of Benefits' (22 February 2017) ('Written submission of EU and its Member States to PrepCom: Marine Genetic Resources, including questions on the sharing of benefits', 22 February 2017) <https://www.un.org/depts/los/biodiversity/prepcom_files/rolling_comp/EU_Written_Submission_on_Marine_Genetic_Resources.pdf> accessed 31 March 2022.

Fedder, Bevis, *Marine Genetic Resources, Access and Benefit Sharing Legal and Biological Perspectives* (Routledge, 2013).

Frakes, Jennifer, 'The Common Heritage of Mankind Principle and the Deep Seabed, Outer Space, and Antarctica: Will Developed and Developing Nations Reach a Compromise?' (2003) 21(2) *Wisconsin International Law Journal* 409–434.

Franklin, Benjamin, 'Constitutional Convention Debate' (Speech, 30 June 1787) in E.H. Scott (ed), *Journal of the Federal Convention Kept by James Madison*; Reprinted from the Edition of 1840 (Albert, Scott & Co, 1893) 278.

French, Duncan, 'Common Concern, Common Heritage and Other Global(-ising) Concepts: Rhetorical Devices, Legal Principles or a Fundamental Challenge?' in Michael Bowman, Peter Davies and Edward Goodwin (eds), *Research Handbook on Biodiversity and Law* (Edward Elgar Publishing, 2016) 334. DOI: https://doi.org/10.4337/9781781004791.00021.

Friedmann, Wolfgang, 'United States Policy and the Crisis of International Law: Some Reflections on the State of International Law' (1965) 59(4) *The American Journal of International Law* 857–871. DOI: 10.2307/2197096.

Gabcíkovo-Nagymaros Project (Hungary v. Slovakia) (1997) *ICJ Rep* 7.

Glover, Adrian G, Helena Wiklund, Chong Chen and Thomas G. Dahlgren, 'Managing a Sustainable Deep-sea 'Blue Economy' Requires Knowledge of What Actually Lives There' (2018) 7 *eLife* e41319: 1-7. DOI: 10.7554/eLife.41319.

Glowka, Lyle, 'The Deepest of Ironies: Genetic Resources, Marine Scientific Research, and the Area' (1996) 12 *Ocean Yearbook* 154–178. DOI: 10.1163/221160096X00111.

Glowka, Lyle, 'Evolving Perspectives on the International Seabed Area's Genetic Resources: Fifteen Years after the 'Deepest of Ironies'' in David Vivas (ed), *Law, Technology & Science for Oceans in Globalisation IUU Fishing, Oil Pollution, Bioprospecting, Outer Continental Shelf* (Brill Online Books & Journals 2010) 401. DOI: https://doi.org/10.1163/ej.9789004180406.i-610.132.

Greiber, Thomas, *Access and Benefit Sharing in Relation to Marine Genetic Resources from Areas Beyond National Jurisdiction: A Possible Way Forward* (Research Project, Federal Agency for Nature Conservation, 2011).

Greiber, Thomas, 'Common Pools for Marine Genetic Resources: A Possible Instrument for a Future Multilateral Agreement Addressing Marine Biodiversity in Areas Beyond National Jurisdiction' in Evanson Chege Kamau and Gerd Winter (eds), *Common Pools of Genetic Resources: Equity and Innovation in International Biodiversity Law* (Routledge, 2013a) 399.

Greiber, Thomas, 'Meaning and Scope' in *IUCN Environmental Law Centre, Information Papers for the Intersessional Workshop on Marine Genetic Resources 2–3 May 2013* (Information Paper 1, IUCN, May 2013b) <https://www.un.org/Depts/los/biodiversityworkinggroup/documents/IUCN%20Information%20Papers%20for%20BBNJ%20Intersessional%20Workshop%20on%20MGR.pdf> accessed 31 March 2022.

Greiber, Thomas, 'Types of Benefits and Benefit-sharing' in *IUCN Environmental Law Centre, Information Papers for the Intersessional Workshop on Marine Genetic Resources 2–3 May 2013* (Information Paper 1, IUCN, May 2013c) <https://www.un.org/Depts/los/biodiversityworkinggroup/documents/IUCN%20Information%20Papers%20for%20BBNJ%20Intersessional%20Workshop%20on%20MGR.pdf> accessed 31 March 2022.

Group of 77, 'Interventions on Behalf of the Group of 77 and China by Mr. Emad Morcos Mattar, Counsellor, Permanent Mission of Egypt to the United Nations, on Agenda Item 7: Marine Genetic Resources, Including Questions on the Sharing of Benefits, at the First Session of the Intergovernmental Conference on an International Legally Binding Instrument under the United Nations Convention on the Law of the Sea on the Conservation and Sustainable Use of Marine Biological Diversity of Areas beyond National Jurisdiction' (New York, 13 September 2018) <http://www.g77.org/statement/getstatement.php?id=180913> accessed 31 March 2022.

Guilloux, Bleuenn, *Marine Genetic Resources, R&D and the Law 1:Complex Objects of Use* (ISTE Ltd, 2018).

Guntrip, Edward, 'The Common Heritage of Mankind: An Adequate Regime for Managing the Deep Seabed?' (2003) 4 *Melbourne Journal of International Law* 376–405.

Harden-Davies, Harriet, 'Deep-sea Genetic Resources: New Frontiers for Science and Stewardship in Areas Beyond National Jurisdiction' (2016) 137 *Deep-sea Research II* 504–513. DOI: 10.1016/j.dsr2.2016.05.005.

Hastings, Colm, 'Time to Set the Record Straight: The Legal Status of Marine Genetic Resources found within the Deep Seabed Area The Freedom of the High Seas, the Common Heritage of Mankind-or Neither?' (LLM Thesis, University of Iceland, 2018).

Heafey, Eve, 'Access and Benefit Sharing of Marine Genetic Resources from Areas Beyond National Jurisdiction: Intellectual Property-Friend, Not Foe' (2014) 14(2) *Chicago Journal of International Law* 493–523.

Horn, Laura, 'Climate Change and the Future Role of the Concept of the Common Concern' (2015) 2(1) *Australian Journal of Environmental Law* 24–56.

Humphries, Fran, Hiroko Muraki Gottlieb, Sarah Laird, Rachel Wynberg, Charles Lawson, Michelle Rourke, Morten Walløe Tvedt, Maria Julia Oliva and Marcel Jaspars, 'A Tiered Approach to the Marine Genetic Resource Governance Framework under the Proposed UNCLOS Agreement for Biodiversity Beyond National Jurisdiction' (2020) 122 *Marine Policy* 103910: 1–14. DOI: 10.1016/j.marpol.2020.103910.

Humphries, Fran, Muriel Rabone and Marcel Jaspars, 'Traceability Approaches for Marine Genetic Resources Under the Proposed Ocean (BBNJ) Treaty' (2021) 8 *Frontiers in Marine Science* 661313: 1–21. DOI: 10.3389/fmars.2021.661313.

'International Seminar on Conservation and Sustainable Use of Marine Biodiversity Beyond National Jurisdiction' (*Summary Report*, German Federal Agency for Nature Conservation and IUCN Environmental Law Centre, 2012).

International Treaty on Plant Genetic Resources for Food and Agriculture, opened for signature on 3 November 2001 (2001) 2400 *UNTS* 303 (entered into force on 29 June 2004) (ITPGRFA).

InterRidge, *InterRidge Statement of Commitment to Responsible Research Practices at Deep-Sea Hydrothermal Vents* (2006).

IUCN, 'Submission by IUCN following the Second Session of the Preparatory Committee on the Development of an International Legally Binding Instrument under the United Nations Convention on the Law of the Sea on the Conservation and Sustainable Use of Marine Biological Diversity of Areas beyond National Jurisdiction' (5 December 2016) ('Written submission of IUCN to PrepCom', 5 December 2016) <https://www.un.org/depts/los/biodiversity/prepcom_files/rolling_comp/IUCN.pdf> accessed 31 March 2022.

Jamaica, 'Submission of the Government of Jamaica on Access and Benefit Sharing Regime for Marine Genetic Resources in Areas beyond National Jurisdiction' (2016) ('Written submission of Jamaica to PrepCom', 2016) <https://www.un

.org/depts/los/biodiversity/prepcom_files/rolling_comp/Jamaica-access_and_benefit_sharing.pdf> accessed 31 March 2022.

Jaspars, Marcel and Abbe E.L. Brown, 'Benefit Sharing: Combining Intellectual Property, Trade Secrets, Science and an Ecosystem-Focused Approach' in Myron H. Nordquist and Ronán Long (eds) *Marine Biodiversity of Areas Beyond National Jurisdiction* (Brill/Nijhoff, 2021) 97–130. DOI: https://doi.org/10.1163/9789004422438_007.

Juniper, S. Kim, 'Technological, Environmental, Social and Economic Aspects' in *IUCN Environmental Law Centre, Information Papers for the Intersessional Workshop on Marine Genetic Resources 2–3 May 2013* (Information Paper 3, IUCN, May 2013) <https://www.un.org/Depts/los/biodiversityworkinggroup/documents/IUCN%20Information%20Papers%20for%20BBNJ%20Intersessional%20Workshop%20on%20MGR.pdf> accessed 31 March 2022.

Kamau, Evanson Chege, 'Access-related Issues' in *IUCN Environmental Law Centre, Information Papers for the Intersessional Workshop on Marine Genetic Resources 2–3 May 2013* (Information Paper 4, IUCN, May 2013) <https://www.un.org/Depts/los/biodiversityworkinggroup/documents/IUCN%20Information%20Papers%20for%20BBNJ%20Intersessional%20Workshop%20on%20MGR.pdf> accessed 31 March 2022.

Kantai, Tallash, Alice Miller and Elisa Morgera, 'Summary of the Ninth Meeting of the Working Group on Marine Biodiversity Beyond Areas of National Jurisdiction: 20–23 January 2015,' *Earth Negotiations Bulletin* (Online Bulletin, 26 January 2015) <https://enb.iisd.org/download/pdf/enb2594e.pdf> accessed 31 March 2022.

Kantai, Tallash, Asheline Appleton, Priscila Pereira de Andrade, Bernard Soubry and Asterios Tsioumanis, 'Summary of the Second Session of the Intergovernmental Conference on the Conservation and Sustainable Use of Marine Biodiversity of Areas Beyond National Jurisdiction: 25 March–5 April 2019' *Earth Negotiations Bulletin* (Online Bulletin, 8 April 2019) <https://enb.iisd.org/download/pdf/enb25195e.pdf> accessed 31 March 2022.

Kimball, Lee, 'Balancing the Interests' (1978) 4 *Environmental Policy and Law* 69–77.

Lawson, Charles, *Regulating Genetic Resources: Access and Benefit Sharing in International Law* (Edward Elgar Publishing, 2012). DOI: https://doi.org/10.4337/9781781001660.

Leary, David, *International Law and the Genetic Resources of the Deep Sea* (Martinus Nijhoff Publishers, 2007).

Leary, David, 'International Law and the Genetic Resources of the Deep Sea' in Davor Vidas (ed), *Law, Technology and Science for Oceans in Globalisation* (Martinus Nijhoff Publishers, 2010) 353. DOI: https://doi.org/10.1163/ej.9789004180406.i-610.115.

Leary, David, 'Agreeing to Disagree on What We Have or Have not Agreed on: The Current State of Play of the BBNJ Negotiations on the Status of Marine Genetic Resources in Areas Beyond National Jurisdiction' (2019) 99 *Marine Policy* 21–29. DOI: 10.1016/j.marpol.2018.10.031.

Leary, David and S. Kim Juniper, 'Addressing the Marine Genetic Resources Issue: Is the Debate Heading in the Wrong Direction?' in Clive Schofield, Seokwoo Lee and Moon-Sang Kwon (eds), *The Limits of Maritime Jurisdiction* (Koninklijke Brill, 2014) 769. DOI: 10.1163/9789004262591.

Ma, Juncai, Linhuan Wu and Ipek Kurtböke, 'Skerman and Beyond: 2019 Status of the Global Catalogue of Microorganisms' (2019) 40(3) *Microbiology Australia* 121–124. DOI: 10.1071/MA19033.

Millicay, Fernanda, 'A Legal Regime for the Biodiversity of the Area' in Myron H. Nordquist (ed), *Law, Science and Ocean Management* (Martinus Nijhoff Publishers, 2007) 739. DOI: https://doi.org/10.1163/ej.9789004162556.i-850.199.

Morgera, Elisa, *Fair and Equitable Benefit-sharing in a New Treaty on Marine Biodiversity: A Principled Approach Towards Partnership Building?* (Working Paper No. 16, Benelex, 2018). DOI: http://dx.doi.org/10.2139/ssrn.3234346.

Morgera, Elisa, Matthias Buck and Elsa Tsioumani, *Unraveling the Nagoya Protocol: A Commentary on the Nagoya Protocol on Access and Benefit-Sharing to the Convention on Biological Diversity* (Brill, 2014) vol 2. DOI: 10.1163/9789004217188.

Morgera, Elisa, Daniela Diz, Tallash Kantai and Asterios Tsioumanis, 'Summary of the First Session of the Preparatory Committee on Marine Biodiversity of Areas Beyond National Jurisdiction: 28 March–8 April 2016' *Earth Negotiations Bulletin* (Online Bulletin, 11 April 2016) <https://enb.iisd.org/download/pdf/enb25106e.pdf> accessed 31 March 2022.

Morgera, Elisa, Asheline Appleton, Tallash Kantai and Asterios Tsioumanis, 'Summary of the Fourth Session of the Preparatory Committee on Marine Biodiversity Beyond Areas of National Jurisdiction: 10–21 July 2017' *Earth Negotiations Bulletin* (Online Bulletin, 24 July 2017) <https://enb.iisd.org/download/pdf/enb25141e.pdf> accessed 31 March 2022.

Morgera, Elisa, Asheline Appleton, Daniela Diz and Asterios Tsioumanis, 'Summary of the First Session of the Intergovernmental Conference on an International Legally Binding Instrument under the UN Convention on the Law of the Sea on the Conservation and Sustainable Use of Marine Biodiversity of Areas Beyond National Jurisdiction 4–17 September 2018' *Earth Negotiations Bulletin* (Online Bulletin, 20 September 2018) <https://enb.iisd.org/download/pdf/enb25179e.pdf> accessed 31 March 2022.

Morris, Anja, 'Marine Genetic Resources in Areas Beyond National Jurisdiction: How Should the Exploitation of the Resources by Regulated' (2018) 22 *New Zealand Journal of Environmental Law* 57–86.

Morris-Sharma, Natalie Y, 'Marine Genetic Resources in Areas Beyond National Jurisdiction: Issues with, in and outside of UNCLOS' (2017) 20(1) *Max Planck Yearbook of United Nations Law Online* 71–97. DOI: 10.1163/13894633_02001004.

Mossop, Joanna, 'Protecting Marine Biodiversity on the Continental Shelf Beyond 200 Nautical Miles' (2007) 38 *Ocean Development and International Law* 283–304. DOI: 10.1080/00908320701530474.

Mulalap, Clement Yow, Tekau Frere, Elise Huffer, Edvard Hviding, Kenneth Paul, Anita Smith and Marjo K. Vierros, 'Traditional knowledge and the BBNJ instrument' (2020) 122 *Marine Policy* 104103. DOI: 10.1016/j.marpol.2020.104103.

Murillo, Jimena, 'Common Concern of Humankind and Its Implications in International Environmental Law' (2008) 5(2) *Macquarie Journal of International and Comparative Environmental Law* 133–148.

'Nagoya Protocol on Access to Genetic Resources and the Fair and Equitable Sharing of Benefits Arising from their Utilization to the Convention on Biological Diversity, Opened for Signature' (2 February 2011), Doc. UNEP/CBD/COP/DEC/X/1 (entered into force 12 October 2014) (Nagoya Protocol).

Norway, 'Preparatory Committee established by General Assembly Resolution 69/292: Development of an International Legally Binding Instrument under the United Nations Convention on the Law of the Sea on the Conservation and Sustainable Use of Marine Biological Diversity of Areas beyond National Jurisdiction, Comments by Norway' (December 2016) ('Written submission of Norway to PrepCom', December 2016) <https://www.un.org/depts/los/biodiversity/prepcom_files/rolling_comp/Norway.pdf> accessed 31 March 2022.

Noyes, John E, 'The Common Heritage of Mankind, Past, Present and Future' (2011) 40 *Denver Journal of International Law and Policy* 447–471.

Oldham, Paul, Stephen Hall, Colin Barnes, Catherine Oldham, Mark Cutter, Natasha Burns and Leonie Kindness, '*Valuing the Deep: Marine Genetic Resources in Areas Beyond National Jurisdiction*' (Technical Report, Department for Environment Food and Rural Affairs, 2014).

Pauchard, Nicolas 'Access and Benefit Sharing under the Convention on Biological Diversity and Its Protocol: What Can Some Numbers Tell Us about the Effectiveness of the Regulatory Regime?' (2017) 6(1) *Resources* 11–26. DOI: 10.3390/resources6010011.

People's Republic of China, 'Written Submission of the Chinese Government on Elements of a Draft Text of an International Legally Binding Instrument under the United Nations Convention on the Law of the Sea on the Conservation and Sustainable Use of Marine Biological Diversity of Areas Beyond National Jurisdiction' (7 March 2017)('Written submission of China to PrepCom, 7 March 2017b) <https://www.un.org/depts/los/biodiversity/prepcom_files/rolling_comp/China.pdf> accessed 31 March 2022.

People's Republic of China, 'Written Submission of the Government of the People's Republic of China on Elements of a Draft Text of an International Legally Binding Instrument under the United Nations Convention on the Law of the Sea on the Conservation and Sustainable Use of Marine Biological Diversity of Areas Beyond National Jurisdiction' (20 April 2017)('Written submission of China to PrepCom 20 April 2017b) <https://www.un.org/depts/los/biodiversity/prepcom_files/streamlined/China.pdf> accessed 31 March 2022.

Permanent Mission of Algeria to the United Nations New York, 'Statement on Behalf of the African Group by H.E. Ambassador Mohammed Bessedik, Deputy Permanent Representative, Chargé d'affaires a.i., At the Third Session of the Intergovernmental Conference on an International Legally Binding Instrument under the United Nations Convention on the Law of the Sea on the Conservation and Sustainable Use of Marine Biological Diversity of Areas beyond National Jurisdiction, General Exchange of Views (Item 5)' (New York, 19 August 2019) <http://statements.unmeetings.org/media2/21996848/algeria-obo-african-group.pdf> accessed 31 March 2022.

Permanent Mission of the Republic of Nauru to the United Nations, 'PSIDS Submission to the Second Meeting of the Preparatory Committee for the Development of an International Legally Binding Instrument under the United Nations Convention on the Law of the Sea on the Conservation and Sustainable Use of Marine Biological Diversity of Areas beyond National Jurisdiction (BBNJ PrepCom)' (29 August 2016) ('Written submission of PSIDS to PrepCom', 29 August 2016) <https://www.un.org/depts/los/biodiversity/prepcom_files/rolling_comp/PSIDS_second.pdf> accessed 31 March 2022.

Prathapan, K. Divakaran, Rohan Pethuyagoda, Kamaljit S. Bawa, Peter H. Raven, Priyadarsanan Dharma Rajan, 'When the Cure Kills–CBD Limits Biodiversity Research' (2018) 360 *Science* 1405–1406. DOI: 10.1126/science.aat9844.

President's Aid to Discussions, UN Doc A/CONF.232/2018/33 (25 June 2018) <https://documents-dds-ny.un.org/doc/UNDOC/GEN/N18/197/15/PDF/N1819715.pdf?OpenElement> accessed 31 March 2022.

Rabitz, Florian, *The Global Governance of Genetic Resources Institutional Change, Structural Constraints* (Routledge, 2017). DOI: 10.4324/9781315271316.

Ramirez-Llodra, E, A. Brandt, R. Danovaro, B. De Mol, E. Escobar, C.R. German, L.A. Levin, P. Martinez Arbizu, L. Menot, P. Buhl-Mortensen, B.E. Narayanaswamy, C.R. Smith, D.P. Tittensor, P.A. Tyler, A. Vanreusel and M. Vecchione, 'Deep, Diverse and Definitely Different: Unique Attributes of the World's Largest Ecosystem' (2010) 7 *Biogeosciences* 2851–2899. DOI: 10.5194/bg-7-2851-2010.

Revised Draft Text of an Agreement under the United Nations Convention on the Law of the Sea on the Conservation and Sustainable Use of Marine Biological Diversity of Areas Beyond National Jurisdiction, UN Doc A/CONF.232/2020/3 (18 November 2019). <https://documents-dds-ny.un.org/doc/UNDOC/GEN/N19/372/88/PDF/N1937288.pdf?OpenElement> accessed 31 March 2022

Ridings, Penelope, 'Redefining Environmental Stewardship to Deliver Governance Frameworks for Marine Biodiversity Beyond National Jurisdiction' (2018) 75(1) *ICES Journal of Marine Science* 435–443. DOI: 10.1093/icesjms/fsx122.

Rogers Alex D, Amy Baco, Elva Escobar-Briones, Duncan Currie, Kristina Gjerde, Judith Gobin, Marcel Jaspars, Lisa Levin, Katrin Linse, Muriel Rabone, Eva Ramirez-Llodra, Javier Sellanes, Timothy M. Shank, Kerry Sink, Paul V.R. Snelgrove, Michelle L. Taylor, Daniel Wagner, Harriet Harden-Davies, 'Marine Genetic Resources in Areas Beyond National Jurisdiction: Promoting Marine Scientific Research and Enabling Equitable Benefit Sharing' (2021) 8 *Frontiers in Marine Science* 667274: 1–22.

Salpin, Charlotte, 'Marine Genetic Resources of Areas Beyond National Jurisdiction: Soul searching and the Art of Balance' in Elisa Morgera and Kati Kulovesi (eds), *Research Handbook on International Law and Natural Resources* (Edward Elgar Publishing, 2016) 411. DOI: https://doi.org/10.4337/9781783478330.00035.

Schoenberg, Pamela, 'A Polarizing Dilemma: Assessing Potential Regulatory Gap-Filling Measures for Arctic & Antarctic Marine Genetic Resource Access & Benefit Sharing' (2009) 42 *Cornell International Law Journal* 271–299.

Scope, Parameters and Feasibility of an International Instrument under the United Nations Convention on the Law of the Sea: Informal Working Document Compiling the Views of Member States, Prepared in Accordance with General Assembly Resolution 68/70 paragraph 201 (4 December 2014) <http://cpps.dyndns.info/cpps-docs-web/circulares/2015/003.Circular%20003-2015_Videoconferencia%20del%20GT-CPPS-B-RGM.pdf> accessed 31 March 2022.

Scovazzi, Tullio, 'The Concept of Common Heritage of Mankind and the Genetic Resources of the Seabed Beyond the Limits of National Jurisdiction' (2007) 14(25) *Agenda Internacional* 11–24.

Scovazzi, Tullio, 'The Rights to Genetic Resources Beyond National Jurisdiction: Challenges for the Ongoing Negotiations at the United Nations' in Catherine Banet (ed) *The Law of the Seabed* (Brill Nijhoff, 2020) 213. DOI: https://doi.org/10.1163/9789004391567_012.

Shelton, Dinah, 'Common Concern of Humanity' (2009) 39(2) *Environmental Policy and Law* 83–86.

'SisGen' <https://sisgen.gov.br/paginas/login.aspx> accessed 31 March 2022.

Soltau, Friedrich, 'Common Concern of Humankind' in Cinnamon P. Carlarne, Kevin R. Gray and Richard Tarasofsky (eds), *The Oxford Handbook of International*

Climate Change Law (Oxford University Press, 2016) 202. DOI: 10.1093/law/9780199684601.003.0010.

Tanaka, Yoshifumi, *The International Law of the Sea* (Cambridge University Press, 2nd ed, 2015). DOI: https://doi.org/10.1017/9781108545907.

Taylor, Prue, 'The Common Heritage of Mankind: A Bold Doctrine Kept Within Strict Boundaries' in David Bollier and Silke Helfrich (eds), *The Wealth of the Commons: A World Beyond Market & State* (Levellers Press, 2012) 566.

Textual Proposals Submitted by Delegations for Consideration at IGC 4, in Response to the Invitation by the President of the Conference in her Note of 18 November 2019, UN Doc A/CONF.232/2020/3 (15 April 2020).

Tladi, Dire, 'The Common Heritage of Mankind and the Proposed Treaty on Biodiversity in Areas Beyond National Jurisdiction: The Choice between Pragmatism and Sustainability' (2015) 25(1) *Yearbook of International Environmental Law* 113–132. DOI: 10.1093/yiel/yvv060.

Tvedt, Morten Walløe and Ane E. Jørem, 'Bioprospecting in the High Seas: Regulatory Options for Benefit Sharing' (2013) 16(3–4) *The Journal of World Intellectual Property* 150–167. DOI: 10.1002/jwip.12010.

United Nations Convention on the Law of the Sea, opened for signature 10 December 1982 1982, 1833 *UNTS* 397 (entered into force 16 November 1994) (UNCLOS).

United Nations Framework Convention on Climate Change, opened for signature 9 May 1992 (1992) 1771 *UNTS* 165 (entered into force 21 March 1994) (UNFCCC).

United Nations General Assembly, *Oceans and the Law of the Sea–Report of the Secretary-General*, UN Doc A/59/62 (4 March 2004).

United Nations General Assembly, *Oceans and the Law of the Sea-Report of the Secretary-General*, UN Doc A/60/63/Add.1 (15 July 2005).

United Nations General Assembly, *Oceans and the Law of the Sea-Report of the Secretary-General*, UN Doc A/62/66/Add.2 (10 September 2007).

Vierros, Marjo, Charlotte Salpin, Claudio Chiarolla and Salvatore Aricò, 'Emerging and Unresolved Issues: Marine Genetic Resources' in Salvatore Arico (ed), *Ocean Sustainability in the 21st Century* (Cambridge University Press, 2015) 198. DOI: https://doi.org/10.1017/CBO9781316164624.012.

Vierros, Marjo, Curtis A. Suttle, Harriet Harden-Davies and Geoff Burton, 'Who Owns the Ocean? Policy Issues Surrounding Marine Genetic Resources' (2016) 25(2) *Association for the Sciences of Limnology and Oceanography* 29–35. DOI: 10.1002/lob.10108.

Voigt-Hanssen, Gaute, 'Current "Light" and "Heavy" Options for Benefit-Sharing in the Context of the United Nations Convention on the Law of the Sea' (2018) 33(4) *The International Journal of Marine and Coastal Law* 683–705. DOI: 10.1163/15718085-12334012.

Warner, Robin, *Protecting the Oceans Beyond National Jurisdiction: Strengthening the International Law Framework* (Martinus Nijhoff, 2009).

Weiss, Edith Brown, 'The Coming Water Crisis: A Common Concern of Humankind' (2012) 1(1) *Transnational Environmental Law* 153–168. DOI: 10.1017/S2047102511000100.

5 Caught in a geopolitical undertow

Marine protected areas beyond national jurisdiction

Introduction

Marine protected areas (MPAs) are a key tool for biodiversity conservation.[1] They support ecological connectivity, boost ecological resilience to climate change and help preserve species and ecosystems.[2] However, MPAs are only part of the solution to the challenges facing BBNJ. MPAs cannot address all existing and emerging threats to deep-sea ecosystems, nor can they achieve all management goals.[3] The designation of high seas MPAs is also an issue fraught with political difficulties. Dodds and Nuttall argue that MPAs are always caught up in a matrix of geopolitical, scientific, legal and environmental factors.[4] It is seen in this chapter that MPAs in the BBNJ context are no exception to this.

Kaye has identified six broad geopolitical issues that may impede progress towards the negotiation of high seas MPAs, namely: (1) the traditional high seas framework, (2) high seas fisheries, (3) geographically disadvantaged States, (4) strategic considerations, (5) deep-seabed issues and (6) marine scientific research (MSR).[5] As the BBNJ process reaches its tail-end, it seems an appropriate time to revisit Kaye's geopolitical factors to determine whether they still pose an obstacle to the establishment of MPAs under an ILBI. This chapter seeks to fill a gap in the literature in two respects. First, Kaye's work was published almost two years before the first meeting of the BBNJ Working Group. This chapter analyses documents submitted by States and their statements made during the on-going negotiations to gain an insight into the geopolitical factors currently at play. Second, at the time of writing, Kaye did not have any high seas MPAs to

1 Inês Aguiar Branco, 'Solving the Potential Conflict: High Seas Marine Protected Areas and Sovereign Rights over the Continental Shelf Beyond 200 Nautical Miles' in M.C. Ribeiro et al (eds), *Global Challenges and the Law of the Sea* (Springer Nature Switzerland, 2020) 423, 425.

2 IUCN, 'Governing Areas beyond National Jurisdiction' (Issues Brief, March 2019) 2.

3 Benjamin S. Halpern, Sarah E. Lester and Karen L. McLead, 'Placing Marine Protected Areas onto the Ecosystem-Based Management Seascape' (2010) 107(43) *Proceedings of the National Academy of Sciences of the United States of America* 18312, 18312.

4 Klaus Dodds and Mark Nuttall, *The Scramble for the Poles* (Polity Press, 2016) 94.

5 Stuart Kaye, 'Implementing High Seas Biodiversity Conservation: Global Geopolitical Considerations' (2004) 28 *Marine Policy* 221.

DOI: 10.4324/b22996-6

consider. The first MPA beyond national jurisdiction, the South Orkney Islands southern shelf MPA, was designated in 2009,[6] almost five years after Kaye's work. Twelve high seas MPAs have now been developed, including two under the 1980 Convention on the Conservation of Antarctic Marine Living Resources (CAMLR Convention).[7] This chapter uses the CAMLR MPAs as a case study to assess how geopolitical considerations influenced, shaped or hindered their development and to identify lessons for future MPAs under an ILBI.

The COVID-19 pandemic has significantly affected the BBNJ negotiation process and engendered some degree of political and economic uncertainty. In this context it is possible that international consensus on the establishment of a network of MPAs might be more difficult to achieve. In other words, MPAs are at risk of being caught up in a geopolitical undertow. In an effort to overcome geopolitical issues, the argument is made for the ILBI to adopt a modern, flexible and compromise approach to MPAs and for this approach to be underpinned by an expert-driven systematic conservation planning process and involve the use of dynamic management tools.

5.1 MPAs in the current legal seascape

5.1.1 An unfinished agenda

In global forums, the international community has committed to the establishment of a network of MPAs covering 10 to 30 per cent of the oceans.[8] For example, in 2010, CBD Parties adopted Aichi Biodiversity Target 11, which requires at least 10 per cent of coastal and marine areas to be conserved through ecologically representative and well-connected systems of protected areas by 2020.[9] The UNGA has also emphasised the importance of MPAs in its annual resolutions. Yet, despite these encouraging steps, only 1.2 per cent of ABNJ fall under actively managed MPAs.[10] To understand the delay in achieving globally agreed targets, the following sections outline the legal and practical challenges inherent in designating MPAs in ABNJ.[11]

6 CCAMLR, 'Protection of the South Orkney Islands Southern Shelf' Conservation Measure 91-03 (2009).

7 Elizabeth M. De Santo, 'Implementation Challenges of Area-Based Management Tools (ABMTs) for Biodiversity beyond National Jurisdiction (BBNJ)' (2018) 97 *Marine Policy* 34, 35.

8 Alan M. Friedlander et al, 'Co-operation between Large-Scale MPAs: Successful Experiences from the Pacific Ocean' (2016) 26 (Suppl. 2) *Aquatic Conservation: Marine and Freshwater Ecosystems* 126, 126.

9 CBD, *Strategic Plan 2011–2020, Aichi Target 11*, UN Doc COP/10/INF/12/Rev.1. This target is reiterated in Goal 14.5 of Sustainable Development Goal 14 of the UN, *Transforming Our World: 2030 Agenda for Sustainable Development.*

10 'Atlas of Marine Protection,' *Marine Conservation Institute* (Web Page, 3 February 2022) <http://www.mpatlas.org>.

11 Glen Wright, Julien Rochette and Elisabeth Druel, 'Marine Protected Areas in Areas beyond National Jurisdiction' in Rosemary Rayfuse (ed), *Research Handbook on International Marine Environmental Law* (Edward Elgar Publishing, 2015) 272, 272.

5.1.2 Lack of a definition

There is no internationally agreed legal definition of MPA. It is an umbrella term covering different management options.[12] These range from no-take marine reserves (where all extractive uses are prohibited) to large multiple-use areas (where some uses are prohibited, others regulated or allowed).[13] MPA terms can also carry different meanings.[14] For example, in Kenya, marine reserves adopt a multiple-use approach, while in Tanzania, they are strictly no-take.[15] An ILBI could remedy this confusion by clearly defining the meaning and scope of MPA terms, perhaps by reference to the IUCN protected area management categories which are recognised by the CBD.[16]

Existing international instruments could also be used to craft a definition of MPA under an ILBI.[17] Article 2 of CBD defines 'protected area' as *a geographically defined area which is designated, regulated and managed to achieve specific conservation objectives.* This definition has garnered increasing support, particularly as it would provide 'consistency and coherence across international regimes.'[18] It also provides a 'flexible notion of MPA,'[19] one broad enough to encompass different management options.

5.1.3 Lack of a global mechanism

Currently, there is no global mechanism to establish binding, multi-sectoral MPAs in ABNJ.[20] Gjerde and Rulska-Domino argue that the environmental obligations in UNCLOS could provide a legal basis for establishing MPAs under an

12 Ingvild Ulrikke Jakobsen, *Marine Protected Areas in International Law: An Arctic Perspective* (Brill Nijhoff, 2016) Queen Mary Studies in International Law, vol 25, 8.
13 Joachim Claudet, 'Food for Thought: Six Conditions under which MPAs Might Not Appear Effective' (2018) 75(3) *ICES Journal of Marine Science* 1172, 1172.
14 Dan Laffoley et al, 'Marine Protected Areas' in Charles Sheppard (ed), *World Seas: An Environmental Evaluation Volume III, Ecological Issues and Environmental Impacts* (Elsevier Ltd, 2nd ed, 2019) 549, 553.
15 Ibid.
16 Nigel Dudley (ed), 'Guidelines for Applying Protected Area Management Categories' (Best Practice Protected Area Guidelines Series No. 21, IUCN, 2008) vii.
17 *Chair's Indicative Suggestions of Clusters of Issues and Questions to Assist Further Discussions in the Informal Working Groups at the Second Session of the Preparatory Committee*, 3.
18 Australia, 'Preparatory Committee on Conservation and Sustainable Use of Marine Biological Diversity of Areas beyond National Jurisdiction (BBNJ): Submission by Australia' (6 December 2016) 3 <https://www.un.org/depts/los/biodiversity/prepcom_files/rolling_comp/Australia.pdf>.
19 Tullio Scovazzi, 'The Negotiations for a Binding Instrument on the Conservation and Sustainable Use of Marine Biological Diversity beyond National Jurisdiction' (2016) 70 *Marine Policy* 188, 189.
20 Amy Hammond and Peter J.S. Jones, 'Protecting the 'Blue Heart of the Planet': Strengthening the Governance Framework for Marine Protected Areas beyond National Jurisdiction' (2021) 127 *Marine Policy* 104260, 1–12, 1.

ILBI.[21] For example, Article 194(5) requires States to adopt *measures* to protect fragile ecosystems. The word 'measures' is 'sufficiently vague and open to include the MPA tool.'[22] However, UNCLOS lacks detail on how MPAs can be identified or designated and how they should be managed or enforced.[23]

5.1.4 The prevailing regional and sectoral approach

To date, the designation of high seas MPAs has taken place under, or in association with, the UN Environment's Regional Seas Programme (RSP). The geographical coverage of these regional bodies is presently limited to four marine spaces: the Southern Ocean (CAMLR), the North-East Atlantic (OSPAR), the Mediterranean Sea (Barcelona Convention) and the South Pacific region (Noumea Convention).[24] MPAs established under regional conventions are only binding on parties to the respective treaty regimes.[25] The legality of these MPAs also 'remains open to question in the absence of a multilateral legal basis supporting their designation.'[26] BBNJ delegates have expressed reservations over the legitimacy of high seas MPAs designated unilaterally or by a group of States.[27] As these RSP conventions also have a limited regulatory mandate, they must cooperate with relevant competent authorities through agreements (i.e. Memorandums of Understanding or Collective Arrangements) to effectively manage high seas MPAs, as has occurred under OSPAR in the North-East Atlantic region.[28]

21 Kristina M. Gjerde and Anna Rulska-Domino, 'Marine Protected Areas beyond National Jurisdiction: Some Practical Perspectives for Moving Ahead' (2012) 27 *The International Journal of Marine and Coastal Law* 351, 356.

22 Marta Chantal Ribeiro, 'Marine Protected Areas: The Case of the Extended Continental Shelf' in *30 Years after the Signature of the United Nations Convention on the Law of the Sea: The Protection of the Environment and the Future of the Law of the Sea: Proceedings of the International Conference, Faculty of Law, University of Porto, 15–17 November 2012* (Coimbra Editora, 2014) 179, 184.

23 Scovazzi (n 19) 189.

24 Kristine Dalaker Kraabel, 'The BBNJ PrepCom and Institutional Arrangements: The Hype about the Hybrid Approach' in Myron H. Nordquist, John Morton Moore and Ronán Long (eds), *The Marine Environment and United Nations Sustainable Development Goal 14* (Brill Nijhoff, 2019) 137, 150.

25 David Freestone, 'The UN Process to Develop an International Legally Binding Instrument under the 1982 Law of the Sea Convention: Issues and Challenges' in David Freestone (ed), *Conserving Biodiversity in Areas beyond National Jurisdiction* (Brill Nijhoff, 2019) 3, 14.

26 Karen N. Scott, 'Conservation on the High Seas: Developing the Concept of the High Seas Marine Protected Areas' (2012) 27 *The International Journal of Marine and Coastal Law* 849, 855.

27 *Letter Dated 8 June 2012 from the Co-Chairs of the Ad Hoc Open-Ended Informal Working Group to the President of the General Assembly*, UN Doc A/67/95 (13 June 2012) annex ('Co-Chairs' Summary of Discussions') [22].

28 Henning von Nordheim, 'Marine Protected Areas: Global Framework, Regional MPA Networks and a National Example' in Markus Salomon and Till Markus (eds), *Handbook on Marine Environment Protection: Science, Impacts and Sustainable Management* (Springer International Publishing, 2018) 871, 886.

Aside from regional initiatives, the prevailing approach in ABNJ is sectoral, with several international organisations having ABMTs at their disposal.[29] RFMO/As can close fisheries; the IMO can designate Particularly Sensitive Sea Areas (PSSAs) and the ISA can designate Areas of Particular Environmental Interest (APEIs). Generally, these sector-specific measures are spatially and/or temporally limited and do not focus on cumulative impacts.[30] With no global mechanism to ensure coordination of sectoral ABMTs, this increases the risk for 'gaps, duplication of efforts and conflicting results.'[31] An ILBI could therefore provide an overarching framework to ensure sectoral tools are comprehensively and consistently applied in ABNJ.[32]

5.2 Are high seas MPAs still caught up in a geopolitical undertow?

5.2.1 Kaye's geopolitical factors

The following sections revisit Kaye's six geopolitical factors to assess whether they still hold the potential to impede the establishment of MPAs under an ILBI or whether new factors have now come to the fore.

5.2.1.1 The traditional high seas framework

Kaye anticipated that the traditional high seas framework in Part VII of UNCLOS would hinder attempts to establish MPAs. The effective protection of a marine site may require significant restrictions to be placed on activities there, and these restrictions may affect the rights of all States to use ABNJ.[33] Accordingly, high seas MPAs do not sit comfortably with proponents of the freedom of the seas, as they can be perceived as another attempt to erode the Grotian doctrine.

The tension between restricting activities in MPAs and pressure from maritime States to retain high seas freedoms harks back to the controversy of 'closed seas' and 'open seas' that dominated 17th-century literature. There is a reluctance on the part of some BBNJ delegations, mainly maritime States, to endorse stringent

29 Glen Wright and Julien Rochette, 'Regional Ocean Governance of Areas beyond National Jurisdiction: Lessons Learnt and Ways Forward' (STRONG High Seas Project, 2019) 14.

30 Rachel Tiller et al, 'The Once and Future Treaty: Towards a New Regime for Biodiversity in Areas beyond National Jurisdiction' (2019) 99 *Marine Policy* 239, 240.

31 Elisabeth Druel et al, 'Paper VI: Options and Approaches for Establishing and Managing Marine Protected Areas in ABNJ' in 'An International Instrument on Conservation and Sustainable Use of Biodiversity in Marine Areas beyond National Jurisdiction Exploring Different Elements to Consider' (Series of Policy Briefs on Scope, Parameters and Feasibility, IUCN, 2003) 39.

32 Glen Wright et al, 'High Seas Fisheries: What Role for a New International Instrument?' (Study No. 03/16, IDDRI, August 2016) 12.

33 Alex G. Oude Elferink, 'The Regime of the Area: Delineating the Scope of Application of the Common Heritage Principle and Freedom of the High Seas' (2007) 22(1) *The International Journal of Marine and Coastal Law* 143, 152.

mandatory protective measures within MPAs, particularly if they will impact high seas freedoms in the long-term.[34] Thus, the Grotian tradition continues to be used as a 'trump card'[35] to reject attempts to elaborate strict regulations within high seas MPAs.

However, we have seen that the Grotian doctrine has been adapted, modified and eroded over the centuries to accommodate different interests, including for conservation measures. UNFSA provides an example of States agreeing to forego high seas freedoms to some extent in the service of a common objective. Why should the issue of the conservation and sustainable use of BBNJ be any different? While high seas freedoms are important considerations, the freedom of the seas should be seen through a modern 21st-century lens and balanced with other interests, including the protection of BBNJ.

5.2.1.2 Strategic considerations

Kaye's second geopolitical factor is strategic considerations. Almost 90 per cent of world trade is carried by the international shipping industry.[36] Associated threats to BBNJ include noise, bio-invasions, wildlife collisions and pollution.[37] Navigation may therefore need to be restricted or prohibited within MPAs to protect BBNJ. Kaye argued that this is likely to be met with strong opposition by maritime States keen to safeguard maritime trade and naval mobility.[38] At a 2018 symposium, Kraska argued that the 'costs to national security interests will check the ambitions for a strong, progressive' ILBI.[39] As the US and other naval forces rely on unimpeded navigational freedom to conduct military operations and freedom of navigation patrols, these maritime powers are likely to insist that MPAs and associated protective measures do not diminish navigational freedoms

34 See, e.g. submissions by Japan and the US for MPAs to be on a temporary basis and 'terminated when their specific targets are achieved' in Elisa Morgera et al, 'PrepCom 4 Highlights: Wednesday 12 July 2017' *Earth Negotiations Bulletin* (Online Bulletin, 13 July 2017) 1 ('PrepCom 4 Highlights: Wednesday 12 July 2017') <https://s3.us-west-2.amazonaws.com/enb.iisd.org/archive/download/pdf/enb25134e.pdf?X-Amz-Content-Sha256=UNSIGNED-PAYLOAD&X-Amz-Algorithm=AWS4-HMAC-SHA256&X-Amz-Credential=AKIA6QW3YWTJ6YORWEEL%2F20220402%2Fus-west-2%2Fs3%2Faws4_request&X-Amz-Date=20220402T055210Z&X-Amz-SignedHeaders=host&X-Amz-Expires=60&X-Amz-Signature=6f58549979bbd122b0c0f87f71411dfa1c1d24d4ef4cc52294b243ebe432c2ee>.

35 Michaela Young, 'Then and Now: Reappraising Freedom of the Seas in Modern Law of the Sea' (2016) 47(2) *Ocean Development & International Law* 165, 171.

36 'Shipping and World Trade' *International Chamber of Shipping* (Web Page, 2020) <https://www.ics-shipping.org/shipping-facts/shipping-and-world-trade>.

37 Bethan C. O'Leary et al, 'Options for Managing Human Threats to High Seas Biodiversity' (2020) 187 *Ocean and Coastal Management* 105110, 1–12, 3.

38 Kaye (n 5) 223–224.

39 Cymie R. Payne, 'Introduction to the Symposium on Governing High Seas Biodiversity' (2018) 112 *AJIL Unbound* 118, 122.

and other military uses of the sea.[40] Arguably, this is even more likely to be the case post-COVID-19.

The effects of the pandemic will impact the regional and global maritime security calculus for decades.[41] The US has grown increasingly worried about China's rising maritime power, and the rivalry between the two nations is escalating, with military standoffs now a regular occurrence in and around the South China Sea.[42] Given the uncertain political and economic climate, maritime States are likely to favour the widest possible retention of navigational freedom, for security and economic reasons.

Navigation-related concerns have been apparent throughout the BBNJ process. During the first Working Group, the US was quick to oppose MPAs conceived as 'no-go zones.'[43] Some delegates argue that ABMTs are already available to protect BBNJ from shipping impacts, including PSSAs and MARPOL Special Areas under the IMO.[44] Resistance to the curtailment of navigational freedoms is also evident in calls for time-bound MPAs. Japan, the US and Russia stress that MPAs should be temporary and 'adjustable to allow for strengthening, weakening or lifting of restrictions.'[45] As national security interests linger in the background of BBNJ negotiations,[46] strategic geopolitical considerations still present an obstacle in efforts to establish high seas MPAs.

The crucial question is whether the strategic concerns of maritime States are valid or just part and parcel of their unwavering support and historical devotion to the Grotian doctrine. Maritime States have already agreed to some level of infringement upon their navigational freedoms by accepting limitations under IMO conventions such as MARPOL.[47] The IMO is responsible for regulating

40 James Kraska, 'National Security Considerations for a Binding Instrument on Managing Biodiversity beyond National Jurisdiction' (2018) 112 *AJIL Unbound* 150, 150.

41 Anil Jai Singh, 'Maritime Security in the Age of the Pandemic: The Naval Dimension,' *The Financial Express* (Online Newspaper, 21 April 2020) <https://www.financialexpress.com/defence/maritime-security-in-the-age-of-the-pandemic-the-naval-dimension/1934426/>.

42 Hu Bo, 'China-US Military Confrontation in the South China Sea: Fact and Fiction,' *The Diplomat* (Online Magazine, 12 June 2020) <https://thediplomat.com/2020/06/china-us-military-confrontation-in-the-south-china-sea-fact-and-fiction/>.

43 Karen Alvarenga et al, 'Marine Biodiversity Working Group Highlights: Thursday, 16 February 2006' *Earth Negotiations Bulletin* (Online Bulletin, 17 February 2006) 2 <https://enb.iisd.org/download/pdf/enb2524e.pdf>.

44 See *Revised Guidelines for the Identification and Designation of Particularly Sensitive Sea Areas*, IMO Assembly Doc A24/Res/982 (1 December 2005); International Convention for the Prevention of Pollution from Ships, as modified by the Protocol 1978 relating thereto, opened for signature 2 November 1973, 1340 UNTS 61 (entered into force 12 October 1984) (MARPOL) Annexes I–V.

45 Elisa Morgera et al, 'PrepCom 4 Highlights: Wednesday 12 July 2017' (n 34) 1; Tallash Kantai et al, 'BBNJ IGC-3 Highlights: Wednesday, 21 August 2019' *Earth Negotiations Bulletin* (Online Bulletin, 22 August 2019) 1 <https://enb.iisd.org/download/pdf/enb25211e.pdf>.

46 Kraska (n 40) 154.

47 The IMO has 174 Member States and 3 Associate Members, including maritime States (the UK, France, the Netherlands, Norway, Russia, the US).

international shipping by setting standards to improve safety and security and prevent pollution.[48] This includes routing, reporting and discharge requirements.[49] The IMO can also designate ABMTs.[50] While the IMO is yet to designate a high seas PSSA and only two MARPOL Special Areas include ABNJ,[51] it is important to acknowledge that it has been granted this authority. A number of high seas areas have been suggested as appropriate for PSSA designation including the Sargasso Sea and polar areas.[52] As States Parties of IMO Conventions account for about 99 per cent of gross tonnage of the world's merchant fleet,[53] IMO regulations are essentially binding on nearly all vessels, and to some extent already limit navigational freedoms.

Under an ILBI, a combination of measures could be adopted within an MPA to minimise shipping impacts on BBNJ, including regulation of speed, noise, anchoring, routing requirements and, if required, the prohibition of navigation at priority protection sites. To ensure the establishment of high seas MPAs does not undermine existing IMO standards and regulations, meaningful consultation with the IMO and the shipping sector is essential to guarantee 'the input of specialised technical expertise' and ensure a balance is maintained between environmental protection and navigational freedoms.[54] A heightened role for the IMO in the BBNJ process, concerning the designation of MPAs, may also go some way to alleviating the strategic concerns of maritime States. However, it may also reignite underlying tensions in the IMO concerning the balance between environmental protection measures and UNCLOS navigational rights and freedoms, as was evident in the controversy over a compulsory pilotage system in the Torres Strait, which triggered protests from maritime States including the US and Singapore.[55]

48 O'Leary et al (n 37) 7.

49 Daniel Wagner et al, 'Coral Reefs of the High Seas: Hidden Biodiversity Hotspots in Need of Protection' (2020) 7 *Frontiers in Marine Science* 1, 9.

50 David Freestone and Viva Harris, 'Particularly Sensitive Sea Areas beyond National Jurisdiction: Time to Chart a New Course?' in Myron H. Nordquist, John Norton Moore and Ronán Long (eds), *International Marine Economy: Law and Policy* (Koninklijke Brill NV, 2017) vol 20, 322, 323.

51 International Maritime Organisation, 'PrepCom 1 Conservation and Sustainable Use of Marine Biological Diversity of ABNJ' ('IMO Policy brief') 3 <https://www.un.org/depts/los/biodiversity/prepcom_files/IMO_Policy_Brief_BBNJ_PrepCom_1.pdf> ('IMO Policy Brief').

52 Freestone and Harris (n 50) 322.

53 IMO Policy Brief (n 51) 2.

54 International Chamber of Shipping, the European Community Shipowners' Associations and the Asian Shipowners' Association, 'Development of an International Legally Binding Instrument under UNCLOS on the Conservation and Sustainable Use of Biological Diversity in Areas beyond National Jurisdiction' (Position Paper, July 2018) <https://www.ecsa.eu/sites/default/files/publications/ics-ecsa-asa%20position%20paper%20on%20unclos%20implementing%20agreement.pdf>.

55 See, generally, Robert C. Beckman, 'PSSAs and Transit Passage – Australia's Pilotage System in the Torres Strait Challenges the IMO and UNCLOS' (2007) 38 *Ocean Development & International Law* 325.

5.2.1.3 High seas fisheries

High seas fisheries are another geopolitical consideration. Kaye argued that distant-water fishing nations will object to restricting access to high seas fisheries and will be unsupportive of MPAs that hamper their freedom to fish or overlap with their fishing grounds.[56] These objections remain.

Even though fishing is the primary activity affecting BBNJ,[57] delegations disagree on whether fisheries issues should fall within an ILBI's mandate. The BBNJ package deal did not explicitly refer to fisheries. This presents a dilemma. If the ILBI excludes fisheries, can it really claim to be a comprehensive instrument for BBNJ protection? Fishing States, including Iceland, Japan and Russia, argue there is no place for fisheries in an ILBI as the existing legal and institutional arrangements adequately protect BBNJ from fishing impacts.[58] Barnes contends that these States suffer from 'status quo bias,'[59] in seeking to safeguard traditional high seas freedoms.

As fishing States continue to fear the BBNJ process will be used as a back-door way of reopening fisheries discussions, these concerns need to be addressed head-on to move the negotiation process forward. These concerns may be alleviated by reinforcing the purpose and legal effect of an ILBI as an implementing agreement to UNCLOS. The drafters of UNCLOS anticipated that States Parties would 'continue to regulate their relations through subsequent treaties' to address new challenges in the law of the sea.[60] Two treaties have been designated as implementing agreements to UNCLOS, the Part XI Agreement and UNFSA. Both were developed to rectify problems or omissions in UNCLOS; however, they differ in the way they implement the Convention.[61] The Part XI Agreement significantly altered the seabed mining regime, with several provisions disapplied, replaced or removed.[62] These modifications were ambiguously drafted to avoid suggestions that amendments were being made to the original UNCLOS text. However, Harrison asks, rhetorically, whether 'the true impact of

56 Kaye (n 5) 222–223.

57 See US submission in *Scope, Parameters and Feasibility of an International Instrument under UNCLOS: Informal Working Document Compiling the Views of Member States, Prepared in Accordance with General Assembly Resolution 68/70 Paragraph 201* (4 December 2014) Addendum 2, 34 ('Informal Working Document').

58 See, e.g. Elisa Morgera, 'PrepCom 1 Highlights: Monday, 28 March 2016' *Earth Negotiations Bulletin* (Online Bulletin, 29 March 2016) 1, 2 <https://enb.iisd.org/download/pdf/enb2597e.pdf>.

59 Richard Alan Barnes, 'Fisheries and ABNJ: Advancing and Enhancing Cooperation' in Tomas Heidar (ed), *New Knowledge and Changing Circumstances in the Law of the Sea* (Brill Nijhoff, 2020) 124, 134 ('Fisheries and ABNJ').

60 James Harrison, *Making the Law of the Sea: A Study in the Development of International Law* (Cambridge University Press, 2011) 85. See, also, UNCLOS, art 311.

61 Anna-Maria Hubert, 'UN General Assembly Resolution to Develop a New Legally Binding Instrument on the Conservation and Sustainable Use of Marine Biological Diversity of Areas beyond National Jurisdiction' (The NCLOS Blog, 17 August 2015).

62 Harrison (n 60) 92.

the 1994 Agreement is anything but a de facto amendment of the law of the sea regime?'[63] This is a view shared by other commentators.[64]

In contrast, the overriding purpose of UNFSA was to respond to the Convention's very general fisheries provisions. The intention was not to revise these provisions, but to fill in gaps left at the conclusion of UNCLOS III.[65] UNFSA achieves this by providing further clarification without amending or disapplying UNCLOS provisions.[66] Arguably, the same overriding purpose lies behind the ILBI. The purpose of an ILBI is not to 'deal with ocean governance matters afresh.'[67] Instead, it is 'to work with existing rules and institutions, shaping them where necessary and harnessing them where appropriate.'[68] This is evident in the language of UNGA resolutions 69/292 and 72/249.[69]

An ILBI will affect fisheries, either directly or indirectly, particularly in respect to MPAs.[70] As has been argued throughout this book, the effectiveness of an ILBI will depend upon the 'integration of all relevant elements impacting' BBNJ.[71] Accordingly, the exclusion of fisheries issues would inevitably prevent the development of an ILBI that addresses ABNJ comprehensively.

5.2.1.4 Marine scientific research (MSR)

MSR is another high seas freedom that could be affected by the designation of MPAs. Kaye labelled this geopolitical consideration 'a subsidiary issue,'[72] and it has remained so in BBNJ discourse on ABMTs. Part XIII of UNCLOS places some limitations on MSR. For example, Article 240 requires all MSR to be conducted for peaceful purposes, using appropriate scientific methods, and not unjustifiably interfere with other legitimate sea uses. Leary argues that any

63 Ibid.
64 See, e.g. David Freestone and Alex G. Oude Elferink, 'Flexibility and Innovation in the Law of the Sea: Will the LOS Convention Amendment Procedures Ever Be Used?' in Alex G. Oude Elferink (ed), *Stability and Change in the Law of the Sea: The Role of the LOSC Convention* (Martinus Nijhoff, 2005) 184.
65 Harrison (n 60) 102.
66 Hubert (n 61).
67 Richard Barnes, David Freestone and David M. Ong, 'The Law of the Sea: Progress and Prospects' in David Freestone, Richard Barnes and David M. Ong (eds), *The Law of the Sea Progress and Prospects* (2006, Oxford University Press) 1, 15.
68 Ibid.
69 See, e.g. *International Legally Binding Instrument under UNCLOS on the Conservation and Sustainable Use of Marine Biological Diversity of Areas beyond National Jurisdiction*, GA Res 72/249, UN Doc A/RES/72/249 (19 January 2018, adopted on 24 December 2017) paras. 6 and 7.
70 Richard Barnes, 'The Proposed LOSC Implementation Agreement on Areas beyond National Jurisdiction and Its Impact on International Fisheries Law' (2016) 31(4) *The International Journal of Marine and Coastal Law* 583, 615.
71 Catherine Blanchard, 'Fragmentation in High Seas Fisheries: Preliminary Reflections on a Global Oceans Governance Approach' (2017) 84 *Marine Policy* 327, 328.
72 Kaye (n 5) 225.

attempt to regulate MSR beyond these limitations would 'undermine a cornerstone' of the traditional high seas framework,[73] and would not be acceptable to proponents of the Grotian tradition.

Historically, a stumbling block for MPA planning has been a lack of spatial data on ABNJ.[74] Highly restrictive MSR regulations within MPAs could reduce BBNJ research.[75] Scientists could therefore miss out on the raw ingredients needed for MPA planning,[76] particularly for identifying priority sites. Having an informed understanding of BBNJ will inevitably improve attempts to protect it through ABMTs. Thus, even though MSR has been treated as a peripheral issue, BBNJ negotiators need to carefully consider this factor in developing an MPA regime under an ILBI.

5.2.1.5 Deep-seabed issues

As species in the water column and seabed are often interlinked, MPAs that cover both maritime zones conserve the marine environment most effectively.[77] As the geographical scope of an ILBI encompasses ABNJ, it is expected that MPAs under the instrument will not be restricted to the high seas water column but will necessarily envelop deep-seabed biodiversity. Kaye argued that this will inevitably provoke the interest of the ISA and potentially re-open controversial questions on whether it should play a role in the designation of MPAs in ABNJ.[78]

The ISA has adopted its own set of spatial management tools, including a network of nine APEI in the Clarion-Clipperton Zone (CCZ).[79] As the CCZ is biodiversity-rich, it is likely to be a priority area for MPAs under an ILBI. This opens up the possibility of separate institutions (the ISA and an ILBI body) overseeing the same protected area, which could lead to conflict and inconsistencies in approach. Of course, the same can be said of other relevant organisations with mandates to establish ABMTs in ABNJ. APEI are therefore emblematic of a much larger geopolitical issue, namely, how will an ILBI interact with existing

73 David Leary, 'Agreeing to Disagree on What We Have or Have Not Agreed on: The Current State of Play of the BBNJ Negotiations on the Status of Marine Genetic Resources in Areas beyond National Jurisdiction' (2019) 99 *Marine Policy* 21, 23.

74 Morgan E. Visalli et al, 'Data-Driven Approach for Highlighting Priority Areas for Protection in Marine Areas beyond National Jurisdiction' (2020) 122 *Marine Policy* 103927, 1–14, 2.

75 Robert Blasiak and Nobuyuki Yagi, 'Shaping an International Agreement on Marine Biodiversity beyond Areas of National Jurisdiction: Lessons from High Seas Fisheries' (2016) 71 *Marine Policy* 210, 213.

76 Visalli et al (n 74) 2.

77 The Pew Charitable Trusts, 'A Path to Creating the First Generation of High Seas Protected Areas' (Report, 31 March 2020) 6.

78 Kaye (n 5) 224.

79 ISA, *Decision of the Council Relating to an Environmental Management Plan for the Clarion-Clipperton Zone*, ISBA/18/C/22 (26 July 2012).

legal instruments and frameworks that already provide for the creation of areas of special protection, without undermining them?

5.2.1.6 The potential to undermine existing arrangements

UNGA resolutions 69/292 and 72/249 explicitly stipulate that an ILBI should not undermine existing legal instruments, frameworks and bodies. However, 'undermine' is an ambiguous term, and divergent views exist on its precise scope and implications.[80] For example, Guatemala and Mexico understand 'not undermining' to mean *not contradicting or weakening* existing mandates.[81] Other delegations, like Iceland, 'adhere to a stricter meaning' and will not accept provisions that will 'change, modify or adapt the mandate and functioning of current structures.'[82]

The debate over the meaning of 'undermine' also taps into a larger dispute concerning the ILBI's institutional arrangements. The concept is often 'wielded as a buffer'[83] by those States that fear the creation of a 'centralised global ocean governance system' analogous to the seabed mining regime administered by the ISA.[84] The US, Norway and Russia are apprehensive about the degree of control a new global mechanism could have over existing bodies.[85] Thus, rather than 'creating another bureaucratic layer,'[86] this group argues that an ILBI should rely on existing regional and sectoral bodies to implement any new obligations and measures to conserve BBNJ.[87] However, this would perpetuate the status quo of oceans governance in ABNJ.[88]

This geopolitically charged issue has the potential to inhibit movement towards an effective MPA regime. Mendenhall et al suggest that the 'not

80 Vito De Lucia, 'Reflecting on the Meaning of "Not Undermining" ahead of IGC-2' (The Blog of the Norwegian Centre for the Law of the Sea, 21 March 2019) <http://site.uit.no/jclos/files/2019/03/JCLOS-Blog-21.3.2019-Reflecting-on-the-meaning-of-not-undermining-ahead-of-IGC-2-3.pdf>.

81 Elisa Morgera et al, 'Summary of the Third Session of the Preparatory Committee on Marine Biodiversity beyond Areas of National Jurisdiction 27 March–7 April 2017' *Earth Negotiations Bulletin* (Online Bulletin, 10 April 2017) 12 ('Summary of PrepCom 3') <https://enb.iisd.org/events/3rd-session-bbnj-preparatory-committee/summary-report-27-march-7-april-2017>.

82 Blanchard (n 71) 328.

83 Barnes, 'Fisheries and ABNJ' (n 59) 134.

84 Freestone (n 25) 31.

85 Zoe Scanlon, 'The Art of "Not Undermining": Possibilities within Existing Architecture to Improve Environmental Protections in Areas beyond National Jurisdiction' (2018) 75(1) *ICES Journal of Marine Science* 405, 408.

86 Elisa Morgera et al, 'Summary of the Second Session of the Preparatory Committee on Marine Biodiversity beyond Areas of National Jurisdiction: 26 August–9 September 2016' *Earth Negotiations Bulletin* (Online Bulletin, 12 September 2016) 17 ('Summary of PrepCom 2') <https://enb.iisd.org/events/2nd-session-bbnj-preparatory-committee/summary-report-26-august-9-september-2016>.

87 Freestone (n 25) 31.

88 Barnes, 'Fisheries and ABNJ' (n 59) 139.

undermine' commitment may actually end up weakening the whole BBNJ process by 'minimising the compliance and implementation functions' an ILBI could feasibly adopt.'[89] To move negotiations forward, BBNJ negotiators could follow UNFSA. Under UNFSA, 'undermine' is interpreted to mean 'undermine the effectiveness or reduce the effectiveness.'[90] Applying this to the BBNJ context, an ILBI should not undermine existing conservation measures, or reduce the effectiveness of existing arrangements.[91] If reducing the effectiveness is the test, there should be no issue with measures adopted under an ILBI that strengthen and elaborate upon existing obligations or that promote the capacity, cooperation and coherence of existing bodies. Such measures will enhance the effectiveness of the current legal and institutional framework, not reduce it.

5.2.1.7 Geographically disadvantaged States

Kaye's last geopolitical factor concerns geographically disadvantaged States. During UNCLOS III geographically disadvantaged and land-locked States coalesced as a single interest group.[92] This group had two main concerns: (1) the right to access and navigate the sea and (2) access to marine resources.[93] Kaye argued that this bloc of States would be sceptical of MPAs that sought to restrict high seas freedoms and impose limitations upon the remaining common resource area.[94] However, there has been little mention of this group in BBNJ discourse on ABMTs. Instead, it has been the concerns of adjacent coastal States, another geopolitical interest group, that have dominated discussions on MPAs.[95]

5.2.1.8 Adjacent coastal States

Some delegations have suggested that adjacent coastal States (those with an EEZ adjacent to a high seas MPA) should be accorded special interests or rights under an ILBI. This is not a new idea.[96] Molenaar points to Articles 63(2), 64–67

89 Elizabeth Mendenhall et al, 'A Soft Treaty, Hard to Reach: The Second Inter-Governmental Conference for Biodiversity beyond National Jurisdiction' (2019) 108 *Marine Policy* 103664, 1–3, 3.
90 Wright et al (n 32) 10.
91 Ibid.
92 R.R. Churchill and A.V. Lowe, *The Law of the Sea* (Manchester University Press, 3rd ed, 1999) 434.
93 Ibid, 433.
94 Kaye (n 5) 223.
95 A number of coastal States are considered geographically disadvantaged because their coastline is short in proportion to their land territory; or the presence of neighbouring States prevents the generation of maritime zones (EEZ or continental shelf) (e.g. Germany, Singapore and Togo); or their EEZ is poor in natural resources (e.g. Jamaica, Nauru and Tanzania)—see, generally, Churchill and Lowe (n 92) 433.
96 Erik J. Molenaar, 'Ocean Governance beyond Boundaries: Origins, Trends, and Current Challenges' in Andrés M. Cisneros-Montemayor, William W.L. Cheung and Yoshitaka Ota

and 116 of UNCLOS and Article 3(1) of UNSFA, which recognise the rights and interests of coastal States over transboundary fish stocks.[97] Similarly, Articles 77(1) and 78(2) of UNCLOS recognise that a coastal State may impose restrictions on high seas bottom fisheries to protect sedentary species on its continental shelf.[98] There are also some interesting parallels between this idea and the concept of preferential fishing rights endorsed by the ICJ in the *Icelandic Fisheries Case*.[99] Of course, that doctrine has since been replaced by the EEZ.

The adjacency issue has been a point of dispute in BBNJ discussions. Some delegates seek a duty to consult adjacent coastal States;[100] however there is disagreement on the weight to be given to their opinion in the decision-making process. The adjacency concept could also 'advance a prioritised coastal State position'[101] and potentially undermine UNCLOS's delicate balance of rights between coastal States and flag States.[102] Coastal States have also proposed consensus voting for decisions on MPAs that overlie their outer continental shelf (OCS). This would essentially give these States a veto power and 'it is foreseeable that given the chance to do so' they will likely reject the creation of an MPA above their OCS.[103] This could have a profound impact on BBNJ located within approximately 12 per cent of ABNJ, where high seas overlie OCS.[104]

Prioritising the rights of coastal States could also 'lead to a push against international review mechanisms' to assess the effectiveness of MPAs designated in proximity to a coastal State.[105] These States are generally resistant to the 'review of their compliance with international obligations in managing their maritime zones'[106] and have been persistently unwilling 'to consider constraints or reforms' within their national waters.[107] The efforts made by the UNGA and FAO to protect VMEs from bottom fishing impacts are a case in point.[108] These efforts

(eds), *Predicting Future Oceans: Sustainability of Ocean and Human Systems Amidst Global Environmental Change* (Elsevier, 2019) 421.

97 Ibid.

98 Ibid.

99 *Fisheries Jurisdiction Case (United Kingdom of Britain and Northern Ireland v Iceland)* (Merits) [1974] ICJ Rep 3, 23 [52]. The ICJ accepted as customary law the concept of preferential fishing rights in adjacent waters in favour of the coastal State which has special dependence on its coastal fisheries.

100 See, e.g. submissions received from the EU, the US, Monaco and Greenpeace in response to the Chair's invitation at PrepCom 2.

101 Alex Oude Elferink, 'Coastal States and MPAs in ABNJ: Ensuring Consistency with the LOSC' in David Freestone (ed), *Conserving Biodiversity in Areas beyond National Jurisdiction* (Brill Nijhoff, 2019) 56, 60.

102 Freestone (n 25) 23.

103 Branco (n 1) 436.

104 Ibid, 434. This figure is based on the assumption that all the OCS claims (excluding overlapping areas) submitted to the CLCS are confirmed by its recommendations.

105 Oude Elferink (n 101) 83.

106 Ibid.

107 Molenaar (n 96) 422.

108 Ibid.

were ultimately confined to the high seas even though more serious impacts were occurring within national waters.[109] The adjacency concept and any special new authority it may confer on coastal States have the potential to hinder the establishment of MPAs under an ILBI. If the demands of coastal States are not met, it could also deter this bloc from participating in the new instrument.

Based on the above analysis, it is clear that high seas MPAs are still caught up in a geopolitical undertow. The majority of Kaye's geopolitical factors continue to impede their negotiation and development in ABNJ. Moreover, several new geopolitical considerations have come to light during the BBNJ process, including the interaction between an ILBI and existing arrangements and the complex issue of adjacency.

5.3 Geopolitical agendas—hindering progress, influencing outcomes

5.3.1 The Southern Ocean—a case study

Section 5.2 of this chapter has provided an up-to-date analysis of the geopolitical factors currently at play in the BBNJ process. Even though this paints a somewhat dismal picture in terms of the obstacles to overcome, BBNJ negotiators will not be starting from scratch. MPAs have been established in ABNJ, including under the CAMLR Convention. The following sections analyse the CAMLR's negotiation process to assess how geopolitical considerations influenced the resulting MPAs. This analysis also provides insight into objections likely to be raised in developing MPAs under an ILBI.

5.3.2 The CAMLR Convention

Since 2002, the Commission for the Conservation of Antarctic Marine Living Resources (CCAMLR) has been committed to establishing a coherent and representative MPA network in accordance with targets set by the UN World Summit on Sustainable Development.[110] After years of dialogue, two significant developments occurred in 2011; the CAMLR Convention area was divided into nine MPA planning domains, and the CCAMLR adopted Conservation Measure 91-04, which provides a general framework for developing a MPA network.[111] Although CAMLR Parties have long agreed, in principle, on the need for MPAs,

109 Ibid.

110 Cassandra M. Brooks et al, 'Reaching Consensus for Conserving the Global Commons: The Case of the Ross Sea, Antarctica' (2019) 13 *Conservation Letters* e12676 1–10, 3 ('Reaching Consensus').

111 Scientific Committee for the Conservation of Antarctic Marine Living Resources, *Report of the Thirtieth Meeting of the Scientific Committee* (SC-CAMLR-XXX) annex 6; CCAMLR, 'General Framework for the Establishment of CCAMLR Marine Protected Areas' Conservation Measure 91-04 (2011).

their development has been complex, slow and fraught with geopolitical issues.[112] Consequently, only two high seas MPAs have been designated under the CAMLR Convention, the first being the South Orkney Islands southern shelf MPA covering 94,000 square kilometres.[113]

5.3.2.1 The South Orkney Islands southern shelf MPA

The South Orkney Islands southern shelf is an important foraging ground for seabirds, a key habitat for krill and contains important benthic ecosystems.[114] In 2009, the UK submitted an initial MPA proposal, designating it a no-take zone, explicitly closed to fishing.[115] This was expected to draw opposition from fishing States. However, key amendments were made to appease their concerns. The original boundaries of the MPA were re-drawn to exclude prime krill fishing grounds.[116] These amended boundaries fail to protect regions adjacent to the Islands which have 'the greatest ecological value.'[117] Fishing interests therefore trumped conservation objectives.

The original proposal was also modified to accommodate future fishing interests.[118] Russia had expressed interest in a possible crab fishery in the northern section of the MPA,[119] which was subsequently excised from the proposal.[120] Ironically, this exploratory crab fishery 'proved fruitless: after almost 80,000 pot hours and 17 sets, only three crabs were caught.'[121] Fisheries interests thereby influenced the final shape of the MPA and arguably hindered its conservation potential. The concessions made to fishing States also set a precedent for future MPA proposals, including for the Ross Sea region.

5.3.2.2 The Ross Sea region MPA

The Ross Sea covers 1.57 million square kilometres of high seas and remains largely untouched by human impacts.[122] The Ross Sea is home to an estimated

112 Wright, Rochette and Druel (n 11) 280.
113 von Nordheim (n 28) 882.
114 Julian Roberts, Aldo Chircop and Siân Prior, 'Area-Based Management on the High Seas: Possible Application of the IMO's Particularly Sensitive Sea Area Concept' (2010) 25 *The International Journal of Marine and Coastal Law* 483, 503.
115 Cassandra M. Brooks, 'Competing Values on the Antarctic High Seas: CCAMLR and the Challenge of Marine-Protected Areas' (2013) 3(2) *The Polar Journal* 277, 282 ('Competing Values').
116 Scott (n 26) 855.
117 Cheryle Hislop and Julia Jabour, 'Quality Counts: High Seas Marine Protected Areas in the Southern Ocean' (2015) 29 *Ocean Yearbook* 166, 180.
118 Brooks et al, 'Reaching Consensus' (n 110) 3.
119 Danielle Smith and Julia Jabour, 'MPAs in ABNJ: Lessons from Two High Seas Regimes' (2017) 75(1) *ICES Journal of Marine Science* 417-425, 418.
120 Ibid.
121 Brooks, 'Competing Values' (n 115) 282.
122 Dodds and Nuttall (n 4) 181.

16,000 species, including the commercially lucrative Patagonian toothfish.[123] In 2012, New Zealand (NZ) and the US submitted independent proposals for a Ross Sea MPA.[124] As the US does not engage in toothfish fishing, its proposal displaced more of the commercial fishery.[125] The submissions were eventually amalgamated into a joint proposal, extending across 2.27 million square kilometres and dividing the MPA into three protection categories:

(1) A General Protection Zone where commercial fishing would be prohibited;
(2) A Special Research Zone, where tightly controlled research toothfish fishing would be allowed, by way of a concession to NZ;
(3) A Spawning Protection Zone, where research fishing would be permitted between December and March to protect winter spawning.[126]

The Ross Sea MPA proposal generated considerable debate.[127] Russia and China were the most vocal opponents.[128] Both States sought to minimise further restrictions on their Southern Ocean fishing aspirations.[129] China argued that MPAs should be of limited duration and opposed no-take zones,[130] while Russia advocated for additional fishing areas within and outside the MPA to offset potential closures.[131]

CCAMLR members were also concerned about the impact the MPA would have on other marine activities, including seabed mining. Despite the indefinite prohibition on Antarctic mining and mineral exploitation,[132] Russia, China and Ukraine have all published statements expressing interest in Antarctica's mineral resources.[133] Dodds and Nuttall suggest China's increase in funding for scientific programmes and research stations indicates a desire to see 'the Antarctic as a resource frontier.'[134] This would also explain China's staunch resistance to the establishment of further MPAs within the region.[135] During Ross Sea negotiations there was also 'an undercurrent of suspicion' that MPAs could be used to

123 Brian Clark Howard, 'World's Largest Marine Reserve Created off Antarctica' *National Geographic* (Online Magazine, 27 October 2016) <https://www.nationalgeographic.com/science/article/ross-sea-marine-protected-area-antarctica>.

124 Brooks, 'Competing Values' (n 115) 285.

125 Ibid.

126 Lauren Wenzel et al, 'Polar Opposites? Marine Conservation Tools and Experiences in the Changing Arctic and Antarctic' (2016) 26 (Suppl.2) *Aquatic Conservation: Marine and Freshwater Ecosystems* 61, 75.

127 Philip N. Trathan, 'Settle Discord over the Southern Ocean' (Pt Correspondence) (2012) 492 *Nature* 186.

128 Howard (n 123).

129 Dodds and Nuttall (n 4) 94.

130 CCAMLR, *Report of the Thirty-Fourth Meeting of the Commission*, (CCAMLR-XXXIV) November 2015.

131 Brooks, 'Reaching Consensus' (n 110) 5.

132 Madrid Protocol, art 7.

133 Dodds and Nuttall (n 4) 139.

134 Ibid, 93.

135 Three proposals are under negotiation in the East Antarctic, Weddell Sea and western Antarctic Peninsula.

'support or extend sovereign claims to Antarctic territory,'[136] despite the sovereignty moratorium in Article 4 of the Antarctic Treaty.

After intense diplomatic efforts, the Ross Sea MPA was adopted by consensus in 2016 and was hailed as a display of 'global environmental leadership.'[137] To achieve this result a number of trade-offs were necessary 'in a bid to achieve consensus through compromise.'[138] The MPA boundaries were adjusted, largely to accommodate fishing interests. The size of the MPA was significantly reduced from 2.27 to 1.55 million square kilometres.[139] The main fishing grounds on and around Iselin Bank were excised from the MPA despite being of high species richness and conservation importance.[140] The Spawning Protection Zone was also removed.[141] The size of the Special Research Zone was expanded in an attempt to appease Russian research fishing interests and a 322,000 square kilometre fishing zone was included, as a direct concession to China.[142] The CCAMLR also agreed to permit krill fishing in the toothfish fishing zone, despite being an important breeding area for Adélie and emperor penguins.[143] Patagonian toothfish areas were also re-opened outside the MPA[144] (Figure 5.1).

The full extent of the conservation value of the Ross Sea MPA is yet to be determined. Brooks et al argue that the most biodiversity-rich areas have been 'left unprotected to accommodate fishing.'[145] Moreover, the MPA may not comprehensively protect the ecological structure and function of the Ross Sea, which was one of its main objectives.[146] The MPA is also of limited duration, with a 35-year expiration date. Nicoll and Day argue that the Ross Sea cannot formally be considered an MPA because it has not been established 'to achieve the long-term conservation of nature.'[147] The IUCN Guidelines define long-term conservation as being in perpetuity rather than a short-term or temporary management strategy.[148] While the short duration of the MPA might be seen 'as a compromise to the notion of protection,'[149] Jabour and Smith argue that it actually 'represents

136 Smith and Jabour (n 119) 419.
137 Howard (n 123).
138 Hislop and Jabour (n 117) 182; Cassandra M. Brooks et al, 'The Ross Sea, Antarctica: A Highly Protected MPA in International Waters' (2021) 134 *Marine Policy* 104795, 1–7, 6.
139 Smith and Jabour (n 119) 419.
140 Brooks, 'Competing Values' (n 115) 289.
141 Wenzel et al (n 126) 75
142 Nengye Liu and Cassandra M. Brooks, 'China's Changing Position towards Marine Protected Areas in the Southern Ocean: Implications for Future Antarctic Governance' (2018) 94 *Marine Policy* 189, 191.
143 Ibid.
144 De Santo (n 7) 37.
145 Brooks et al 'Reaching Consensus' (n 110) 9.
146 Ibid.
147 Rob Nicoll and Jon C. Day, 'Correct Application of the IUCN Protected Area Management Categories to the CCAMLR Convention Area' (2017) 77 *Marine Policy* 9, 11.
148 Ibid.
149 Julia Jabour and Danielle Smith, 'The Ross Sea Region Marine Protected Areas: Can It Be Successfully Managed?' (2018) 32 *Ocean Yearbook* 190, 204.

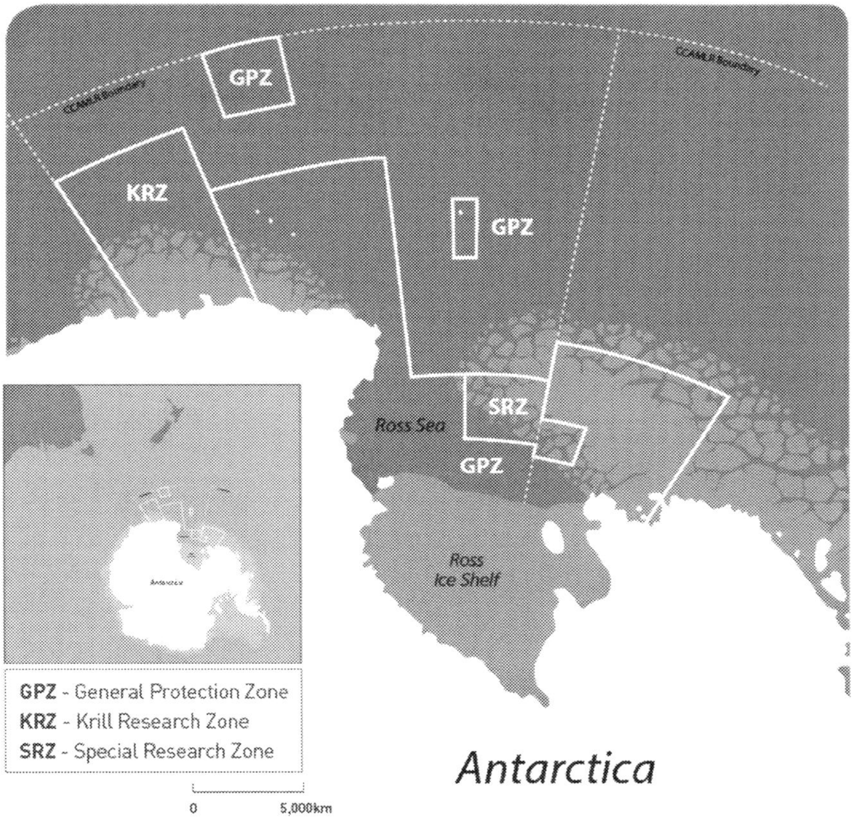

Figure 5.1 The Ross Sea region MPA ©. Image reproduced with the permission of the New Zealand Ministry of Foreign Affairs and Trade.

the realpolitik' of MPA negotiations.[150] This appears to be the stance taken by certain delegates in the BBNJ process. Several States continue to view the issue of duration as one directly linked to the strength of protection measures. Others argue that MPAs established on an eternal basis will provide no incentive for further scientific or financial investments at these sites.[151]

The case study of the CAMLR MPAs demonstrate the significant role geopolitical factors can play in shaping MPAs, in terms of their size, boundaries and duration, and influencing their outcome in terms of protective measures. Fishing

150 Ibid.
151 Tallash Kantai et al, 'BBNJ IGC-3 Highlights: Tuesday 27 August 2019' *Earth Negotiations Bulletin* (Online Bulletin, 28 August 2019) 2 <https://enb.iisd.org/download/pdf/enb25215e.pdf>.

interests took priority in both the South Orkney Islands and Ross Sea region. This arguably diminished the overall conservation value of these MPAs. Taking these lessons on board, BBNJ negotiators will need to find an appropriate balance between achieving conservation aims, whilst minimising the impact on high seas users.

5.4 MPAs under an ILBI—clearing a path through compromise

The following sections examine the various stages of the MPA process and offer suggestions on how BBNJ negotiators could, in effect, readjust the sails, to navigate a path through a persistently difficult geopolitical seascape.

5.4.1 The MPA process

First, BBNJ negotiators need to decide upon the process for the establishment of MPAs, including the institutions or bodies to be involved. One option is for an ILBI to adopt a 'global model.' A centralised decision-making body, in the form of a new or existing organisation, could be tasked with identifying, designating, managing and enforcing MPAs.[152] Some delegates warn that a global model risks undermining existing bodies and frameworks.[153] The other option is to maintain the prevailing regional and sectoral approach. Some States argue that existing bodies are the most efficient means for regulating MPAs due to their prior knowledge and experience.[154] However, Freestone contends that regional and sectoral organisations are too narrowly focused on their particular region or sector and lack the ability 'to perform a wider biodiversity or ecosystem-stewardship role.'[155]

A better approach lies in the adoption of a 'hybrid model,' such as the one proposed by NZ during PrepCom.[156] Under a hybrid approach, an ILBI could set out internationally agreed standards and obligations at the global level, which could then be implemented by States at the regional and sectoral levels.[157] This would give existing bodies a greater role, granting them the authority to establish MPAs,[158]

152 *Chair's Streamlined Non-Paper on Elements of a Draft Text of an International Legally-Binding Instrument under UNCLOS*, (2007) 21 ('Chair's Streamlined Non-Paper').

153 See, e.g. Iceland submission in Elisa Morgera et al, 'Summary of PrepCom 2' (n 86) 7.

154 Achinthi C. Vithanage, 'A Deep Dive into the High Seas: Harmonizing Regional Frameworks for Marine Protected Areas with the UNCLOS Convention on the Conservation and Sustainable Use of Marine Biological Diversity in Areas beyond National Jurisdiction' (2017) 28(1) *Yearbook of International Environmental Law* 63, 73.

155 Freestone (n 25) 32

156 See New Zealand, 'Preparatory Committee on Conservation and Sustainable Use of Marine Biological Diversity of Areas beyond National Jurisdiction: New Zealand Submission' (December 2016) 1 and 5 <https://www.un.org/depts/los/biodiversity/prepcom_files/rolling_comp/New_Zealand.pdf>.

157 Ibid, 1.

158 *Chair's Overview of the Third Session of the Preparatory Committee*, 12.

while providing international oversight of their decision-making and implementation functions.[159]

Another alternative is Vithanage's amalgamated global-hybrid approach. Pursuant to this model, a global commission, similar to CCAMLR, could oversee MPA proposals and set minimum standards for their designation, implementation and enforcement.[160] If a proposal falls within the mandate of an existing regional or sectoral organisation, the commission could delegate its duties to the relevant body.[161] This could be on the proviso that the commission's minimum standards are met and subject to oversight.[162] Where such a body does not exist or is unable to comply with minimum standards, the commission could step in to 'shoulder the responsibilities' of the process.[163]

A hybrid model offers a pragmatic approach, one that balances international guidance and oversight, whilst utilising and respecting the mandates of existing bodies.[164] A hybrid approach could also assist in integrating biodiversity considerations into regional and sectoral processes, thereby promoting 'a holistic and cross-sectoral approach' to the management of ABNJ.[165] More critically, a hybrid approach could assist in resolving geopolitical issues associated with the interplay between an ILBI and existing arrangements.

5.4.2 Identification of priority protection areas

BBNJ negotiators also need to decide how MPAs will be identified. As ABNJ remain poorly understood, a precautionary approach is required, one that 'includes appropriate protection of areas that are representative of targeted habitat as well as ecologically, biologically and scientifically important.'[166] With a view to avoiding duplication, the identification of protection sites should be based on agreed scientific criteria developed under existing instruments and frameworks, including the criteria used to identify VMEs, PSSAs and Ecologically or Biologically Significant Areas (EBSAs) (see Appendix 5).

5.4.2.1 Limitations of a VME-focused approach

The VME concept could be a particularly useful resource for identifying conservation priority areas. However, as it focuses predominately on spatially confined

159 Ibid. The institutional arrangements under an ILBI could comprise a decision-making body (i.e. a COP), a Secretariat and a Scientific and Technical body.

160 Vithanage (n 154) 81.

161 Ibid.

162 Ibid.

163 Ibid, 81–82.

164 Ibid, 81.

165 See *Revised Draft Text of an Agreement under UNCLOS on the Conservation and Sustainable Use of Marine Biological Diversity of Areas beyond National Jurisdiction*, UN Doc A/CONF.232/2020/3, art 14(a) ('*Revised Draft Negotiating Text*').

166 Kathryn J. Mengerink et al, 'A Call for Deep-Ocean Stewardship' (2014) 344(6185) *Science* 696, 697.

marine ecosystems, it is important to recognise its limitations in respect to environmental protection in ABNJ. The VME concept shares similarities with the 'Biodiversity Hotspot' approach to terrestrial conservation, and some of the criticisms levelled at this approach also apply to the VME concept. The term 'Biodiversity Hotspot' was coined in the 1980s in two seminal papers by Norman Myers.[167] Biodiversity hotspots were defined as areas with unusually high levels of endemic species that had also suffered severe habitat loss.[168] Using the principles of irreplaceability and vulnerability, Myers identified 18 geographical regions as conservation priorities.[169]

The hotspot approach emphasises species richness, resulting 'in high levels of protection for a few species-rich areas.'[170] However, evidence from both marine and terrestrial environments shows that species hotspots do not always align with hotspots of endemism or threat.[171] Focusing exclusively on hotspots runs the risk of leaving other equally important marine areas unprotected and may inadvertently alter the course of evolution.[172] The protection of hotspots 'at small scales favours species that can live in relatively restricted areas.'[173] Thus, species that migrate or that are not spatially confined 'will suffer disproportionate extinction.'[174] Smith et al argue for a more comprehensive approach that includes 'regions important to the generation and maintenance of biodiversity, regardless of whether they are 'species-rich''[175] or contain 'indicator species' as is the case with VMEs.

An over-reliance upon biodiversity hotspots or VMEs to set conservation priorities also ignores the need to preserve adaptive variation across environments.[176]

167 Norman Myers, 'Threatened Biotas: "Hotspots" in Tropical Forests' (1988) 8(3) *Environmentalist* 187; Norman Myers, 'The Biodiversity Challenge: Expanded Hot-Spots Analysis' (1990) 10(4) *Environmentalist* 243.

168 Peter Kareiva and Michelle Marvier, 'Conserving Biodiversity Coldspots' (2003) 91(4) *American Scientist* 344, 344.

169 Russell A. Mittermeier et al, 'Global Biodiversity Conservation: The Critical Role of Hotspots' in Frank E. Zachos and Jan Christian Habel (eds), *Biodiversity Hotspots Distribution and Protection of Conservation Priority Areas* (Springer Berlin Heidelberg, 2011) 3, 5. Globally, there are 36 biodiversity hotspots.

170 Kareiva and Marvier (n 168) 348.

171 See, e.g. Clinton N. Jenkins, Stuart L. Pimm and Lucas N. Joppa, 'Global Patterns of Terrestrial Vertebrate Diversity and Conservation' (2013) 110(28) *Proceedings of the National Academy of Sciences of the United States of America* E2602-10; C. David L. Orme et al, 'Global Hotspots of Species Richness Are Not Congruent with Endemism or Threat' (2005) 436(7053) *Nature* 1016–1019; Terry P. Hughes, David R. Bellwood and Sean R. Connolly, 'Biodiversity Hotspots, Centres of Endemicity, and the Conservation of Coral Reefs' (2002) 5(6) *Ecology Letters* 775–784.

172 Kareiva and Marvier (n 168) 349.

173 Ibid.

174 Ibid.

175 Thomas B. Smith et al, 'Biodiversity Hotspots and beyond: The Need for Preserving Environmental Transitions' (2001) 16(8) *Trends in Ecology and Evolution* 431, 431.

176 Ibid.

Climate change is altering marine species distribution with large-scale shifts already occurring.[177] Evidence suggests that changes in 'ocean temperature will continue to play a role in where commercially and recreationally important species find suitable habitat.'[178] Thus, 'the hotspots of today are unlikely to be the hotspots of tomorrow.'[179] Smith et al maintain that 'maximising adaptive variation' is the only 'hope to preserve the evolutionary response' to climate change effects and this will require a conservation strategy that focuses on both hotspots and associated transitional zones.[180]

While biodiversity hotspots and VMEs are appealing concepts, they are not a 'silver bullet' for conservation as they only provide a partial response.[181] Instead, these concepts should be included in 'an armoury'[182] of conservation tools and complemented by other strategies that 'fully reflect the spectrum of variability seen in the open ocean and deep-seabed.'[183] For example, an ILBI should encourage the use of modern management tools, such as a network of mobile MPAs.[184] The boundaries of mobile MPAs shift across space and time to protect dynamic habitats and migratory species in an ever-changing marine environment.[185] Mobile MPAs could also protect connectivity corridors between static MPAs, by offering protection to species or habitats that move outside fixed boundaries due to the effects of anthropogenic stressors.[186]

5.4.3 *Designation process*

Turning to the designation process, it is generally agreed that MPA proposals should be submitted by States Parties to the Secretariat of an ILBI.[187] At a minimum, a MPA proposal should include:

177 Kristin M. Kleisner et al, 'Marine Species Distribution Shifts on the U.S. Northeast Continental Shelf under Continued Ocean Warming' (2017) 153 *Progress in Oceanography* 24.

178 NOAA Northeast Fisheries Science Center, 'Marine Species Distribution Shifts Will Continue under Ocean Warming: Changes Impact Local Fishing Communities, Resource Management,' *Science Daily* (Web Page, 27 May 2017) <https://www.sciencedaily.com/releases/2017/05/170527110628.htm>.

179 Smith et al (n 175) 431.

180 Ibid.

181 Paul Jepsen and Susan Canney, 'Biodiversity Hotspots: Hot for What?' (2001) 10(3) *Global Ecology and Biogeography* 225, 227.

182 Ibid.

183 Guillermo Ortuño Crespo et al, 'Beyond Static Spatial Management: Scientific and Legal Considerations for Dynamic Management in the High Seas' (2020) 122 Marine Policy 104102, 1–10, 2.

184 Sara M. Maxwell et al, 'Mobile Protected Areas for Biodiversity on the High Seas' (2020) 367 (6475) *Science* 252.

185 Ibid.

186 Ibid, 253.

187 *Statement by the President of the Conference at the Closing of IGC 3*, UN Doc A/CONF.232/2019/10 (13 September 2019) [20]. This could be in collaboration with other States and stakeholders.

a) The geographic or spatial boundaries;
b) An evaluation of the current state of the marine environment and a description of human activities in the area;
c) A statement of conservation objectives.[188]

It would also be prudent to require a description of the activities that will be limited or prohibited in the proposed MPA, including information relating to possible infringement on high seas freedoms as well as socio-economic costs and mitigation measures. This could assist in finding an appropriate balance between conservation objectives and minimising impact upon other high seas users.

A growing body of evidence suggests that ABNJ and coastal waters are tightly linked via ecological and ocean circulation connectivity and that activities in ABNJ are impacting coastal maritime zones.[189] This connectivity raises implications for a coastal State in respect to the management of activities in MPAs established adjacent to its EEZ or above its OCS. As MPAs are most successful when they involve relevant stakeholders in their development and implementation,[190] an ILBI should provide an obligation to consult adjacent coastal States and take their interests into account. For example, a coastal State may have established ABMTs above its OCS to protect biodiversity. An ILBI should respect existing ABMTs imposed by coastal States to avoid undermining their economic and political interests.[191]

5.4.4 Decision-making

Scientific evidence suggests that MPAs 'yield the greatest conservation benefits when they are large, highly protected, isolated, well-enforced and long-standing.'[192]

188 Costa Rica and Monaco, 'Joint Submission on Marine Protected Areas' (31 August 2016) 3 <https://www.un.org/depts/los/biodiversity/prepcom_files/Costa_Rica_Monaco_BBNJ_Submission_MPAs.pdf>.

189 Ekaterina Popova et al, 'Ecological Connectivity between the Areas beyond National Jurisdiction and Coastal Waters: Safeguarding Interests of Coastal Communities in Developing Countries' (2019) 104 *Marine Policy* 90, 91.

190 United States of America, 'Views Expressed by the United States Delegation Related to Certain Key Issues under Discussion at the Second Session of the Preparatory Committee on the Development of an International Legally Binding Instrument under the United Nations Convention on the Law of the Sea on the Conservation and Sustainable Use of Marine Biological Diversity' (9 September 2016) 4 ('Views Expressed by US Delegation') <https://www.un.org/depts/los/biodiversity/prepcom_files/USA_Submission_of_Views_Expressed.pdf>.

191 See *Revised Draft Negotiating Text* (n 165) art 15(4); Permanent Mission of the Federated States of Micronesia to the United Nations, 'Views of the Government of the Federated States of Micronesia on the Elements of a Draft Text of an International Legally Binding Instrument under the United Nations Convention on the Law of the Sea on the Conservation and Sustainable Use of Marine Biological Diversity of Areas beyond National Jurisdiction'(14 March 2016) 4 <https://www.un.org/depts/los/biodiversity/prepcom_files/Federated_States_of_Micronesia.pdf>.

192 The Pew Charitable Trusts, 'How MPAs Safeguard the High Seas' (Brief, July 2019) 3 <https://www.pewtrusts.org/-/media/assets/2019/08/how_mpas_safeguard_the_high_seas_issue_brief_v1b.pdf>.

Certain delegates are therefore keen to see a network of marine reserves designated under an ILBI as these carry the highest level of protection.[193] However, maritime and fishing States, with a deep-seated desire to limit and prevent further restrictions on high seas freedoms, are unlikely to agree to a network of only marine reserves. For example, Russia and China argue that MPAs 'should not follow a uniform methodology,'[194] while the US insists that MPAs should 'allow for varying levels of ecosystem management' based on the characteristics of specific areas.[195]

When defining the scope of the BBNJ negotiations, States were encouraged to establish a global system of effectively managed MPAs *and* reserves.[196] The purpose of an ILBI is not to close all high seas areas to human activities as this would only 'create conflict with other societal needs.'[197] Instead, to be universally acceptable, an ILBI will need to embrace different types of management options for MPAs. Some marine sites will necessarily require strict protection, while others may function with less restrictive management approaches.[198] As Wells et al argue, partially protected areas can 'have positive ecological effects' and could be 'a valuable tool in places where exclusion of all extractive activities is not a socio-economically and politically viable option.'[199] Accordingly, as with the other elements of the package deal, trade-offs will inevitably need to be a core part of MPA planning in the BBNJ context.

An ILBI should therefore adopt a modern and flexible approach to MPAs underpinned by an 'expert-driven systematic conservation planning process.'[200] The ISA has advanced this approach as part of a collaborative stakeholder initiative to develop science-based recommendations on the delineation of protected sites in the CCZ.[201] The stakeholders developed the recommendations:

> by applying ecosystem-based management principles together with spatial analysis of biophysical and social datasets, which helped assess trade-offs in

193 Bruce Barcott, 'The Unfulfilled Promise of the World's Marine Protected Areas' on Yale School of Forestry and Environmental Studies, *Yale Environment 360* (Online Magazine, 16 June 2011) <https://e360.yale.edu/features/fulfilling_the_great_promise_of_worlds_marine_protected_areas>.

194 *Letter Dated 30 June 2011 from the Co-Chairs of the Ad Hoc Open-Ended Informal Working Group to the President of the General Assembly*, UN Doc A/66/119 (30 June 2011) annex ('Recommendations of the Ad Hoc Open-Ended Informal Working Group') [26].

195 Views expressed by US Delegation (n 190) 3.

196 Submission of Costa Rica in 'Informal Working Document' (n 57) [20]. Emphasis added.

197 Dudley (n 16) 44.

198 Ibid, 3.

199 Sue Wells et al, 'Building the Future of MPAs: Lessons from History' (2016) 26 (Supplement Article 2) *Aquatic Conservation: Marine and Freshwater Ecosystems* 101, 115.

200 L.M. Wedding et al, 'From Principles to Practice: A Spatial Approach to Systematic Conservation Planning in the Deep Sea' (2013) 280 *Proceedings of the Royal Society of Biological Sciences* 1–10, 1.

201 Ibid.

the planning region and ultimately select an approach that best balanced the competing interests of biodiversity protection and resource use.[202]

A systematic conservation planning approach could assist in striking a balance between different competing interests. BBNJ negotiators could also make use of a recent project funded by the Pew Charitable Trusts and led by scientists at the University of California, which uses data-driven analysis to identify marine sites of conservation value.[203] A state-of-the-art algorithm (prioritizr R) integrates 55 global data layers of conservation features which can be grouped into 6 broad categories and 1 'cost' layer.[204] The conservation features include: (1) species richness, (2) species extinction risk, (3) seamounts, (4) hydrothermal vents, (5) seafloor habitat diversity and (6) productivity.[205] The cost layer is commercial fishing.[206] The algorithm searches for a solution area that protects at least 30 per cent of the conservation features in each layer while minimising overlap with highly fished sites.[207] Using this algorithm, scientists identified over 52 million square kilometres of the ocean as high-priority regions for spatial protection and 73 per cent of this area remained the same even when the cost layer was applied.[208] This could be a valuable data resource tool for determining where MPAs should be established under an ILBI.

As an expert-driven systematic conservation planning process accounts for a variety of objectives and maritime uses, this approach could appeal to maritime and fishing States, as it could result 'in a smaller footprint of restrictive management of human activities' in ABNJ.[209] This group of States may be more inclined to endorse and join an ILBI if attempts are made to accommodate their interests, whether they be navigational, fishing or otherwise. As was the case during UNCLOS III, a package deal of differentiated management approaches to MPAs will be required in order to keep these States at the negotiating table.[210]

5.5 Conclusion

When MPAs are science-based, carefully designed, fully implemented and managed effectively, they can enhance ecosystem resilience, create meaningful links across habitats and preserve biodiversity.[211] MPAs form 'the cornerstones of virtually all national and international conservation strategies.'[212] However,

202 Ibid, 2.
203 The Pew Charitable Trusts (n 77) 3.
204 Ibid, 7.
205 Ibid.
206 Ibid.
207 Ibid, 9.
208 Visalli et al (n 74) 1 and 7.
209 Maxwell et al (n 184) 254.
210 Summary of PrepCom 2 (n 153) 19.
211 Views Expressed by the US delegation (n 190) 3.
212 Dudley (n 16) 2.

geopolitically charged issues continue to impede the establishment of MPAs in ABNJ. Taking Kaye's assessment of the key geopolitical factors of relevance to high seas protection as a starting point, this chapter has assessed the extent to which these and additional factors continue to influence the negotiation and development of MPAs under an ILBI. Using the CAMLR MPAs as a case study, this chapter showed how geopolitical factors have the power to hinder progress and influence outcomes in MPA negotiations. Thus, to arrive at a satisfactory outcome, BBNJ negotiators will need to find a way to navigate a path through a persistently difficult geopolitical seascape.

This chapter has suggested a number of compromise solutions that could assist in bridging the divide between MPAs and high seas freedoms. First, in order to alleviate the navigational and strategic concerns of maritime States, this chapter proposes a heightened role for the IMO under an ILBI in respect to the designation of MPAs, to guarantee the input of specialised technical expertise and to ensure that a balance is maintained between BBNJ protection and the preservation of high seas navigational freedoms.

Second, the purpose and legal effect of an ILBI as an 'implementing agreement' to UNCLOS should be continually reinforced in BBNJ discussions to reassure fishing States that the development of an ILBI will not be used as a surreptitious way of reopening fisheries discussions or to deal with ocean governance matters afresh.

This leads onto the third compromise solution which concerns the interpretation of the ambiguous term 'undermine.' BBNJ negotiators should follow the interpretation adopted in UNFSA, wherein 'undermine' is taken to mean 'undermine the effectiveness or reduce the effectiveness.'[213] Measures adopted under an ILBI that strengthen and elaborate upon existing obligations or promote the capacity, cooperation and coherence of existing bodies, should be understood as enhancing the effectiveness of the current legal and institutional framework, not reducing it. The adoption of a hybrid model could also assist in resolving the geopolitical issues associated with the interplay between an ILBI and existing arrangements.

Lastly, while the adjacency issue is sure to stoke fears of creeping jurisdiction, MPAs are most successful when they involve relevant stakeholders in their development and implementation. Thus, an ILBI should provide an obligation to consult adjacent coastal States and take their interests into account when a high seas MPA is to be established in proximity to a coastal State.[214]

The inevitable conflict between MPAs and high seas freedoms will not be resolved by simply 'giving precedence to the protection of the marine environment.'[215] An effective regime for the protection of BBNJ will require, to

213 Wright et al (n 32) 10.

214 Oude Elferink (n 101) 83.

215 Nele Matz-Lück and Johannes Fuchs, 'The Impact of OSPAR on Protected Area Management beyond National Jurisdiction: Effective Regional Cooperation or a Network of Paper Parks?' (2014) 49 *Marine Policy* 155, 156.

some extent, the 'circumscribing of traditional high seas freedoms'[216] and compromise solutions. In order to keep a key bloc of maritime and fishing States at the negotiating table, BBNJ negotiators will need to strike the right balance between achieving conservation aims whilst minimising impacts on high seas users. At the same time, BBNJ negotiators need to be careful to avoid creating a network of 'paper parks,' being noble in name but offering no real protection.[217] Paper parks will be created if 'MPAs are designated in areas with low biodiversity value or few human activities.'[218] While the geopolitical obstacles in this chapter are substantial, they are not insurmountable.[219] In an effort to overcome geopolitical challenges, this chapter has argued for an ILBI to adopt a modern, flexible and compromise approach to high seas MPAs and for this approach to be underpinned by an expert-driven systematic conservation planning process and involve the use of innovative data resource and management tools. This approach could offer a pragmatic path forward and assist in preventing MPAs under an ILBI from being caught up in a geopolitical undertow.

References

Alvarenga, Karen, et al., 'Marine Biodiversity Working Group Highlights: Thursday, 16 February 2006' *Earth Negotiations Bulletin* (online, 17 February 2006) <https://enb.iisd.org/download/pdf/enb2524e.pdf> accessed 31 March 2022.

'Australia Preparatory Committee on Conservation and Sustainable Use of Marine Biological Diversity of Areas beyond National Jurisdiction (BBNJ): Submission by Australia' (6 December 2016) ('Written submission of Australia to PrepCom') <https://www.un.org/depts/los/biodiversity/prepcom_files/rolling_comp/Australia.pdf> accessed 31 March 2022.

Barcott, Bruce, 'The Unfulfilled Promise of the World's Marine Protected Areas' on Yale School of Forestry and Environmental Studies' *Yale Environment* 360 <https://e360.yale.edu/features/fulfilling_the_great_promise_of_worlds_marine_protected_areas> accessed 31 March 2022.

Barnes, Richard, 'The Proposed LOSC Implementation Agreement on Areas Beyond National Jurisdiction and Its Impact on International Fisheries Law' (2016) 31(4) *The International Journal of Marine and Coastal Law* 583–619. DOI: 10.1163/15718085-12341411.

Barnes, Richard, David Freestone and David M. Ong, 'The Law of the Sea: Progress and Prospects' in Richard Barnes, David Freestone and David M Ong (eds), *The Law of the Sea Progress and Prospects* (Oxford University Press, 2006) 1. DOI: 10.1093/acprof:oso/9780199299614.003.0001.

Barnes, Richard Alan, 'Fisheries and ABNJ: Advancing and Enhancing Cooperation' in Tomas Heidar (ed), *New Knowledge and Changing Circumstances in the Law of the*

216 Kaye (n 5) 221.

217 Gjerde and Rulska-Domino (n 21) 357.

218 Bethan C. O'Leary et al, 'Effective Coverage Targets for Ocean Protection' (2016) 9(6) *Conservation Letters* 398, 402.

219 Kaye (n 5) 225.

Sea (Brill Nijhoff, 2020) 124. DOI: https://doi.org/10.1163/9789004437753_009.

Beckman, Robert C., 'PSSAs and Transit Passage: Australia's Pilotage System in the Torres Strait Challenges the IMO and UNCLOS' (2007) 38 *Ocean Development & International Law* 325–357. DOI: 10.1080/00908320701641552.

Blanchard, Catherine, 'Fragmentation in High Seas Fisheries: Preliminary Reflections on a Global Oceans Governance Approach' (2017) 84 *Marine Policy* 327–332. DOI: 10.1016/j.marpol.2017.06.017.

Blasiak, Robert and Nobuyuki Yagi, 'Shaping an International Agreement on Marine Biodiversity Beyond Areas of National Jurisdiction: Lessons from High Seas Fisheries' (2016) 71 *Marine Policy* 210–216. DOI: 10.1016/j.marpol.2016.06.004.

Bo, Hu 'China-US Military Confrontation in the South China Sea: Fact and Fiction' *The Diplomat* (Online Magazine, 12 June 2020) <https://thediplomat.com/2020/06/china-us-military-confrontation-in-the-south-china-sea-fact-and-fiction/> accessed 31 March 2022.

Branco, Inês Aguiar, 'Solving the Potential Conflict: High Seas Marine Protected Areas and Sovereign Rights Over the Continental Shelf Beyond 200 Nautical Miles' in Marta Chantal Ribeiro, Fernando Loureiro Bastos and Tore Henriksen (eds) *Global Challenges and the Law of the Sea* (Springer Nature Switzerland, 2020) 423. DOI: https://doi.org/10.1007/978-3-030-42671-2_22.

Brooks, Cassandra M., 'Competing Values on the Antarctic High Seas: CCAMLR and the Challenge of Marine-protected Areas' (2013) 3(2) *The Polar Journal* 277–300. DOI: 10.1080/2154896X.2013.854597.

Brooks, Cassandra M., Larry B. Crowder, Henrik Österblom and Aaron L. Strong, 'Reaching Consensus for Conserving the Global Commons: The Case of the Ross Sea, Antarctica' (2019) 13 *Conservation Letters* e12676: 1–10. DOI: 10.1111/conl.12676.

Brooks, Cassandra M., Evan Bloom, Andrea Kavanagh, Emily S. Nocito, George M. Watters and John Weller, 'The Ross Sea, Antarctica: A Highly Protected MPA in International Waters' (2021) 134 *Marine Policy* 104795: 1–7. DOI: https://doi.org/10.1016/j.marpol.2021.104795.

CBD, *Strategic Plan 2011–2020, Aichi Target 11*, UN Doc COP/10/INF/12/Rev.1 (14 March 2011).

CCAMLR, 'Protection of the South Orkney Islands Southern Shelf' (2009) 91(3) *Conservation Measure* 1-2.

CCAMLR, 'General Framework for the Establishment of CCAMLR Marine Protected Areas' (2011) *Conservation Measure* 91(4) 1-4.

CCAMLR, *Report of the Thirty-Fourth Meeting of the Commission* (CCAMLR-XXXIV, November 2015).

Chair's Indicative Suggestions of Clusters of Issues and Questions to Assist Further Discussions in the Informal Working Groups at the Second Session of the Preparatory Committee <https://www.un.org/Depts/los/biodiversity/prepcom_files/IWGs_Indictive_Issues_and_Questions.pdf> accessed 31 March 2022.

Chair's Overview of the Third Session of the Preparatory Committee, <https://www.un.org/Depts/los/biodiversity/prepcom_files/Chair_Overview.pdf> accessed 31 March 2022.

Chair's Streamlined non-paper on Elements of a Draft Text of an International Legally-binding Instrument under the United Nations Convention on the Law of the Sea on the Conservation and Sustainable Use of Marine Biological Diversity of Areas Beyond National Jurisdiction Fourth Session of the PrepCom (10–21 July 2017) <https://www.un.org/depts/los/biodiversity/prepcom_files/Chairs_streamlined_non-paper_to_delegations.pdf> accessed 31 March 2022.

Churchill, R.R., and A.V. Lowe, *The Law of the Sea* (Manchester University Press, 3rd ed, 1999).

Claudet, Joachim, 'Food for Thought Six Conditions under Which MPAs Might Not Appear Effective' (2018) 75(3) *ICES Journal of Marine Science* 1172–1174. DOI: 10.1093/icesjms/fsx074.

Costa Rica and Monaco, 'Joint Submission on Marine Protected Areas' (31 August 2016) ('Written submission of Costa Rica and Monaco to PrepCom') <https://www.un.org/depts/los/biodiversity/prepcom_files/Costa_Rica_Monaco_BBNJ_Submission_MPAs.pdf> accessed 31 March 2022.

Crespo, Guillermo Ortuño, Joanna Mossop, Daniel Dunn, Kristina Gjerde, Elliot Hazen, Gabriel Reygondeau, Robin Warner, Derek Tittensor and Patrick Halpin, 'Beyond Static Spatial Management: Scientific and Legal Considerations for Dynamic Management in the High Seas' (2020) 122 *Marine Policy* 104102: 1–10. DOI: 10.1016/j.marpol.2020.104102.

De Lucia, Vito, 'Reflecting on the Meaning of "Not Undermining" Ahead of IGC-2' (The Blog of the Norwegian Centre for the Law of the Sea, 21 March 2019) <https://site.uit.no/nclos/2019/03/21/reflecting-on-the-meaning-of-not-undermining-ahead-of-igc-2/> accessed 31 March 2022.

De Santo, Elizabeth M., 'Implementation Challenges of Area-based Management Tools (ABMTs) for Biodiversity Beyond National Jurisdiction (BBNJ)' (2018) 97 *Marine Policy* 34–43. DOI: 10.1016/j.marpol.2018.08.034.

Dodds, Klaus and Mark Nuttall, *The Scramble for the Poles* (Polity Press, 2016).

Druel, Elisabeth, 'Paper VI: Options and Approaches for Establishing and Managing Marine Protected Areas in ABNJ' in IUCN (ed), *An International Instrument on Conservation and Sustainable Use of Biodiversity in Marine Areas Beyond National Jurisdiction Exploring Different Elements to Consider* (Series of Policy Briefs on Scope, Parameters and Feasibility, IUCN, 2003).

Dudley, Nigel (ed), *Guidelines for Applying Protected Area Management Categories* (Best Practice Protected Area Guidelines Series No. 21, IUCN, 2008).

FAO, *International Guidelines for the Management of Deep-Sea Fisheries in the High Seas* (FAO, 2009).

Fisheries Jurisdiction Case (United Kingdom of Britain and Northern Ireland v Iceland) (Merits) (1974) *ICJ Rep* 3.

Freestone, David, 'The UN Process to Develop an International Legally Binding Instrument under the 1982 Law of the Sea Convention: Issues and Challenges' in David Freestone (ed), *Conserving Biodiversity in Areas Beyond National Jurisdiction* (Brill Nijhoff, 2019) 3. DOI: https://doi.org/10.1163/9789004391703_002.

Freestone, David and Alex G. Oude Elferink, 'Flexibility and Innovation in the Law of the Sea: Will the LOS Convention Amendment Procedures Ever Be Used' in Alex G. Oude Elferink (ed), *Stability and Change in the Law of the Sea: The Role of the LOSC Convention* (Martinus Nijhoff, 2005) 184.

Freestone, David and Viva Harris, 'Particularly Sensitive Sea Areas Beyond National Jurisdiction: Time to Chart a New Course?' in Myron H. Nordquist, John Norton

Moore and Ronán Long (eds), *International Marine Economy: Law and Policy* (Koninklijke Brill NV, 2017) vol 20, 322. DOI: 10.1163/9789004323445.

Friedlander, Alan M., Daniel Wagner, Carlos F. Gaymer, T. 'Auluni Wilhelm, Nai'A Lewis, Samantha Brooke, Kekuewa Kikiloi and Ole Varmer, 'Co-operation Between Large-scale MPAs: Successful Experiences from the Pacific Ocean' (2016) 26 (Suppl. 2) *Aquatic Conservation: Marine and Freshwater Ecosystems* 126–141. DOI: 10.1002/aqc.2645.

Gjerde, Kristina M. and Anna Rulska-Domino, 'Marine Protected Areas Beyond National Jurisdiction: Some Practical Perspectives for Moving Ahead' (2012) 27 *The International Journal of Marine and Coastal Law* 351–373. DOI: 10.1163/157180812X633636.

Halpern, Benjamin S., Sarah E. Lester and Karen L. McLead, 'Placing Marine Protected Areas onto the Ecosystem-Based Management Seascape' (2010) 107(43) *Proceedings of the National Academy of Sciences of the United States of America* 18312–18317. DOI: 10.1073/pnas.0908503107.

Hammond, Amy and Peter J.S. Jones, 'Protecting the 'Blue Heart of the Planet': Strengthening the Governance Framework for Marine Protected Areas Beyond National Jurisdiction' (2021) 127 *Marine Policy* 104260: 1–12. DOI: https://doi.org/10.1016/j.marpol.2020.104260.

Harrison, James, *Making the Law of the Sea: A Study in the Development of International Law* (Cambridge University Press, 2011). DOI: https://doi.org/10.1017/CBO9780511974908.

Hislop, Cheryle and Julia Jabour, 'Quality Counts: High Seas Marine Protected Areas in the Southern Ocean' (2015) 29 *Ocean Yearbook* 166–191. DOI: 10.1163/22116001-02901009.

Howard, Brian Clark, 'World's Largest Marine Reserve Created Off Antarctica' *National Geographic* (Online Magazine, 27 October 2016) <https://www.nationalgeographic.com/science/article/ross-sea-marine-protected-area-antarctica> accessed 31 March 2022.

Hubert, Anna-Maria 'UN General Assembly Resolution to Develop a New Legally Binding Instrument on the Conservation and Sustainable Use of Marine Biological Diversity of Areas Beyond National Jurisdiction' (The NCLOS Blog, 17 August 2015) <https://site.uit.no/nclos/2015/08/17/un-general-assembly-resolution-to-develop-a-new-legally-binding-instrument-on-the-conservation-and-sustainable-use-of-marine-biological-diversity-of-areas-beyond-national-jurisdiction/> accessed 31 March 2022.

Hughes, Terry P., David R. Bellwood and Sean R. Connolly, 'Biodiversity Hotspots, Centres of Endemicity, and the Conservation of Coral Reefs' (2002) 5(6) *Ecology Letters* 775–784. DOI: 10.1046/j.1461-0248.2002.00383.x.

Iceland, 'Iceland's Written Submission to the Preparatory Committee Established by the General Assembly Resolution 69/292: Development of an International Legally Binding Instrument under the United Nations Convention on the Law of the Sea on the Conservation and Sustainable Use of Marine Biological Diversity Beyond National Jurisdiction' (December 2016) <https://www.un.org/depts/los/biodiversity/prepcom_files/rolling_comp/Iceland.pdf> accessed 31 March 2022.

IMO, *Revised Guidelines for the Identification and Designation of Particularly Sensitive Sea Areas*, Resolution A.982(24) (1 December 2005).

IMO, *PrepCom 1 Conservation and Sustainable Use of Marine Biological Diversity of ABNJ* (Policy brief, 2016) <https://www.un.org/depts/los/biodiversity/prepcom_files/IMO_Policy_Brief_BBNJ_PrepCom_1.pdf> accessed 31 March 2022.

International Chamber of Shipping and the European Community Shipowners' Association and the Asian Shipowners' Association, 'Development of an International Legally Binding Instrument Under UNCLOS on the Conservation and Sustainable Use of Biological Diversity in Areas Beyond National Jurisdiction' (Position Paper, July 2018) <https://www.ecsa.eu/sites/default/files/publications/ics-ecsa-asa%20position%20paper%20on%20unclos%20implementing%20agreement.pdf> accessed 31 March 2022.

International Convention for the Prevention of Pollution from Ships, as amended by the 1978 Protocol, opened for signature 2 November 1973 (1973) 1340 *UNTS* 61 (entered into force 12 October 1984) (MARPOL).

International Legally Binding Instrument under the United Nations Convention on the Law of the Sea on the Conservation and Sustainable Use of Marine Biological Diversity of Areas Beyond National Jurisdiction, GA Res 72/249, UN Doc A/RES/72/249 (19 January 2018, adopted on 24 December 2017).

ISA, *Decision of the Council relating to an environmental management plan for the Clarion-Clipperton Zone*, ISBA/18/C/22 (ISA, 26 July 2012).

IUCN, *Governing Areas Beyond National Jurisdiction* (Issues Brief, IUCN, March 2019).

Jabour, Julia and Danielle Smith, 'The Ross Sea Region Marine Protected Areas: Can It be Successfully Managed?' (2018) 32 *Ocean Yearbook* 190–205. DOI: 10.1163/22116001-03201008.

Jakobsen, Ingvild Ulrikke, *Marine Protected Areas in International Law: An Arctic Perspective* (Brill/Nijhoff, 2016) Queen Mary Studies in International Law, vol 25.

Jenkins, Clinton N., Stuart L. Pimm and Lucas N. Joppa, 'Global Patterns of Terrestrial Vertebrate Diversity and Conservation' (2013) 110(28) *Proceedings of the National Academy of Sciences of the United States of America* E2602–2610. DOI: 10.1073/pnas.1302251110.

Jepsen, Paul and Susan Canney, 'Biodiversity Hotspots: Hot for What?' (2001) 10(3) *Global Ecology and Biogeography* 225–227. DOI: 10.1046/j.1466-822x.2001.00255.x.

Kantai, Tallash, Jennifer Bansard, Tasha Goldberg, Katarina Hovden and Asterios Tsioumanis, 'BBNJ IGC-3 Highlights: Wednesday, 21 August 2019' *Earth Negotiations Bulletin* (Online Bulletin, 22 August 2019a) <https://enb.iisd.org/download/pdf/enb25211e.pdf> accessed 31 March 2022.

Kantai, Tallash, Jennifer Bansard, Tasha Goldberg, Katarina Hovden and Asterios Tsioumanis, 'BBNJ IGC-3 Highlights: Tuesday 27 August 2019' *Earth Negotiations Bulletin* (Online Bulletin, 28 August 2019b) <https://enb.iisd.org/download/pdf/enb25215e.pdf> accessed 31 March 2022.

Kareiva, Peter and Michelle Marvier, 'Conserving Biodiversity Coldspots' (2003) 91 *American Scientist* 344–351. DOI: 10.1511/2003.4.344.

Kaye, Stuart, 'Implementing High Seas Biodiversity Conservation: Global Geopolitical Considerations' (2004) 28 *Marine Policy* 221–226. DOI: 10.1016/j.marpol.2003.09.001.

Kleisner, Kristin M., Michael J. Fogarty, Sally McGee, Jonathan A. Hare, Skye Moret, Charles T. Perretti and Vincent S. Saba, 'Marine Species Distribution Shifts on the

U.S. Northeast Continental Shelf under Continued Ocean Warming' (2017) 153 *Progress in Oceanography* 24–36. DOI: 10.1016/j.pocean.2017.04.001.

Kraabel, Kristine Dalaker, 'The BBNJ PrepCom and Institutional Arrangements: The Hype about the Hybrid Approach' in Myron H. Nordquist, John Morton Moore and Ronán Long (eds), *The Marine Environment and United Nations Sustainable Development Goal 14* (Brill, 2019) 137. DOI: https://doi.org/10.1163/9789004366619_012.

Kraska, James, 'National Security Considerations for a Binding Instrument on Managing Biodiversity Beyond National Jurisdiction' (2018) 112 *AJIL Unbound* 150–154. DOI: 10.1017/aju.2018.43.

Laffoley, Dan, John M. Baxter, Jon C. Day, Lauren Wenzel, Paula Bueno and Katherine Zischka, 'Marine Protected Areas' in Charles Sheppard (ed) *World Seas: An Environmental Evaluation Volume III, Ecological Issues and Environmental Impacts* (Elsevier Ltd, 2nd ed, 2019) 549.

Leary, David, 'Agreeing to Disagree on What We Have or Have Not Agreed on: The Current State of Play of the BBNJ Negotiations on the Status of Marine Genetic Resources in Areas Beyond National Jurisdiction' (2019) 99 *Marine Policy* 21–29. DOI: 10.1016/j.marpol.2018.10.031.

Letter Dated 30 June 2011 from the Co-Chairs of the Ad Hoc Open-ended Informal Working Group to the President of the General Assembly, UN Doc A/66/119 (30 June 2011) <https://documents-dds-ny.un.org/doc/UNDOC/GEN/N11/397/64/PDF/N1139764.pdf?OpenElement> accessed 31 March 2022.

Letter Dated 8 June 2012 from the Co-Chairs of the Ad Hoc Open-ended Informal Working Group to the President of the General Assembly, UN Doc A/67/95 (13 June 2012) annex ('Co-Chairs' Summary of discussions') <https://documents-dds-ny.un.org/doc/UNDOC/GEN/N12/372/82/PDF/N1237282.pdf?OpenElement> accessed 31 March 2022.

Liu, Nengye and Cassandra M. Brooks, 'China's Changing Position Towards Marine Protected Areas in the Southern Ocean: Implications for Future Antarctic Governance' (2018) 94 *Marine Policy* 189–195. DOI: 10.1016/j.marpol.2018.05.011.

Marine Conservation Institute,'Atlas of Marine Protection' (Web Page, 3 February 2022) <http://www.mpatlas.org> accessed 31 March 2022.

Matz-Lück, Nele and Johannes Fuchs, 'The Impact of OSPAR on Protected Area Management Beyond National Jurisdiction: Effective Regional Cooperation or a Network of Paper Parks?' (2014) 49 *Marine Policy* 155–166. DOI: 10.1016/j.marpol.2013.12.001.

Maxwell, Sara M., Kristina M. Gjerde, Melinda G. Conners and Larry B. Crowder, 'Mobile Protected Areas for Biodiversity on the High Seas' (2020) 367(6475) *Science* 252–254. DOI: 10.1126/science.aaz9327.

Mendenhall, Elizabeth, Elizabeth De Santo, Elizabeth Nyman and Rachel Tiller, 'A Soft Treaty, Hard to Reach: The Second Inter-governmental Conference for Biodiversity Beyond National Jurisdiction' (2019) 108 *Marine Policy* 103664: 1–3. DOI: 10.1016/j.marpol.2019.103664.

Mengerink, Kathryn J., Cindy L. Van Dover, Jeff Ardron, Maria Baker, Elva Escobar-Briones, Kristina Gjerde, J. Anthony Koslow, Eva Ramirez-Llodra, Ana Lara-Lopez, Dale Squires, Tracey Sutton, Andrew K. Sweetman and Lisa A. Levin, 'A Call for Deep-Ocean Stewardship' (2014) 344(6185) *Science* 696–698. DOI: 10.1126/science.1251458.

Mittermeier, Russell A., Will R. Turner, Frank W. Larsen, Thomas M. Brooks and Claude Gascon, 'Global Biodiversity Conservation: The Critical Role of Hotspots' in Frank E. Zachos and Jan Christian Habel (eds), *Biodiversity Hotspots Distribution and Protection of Conservation Priority Areas* (Springer, 2011) 3. DOI: https://doi.org/10.1007/978-3-642-20992-5_1.

Molenaar, Erik J., 'Ocean Governance Beyond Boundaries: Origins, Trends and Current Challenges' in Andres M. Cisneros-Montemayor, William W.L. Cheung and Yoshitaka Ota (eds), *Predicting Future Oceans: Sustainability of Ocean and Human Systems Amidst Global Environmental Change* (Elsevier, 2019) 419. DOI: https://doi.org/10.1016/B978-0-12-817945-1.00040-X.

Morgera, Elisa, Daniela Diz, Tallash Kantai and Asterios Tsioumanis, 'PrepCom 1 Highlights: Monday, 28 March 2016,' *Earth Negotiations Bulletin* (Online Bulletin, 29 March 2016a) <https://enb.iisd.org/download/pdf/enb2597e.pdf> accessed 31 March 2022.

Morgera, Elisa, Daniela Diz, Tallash Kantai and Asterios Tsioumanis, 'Summary of the Second Session of the Preparatory Committee on Marine Biodiversity Beyond Areas of National Jurisdiction: 26 August – 9 September 2016' *Earth Negotiations Bulletin* (Online Bulletin, 12 September 2016b) <https://enb.iisd.org/download/pdf/enb25118e.pdf> accessed 31 March 2022.

Morgera, Elisa, Asheline Appleton, Tallash Kantai and Asterios Tsioumanis, 'Summary of the Third Session of the Preparatory Committee on Marine Biodiversity beyond Areas of National Jurisdiction 27 March –7 April 2017' *Earth Negotiations Bulletin* (Online Bulletin, 10 April 2017a) <https://enb.iisd.org/download/pdf/enb25129e.pdf> accessed 31 March 2022.

Morgera, Elisa, Asheline Appleton, Tallash Kantai and Asterios Tsioumanis, 'PrepCom 4 Highlights: Wednesday 12 July 2017' *Earth Negotiations Bulletin* (Online Bulletin, 13 July 2017b) <https://enb.iisd.org/download/pdf/enb25134e.pdf> accessed 31 March 2022.

Myers, Norman, 'Threatened Biotas: "Hotspots" in Tropical Forests' (1988) 8(3) *Environmentalist* 187–208. DOI: https://doi.org/10.1007/BF02240252.

Myers, Norman, 'The Biodiversity Challenge: Expanded Hot-spots Analysis' (1990) 10(4) *Environmentalist* 243–256. DOI: 10.1007/BF02239720.

New Zealand, 'Preparatory Committee on Conservation and Sustainable Use of Marine Biological Diversity of Areas beyond National Jurisdiction: New Zealand Submission' (December 2016) ('Written submission of New Zealand to PrepCom') <https://www.un.org/depts/los/biodiversity/prepcom_files/rolling_comp/New_Zealand.pdf> accessed 31 March 2022.

Nicoll, Rob and Jon C. Day, 'Correct Application of the IUCN Protected Area Management Categories to the CCAMLR Convention Area' (2017) 77 *Marine Policy* 9–12. DOI: 10.1016/j.marpol.2016.11.035.

NOAA Northeast Fisheries Science Centre, 'Marine Species Distribution Shifts Will Continue under Ocean Warming: Changes Impact Local Fishing Communities, Resource Management,' *Science Daily* (Web Page, 27 May 2017) <https://www.sciencedaily.com/releases/2017/05/170527110628.htm> accessed 31 March 2022.

O'Leary, Bethan C., 'Effective Coverage Targets for Ocean Protection' (2016) 9(6) *Conservation Letters* 398–404. DOI: 10.1111/conl.12247.

O'Leary, Bethan C., George Hoppit, Adam Townley, Harriet L. Allen, Christina J. McIntyre and Callum M. Roberts, 'Options for Managing Human Threats to

High Seas Biodiversity' (2020) 187 *Ocean and Coastal Management* 105110: 1–12. DOI: 10.1016/j.ocecoaman.2020.105110.

Orme, C. David L, Richard G. Davies, Malcolm Burgess, Felix Eigenbrod, Nicola Pickup, Valerie A. Olson, Andrea J. Webster, Tzung-Su Ding, Pamela C. Rasmussen, Robert S. Ridgely, Ali J. Stattersfield, Pete M. Bennett, Tim M. Blackburn, Kevin J. Gaston, Ian P.F. Owens, 'Global Hotspots of Species Richness Are Not Congruent with Endemism or Threat' (2005) 436(7053) *Nature* 1016–1019. DOI: 10.1038/nature03850.

Oude Elferink, Alex, 'The Regime of the Area: Delineating the Scope of Application of the Common Heritage Principle and Freedom of the High Seas' (2007) 22(1) *The International Journal of Marine and Coastal Law* 143–176. DOI: 10.1163/157180807781475272.

Oude Elferink, Alex, 'Coastal States and MPAs in ABNJ: Ensuring Consistency with the LOSC' in David Freestone (ed), *Conserving Biodiversity in Areas Beyond National Jurisdiction* (Brill Nijhoff, 2019) 56. DOI: https://doi.org/10.1163/9789004391703_004.

Payne, Cymie R., 'Introduction to the Symposium on Governing High Seas Biodiversity' (2018) 112 *AJIL Unbound* 118–122. DOI: 10.1017/aju.2018.49.

Permanent Mission of the Federated States of Micronesia to the United Nations, 'Views of the Government of the Federated States of Micronesia on the Elements of a Draft Text of an International Legally Binding Instrument under the United Nations Convention on the Law of the Sea on the Conservation and Sustainable Use of Marine Biological Diversity of Areas beyond National Jurisdiction' (14 March 2016) ('Written submission of the Federated States of Micronesia to PrepCom') <https://www.un.org/depts/los/biodiversity/prepcom_files/Federated_States_of_Micronesia.pdf> accessed 31 March 2022.

Popova, Ekaterina, David Vousden, Warwick H.H. Sauer, Essam Y. Mohammed, Valerie Allain, Nicola Downey-Breedt, Ruth Fletcher, Kristina M. Gjerde, Patrick N. Halpin, Stephen Kelly, David Obura, Gretta Pecl, Michael Roberts, Dionysios E. Raitsos, Melita Samoilys, Ussif Rashid Sumaila, Sean Tracey and Andrew Yool, 'Ecological Connectivity Between Areas Beyond National Jurisdiction and Coastal Waters: Safeguarding Interests of Coastal Communities in Developing Countries' (2019) 104 *Marine Policy* 90–102. DOI: 10.1016/j.marpol.2019.02.050.

Revised Draft Text of an Agreement under the United Nations Convention on the Law of the Sea on the Conservation and Sustainable Use of Marine Biological Diversity of Areas Beyond National Jurisdiction, UN Doc A/CONF.232/2020/3 (18 November 2019) <https://documents-dds-ny.un.org/doc/UNDOC/GEN/N19/372/88/PDF/N1937288.pdf?OpenElement> accessed 31 March 2022.

Ribeiro, Marta Chantal, 'Marine Protected Areas: The Case of the Extended Continental Shelf' in Marta Chantal Ribeiro (ed), 30 Years After the Signature of the United Nations Convention on the Law of the Sea: The Protection of the Environment and the Future of the Law of the Sea: Proceedings of the International Conference, Faculty of Law, University of Porto, 15–17 November 2012 (Coimbra Editora, 2014) 179.

Roberts, Julian, Aldo Chircop and Siân Prior, 'Area-based Management on the High Seas: Possible Application of the IMO's Particularly Sensitive Sea Area Concept' (2010) 25 *The International Journal of Marine and Coastal Law* 483–522. DOI: 10.1163/157180810X525403.

Scanlon, Zoe, 'The Art of "not Undermining": Possibilities Within Existing Architecture to Improve Environmental Protections in Areas Beyond National Jurisdiction' (2017) 75(1) *ICES Journal of Marine Science* 405–416. DOI: 10.1093/icesjms/fsx209.

Scientific Committee for the Conservation of Antarctic Marine Living Resources, *Report of the Thirtieth Meeting of the Scientific Committee* (SC-CAMLR-XXX).

Scope, Parameters and Feasibility of an International Instrument under the United Nations Convention on the Law of the Sea: Informal Working Document Compiling the Views of Member States, Prepared in Accordance with General Assembly Resolution 68/70 Paragraph 201 (4 December 2014) <http://cpps.dyndns.info/cpps-docs-web/circulares/2015/003.Circular%20003-2015_Videoconferencia%20del%20GT-CPPS-B-RGM.pdf> accessed 31 March 2022.

Scott, Karen N., 'Conservation on the High Seas: Developing the Concept of the High Seas Marine Protected Areas' (2012) 27 *The International Journal of Marine and Coastal Law* 849–857. DOI: 10.1163/15718085-12341243.

Scovazzi, Tullio, 'The Negotiations for a Binding Instrument on the Conservation and Sustainable Use of Marine Biological Diversity Beyond National Jurisdiction' (2016) 70 *Marine Policy* 188–191. DOI: 10.1016/j.marpol.2016.04.007.

'Shipping and World Trade' *International Chamber of Shipping* (Web Page, 2020) <https://www.ics-shipping.org/shipping-facts/shipping-and-world-trade> accessed 31 March 2022.

Singh, Anil Jai, 'Maritime Security in the Age of the Pandemic: The Naval Dimension,' *The Financial Express* (Online Newspaper, 21 April 2020) <https://www.financialexpress.com/defence/maritime-security-in-the-age-of-the-pandemic-the-naval-dimension/1934426/> accessed 31 March 2022.

Smith, Danielle and Julia Jabour, 'MPAs in ABNJ: Lessons from Two High Seas Regimes' (2017) 75(1) *ICES Journal of Marine Science* 417–425. DOI: 10.1093/icesjms/fsx189.

Smith, Thomas B., Salit Kark, Christopher J. Schneider, Robert K. Wayne and Craig Moritz, 'Biodiversity Hotspots and Beyond: The Need for Preserving Environmental Transitions' (2001) 16(8) *Trends in Ecology and Evolution* 431–431. DOI: 10.1016/S0169-5347(01)02201-7.

Statement by the President of the Conference at the Closing of the Third Session of the Intergovernmental Conference on an International Legally Binding Instrument under the United Nations Convention on the Law of the Sea on the Conservation and Sustainable Use of Marine Biological Diversity of Areas Beyond National Jurisdiction, UN Doc A/CONF.232/2019/10 (13 September 2019) <https://documents-dds-ny.un.org/doc/UNDOC/GEN/N19/281/55/PDF/N1928155.pdf?OpenElement> accessed 31 March 2022.

The Pew Charitable Trusts, 'How MPAs Safeguard the High Seas' (Brief, July 2019) <https://www.pewtrusts.org/-/media/assets/2019/08/how_mpas_safeguard_the_high_seas_issue_brief_v1b.pdf> accessed 31 March 2022.

The Pew Charitable Trusts, 'A Path to Creating the First Generation of High Seas Protected Areas' (Report, 31 March 2020) <https://www.pewtrusts.org/-/media/assets/2020/04/highseas_mpa_report.pdf> accessed 31 March 2022.

Tiller, Rachel, 'Elizabeth De Santo, Elizabeth Mendenhall, Elizabeth Nyman, 'The Once and Future Treaty: Towards a New Regime for Biodiversity in Areas Beyond National Jurisdiction' (2019) 99 *Marine Policy* 239–242. DOI: 10.1016/j.marpol.2018.10.046.

Trathan, Philip N., 'Settle discord over the Southern Ocean' (Pt Correspondence) (2012) 492 *Nature* 186. DOI: 10.1038/492186b.

United Nations General Assembly, *Transforming our World: The 2030 Agenda for Sustainable Development*, UN Doc. A/RES/70/1 (2015).

United States of America, 'Views Expressed by the United States Delegation Related to Certain Key Issues under Discussion at the Second Session of the Preparatory Committee on the Development of an International Legally Binding Instrument under the United Nations Convention on the Law of the Sea on the Conservation and Sustainable Use of Marine Biological Diversity' (9 September 2016) ('Views Expressed by the US Delegation') <https://www.un.org/depts/los/biodiversity/prepcom_files/USA_Submission_of_Views_Expressed.pdf> accessed 31 March 2022.

Visalli, Morgan E., Benjamin D. Best, Reniel B. Cabral, William W.L. Cheung, Nichola A. Clark, Cristina Garilao, Kristin Kaschner, Kathleen Kesner-Reyes, Vicky W.Y. Lam, Sara M. Maxwell, Juan Mayorga, Holly V. Moeller, Lance Morgan, Guillermo Ortuño Crespo, Malin L. Pinsky, Timothy D. White, Douglas J. McCauley, 'Data-driven Approach for Highlighting Priority Areas for Protection in Marine Areas Beyond National Jurisdiction' (2020) 122 *Marine Policy* 103927: 1–14. DOI: 10.1016/j.marpol.2020.103927.

Vithanage, Achinthi C., 'A Deep Dive into the High Seas: Harmonizing Regional Frameworks for Marine Protected Areas with the UNCLOS Convention on the Conservation and Sustainable Use of Marine Biological Diversity in Areas beyond National Jurisdiction' (2017) 28(1) *Yearbook of International Environmental Law* 63–84. DOI: 10.1093/yiel/yvy085.

Von Nordheim, Henning, 'Marine Protected Areas: Global Framework, Regional MPA Networks and a National Example' in Markus Salomon and Till Markus (eds), *Handbook on Marine Environment Protection: Science, Impacts and Sustainable Management* (Springer International Publishing AG, 2018) 871. DOI: https://doi.org/10.1007/978-3-319-60156-4_46.

Wagner, Daniel, Alan M. Friedlander, Richard L. Pyle, Cassandra M. Brooks, Kristina M. Gjerde, T. 'Aulani Wilhelm, 'Coral Reefs of the High Seas: Hidden Biodiversity Hotspots in Need of Protection' (2020) 7 *Frontiers in Marine Science* 567428: 1–13. DOI: 10.3389/fmars.2020.567428.

Wedding, L.M, A.M. Friedlander, J.N. Kittinger, L. Watling, S.D. Gaines, M. Bennett, S.M. Hardy and C.R. Smith, 'From Principles to Practice: A Spatial Approach to Systematic Conservation Planning in the Deep Sea' (2013) 280(1773) *Proceedings of the Royal Society of Biological Sciences* 20131684: 1–10. DOI: 10.1098/rspb.2013.1684.

Wells, Sue, G. Carleton Ray, Kristina M. Gjerde, Alan T. White, Nyawira Muthiga, Creel Bezaury, E. Juan, Billy D. Causey, Jerry Mccormick-Ray, Rod Salm, Sue Gubbay, Graeme Kelleher and Joe Reti, 'Building the Future of MPAs: Lessons from History' (2016) 26(Supplement Article 2) *Aquatic Conservation: Marine and Freshwater Ecosystems* 101–125. DOI: 10.1002/aqc.2680.

Wenzel, Lauren, Neil Gilbert, Lyn Goldworthy, Clive Tesar, Martha Mcconnell and Melis Okter, 'Polar Opposites? Marine Conservation Tools and Experiences in the Changing Arctic and Antarctic' (2016) 26(Suppl.2) *Aquatic Conservation: Marine and Freshwater Ecosystems* 61–84. DOI: 10.1002/aqc.2649.

Wright, Glen and Julien Rochette, 'Regional Ocean Governance of Areas Beyond National Jurisdiction: Lessons Learnt and Ways Forward' (STRONG High Seas Project, 2019) <https://www.iddri.org/sites/default/files/PDF/Publications/

Hors%20catalogue%20Iddri/strong%20high%20seas%20-%20regional %20governance%20ABNJ_1.pdf> accessed 31 March 2022.

Wright, Glen, Julien Rochette and Elisabeth Druel, 'Marine Protected Areas in Areas Beyond National Jurisdiction' in Rosemary Rayfuse (ed), *Research Handbook on International Marine Environmental Law* (Edward Elgar Publishing, 2015) 272. DOI: 10.4337/9781781004777.00023.

Wright, Glenn, Julien Rochette, Lucie Blom, Duncan Currie, Carole Durussel, Kristina Gjerde and Sebastian Unger, *High Seas Fisheries: What Role for a New International Instrument?* (Study No. 03/16, IDDRI, August 2016).

Young, Michaela, 'Then and Now: Reappraising Freedom of the Seas in Modern Law of the Sea' (2016) 47(2) *Ocean Development & International Law* 165–185. DOI: 10.1080/00908320.2016.1159088.

6 Environmental impact assessments

Devising a recipe for environmentally sustainable decision-making under an ILBI

Introduction

The age-old axiom, 'an ounce of prevention is worth a pound of cure,' is as true today as it was in 1735, when Benjamin Franklin first employed the adage to advocate for a fire-fighting organisation in colonial Philadelphia.[1] Franklin argued that the prevention of a catastrophic city-wide fire was preferable to rebuilding a burned city from scratch.[2] Today, Franklin's maxim is particularly fitting in the BBNJ context. Anthropogenic activities in ABNJ have the potential to significantly or irreparably harm deep-sea ecosystems and their associated biodiversity.[3] Realistically, activities in ABNJ will inevitably result in some biodiversity loss. The difficult decision for BBNJ negotiators is deciding the extent of loss to be tolerated. If a majority of States seek to continue to engage in these activities, the decision could be that some loss, perhaps substantial loss, will be deemed acceptable. This chapter focuses on how biodiversity loss could be mitigated through environmentally sustainable decision-making.

Since the 1960s, a suite of proactive, anticipatory and precautionary mechanisms have emerged to address environmental issues in a preventative manner.[4] One of the most important tools in this effort is the process known as Environmental Impact Assessment (EIA).[5] In general terms, EIA is a legal technique that analyses

1 Benjamin Franklin, 'On Protection of Towns from Fire', *Pennsylvania Gazette* (4 February 1735); 'The Electric Ben Franklin—In Case of Fire' *UShistory.org* (Web Page, 4 July 1995) <http://www.ushistory.org/franklin/philadelphia/fire.htm>.

2 'Citizen Ben-Firefighter' PBS.org (Web Site, 2002) <http://www.pbs.org/benfranklin/l3_citizen_firefighter.html>

3 Robin Warner, 'Conserving Marine Biodiversity in Areas beyond National Jurisdiction: Co-Evolution and Interaction with the Law of the Sea' in Donald Rothwell et al (eds), *The Oxford Handbook of the Law of the Sea* (Oxford University Press, 2015) 752, 753 ('Conserving Marine Biodiversity').

4 Young-il Song, 'Environmental Impact Assessment in Korea' (2004) II(2) *Korea Environmental Policy Bulletin* 1, 1.

5 Impact assessment encompasses a range of techniques including EIA and Strategic Environmental Assessment (SEA). This chapter focuses on EIA. BBNJ delegations remain divided on whether to integrate SEA provisions into an ILBI; see, e.g. Tallash Kantai et al, 'Summary of the Third Session of the Intergovernmental Conference on the Conservation and

DOI: 10.4324/b22996-7

the impact of a proposed activity to assist in determining whether it should proceed and under what conditions.[6] The process is designed to predict impacts at an early stage, find ways to reduce adverse impacts and present the predictions and options to decision-makers usually via an Environmental Impact Statement (EIS).[7]

There is an impressive architecture already in place concerning the conduct of EIA in the marine environment, emanating from global instruments (UNCLOS and CBD), regional instruments (Espoo Convention[8] and Madrid Protocol) and sectoral guidelines. EIA has also been the subject of international jurisprudence. In its 2011 Advisory Opinion, the Seabed Disputes Chamber of ITLOS confirmed that EIA is a general obligation under customary international law and a direct obligation under Article 206 of UNCLOS.[9] Yet, there is no overarching framework for the application of EIA in ABNJ.

The development of an ILBI presents an opportunity to formulate a recipe for environmentally sustainable decision-making in ABNJ. This chapter lays out key ingredients required for an effective EIA framework and argues that internationally accepted standards, processes and protocols found within the existing law framework could be used to shape and underpin EIA ingredients under an ILBI and appropriately adjusted to suit the BBNJ context.

EIA has been labelled the 'low-hanging fruit' of the BBNJ negotiations.[10] However, this is a misconception, as it remains a contentious issue. There is a continued unwillingness, on the part of some States, 'to subject themselves to what they consider to be unnecessary and intrusive' EIA procedures.[11] Delegates also disagree on the extent to which the EIA process should be internationalised under an ILBI. BBNJ negotiators will need to strike the right balance between ensuring protection without imposing overly onerous regulatory requirements. Thus, in keeping with the other elements of the package deal, this balance can be achieved through compromise.

Sustainable Use of Marine Biodiversity of Areas beyond National Jurisdiction: 19–30 August 2019' *Earth Negotiations Bulletin* (Online Bulletin, 2 September 2019) 11 ('Summary of IGC 3') <https://enb.iisd.org/events/3rd-session-intergovernmental-conference-igc-conservation-and-sustainable-use-marine/summary>.

6 Oxford University Press, *Max Planck Encyclopedias of International Law* (online at 1 November 2020) Environmental Impact Assessment [2].

7 'What Is Impact Assessment?' *Convention on Biological Diversity* (Web Page, 27 April 2010) <https://www.cbd.int/impact/whatis.shtml>.

8 The Espoo Convention focuses on environmental assessment of transboundary impacts and does not apply to ABNJ, see art 1(viii).

9 *Responsibilities and Obligations of States Sponsoring Persons and Entities with Respect to Activities in the Area* (Advisory Opinion) (Seabed Disputes Chamber, Case No 17, 1 February 2011) 50 [145]–[148]. See, also, *Pulp Mills on the River Uruguay (Argentina v. Uruguay) (Judgment)* [2010] ICJ Rep 14, 73 [204].

10 Glen Wright et al, 'The Long and Winding Road: Negotiating a Treaty for the Conservation and Sustainable Use of Marine Biodiversity in Areas beyond National Jurisdiction' (Study No. 8/2018, IDDRI, August 2018) 59.

11 Philippe Sands and Jacqueline Peel, *Principles of International Environmental Law* (Cambridge University Press, 3rd ed, 2012) 623.

6.1 A recipe for the scope of EIA

6.1.1 Defining EIA

As there is no internationally agreed definition for EIA, the first key ingredient is a definition of this term. The President's Aid to Negotiations defines EIA as:

> a process to evaluate the environmental impacts of an activity to be carried out in areas beyond national jurisdiction, with an effect on areas within or beyond national jurisdiction, taking into account interrelated socio-economic, cultural and human health impacts, both beneficial and adverse.[12]

This broad definition draws heavily upon the CBD's Revised Voluntary Guidelines for the Consideration of Biodiversity in Environmental Impact Assessment and Strategic Environmental Assessment in Marine and Coastal Areas (CBD Guidelines)[13] and has garnered increasing support from BBNJ delegates, including the G77/China bloc.[14] However, some States are reluctant to commit to a definition 'before deciding on the substance of EIA.'[15] An ILBI's definition should be consistent with other relevant international instruments as this will enhance coherence across regimes.

Existing instruments could also assist in defining other key EIA terms. For example, the definition of 'impact' under the Espoo Convention could significantly enlarge the scope of EIA under an ILBI to include impacts on cultural heritage or socio-economic conditions.[16] Similarly, a definition of 'environment' could fully incorporate the concept of biodiversity as defined by the CBD, to ensure that an EIA considers the different levels of biodiversity, as well as ecosystem structure and functioning.[17]

12 *President's Aid to Negotiations*, UN Doc A/CONF.232/2019/1 (3 December 2018) Part II, 1(19).

13 CBD, *Decision Adopted by the Conference of the Parties to the Convention on Biological Diversity at its Eighth Meeting*, UNEP/CBD/COP/DEC/VIII/28 (15 June 2006) annex ('Impact Assessment: Voluntary Guidelines on Biodiversity Inclusive Impact Assessment') 5 [5].

14 See, e.g. The Group of 77, 'Development of an International Legally Binding Instrument under the United Nations Convention on the Law of the Sea on the Conservation and Sustainable Use of Marine Biological Diversity of Areas beyond National Jurisdiction (A/RES/69/292): Group of 77 and China's Written Submission' (5 December 2016) 3 <https://www.un.org/depts/los/biodiversity/prepcom_files/rolling_comp/Group_of_77_and_China.pdf>.

15 See US submission in Tallash Kantai et al, 'Summary of the Second Session of the Intergovernmental Conference on the Conservation and Sustainable Use of Marine Biodiversity of Areas beyond National Jurisdiction: 25 March–5 April 2019' *Earth Negotiations Bulletin* (Online Bulletin, 8 April 2019) 15 <https://enb.iisd.org/events/2nd-session-intergovernmental-conference-igc-conservation-and-sustainable-use-marine/summary>.

16 See Espoo Convention, art 1(vii); Neil Craik, *The International Law of Environmental Impact Assessment: Process, Substance and Integration* (Cambridge University Press, 2008) 141 ('International Law of EIA').

17 CBD, art 2; CBD Secretariat, Netherlands Commission for Environmental Assessment, Biodiversity in Impact Assessment, 'Background Document to CBD Decision VIII/28: Voluntary Guidelines on Biodiversity-Inclusive Impact Assessment' (2006) 9.

6.1.2 Objective and guiding principles

The next key ingredient is an objective to test the outcome of an EIA. Barritt and Viñuales argue that a general objective under an ILBI could assist decision-makers in deciding whether to permit activities or impose conditions.[18] The general objective in the Madrid Protocol could serve as a template. Under the Protocol, the protection of the Antarctic environment and its associated ecosystems are to be fundamental considerations in the planning and conduct of activities.[19] The Protocol also lists particular outcomes to avoid, including adverse effects on climate and detrimental changes in the distribution, abundance or productivity of fauna and flora.[20] Echoing the Madrid Protocol, an ILBI could provide that activities in ABNJ are to be planned and conducted so as to avoid significant and harmful changes to BBNJ taking into account the precautionary principle and ecosystem approach.[21]

Irrespective of the general objective chosen, the EIA components of an ILBI should also be consistent with the overarching objective of the instrument, namely, the long-term conservation and sustainable use of BBNJ.[22]

6.1.3 Cumulative impacts

The assessment of cumulative impacts is another important ingredient for environmentally sustainable decision-making, as it is critical to understanding the ability of marine ecosystems to cope with multiple stressors, including climate change effects.[23] As one delegate stated during IGC 1: 'If cumulative effects are not adequately addressed under an ILBI, what are we here for?'[24] While cumulative impact assessments are common practice within national waters, there are no global mechanisms in place for these assessments in ABNJ.[25]

18 Emily Barritt and Jorge E. Viñuales, 'Legal Scan: A Conservation Agenda for Biodiversity beyond National Jurisdiction' (Cambridge Centre for Environment, Energy and Natural Resource Governance, University of Cambridge, May 2016) 79.
19 Madrid Protocol, art 3(2)(a).
20 Madrid Protocol, art 3(2)(b)(i)–(vi).
21 Duncan E.J. Currie, 'Key Components and Best Practices for Environmental Impact Assessments and Strategic Environmental Assessments' (Working Paper, High Seas Alliance, 23 August 2016) 2.
22 Robin Warner, 'Environmental Assessment in Marine Areas beyond National Jurisdiction' in Rosemary Rayfuse (ed), *Research Handbook on International Marine Environmental Law* (Edward Elgar Publishing, 2015) 291, 311 ('Environmental Assessment').
23 Elisa Morgera et al, 'Summary of the First Session of the Intergovernmental Conference on an International Legally Binding Instrument under the UN Convention on the Law of the Sea on the Conservation and Sustainable Use of Marine Biodiversity of Areas beyond National Jurisdiction 4–17 September 2018' *Earth Negotiations Bulletin* (Online Bulletin, 20 September 2018) 16 ('Summary of IGC 1') <https://enb.iisd.org/events/1st-session-intergovernmental-conference-igc-international-legally-binding-instrument-12>.
24 Ibid.
25 Elisabeth Druel, 'Environmental Impact Assessments in Areas beyond National Jurisdiction' (Study No. 01/13, IDDRI, January 2013) 32; Glen Wright et al, 'The Long and Winding

An ILBI should provide a clear obligation to assess cumulative impacts in the conduct of EIA. Some delegations argue for cumulative impacts to be assessed 'as far as practicable' or 'as far as possible,'[26] while others believe the inclusion of this phrasing would create a significant loophole in addressing cumulative impacts.[27] It is not clear whether the inclusion of this phrasing is to qualify the obligation or account for the differing capacities among States to carry out such an assessment. It may be an attempt to appease a key bloc of States that oppose the consideration of processes originating from land-based activities, such as climate change.[28] Russia, for example, maintains that EIA under an ILBI should not be related to global processes (i.e. ocean acidification or global warming) as these depend on many factors and their regulation is already carried out within competent international structures.[29] However, as climate change may cause irreversible damage to BBNJ, it would be far preferable for an ILBI to use EIA as a way to monitor and mitigate the adverse impacts of these pressures. At a bare minimum, EIA under an ILBI should take into account the *full* range of impacts of an activity including direct and indirect secondary effects.[30]

To assist in identifying cumulative impacts, BBNJ negotiators could include a recommended set of questions in an Annex to the ILBI. These questions could be modelled on those contained in the Revised Guidelines for Environmental Impact Assessment in Antarctica.[31] For example, proponents of an activity could be required to answer the following questions in preparing an EIS:

(1) What activities have been undertaken, are currently being undertaken or are likely to be undertaken at the activity site?
(2) Is there a temporal or spatial overlap (or a combination) with other activities in the area that may result in particular impacts?
(3) What effects from the proposed activity may contribute to cumulative impacts?
(4) What cumulative impacts are likely to occur?[32]

Road Continues: Towards a New Agreement on High Seas Governance' (Study No. 01/16, IDDRI, March 2016) 35. A few notable exceptions include The Antarctic Treaty System, ISA's Environmental Management Plan of the CCZ and the bottom fishing provisions under UNGA Resolutions.

26 *Chair's Streamlined Non-Paper on Elements of a Draft Text of an International Legally-Binding Instrument under UNCLOS*, (2007) 31 [162] ('*Chair's Streamlined Non-Paper*').

27 See, e.g. *Textual Proposals Submitted by Delegations for Consideration at IGC4, in Response to the Invitation by the President of the Conference in Her Note of 18 November 2019*, UN Doc A/CONF.232/2020/3 (15 April 2020) OceanCare on art 25, 243.

28 *Statement by the President of the Conference at the Closing of IGC 1*, UN Doc A/CONF.232/2018/7 (20 September 2018) 18 ('*IGC 1 Closing Statement*').

29 *Chair's Streamlined Non-Paper* (n 26) 31 [161].

30 New Zealand, 'Preparatory Committee on Conservation and Sustainable Use of Marine Biological Diversity of Areas beyond National Jurisdiction: New Zealand Submission' (December 2016) 7 ('Written Submission of New Zealand to PrepCom') <https://www.un.org/depts/los/biodiversity/prepcom_files/rolling_comp/New_Zealand.pdf>.

31 ATCM, *Resolution 1*, ATCM XXXIX - CEP XIX (1 June 2016) annex ('Revised Guidelines for Environmental Impact Assessment in Antarctica') 17 [3.3.3].

32 Ibid.

6.2 A recipe for 'when' to conduct EIA

6.2.1 Defining the obligation

One of the most important ingredients for inclusion in an ILBI will be a clear and explicit obligation to conduct EIA. Article 206 of UNCLOS already imposes a general obligation on States to assess the potential effects of planned activities under their jurisdiction or control which may cause substantial pollution of or significant and harmful changes to the marine environment. To trigger the obligation, a State must have *reasonable grounds* for believing the planned activity may have these potential effects.[33] The language of reasonableness appears to grant States a broad discretion;[34] however Craik argues that it provides an objective standard for determining whether the requisite threshold has been met.[35] Article 206 also requires an EIA to be carried out *as far as practicable*. This does not qualify the obligation.[36] Instead, this limitation 'impacts the level of detail and depth' of an EIA and is sensitive to differing capacities among States.[37]

As there is already an established obligation to conduct EIA under both customary and conventional international law,[38] these two sources could be used to underpin an obligation under an ILBI, requiring States to assess the potential effects of planned activities under their jurisdiction or control in ABNJ.[39] However, it will not be sufficient to simply rehash the general obligation in Article 206. Details on the content of this obligation will be required to operationalise this provision and fill the gaps left by UNCLOS.[40] For example, an ILBI should clearly set out *when* to conduct an EIA.

Article 206 provides two ambiguous thresholds, namely, 'substantial pollution of' or 'significant and harmful changes to the marine environment.' An ILBI should operationalise these generic formulae through specific definitions and criteria.[41] The definition of 'significant adverse impacts' in the DSF Guidelines, for

33 Eike Blitza, 'Section 4 Monitoring and Environmental Assessment' in Alexander Proelss et al (eds), *United Nations Convention on the Law of the Sea A Commentary* (Hart Publishing, 2017) 1356, 1373.

34 Lingjie Kong, 'Environmental Impact Assessment under the United Nations Convention on the Law of the Sea' (2011) 10 *Chinese Journal of International Law* 651, 659.

35 Craik, 'International Law of EIA' (n 16) 98.

36 Alex Oude Elferink, 'Environmental Impact Assessment in Areas beyond National Jurisdiction' 27(2) (2012) *The International Journal of Marine and Coastal Law* 449, 456.

37 Craik, 'International Law of EIA' (n 16) 99.

38 Robin Warner, 'Tools to Conserve Ocean Biodiversity: Developing the Legal Framework for Environmental Impact Assessment in Marine Areas beyond National Jurisdiction' (2012) 26(1) *Ocean Yearbook* 317, 335 ('Tools to Conserve').

39 *President's Aid to Negotiations* (n 12) 32 [5.1].

40 Druel (n 25) 34.

41 European Union, 'Development of an International Legally-Binding Instrument under UNCLOS on the Conservation and Sustainable Use of Marine Biological Diversity of Areas beyond National Jurisdiction (BBNJ Process), Written Submission of EU and Its Member States: Environmental Impact Assessments' (15 February 2017) 4 [18] ('Written Submission of EU and Its Member States to PrepCom: Environmental Impact Assessments')

example, could be adapted to suit the BBNJ context and assist in defining the UNCLOS threshold of 'significant and harmful changes to the marine environment.' According to the DSF Guidelines, 'significant adverse impacts' compromise ecosystem integrity in a manner that:

(i) Impairs the ability of affected populations to replace themselves;
(ii) Degrades the long-term natural productivity of habitats;
(iii) Causes, on more than a temporary basis, significant loss of species richness, habitat or community types.[42]

Although this definition was developed to target impacts of deep-sea fisheries on VMEs, these same impacts would arguably constitute significant and harmful changes to BBNJ more generally. This could be used as a starting point for formulating a broader definition under an ILBI, one that covers potential impacts from any or all activities in ABNJ.

The DSF Guidelines also include a list of criteria to determine the scale and significance of an impact, which include (1) its intensity or severity, (2) its spatial extent, (3) the sensitivity/vulnerability of the ecosystem, (4) the ecosystem's ability to recover from harm and recovery rate, (5) the extent to which ecosystem functions may be altered and (6) timing and duration.[43] A scientific and technical body could tailor these criteria to suit the unique characteristics of ABNJ, and this could be used to determine whether an impact is likely to result in significant and harmful changes to BBNJ. In this way, the DSF Guidelines effectively fill out the existing obligation in Article 206 of UNCLOS.

Delegates, however, remain divided on who should bear the ultimate responsibility of conducting an EIA under an ILBI. The first option is for the proponent of the activity to undertake this task. Norway argues that the best results are often achieved when there is a close link between the EIA and the entity that intends to undertake the activity in question.[44] The second option has proven controversial and would involve the EIA being carried out by an independent consultant appointed by a panel of experts designated by an ILBI's scientific and technical body.[45] While this would provide a level of international scrutiny and oversight, it attempts to internationalise the EIA process and is likely to meet with objections

<https://www.un.org/depts/los/biodiversity/prepcom_files/rolling_comp/EU_Written_Submission_on_Environmental_Assessments.pdf>.

42 Ibid, 4 [17].

43 Ibid, 4–5 [18].

44 Norway, 'Preparatory Committee established by General Assembly Resolution 69/292: Development of an International Legally Binding Instrument under the United Nations Convention on the Law of the Sea on the Conservation and Sustainable Use of Marine Biological Diversity of Areas beyond National Jurisdiction: Comments by Norway' (December 2016) 12 <https://www.un.org/depts/los/biodiversity/prepcom_files/rolling_comp/Norway.pdf>.

45 *President's Aid to Negotiations* (n 12) 38 [5.4(1)(c)(i)].

from maritime (flag) States. The third option is for the responsibility to rest with flag States. This is consistent with UNCLOS wherein State Parties are obliged to assess activities under their jurisdiction or control.

By way of compromise, an ILBI could require the proponent of the activity to conduct the EIA under the flag States' oversight and review.[46] In an effort to 'deter EIA of convenience,'[47] the State(s) with jurisdiction over the proponent, by reason of flag, nationality or beneficial ownership, could bear the responsibility of ensuring the EIA is carried out pursuant to ILBI terms.[48] The flag State could be given the option to engage a third party (i.e. a research institution or private company) to carry out the EIA, at the cost of the proponent.[49] This compromise solution is more likely to appeal to the interests of maritime (flag) States as the EIA process will remain under the direction and control of the relevant State(s) with jurisdiction.

6.2.2 Activities that require EIA

Next, an ILBI will require a screening mechanism to determine which activities are subject to EIA. BBNJ delegates have struggled to reach agreement on this issue. The following discussion analyses various options open to BBNJ negotiators and argues that a combination of screening methods could offer the optimal approach.

6.2.2.1 EIA mandatory for all activities

The Federated States of Micronesia support mandatory EIA for all activities in ABNJ, with no minimum threshold of impact required.[50] This is likely to be seen as an overly burdensome and costly exercise and Singapore has cautioned against such an interventionist approach.[51] While there is growing recognition that more drastic conservation measures are necessary to protect BBNJ, a mandatory EIA

46 Australia, 'Preparatory Committee on Conservation and Sustainable Use of Marine Biological Diversity of Areas beyond National Jurisdiction (BBNJ): Submission by Australia' (6 December 2016) 8 <https://www.un.org/depts/los/biodiversity/prepcom_files/rolling_comp/Australia.pdf> ('Written Submission of Australia to PrepCom').

47 Natural Resources Defense Council (NRDC) on behalf of the High Seas Alliance, 'Intervention on EIAs' Statement to the First Session of the Intergovernmental Conference (11 September 2018) 1 <http://www.highseasalliance.org/wp-content/uploads/2013/04/4.-NRDC-on-behalf-of-the-High-Seas-Alliance-Intervention-on-EIAs-.pdf> ('High Seas Alliance Intervention').

48 *Chair's Non-Paper on Elements of a Draft Text of an International Legally-Binding Instrument under UNCLOS on the Conservation and Sustainable Use of Marine Biological Diversity of Areas beyond National Jurisdiction* (28 February 2017) 64 ('*Chair's Non-Paper*').

49 *President's Aid to Negotiations* (n 12) 37–38 [5.4(1)(c)(i)].

50 *Chair's Non-Paper* (n 48) 65.

51 Tallash Kantai et al, 'BBNJ IGC-2 Highlights: Friday 29 March 2019' *Earth Negotiations Bulletin* (Online Bulletin, 1 April 2019) 2 <https://enb.iisd.org/download/pdf/enb25190e.pdf>.

requirement applicable to all activities could be perceived as a direct attack on traditional high seas freedoms and is likely to dissuade a key bloc of maritime States from signing on to the instrument.

A mandatory approach also ignores the fact that not all activities pose the same degree of threat to BBNJ. Instead, EIA should be triggered according to the level of harm an activity poses to ABNJ, and this will require a distinction to be made between different types of activities.

6.2.2.2 A list approach

Like the Espoo Convention, an Annex to the ILBI could include a list of activities that have been pre-determined as likely to reach the requisite threshold of harm and always require EIA.[52] Alternatively, BBNJ negotiators could use the reverse list approach adopted in the 1996 Protocol to the 1972 Convention on the Prevention of Marine Pollution by Dumping of Wastes and Other Matter (London Convention).[53] The London Convention[54] originally adopted a permissive approach to ocean dumping.[55] Thus, with the exception of wastes listed on a prohibited black list, 'almost anything can be dumped at sea as long as a permit is obtained from a Contracting Party.'[56] To provide greater protection to the marine environment and transition to a precautionary approach to ocean dumping, the 1996 Protocol provided a reverse list.[57] Only those wastes or matter in the reverse list may be disposed of at sea and only after a detailed waste assessment has been carried out.[58] Applying this to the BBNJ context, an ILBI could provide a list of activities that may proceed in ABNJ but only after an EIA has been undertaken.

A list of activities under an ILBI should be non-exhaustive and provide a process for regular updating to reflect new and emerging activities that may, at a later date, be determined to have a significant impact on BBNJ.[59] An ILBI could also

52 Pursuant to art 2(3) of Espoo Convention, a Party of Origin is required to conduct an EIA for the 17 activities listed in Appendix I, which have been pre-determined as likely to cause a significant adverse transboundary impact.

53 Protocol to the Convention on the Prevention of Marine Pollution by Dumping of Wastes and Other Matter, opened for signature 7 November 1996, (1997) 36 ILM 1 (entered into force 24 March 2006).

54 Convention on the Prevention of Marine Pollution by Dumping of Wastes and Other Matter, opened for signature on 29 December 1972, (1972) 1046 UNTS 120 (entered into force 30 August 1975.

55 David L. VanderZwaag, 'The International Control of Ocean Dumping: Navigating from Permissive to Precautionary Shores' in Rosemary Rayfuse (ed), *Research Handbook on International Marine Environmental Law* (Edward Elgar Publishing Limited, 2015) 132, 132.

56 Ibid.

57 Ibid.

58 Alan Sielen, 'The New International Rules on Ocean Dumping: Promise and Performance (Part 1)' (2009) 21 *Georgetown International Environmental Law Review* 295, 321–324.

59 IUCN, 'Recommendations for the Intergovernmental Conference: First Session of the Intergovernmental Conference on an International Legally Binding Instrument under the United Nations Convention on the Law of the Sea on Conservation and Sustainable Use

provide a process for parties to add other activities to the list against specified criteria.[60] These criteria could specify whether the activity has the potential to adversely affect BBNJ alone or in combination with other activities.[61] BBNJ negotiators could also consider listing activities that are exempt from EIA requirements. For example, the ISA's Recommendations for the Guidance of Contractors for the Assessment of the Possible Environmental Impacts Arising from Exploration for Marine Minerals in the Area (ISA Recommendations) contains a list of exploration activities that have been pre-determined not to have the potential to provoke serious harm to the marine environment and thus do not require EIA.[62]

A list of activities that automatically require EIA could promote certainty for States and proponents of activities and make it easier to monitor compliance.[63] However, Australia argues that the development of a list will be burdensome and difficult to keep up-to-date.[64] Moreover, the effect of an activity could differ depending on its location and 'in the context of multiple and cumulative impacts.'[65] Australia argues that some activities could 'appear benign' at first 'but if conducted in a hypersensitive environment' (i.e. EBSAs or VMEs) they may have significant impacts for which stronger conservation measures are needed.[66] On this basis, the High Seas Alliance argues that the list approach to screening does 'not reflect the basic tenet of impact assessment,'[67] namely, that an activity's impact can vary 'depending on the nature of the receiving environment.'[68] This is particularly relevant to BBNJ, as less is known about its 'sensitivities to impacts,' and how those sensitivities may 'vary in time and space or by activity.'[69]

---

of Marine Biological Diversity of Areas beyond National Jurisdiction, New York, September 4-17, 2018' (Recommendations Paper, 2018) 10 <https://www.iucn.org/sites/dev/files/content/documents/iucn_bbnj_recommendation_paper_draft_21_aug_2018_3.pdf> ('IUCN recommendations for IGC').

60 Currie (n 21) 3. See, e.g. Espoo Convention, art 2(5) and Appendix III which includes general criteria to determine the environmental significant of activities not listed in Appendix I.

61 IUCN, 'An International Instrument on Conservation and Sustainable Use of Biodiversity in Marine Areas beyond National Jurisdiction – Matrix of Suggestions' (Recommendations Paper, 16 December 2015) 25 <https://www.iucn.org/downloads/iucn_bbnj_matrix_december_2015.pdf> ('Matrix of Suggestions').

62 ISA, *Recommendations for the Guidance of Contractors for the Assessment of the Possible Environmental Impacts Arising from Exploration for Marine Minerals in the Area*, ISBA/19/LTC/8 (1 March 2013) 6 [18] ('*ISA Recommendations*').

63 IUCN Recommendations for IGC (n 59) 10.

64 Written Submission of Australia to PrepCom (n 46) 7.

65 High Seas Alliance Intervention (n 47) 2.

66 Written Submission of Australia to PrepCom (n 46) 7.

67 High Seas Alliance Intervention (n 47) 2.

68 CBD, *Marine and Coastal Biodiversity: Revised Voluntary Guidelines for the Consideration of Biodiversity in Environmental Impact Assessments and Strategic Environmental Assessments in Marine and Coastal Areas*, UNEP/CBD/COP/11/23 (21 August 2012) annex ('Voluntary Guidelines for the Consideration of Biodiversity in Environmental Impact Assessments (EIAs) in Marine and Coastal Areas') (21 August 2012) UNEP/CBD/COP/11/23, 7 [10(a)] ('*CBD Revised Guidelines*').

69 Ibid.

6.2.2.3 A threshold test

In contrast, Australia supports a defined threshold to trigger EIA, based on a certain level of harm.[70] As most activities will have 'measurable, but not serious impacts,'[71] the severity of effects on the marine environment could be balanced against the right of States to carry out activities without unreasonable interference.[72] Many delegates are keen to apply the qualitative threshold in Article 206 of UNCLOS. However, an ILBI could draw upon other thresholds including the Espoo Convention's 'significant adverse effects'[73] or the DSF Guideline's 'significant adverse impacts.'[74]

While the 'significance' threshold has gained widespread approval in global and regional instruments, BBNJ delegates have also pointed to the benefits of a tiered threshold approach.[75] An ILBI could mirror the multi-layered approach to assessment under the Madrid Protocol, with increasing EIA requirements based on the level of potential harm or the geographical location of where impacts are likely to occur.[76]

Under this approach, an activity having 'more than a minor or transitory effect' on BBNJ could require an EIA under an ILBI.[77] This threshold could also be used as a criterion for assessing 'significance' under the instrument. Thus, BBNJ negotiators could use a step-wise approach to screening. The lower threshold of 'minor or transitory impact' could be used to trigger an initial assessment. If this assessment determines an activity is likely to result in significant and harmful changes to BBNJ, then a comprehensive EIA could be required as a result. A step-wise approach may be prudent in the BBNJ context, given the large knowledge gaps concerning ABNJ. Regardless of the threshold chosen, an ILBI will need to set out relevant criteria for determining whether an activity has reached the requisite threshold.

6.2.2.4 Geographical areas

BBNJ negotiators could also adopt a geographical approach to screening and include a list of areas where EIA is mandatory. Again, drawing inspiration from the Madrid Protocol, an ILBI could require an initial screening to determine the

70 *Chair's Non-Paper* (n 48) 65.
71 Neil Craik, 'International EIA Law and Geoengineering: Do Emerging Technologies Require Special Rules' (2015) 5 *Climate Law* 111, 128.
72 Ibid.
73 See, also, CBD, art 14.
74 See, also, Principle 17 of the Rio Declaration and Sustainable Development Goal 14.2.
75 *IGC 1 Closing Statement* (n 28) 17. The African Group, CARICOM, Brazil, New Zealand, India and more recently China and Japan have indicated support for a threshold based on the Madrid Protocol.
76 *Chair's Non-Paper* (n 48) 66.
77 High Seas Alliance Intervention (n 47) 2.

'characteristics of the area where the activity is intended to take place, as well as where the potential effects are going to be felt.'[78] If the activity is located in or adjacent to an MPA, EBSA, VME or ecological corridor, an EIA could be required, 'regardless of whether the impacts are expected to be minimal.'[79] The geographical approach emphasises 'the sensitivity of the receiving environment' rather than the type of activity.[80]

However, certain delegates, including the US, oppose geographical provisions for EIA.[81] Singapore, Canada, Japan and New Zealand also prefer a threshold test. These States argue for the same threshold to be used across all activities and areas to ensure uniformity.[82] For example, the EU and its Member States as well as the Republic of Korea both question the need for Article 27 in the Revised Draft Negotiating Text which provides for EIAs to be required for planned activities taking place in areas identified as requiring protection or special attention by other relevant instruments and competent bodies, such as areas identified as EBSAs or VMEs.[83] These States take the view that there is no need to have a specific provision on this issue.[84] While there has been limited support for this provision, there has been an emerging consensus that the characteristics of an area should be taken into account either in the EIA screening process and/or in the determination of whether an activity meets the relevant threshold defined in the ILBI.[85]

6.2.3 Combining screening mechanisms—a compromise approach

Rather than seeking unanimous support for a single screening mechanism, this book suggests a combination of screening methods tailored to suit BBNJ. In practical terms, this could operate as follows. First, following the Espoo Convention, an ILBI could provide a list of activities that automatically require an EIA. This list should comprise activities that have been pre-determined as likely to reach the UNCLOS thresholds of substantial pollution of or significant and harmful changes to the marine environment. For activities that are not listed,

78 *President's Aid to Negotiations* (n 12) 36 [5.3].
79 Ibid.
80 *CBD Revised Guidelines* (n 68) 7 [10(b)].
81 See, e.g. Morgera et al, 'Summary of IGC 1' (n 23) 10.
82 Ibid.
83 *Textual Proposals Submitted by Delegations for Consideration at IGC 4, in Response to the Invitation by the President of the Conference in Her Note of 18 November 2019*, UN Doc A/CONF.232/2020/3 (15 April 2020) EU and its member States; Republic of Korea on art 27, 247.
84 Ibid.
85 Tallash Kantai and Paolo Bettelli, 'Summary of the Fourth Session of the Intergovernmental Conference on the Conservation and Sustainable Use of Marine Biodiversity of Areas beyond National Jurisdiction: 7-18 March 2022' *Earth Negotiations Bulletin* (Online Bulletin, 21 March 2022) 9 <https://enb.iisd.org/sites/default/files/2022-03/enb25225e.pdf>; Kantai et al, 'Summary of IGC 3' (n 5) 11.

an ILBI should adopt a tiered approach based on the Madrid Protocol. The lower threshold of 'minor or transitory impact' could be used to trigger an initial assessment, to determine whether significant impacts are likely. A defined set of criteria, modelled on Appendix III of the Espoo Convention, could be used to determine the environmental significance of activities not listed. This could include consideration of the following factors:

- The size of the area of the activity or the volume of water affected;
- Its proposed location (i.e. will the activity take place in or close to an MPA, EBSA or VME?);
- Its effects (i.e. will it increase the risk of extinction of genotypes or species or lead to the loss of habitats or ecosystems?).[86]

If the initial assessment discloses the activity is likely to result in significant impacts, then the activity should be treated as a listed activity and subject to a comprehensive EIA. In addition, BBNJ negotiators could also consider a list of geographical areas that automatically require EIA or alternatively provide a lower screening threshold for these areas.[87] This aligns with the CBD's Guidelines which recommend different thresholds for different deep-sea areas and ecosystem features.[88] A one-size-fits-all threshold is not appropriate as it fails to take into account the rich array of biodiversity and the unique ecosystems of ABNJ.

6.3 A recipe for 'how' to conduct EIA in ABNJ

6.3.1 The EIA process

While Article 206 of UNCLOS sets out a general obligation to conduct EIA, it provides no guidance on its content nor does it provide fixed standards for how an EIA should be carried out.[89] States are afforded the discretion to determine these matters. However, this is not unlimited.[90] In *Pulp Mills*, the ICJ held that States are bound by certain minimum requirements, namely, EIA should consider the nature and magnitude of the proposed activity as well as its likely adverse impact on the environment.[91] In addition, due diligence should be exercised in the conduct of EIA.[92] In this way, 'a certain level of vigilance is required' for

86 Warner, 'Tools to Conserve' (n 38) 327.
87 Warner, 'Conserving Marine Biodiversity' (n 3) 773.
88 *CBD Revised Guidelines* (n 68) 8 [13].
89 Kong (n 34) 660.
90 Blitza (n 33) 1376.
91 *Pulp Mills on the River Uruguay (Argentina v. Uruguay) (Judgment)* [2010] ICJ Rep 14, 73 [205].
92 Lene Korseberg, 'The Law-Making Effects of the FAO Deep-Sea Fisheries Guidelines' (2018) 67 *International and Comparative Law Quarterly* 801, 819.

both its content and application.[93] Article 206 lacks detail in respect to both aspects of the procedure, and this could explain why it is one of the most poorly implemented provisions of the Convention.[94] The development of an ILBI offers the opportunity to operationalise Article 206 by providing a recipe for *how* to conduct an EIA in ABNJ.

The Pacific Small Island Developing States argue that an effective EIA process needs to be grounded on a good governance mechanism and contain the following key ingredients:

1. A clear set of procedural steps;
2. A clear outline of the respective roles, authority and responsibility of States, proponents, relevant bodies and other stakeholders in the decision-making process;
3. A clear scope of terms of reference for the content of the EIA, especially in the preparation of the EIS;
4. A process that is participatory in nature and engages all relevant stakeholders;
5. A process that provides for a certain level of international scrutiny and oversight;
6. A process that includes review, monitoring, enforcement and compliance provisions.[95]

The following sections of this chapter address each key ingredient and demonstrate how existing EIA measures could assist to shape and underpin these essential components in an ILBI.

6.3.1.1 A clear set of general procedural steps

The EIA process is generally split into a number of different stages. The International Association for Impact Assessment (IAIA) defines the process in ten steps:

(i) Screening;
(ii) Scoping;
(iii) Examination of alternatives;
(iv) Impact analysis;
(v) Mitigation and impact analysis;

93 Ibid, 820 referring to *Pulp Mills on the River Uruguay (Argentina v. Uruguay) (Judgment)* [2010] ICJ Rep 14, 73 [197].

94 Wright et al (n 10) 36.

95 Pacific Small Island Developing States (PSIDS), 'PSIDS Submission to the Second Meeting of the Preparatory Committee for the Development of an International Legally Binding Instrument under the United Nations Convention on the Law of the Sea on the Conservation and Sustainable Use of Marine Biological Diversity of Areas beyond National Jurisdiction (BBNJ PrepCom)' (August 2016) 11 <https://www.un.org/depts/los/biodiversity/prepcom_files/rolling_comp/PSIDS_second.pdf>.

(vi) Evaluation of significance of impacts that cannot be mitigated;
(vii) Preparation of EIS;
(viii) Review of EIS;
(ix) Decision-making;
(x) Follow up.[96]

The IAIA model effectively teases out the various elements of EIA found in most domestic legislation and international agreements. In some cases, the ten steps go by other names or several are combined into a single step.[97] BBNJ delegates generally agree on the usefulness of including a set of procedural steps for EIA under an ILBI.[98] In effect, this would enable 'proposers of an activity to know what the EIA should cover and reviewing agencies [to know] what to expect.'[99] A large number of delegates support the procedural steps in Section III of the PrepCom Report, consisting of screening, scoping, impact assessment and evaluation, EIS reporting, decision-making, review and monitoring.[100]

However, delegates remain divided on whether an ILBI should contain detailed rules for each step of the EIA process. New Zealand has warned against an overly prescriptive approach, as the content of an EIA may differ between activities and areas.[101] Details for each step of the process could be developed at a later stage by a scientific and technical body and included in best-practice guidelines or supplemental recommendations. The CBD's Guidelines could offer inspiration, particularly in respect to integrating biodiversity-inclusive considerations into each stage of the EIA process. The ISA Recommendations could also provide guidance on the type of information to include at each step, including observations and measurements to be made during and after the performance of a specific activity and the procedure to follow in the acquisition of oceanographic and environmental baseline data.[102] For example, the ISA Recommendations suggest that contractors should observe and measure the abundance and diversity of benthic communities, changes in behaviour of key species, water currents and how organisms respond to circulation changes.[103] Some of this information is directly relevant to BBNJ. An ILBI could also provide a Code of Conduct for undertaking EIA in particularly sensitive or vulnerable marine areas.

96 International Association for Impact Assessment, 'Principles of Environmental Impact Assessment Best Practice' (Web Page, January 1999) [2.3] <https://www.iaia.org/uploads/pdf/principlesEA_1.pdf>.
97 Druel (n 25) 13.
98 Written Submission of EU and Its Member States to PrepCom: Environmental Impact Assessments (n 31) 4 [18].
99 Written Submission of New Zealand to PrepCom (n 30) 7.
100 *IGC 1 Closing Statement* (n 28) 18.
101 Written Submission of New Zealand to PrepCom (n 30) 7.
102 *ISA Recommendations* (n 62) 4–6 [14]–[15], 10–11 [29]–[30].
103 Ibid, 10 [30(b)and (j)].

6.3.1.2 *A clear outline of roles and responsibilities in the decision-making process coupled with a level of international scrutiny and oversight*

BBNJ negotiators also need to decide to what degree the EIA process should be internationalised under an ILBI. Some delegates have called for States to be responsible for the entire EIA process in order 'to promote efficiency and timeliness.'[104] The EU argues that a State Party should be responsible for:

a) Deciding that an EIA is required (based on requisite thresholds or criteria);
b) Ensuring that an EIA is carried out (in accordance with ILBI terms) prior to engaging in or authorising an activity;
c) Ensuring that any harmful effects are identified and taken into account in the decision-making process;
d) Monitoring the effects of an activity after the EIA and ensuring compliance with any conditions (i.e. prevention, mitigation or compensation measures);
e) Making the EIS and any subsequent monitoring results publicly available.[105]

Other delegations call for the establishment of institutional arrangements to manage the EIA process, to provide a degree of international scrutiny and oversight and to promote global coherence by ensuring ILBI's standards are met.[106] These States propose a supranational management regime, whereby the EIA process is managed by a specially constituted body established under the ILBI.[107] This body, however, is likely to become quickly overloaded if it is responsible for the management of the entire EIA process.[108]

To break the deadlock on this issue, this book proposes a multi-layered management approach, similar in format to the Madrid Protocol. This could take the following form under an ILBI:

1. States could govern the EIA process for activities under their jurisdiction or control that are likely to have a *minor or transitory impact.* A compliance committee could provide limited oversight to ensure consistency in approach.[109] This committee could review EIA procedures and identify instances of failure to comply with ILBI obligations.[110]

104 *IGC 1 Closing Statement* (n 28) 18.
105 Written Submission of EU and Its Member States to PrepCom: Environmental Impact Assessments (n 31) 5–6 [25].
106 See, e.g. High Seas Alliance submission in *Chair's Non-Paper* (n 48) 71.
107 Barritt and Viñuales (n 18) 84.
108 Ibid.
109 Ibid.
110 Ibid. See, e.g. Article 30(3) of *Revised Draft Negotiating Text* which provides that if a State Party determines that an EIA is not required for a planned activity under its jurisdiction or control, it must provide information to support that conclusion. This provision is supported by the G77/China bloc, CLAM, PSIDS, the African Group, New Zealand, Norway, Indonesia and the High Seas Alliance; see Kantai et al, 'Summary of IGC 3' (n 5) 12.

2. A scientific and technical body could oversee the EIA process for activities likely to have ***more than a minor or transitory impact*** or that are ***likely to occur in a particularly sensitive or vulnerable marine area***. This body could operate as an independent entity or as a subsidiary body, akin to the Committee for Environmental Protection to the Antarctic Treaty or the ISA's Legal and Technical Commission. It could undertake practical tasks including reviewing EIAs and providing advice to the relevant decision-making body on whether and how the proposed activity should proceed.

The above proposal provides an appropriate compromise, one that ensures protection by introducing a certain degree of international scrutiny and oversight to the EIA process.

While the Madrid Protocol offers a distinctive approach to EIA, it is important to recognise its flaws so that these are not replicated in an ILBI. The threshold of 'minor or transitory impact' is not defined in the Madrid Protocol and no clarification is provided on what constitutes more than or less than 'minor or transitory.'[111] Lyons argues that this ambiguity was deliberate so as to achieve consensus.[112] However, this has arguably weakened the Madrid Protocol's EIA process. Even though this issue has been discussed at several Antarctic Treaty Consultative Meetings (ATCM), parties have found it difficult to find a comprehensive definition that would cover the broad range of activities and impacts in Antarctica. At the 1997 ATCM, New Zealand suggested that 'minor' refers to the magnitude of the impact, whilst 'transitory' relates to its duration.[113] This fails to shed light on the level of impact or damage to the environment that will be deemed acceptable and for what duration? Should BBNJ negotiators elect to use the Protocol's threshold, greater clarity will be required in respect to these terms to assist parties in determining at what level activities are submitted for assessment (i.e. initial or comprehensive assessment) and how the assessments are to be conducted in ABNJ. Specific definitions will need to be adapted to suit the BBNJ context.

The Madrid Protocol also fails to specify triggers for each tier of the screening process.[114] As a consequence, national competent authorities make their own decision on the required level of assessment on a case-by-case basis.[115]

111 Timothy J. Ensminger et al, 'Environmental Impact Assessment under the National Environmental Policy Act and the Protocol on Environmental Protection to the Antarctic Treaty' (1999) 24(1) *Environmental Management* 13, 13 and 19.

112 D. Lyons, 'Environmental Impact Assessment in Antarctica under the Protocol on Environmental Protection' (1993) 29 *Polar Record* 111, 111.

113 Ruth Davis and Edmund Lee, 'Marine Environmental Protection and the Southern Ocean' in Alex G. Oude Elferink and Donald Rothwell (eds), *The Law of the Sea and Polar Maritime Delimitation and Jurisdiction* (Kluwer Law International, 2001) 201, 219.

114 Alan D. Hemmings and Lorne K. Kriwoken, 'High Level Antarctic EIA under the Madrid Protocol: State Practice and the Effectiveness of the Comprehensive Environmental Evaluation Process' (2010) 10 *International Environmental Agreements* 187, 191.

115 Kees Bastmeijer, 'Implementing the Environmental Protocol Domestically: An Overview' in Davor Vidas (ed) *Implementing the Environmental Protection Regime for the Antarctic* (Springer Netherlands, 2000) 287, 299.

This has led to standardisation issues between Contracting Parties.[116] Differing interpretations of the minor or transitory threshold could lead to a party taking the easiest option (i.e. an Initial Environmental Evaluation (IEE) instead of a Comprehensive Environmental Evaluation (CEE)).[117] For instance, questions surround Russia's use of an IEE for a proposed snow runway in the Larsemann Hills of East Antarctica with many questioning whether it required a CEE.[118] Similarly, when Italy presented two IEEs for activities at its Ross Sea station, including an ice runway, some Member States felt the project warranted a CEE.[119] Without appropriate guidance and oversight, the same issue could arise under an ILBI. This is where a compliance committee could step in to review the EIA procedures of States and identify instances of failure to comply with the ILBI's requirements. Moreover, even though the ATCM has adopted guidelines for EIA to ensure a level of consistency, these guidelines are voluntary and have not resolved 'inherent ambiguities' in the interpretation of EIA obligations under the Madrid Protocol.[120] To standardise EIA in ABNJ, an ILBI should incorporate binding operational guidelines in an Annex to ensure EIAs are carried out in a consistent and effective manner.

6.3.1.3 A clear scope of the terms of reference of an EIA

Once an EIA is triggered, a scoping process is carried out to determine its 'focus, depth and terms of reference.'[121] Scoping is generally used to identify issues arising from the proposed activity that are likely to have a significant environmental impact and describe alternatives that may 'avoid, mitigate, or compensate adverse impacts.'[122]

Scoping also plays a critical role in defining the terms of reference for the EIS. The content of an EIS tends to vary as 'different activities will have different consequences and therefore will require the consideration of different pieces of information.'[123] Some delegates warn against an ILBI being too prescriptive in the level of detail required in an EIS.[124] The EU argues that an ILBI should only

116 Kees Bastmeijer and Ricardo Roura, 'Environmental Impact Assessment in Antarctica' in Kees Bastmeijer and Timo Koivurova (eds), *Theory and Practice of Transboundary Environmental Impact Assessment* (Martinus Nijhoff Publishers, 2008) 175, 183.

117 Ibid.

118 Hemmings and Kriwoken (n 114) 191.

119 Ibid.

120 Ibid.

121 Robin Warner, 'Paper VIII–Options for Environmental Impact Assessment Elements' in 'An International Instrument on Conservation and Sustainable Use of Biodiversity in Marine Areas beyond National Jurisdiction Exploring Different Elements to Consider' (Series of Policy Briefs on Scope, Parameters and Feasibility, IUCN, 2003) 68.

122 Ibid.

123 Barritt and Viñuales (n 18) 78.

124 See, e.g. Fiji submission in Morgera et al, 'Summary of IGC 1' (n 23) 10.

specify basic content.[125] In contrast, the IUCN argues for some level of detail to set minimum standards.[126]

Appendix II of the Espoo Convention provides a good starting point for setting minimum requirements. It specifies that an EIS should include:

(a) A description of the proposed activity;
(b) A description of the environment, including specific information necessary for identifying and assessing the environmental effects of the activity;
(c) A description of practical alternatives;
(d) An assessment of the likely or potential environmental impacts of the activity, including direct, indirect, cumulative, short-term and long-term effects;
(e) An identification and description of measures available to mitigate adverse impacts and an assessment of those measures;
(f) Gaps in knowledge and uncertainties which may be encountered in compiling the required information;
(g) An indication of whether the environment of a State or ABNJ is likely to be affected by the activity or alternatives;
(h) A brief, non-technical summary of the information above.

In addition, the Espoo Convention provides that parties should also include an outline for monitoring and management programmes and any plans for post-project analysis.[127]

The content of the EIS should also be tailored to the peculiarities of assessing impacts on BBNJ. The CBD's Revised Voluntary Guidelines could assist as they 'elaborate on the types of impacts and alternatives that should be identified and examined in a biodiversity-inclusive EIA report.'[128] Drawing on these guidelines, EIS under an ILBI could also require:

- A description of expected biophysical changes (in water, air, flora and fauna);
- A determination of the spatial and temporal scale of each biophysical change and any effects on ecosystem connectivity;
- A description of ecosystems that lie within the range of influence of a biophysical change;
- A determination of whether biophysical changes are likely to have adverse impacts on BBNJ in terms of composition, structure and key processes;
- Consideration of no net biodiversity loss alternatives and measures to enhance biodiversity;
- Baseline data for the marine area affected.[129]

125 Ibid, 11.
126 IUCN recommendations for IGC (n 59) 10.
127 Espoo Convention, Appendix II (h).
128 Warner, 'Tools to Conserve' (n 38) 322–323.
129 *CBD Revised Guidelines* (n 68) 13–14 [25] and 6 [8(b)].

Key institutions under the ILBI, including a scientific and advisory body or a COP could also work with existing global, regional and sectoral organisations to incorporate biodiversity-inclusive considerations into their respective EIA regimes.[130]

6.3.1.4 *A participatory process that engages all relevant stakeholders*

As environmental challenges in ABNJ are complex, uncertain, multi-scale and affect multiple stakeholders, an ILBI should endeavour to facilitate a transparent decision-making process, one that is 'flexible to changing circumstances' and takes into account a diversity of knowledge and experience.[131] The right to participate in environmental decision-making is increasingly regarded as a democratic right.[132] It is enshrined in the United Nations Economic Commission for Europe's 1998 Convention on Access to Information, Public Participation in Decision-Making and Access to Justice in Environmental Matters,[133] and recognised in various bilateral and multilateral treaties and non-binding instruments.[134] For example, Principle 10 of the Rio Declaration describes three pillars that are considered to form 'a right of participation' in environmental decisions:

> Environmental issues are best handled with participation of all concerned citizens, at the relevant level. At the national level, each individual shall have appropriate access to information concerning the environment that is held by public authorities ... and the opportunity to participate in decision-making processes. States shall facilitate and encourage public awareness and participation by making information widely available. Effective access to judicial and administrative proceedings, including redress and remedy, shall be provided.

Collectively these three pillars strengthen 'environmental democracy' by enabling relevant stakeholders to have a say in decisions affecting the environment.[135] Participation should therefore be seen as a prerequisite for effective EIA under an ILBI. This inevitably raises the question of who qualifies as an interested stake-

130 Robin Warner, 'Oceans in Transition: Incorporating Climate-Change Impacts into Environmental Impact Assessment for Marine Areas beyond National Jurisdiction' (2018) 45 *Ecology Law Quarterly* 31, 49.
131 Mark S. Reed, 'Stakeholder Participation for Environmental Management: A Literature Review' (2008) 141(10) *Biological Conservation* 2417, 2418.
132 Ibid.
133 Convention on Access to Information, Public Participation in Decision-Making and Access to Justice in Environmental Matters, opened for signature 25 June 1998, 2161 UNTS 447 (entered into force 30 October 2001).
134 See, e.g. UNFCCC, art 6 and the Cartagena Protocol on Biosafety to the Convention on Biological Diversity, opened for signature 29 January 2000, 39 ILM 1027 (entered into force 11 September 2003) art 23.
135 Leslie-Anne Duvic-Paoli, 'The Status of the Right to Public Participation in International Environmental Law: An Analysis of the Jurisprudence' (2013) 23(1) *Yearbook of International Environmental Law* 80, 80.

holder in ABNJ.[136] The President's Aid to Negotiations provides an extensive list of potential stakeholders, which includes all States, global, regional and sectoral bodies, indigenous peoples and local communities with traditional knowledge, research and academic institutions, industry and civil society.[137]

Once stakeholders have been identified, it will be necessary to determine how they can participate in the EIA process. For this, one must look at the different rungs on 'the ladder of participation.'[138] The bottom rung is the communication or dissemination of information to relevant stakeholders. Pursuant to Article 206 of UNCLOS States are required to communicate EIA results via the mechanisms provided in Article 205. A State can either publish the report or provide it to a competent international organisation who in turn makes it available to all States. Article 205 provides no explanation as to what 'publish' means in this context, although Craik notes that earlier drafts of the provision refer to the term 'disseminate.'[139] The alternative mechanism of communicating EIA results is 'equally vague,' with no indication as to what qualifies as a 'competent international organisation.'[140] There are also no timescales provided in UNCLOS for the publication or provision of an EIS. An ILBI could build on these existing UNCLOS provisions by nominating 'competent international organisations' or requiring relevant documentation to be published in an EIA database.[141] This database could be accessible to relevant stakeholders and provide a central repository of EIA data including baseline data on ABNJ.[142]

The next rung on the ladder of participation is consultation with relevant stakeholders. The general obligation to consult with stakeholders before a decision is made to proceed with an activity is recognised in Principle 7 of the 1987 UNEP Goals and Principles on Environmental Impact Assessment.[143] According to Principle 7, government agencies, civil society, experts in relevant disciplines and interested groups should be given the opportunity to comment on the EIA. A number of consultation options have been discussed during BBNJ negotiations. One option is for consultation to exist at each stage of the EIA process, beginning with the scoping stage.[144] An ILBI could follow the Espoo Convention and

136 Warner, 'Environmental Assessment,' (n 22) 294.

137 *President's Aid to Negotiations* (n 12) 28 [4.3.2].

138 Reed (n 131) 2419 referring to Sherry R. Arnstein, 'A Ladder of Citizenship Participation' (1969) 26 *Journal of the American Institute of Planners* 216–233.

139 Craik, 'International Law of EIA' (n 16) 145.

140 Ibid.

141 Canada, 'Canada's Views Related to Certain Elements under Discussion by the Preparatory Committee established by United Nations General Assembly Resolution 69/292' (2016) 3 <https://www.un.org/depts/los/biodiversity/prepcom_files/rolling_comp/Canada.pdf>. An EIA database has been established under the Antarctic Treaty System and provides access to IEEs and CEEs.

142 Written Submission of New Zealand to PrepCom (n 30) 6.

143 UNEP, United Nations Environment Programme Goals and Principles of EIA, adopted by decision 14/25 of the Governing Council of UNEP (17 June 1987).

144 'High Seas Alliance Recommendations for Environmental Impact Assessment under the New Legally Binding Instrument' (HAS Briefing, March 2018) 1 <http://www.high-

allow relevant stakeholders to participate in the EIA process, including the preparation of the EIS, and provide them with the opportunity to make comments or objections. As Hubert argues, 'the exchange of views and information between a wider range of participants … may lend greater legitimacy and accountability' to the EIA process.[145] An ILBI could also require stakeholder comments to be taken into account in decision-making. This obligation could be operationalised by:

1. Requiring all proposals, comments and reviews of EIAs to be made publicly available (i.e. in an EIA database);
2. Requiring the decision-making body to justify their final decision by providing reasons, considerations and evidence on how comments or objections have been taken into account.[146] The IUCN, for example, has suggested that the final decision on whether and how the activity goes ahead should be reported as this will contribute to the 'integrity of the EIA process and to the database of knowledge for future EIAs, including cumulative impacts analysis.'[147]

The type and frequency of consultation with relevant stakeholders should also 'reflect the activity's level of risk and its anticipated impacts.'[148] The above approach to consultation is preferable as it ensures full transparency in the decision-making process as well as scrutiny and oversight by the international community. Arguably, it will also improve the quality of environmental decision-making by making the process more balanced and open.

6.3.1.5 Review, monitoring and compliance provisions

No EIA process is complete without an effective monitoring and review component.[149] As environmental conditions change over time, it is important to continue monitoring the on-going risks and impacts of an authorised activity.[150] The

---

seasalliance.org/wp-content/uploads/2013/04/HSA-EIA-recommendations_March-2018.pdf>.

145 Anna-Maria Hubert, 'UN General Assembly Resolution to Develop a New Legally Binding Instrument on the Conservation and Sustainable Use of Marine Biological Diversity of Areas beyond National Jurisdiction' (The University of Calgary Faculty of Law Blog, 14 August 2015) 3.

146 Craik, 'International Law of EIA' (n 16) 151.

147 *Textual Proposals Submitted by Delegations for Consideration at IGC 4, in Response to the Invitation by the President of the Conference in Her Note of 18 November 2019*, UN Doc A/CONF.232/2020/3 (15 April 2020) IUCN on art 36, 279.

148 *President's Aid to Negotiations* (n 12) 39 [5.4(f)(ii)(a)].

149 WWF, 'Taking a Risk Management Approach to Strategic Environmental Assessment and Environmental Impact Assessment for BBNJ' (Paper prepared for the Second BBNJ Prep Com, August 2016) 5 <https://www.un.org/depts/los/biodiversity/prepcom_files/WWF_BBNJ_Prep_Com2_2016.pdf>.

150 Yoshifumi Tanaka, 'The South China Sea Arbitration: Environmental Obligations under the Law of the Sea Convention' (2018) 27(1) *Review of European, Comparative & International Environmental Law* 90, 93.

activities that make up a monitoring system are commonly grouped together under the heading 'EIA follow up' and include monitoring, compliance, enforcement and environmental auditing.[151]

UNCLOS provides for post-project monitoring and surveillance. Article 204 requires States to monitor the risks or effects of pollution. However, it is not clear whether this obligation extends to wider impacts on BBNJ. In *Pulp Mills*, the ICJ held that the obligation to conduct an EIA is a 'continuous one' and the monitoring of an activity's effects should be undertaken, 'where necessary, throughout the life of a project.'[152] Arguably, the duty to monitor is implicit in the obligation to conduct EIA under Article 206 of UNCLOS.[153] Harrison contends that this duty may also be implicit in other UNCLOS provisions, including the overarching obligation to protect and preserve the marine environment in Article 192.[154] Thus, building on Articles 204 and 206 of UNCLOS, an ILBI could require State Parties to ensure that the impacts of authorised activities in ABNJ are continuously monitored, reported on and reviewed.

While there is general recognition of the need to include some form of post-project analysis under an ILBI, disagreement remains on whether it should be internationalised. Some delegates argue States should be responsible for post-EIA monitoring, as well as compliance with any conditions. These States maintain that bodies established under an ILBI (i.e. scientific and technical body or compliance committee) should provide advice only.[155] Other delegates argue that the structural mechanism for monitoring and review will 'require scientific expertise, knowledge of on-going and cumulative impacts from activities, and independence to ensure accountability and transparency.'[156]

An ILBI should require State Parties to submit a report detailing their compliance with EIA-related provisions.[157] This could be submitted to a dedicated compliance committee on an annual basis. While delegations broadly support making reports publicly available, views differ on requiring reports to be submitted to the COP or a subsidiary body, such as a compliance committee.[158] This work suggests that a compliance committee, assisted by a scientific and technical body, could be tasked with preparing an annual report that evaluates States' compliance with EIA obligations, identifying instances of non-compliance and publishing this report publicly.[159] A compliance and review committee could also make rec-

151 *CBD Revised Guidelines* (n 68) 21 [44].

152 *Pulp Mills on the River Uruguay (Argentina v. Uruguay) (Judgment)* [2010] ICJ Rep 14, 73 [205]; James, Harrison, *Saving the Oceans through Law: The International Legal Framework for the Protection of the Marine Environment* (Oxford University Press, 2017) 35.

153 Harrison (n 152) 35.

154 Ibid.

155 See, e.g. Written Submission of G77 and China to PrepCom (n 14) 4.

156 IUCN recommendations for IGC (n 59) 12.

157 *Chair's Streamlined Non-Paper* (n 26) 36 [202].

158 Kantai et al, 'Summary of IGC 3' (n 5) 14.

159 Ibid.

ommendations on ways to address any adverse impacts arising from an authorised activity. In this way, a compliance and review committee could provide a level of international scrutiny to the EIA process to ensure that States continue to abide with their obligations under the ILBI.

6.4 Conclusion

EIA is universally recognised as a key mechanism for environmental management.[160] A large number of international, regional and sectoral instruments, both binding and non-binding, include and further define the requirement of EIA, particularly in respect to marine areas. The analysis undertaken in this chapter has demonstrated that existing EIA measures could be used to underpin and shape key ingredients of an overarching recipe for environmentally sustainable decision-making in ABNJ. The development of an ILBI presents the opportunity to build on pre-existing UNCLOS obligations and provide for an EIA process that is biodiversity-inclusive, transparent and subject to some form of international scrutiny and oversight.[161]

References

Arnstein, Sherry R., 'A Ladder of Citizenship Participation' (1969) 35(4) *Journal of the American Institute of Planners* 216–224. DOI: https://doi.org/10.1080/01944366908977225.

ATCM, *Revised Guidelines for Environmental Impact Assessment in Antarctica*, Res 1, ATCM XXXIX - CEP XIX (ATCM, 1 June 2016).

Australia, 'Preparatory Committee on Conservation and Sustainable Use of Marine Biological Diversity of Areas beyond National Jurisdiction (BBNJ): Submission by Australia' (6 December 2016) https://www.un.org/depts/los/biodiversity/prepcom_files/rolling_comp/Australia.pdf accessed 31 March 2022 ('Written Submission of Australia to PrepCom').

Barritt, Emily and Jorge E. Viñuales, *Legal Scan: A Conservation Agenda for Biodiversity Beyond National Jurisdiction* (Cambridge Centre for Environment, Energy and Natural Resource Governance, University of Cambridge, May 2016).

Bastmeijer, Kees, 'Implementing the Environmental Protocol Domestically: An Overview' in Davor Vidas (ed) *Implementing the Environmental Protection Regime for the Antarctic* (Springer Netherlands, 2000) 287. DOI: https://doi.org/10.1007/978-94-011-4319-6_16.

Bastmeijer, Kees and Ricardo Roura, 'Environmental Impact Assessment in Antarctica' in Kees Bastmeijer and Timo Koivurova (eds), *Theory and Practice of Transboundary Environmental Impact Assessment* (Martinus Nijhoff Publishers, 2008) 175.

160 Richard K. Morgan, 'Environmental Impact Assessment: The State of the Art' (2012) 30(1) *Impact Assessment and Project Appraisal* 5, 6.

161 Warner, 'Environmental Assessment' (n 22) 307.

Blitza, Eike, 'Section 4 Monitoring and Environmental Assessment' in Alexander Proelss et al (ed), *United Nations Convention on the Law of the Sea A Commentary* (Hart Publishing, 2017) 1356.

Canada, 'Canada's Views Related to Certain Elements under Discussion by the Preparatory Committee established by United Nations General Assembly Resolution 69/292' (2016) <https://www.un.org/depts/los/biodiversity/prepcom_files/rolling_comp/Canada.pdf> accessed 31 March 2022.

Cartagena Protocol on Biosafety to the Convention on Biological Diversity, opened for signature 29 January 2000 (2000) 39 *ILM* 1027 (entered into force 11 September 2003).

CBD, *Decision Adopted by the Conference of the Parties to the Convention on Biological Diversity at its Eighth Meeting*, UNEP/CBD/COP/DEC/VIII/28 (CBD, 15 June 2006).

CBD, 'Revised Voluntary Guidelines for the Consideration of Biodiversity in Environmental Impact Assessments and Strategic Environmental Assessments in Marine and Coastal Areas' (21 August 2012) UNEP/CBD/COP/11/23.

Chair's non-paper on Elements of a Draft Text of an International Legally-binding Instrument under the United Nations Convention on the Law of the Sea on the Conservation and Sustainable Use of Marine Biological Diversity of Areas Beyond National Jurisdiction Third Session of the PrepCom (27 March–7 April 2017) (28 February 2017) <https://www.un.org/Depts/los/biodiversity/prepcom_files/Chair_non_paper.pdf> accessed 31 March 2022.

Chair's Streamlined non-paper on Elements of a Draft Text of an International Legally-binding Instrument under the United Nations Convention on the Law of the Sea on the Conservation and Sustainable Use of Marine Biological Diversity of Areas Beyond National Jurisdiction Fourth Session of the PrepCom (10-21 July 2017) <https://www.un.org/depts/los/biodiversity/prepcom_files/Chairs_streamlined_non-paper_to_delegations.pdf> accessed 31 March 2022.

'Citizen Ben-Firefighter' *PBS.org* (Web Site, 2002) <http://www.pbs.org/benfranklin/l3_citizen_firefighter.html> accessed 31 March 2022.

Convention on Access to Information, Public Participation in Decision-Making and Access to Justice in Environmental Matters, opened for signature 25 June 1998 (1998) 2161 *UNTS* 447 (entered into force 30 October 2001).

Convention on Biological Diversity, opened for signature 5 June 1992 (1992) 1760 *UNTS* 143 (entered into force 29 December 1993) (CBD).

Convention on Environmental Impact Assessment in a Transboundary Context, opened for signature 25 February 1991 (1991) 30 *ILM* 802 (entered into force 10 September 1997) (Espoo Convention).

Convention on the Prevention of Marine Pollution by Dumping of Wastes and Other Materials, opened for signature 29 December 1972 (1972) 1046 *UNTS* 120 (entered into force 30 August 1975).

Craik, Neil, *The International Law of Environmental Impact Assessment: Process, Substance and Integration* (Cambridge University Press, 2008). DOI: https://doi.org/10.1017/CBO9780511494611.

Craik, Neil, 'International EIA Law and Geoengineering: Do Emerging Technologies Require Special Rules' (2015) 5 *Climate Law* 111–141. DOI: 10.1163/18786561-00504002.

Currie, Duncan E.J., 'Key Components and Best Practices for Environmental Impact Assessments and Strategic Environmental Assessments' (Working Paper,

High Seas Alliance, 23 August 2016) <https://fundingtheocean.org/reports/key-components-and-best-practices-for-environmental-impact-assessments/> accessed 31 March 2022.

Davis, Ruth and Edmund Lee, 'Marine Environmental Protection and the Southern Ocean' in Alex G. Oude Elferink and Donald Rothwell (eds) *The Law of the Sea and Polar Maritime Delimitation and Jurisdiction* (Kluwer Law International, 2001) 201.

Druel, Elisabeth, *Environmental Impact Assessments in Areas Beyond National Jurisdiction* (Study No. 01/13, IDDRI, January 2013).

Duvic-Paoli, Leslie-Anne, 'The Status of the Right to Public Participation in International Environmental Law: An Analysis of the Jurisprudence' (2013) 23(1) *Yearbook of International Environmental Law* 80–105. DOI: 10.1093/yiel/yvt062.

Ensminger, Timothy J, Lance N. McCold and J. Warren Webb, 'Environmental Impact Assessment under the National Environmental Policy Act and the Protocol on Environmental Protection to the Antarctic Treaty' (1999) 24(1) *Environmental Management* 13–23. DOI: 10.1007/s002679900211.

European Union, 'Development of an International Legally-Binding Instrument under UNCLOS on the Conservation and Sustainable Use of Marine Biological Diversity of Areas beyond National Jurisdiction (BBNJ Process), Written Submission of EU and Its Member States: Environmental Impact Assessments' (15 February 2017) 4 [18] ('Written Submission of EU and Its Member States to PrepCom: Environmental Impact Assessments') <https://www.un.org/depts/los/biodiversity/prepcom_files/rolling_comp/EU_Written_Submission_on_Environmental_Assessments.pdf> accessed 31 March 2022.

Franklin, Benjamin, 'On Protection of Towns from Fire', *Pennsylvania Gazette* (4 February 1735).

Harrison, James, *Saving the Oceans Through Law: The International Legal Framework for the Protection of the Marine Environment* (Oxford University Press, 2017). DOI: 10.1093/law/9780198707325.001.0001.

Hemmings, Alan D. and Lorne K. Kriwoken, 'High level Antarctic EIA under the Madrid Protocol: State Practice and the Effectiveness of the Comprehensive Environmental Evaluation Process' (2010) 10 *International Environmental Agreements* 187–208. DOI: 10.1007/s10784-010-9119-5.

High Seas Alliance, 'High Seas Alliance Recommendations for Environmental Impact Assessment under the New Legally Binding Instrument' (HAS Briefing, March 2018) <https://www.highseasalliance.org/wp-content/uploads/2013/04/HSA-EIA-recommendations_March-2018.pdf> accessed 31 March 2022.

Hubert, Anna-Maria 'UN General Assembly Resolution to Develop a New Legally Binding Instrument on the Conservation and Sustainable Use of Marine Biological Diversity of Areas Beyond National Jurisdiction' (*The University of Calgary Faculty of Law Blog*, 13 August 2015) <https://ablawg.ca/wp-content/uploads/2015/08/Blog_AMH_LOSC_generalresolution_August-2015.pdf> accessed 31 March 2022.

International Association for Impact Assessment, 'Principles of Environmental Impact Assessment Best Practice' (Web Page, January 1999) <https://www.iaia.org/uploads/pdf/principlesEA_1.pdf> accessed 31 March 2022.

ISA, *Recommendations for the Guidance of Contractors for the Assessment of the Possible Environmental Impacts Arising from Exploration for Marine Minerals in the Area*, ISBA/19/LTC/8 (ISA, 1 March 2013) vol. 6, 18.

IUCN, 'An International Instrument on Conservation and Sustainable Use of Biodiversity in Marine Areas beyond National Jurisdiction: Matrix of Suggestions' (16 December 2015) 25 <https://www.iucn.org/downloads/iucn_bbnj_matrix_december_2015.pdf> accessed 31 March 2022.

IUCN, 'Recommendations for the Intergovernmental Conference: First Session of the Intergovernmental Conference on an International Legally Binding Instrument under the United Nations Convention on the Law of the Sea on Conservation and Sustainable Use of Marine Biological Diversity of Areas beyond National Jurisdiction, New York, September 4-17, 2018' (Recommendations Paper, 2018) <https://www.iucn.org/sites/dev/files/content/documents/iucn_bbnj_recommendation_paper_draft_21_aug_2018_3.pdf> accessed 31 March 2022.

Kantai, Tallash, Asheline Appleton, Priscila Pereira de Andrade, Bernard Soubry and Asterios Tsioumanis, 'BBNJ IGC-2 Highlights: Friday 29 March 2019' *Earth Negotiations Bulletin* (Online Bulletin, 1 April 2019a) <https://enb.iisd.org/download/pdf/enb25190e.pdf> accessed 31 March 2022.

Kantai, Tallash, Asheline Appleton, Priscila Pereira de Andrade, Bernard Soubry and Asterios Tsioumanis, 'Summary of the Second Session of the Intergovernmental Conference on the Conservation and Sustainable Use of Marine Biodiversity of Areas Beyond National Jurisdiction: 25 March–5 April 2019' *Earth Negotiations Bulletin* (Online Bulletin, 8 April 2019b) <https://enb.iisd.org/download/pdf/enb25195e.pdf> accessed 31 March 2022.

Kantai, Tallash, Jennifer Bansard, Tasha Goldberg, Katarina Hovden and Asterios Tsioumanis, 'Summary of the Third Session of the Intergovernmental Conference on the Conservation and Sustainable Use of Marine Biodiversity of Areas Beyond National Jurisdiction: 19–30 August 2019' *Earth Negotiations Bulletin* (Online Bulletin, 2 September 2019) <https://enb.iisd.org/download/pdf/enb25218e.pdf> accessed 31 March 2022.

Kantai, Tallash and Paolo Bettelli, 'Summary of the Fourth Session of the Intergovernmental Conference on the Conservation and Sustainable Use of Marine Biodiversity of Areas beyond National Jurisdiction: 7-18 March 2022' *Earth Negotiations Bulletin* (Online Bulletin, 21 March 2022) 9 < https://enb.iisd.org/sites/default/files/2022-03/enb25225e.pdf> accessed 31 March 2022.

Kong, Lingjie, 'Environmental Impact Assessment under the United Nations Convention on the Law of the Sea' (2011) 10 *Chinese Journal of International Law* 651–669. DOI: 10.1093/chinesejil/jmr014.

Korseberg, Lene, 'The Law-Making Effects of the FAO Deep-Sea Fisheries Guidelines' (2018) 67 *International and Comparative Law Quarterly* 801–832. DOI: 10.1017/S0020589318000192.

Lyons, D, 'Environmental Impact Assessment in Antarctica under the Protocol on Environmental Protection' (1993) 29 *Polar Record* 111–120. DOI: 10.1017/S0032247400023561.

Morgan, Richard K, 'Environmental Impact Assessment: The State of the Art' (2012) 30(1) *Impact Assessment and Project Appraisal* 5–14. DOI: 10.1080/14615517.2012.661557.

Morgera, Elisa, Asheline Appleton, Daniela Diz and Asterios Tsioumanis, 'Summary of the First Session of the Intergovernmental Conference on an International Legally Binding Instrument under the UN Convention on the Law of the Sea on the Conservation and Sustainable Use of Marine Biodiversity of Areas Beyond National Jurisdiction 4–17 September 2018' *Earth Negotiations Bulletin* (Online

Bulletin, 20 September 2018) <https://enb.iisd.org/download/pdf/enb25179e.pdf> accessed 31 March 2022.

Natural Resources Defense Council (NRDC) on behalf of the High Seas Alliance, 'Intervention on EIAs' (Statement to the First Session of the Intergovernmental Conference, 11 September 2018) <https://www.highseasalliance.org/wp-content/uploads/2013/04/4.-NRDC-on-behalf-of-the-High-Seas-Alliance-Intervention-on-EIAs-.pdf> accessed 31 March 2022.

New Zealand, 'Preparatory Committee on Conservation and Sustainable Use of Marine Biological Diversity of Areas beyond National Jurisdiction: New Zealand Submission' (December 2016) (December 2016) ('Written Submission of New Zealand to PrepCom') <https://www.un.org/depts/los/biodiversity/prepcom_files/rolling_comp/New_Zealand.pdf> accessed 31 March 2022.

Norway, 'Preparatory Committee established by General Assembly Resolution 69/292: Development of an International Legally Binding Instrument under the United Nations Convention on the Law of the Sea on the Conservation and Sustainable Use of Marine Biological Diversity of Areas beyond National Jurisdiction: Comments by Norway'(December 2016) <https://www.un.org/depts/los/biodiversity/prepcom_files/rolling_comp/Norway.pdf> accessed 31 March 2022.

Oude Elferink, Alex, 'Environmental Impact Assessment in Areas Beyond National Jurisdiction' 27(2) (2012) *The International Journal of Marine and Coastal Law* 449–480. DOI: 10.1163/157180812X636598.

Oxford University Press, 'Environmental Impact Assessment' in *Max Planck Encyclopedias of International Law* (online at 1 November 2020)

Pacific Small Island Developing States (PSIDS), 'PSIDS Submission to the Second Meeting of the Preparatory Committee for the Development of an International Legally Binding Instrument under the United Nations Convention on the Law of the Sea on the Conservation and Sustainable Use of Marine Biological Diversity of Areas beyond National Jurisdiction (BBNJ PrepCom)' (August 2016) <https://www.un.org/depts/los/biodiversity/prepcom_files/rolling_comp/PSIDS_second.pdf> accessed 31 March 2022.

President's Aid to Negotiations, UN Doc A/CONF.232/2019/1 (3 December 2018) <https://documents-dds-ny.un.org/doc/UNDOC/GEN/N18/413/20/PDF/N1841320.pdf?OpenElement> accessed 31 March 2022.

'Protocol on Environmental Protection to the Antarctic Treaty, Opened for Signature 4 October 1991, (1991) 30 *ILM* 1461 (entered into force 14 January 1998) (Madrid Protocol).

'Protocol to the Convention on the Prevention of Marine Pollution by Dumping of Wastes and Other Matter, Opened for Signature 7 November 1996' (1997) 36 *ILM* 1 (entered into force 24 March 2006).

Pulp Mills on the River Uruguay (Argentina v. Uruguay) (Judgment) (2010) *ICJ Rep* 14.

Reed, Mark S, 'Stakeholder Participation for Environmental Management: A Literature Review' (2008) 141(10) *Biological Conservation* 2417–2431. DOI: 10.1016/j.biocon.2008.07.014.

Responsibilities and Obligations of States Sponsoring Persons and Entities with Respect to Activities in the Area (Advisory Opinion) (Seabed Disputes Chamber, Case No. 17, 1 February 2011).

Sands, Philippe and Jacqueline Peel, *Principles of International Environmental Law* (CUP, 3rd ed, 2012).

Secretariat of the Convention on Biological Diversity, Netherlands Commission for Environmental Assessment, '*Biodiversity in Impact Assessment, Background Document to CBD Decision VIII/28: Voluntary Guidelines on Biodiversity-Inclusive Impact Assessment* (CBD Technical Series No. 26, 2006).

Sielen, Alan, 'The New International Rules on Ocean Dumping: Promise and Performance (Part 1)' (2009) 21 *Georgetown International Environmental Law Review* 295–336.

Song, Young-il, 'Environmental Impact Assessment in Korea' (2004)II(2) *Korea Environmental Policy Bulletin* 1.

Statement by the President of the Conference at the Closing of the First Session of the Intergovernmental Conference on an International Legally Binding Instrument under the United Nations Convention on the Law of the Sea on the Conservation and Sustainable Use of Marine Biological Diversity of Areas Beyond National Jurisdiction, UN Doc A/CONF.232/2018/7 (20 September 2018) <https://documents-dds-ny.un.org/doc/UNDOC/GEN/N18/294/09/PDF/N1829409.pdf?OpenElement> accessed 31 March 2022.

Tanaka, Yoshifumi, 'The South China Sea arbitration: Environmental obligations under the Law of the Sea Convention' (2018) 27 *Review of European, Comparative & International Environmental Law* 90–96. DOI: 10.1111/reel.12229.

Textual Proposals Submitted by Delegations for Consideration at IGC4, in Response to the Invitation by the President of the Conference in Her Note of 18 November 2019, UN Doc A/CONF.232/2020/3 (15 April 2020).

'The Electric Ben Franklin-In Case of Fire' *UShistory.org* (Web Page, 4 July 1995) <http://www.ushistory.org/franklin/philadelphia/fire.htm> accessed 31 March 2022.

The Group of 77, 'Development of an International Legally Binding Instrument under the United Nations Convention on the Law of the Sea on the Conservation and Sustainable Use of Marine Biological Diversity of Areas beyond National Jurisdiction (A/RES/69/292): Group of 77 and China's Written Submission' (5 December 2016) 3 <https://www.un.org/depts/los/biodiversity/prepcom_files/rolling_comp/Group_of_77_and_China.pdf> accessed 31 March 2022.

UNEP, *1987 Goals and Principles of Environmental Impact Assessment, Decision 14/25 of the Governing Council of UNEP* (UNEP, 17 June 1987).

United Nations Framework Convention on Climate Change, opened for signature 9 May 1992 (1992) 1771 *UNTS* 165 (entered into force 21 March 1994) (UNFCCC).

United Nations General Assembly, *Transforming our World: The 2030 Agenda for Sustainable Development*, UN Doc. A/RES/70/1 (2015).

VanderZwaag, David L, 'The International Control of Ocean Dumping: Navigating from Permissive to Precautionary Shores' in Rayfuse, Rosemary (ed) *Research Handbook on International Marine Environmental Law* (Edward Elgar Publishing Limited, 2015) 132. DOI: https://doi.org/10.4337/9781781004777.00014.

Warner, Robin, 'Paper VIII—Options for Environmental Impact Assessment Elements' in *An International Instrument on Conservation and Sustainable Use of Biodiversity in Marine Areas Beyond National Jurisdiction Exploring Different Elements to Consider* (Series of Policy Briefs on Scope, Parameters and Feasibility, IUCN, 2003).

Warner, Robin, 'Tools to Conserve Ocean Biodiversity: Developing the Legal Framework for Environmental Impact Assessment in Marine Areas Beyond

National Jurisdiction' (2012) 26(1) *Ocean Yearbook* 317–341. DOI: 10.1163/22116001-92600087.

Warner, Robin, 'Conserving Marine Biodiversity in Areas Beyond National Jurisdiction: Co-Evolution and Interaction with the Law of the Sea' in Donald Rothwell et al (eds), *The Oxford Handbook of the Law of the Sea* (Oxford University Press, 2015) 752. DOI: 10.1093/law/9780198715481.003.0033.

Warner, Robin, 'Environmental Assessment in Marine Areas Beyond National Jurisdiction' in Rosemary Rayfuse (ed), *Research Handbook on International Marine Environmental Law* (Edward Elgar Publishing Limited, 2015) 291. DOI: https://doi.org/10.4337/9781781004777.00024.

Warner, Robin, 'Oceans in Transition: Incorporating Climate-Change Impacts into Environmental Impact Assessment for Marine Areas beyond National Jurisdiction' (2018) 45 *Ecology Law Quarterly* 31–51. DOI: http://dx.doi.org/10.15779/Z38M61BQ0J.

'What is Impact Assessment?' *Convention on Biological Diversity* (Web Page, 27 April 2010) <https://www.cbd.int/impact/whatis.shtml> accessed 31 March 2022.

Wright, Glen, Julien Rochette, Elisabeth Druel and Kristina Gjerde, *The Long and Winding Road Continues: Towards a New Agreement on High Seas Governance* (Study No. 01/16, IDDRI, March 2016).

Wright, Glen, Julien Rochette, Kristina Gjerde and Isabel Seeger, *The Long and Winding Road: Negotiating a Treaty for the Conservation and Sustainable Use of Marine Biodiversity in Areas Beyond National Jurisdiction* (Study No. 8/2018, IDDRI, August 2018).

WWF, 'Taking a Risk Management Approach to Strategic Environmental Assessment and Environmental Impact Assessment for BBNJ' (Paper prepared for the Second BBNJ Prep Com, August 2016) <https://www.un.org/depts/los/biodiversity/prepcom_files/WWF_BBNJ_Prep_Com2_2016.pdf> accessed 31 March 2022.

7 Time to wake the Sleeping Giant

Implementing capacity-building and marine technology transfer in an ILBI

Introduction

> *In the end the only certainty is that, without a renewed and strong compromise between States with respect to capacity-building and the transfer of marine technology, the formula enshrined in LOSC will be merely revisited without the necessary transformation required by developing States.*[1]

Greater scientific knowledge of BBNJ will be required to ensure its long-term conservation and sustainable use. BBNJ research relies on skilled individuals, appropriate infrastructure and financial resources.[2] Many countries lack the capacity to participate in this research and can miss out on benefits from the discovery of new ocean life, habitats and processes.[3] Capacity limitations could also severely constrain the ability of developing States to fully and effectively enjoy rights granted under an ILBI.

UNCLOS framers recognised the 'differing ability of States to benefit from the ocean'[4] and were keenly aware of the need for capacity-building and technology transfer (CBTT).[5] This is evident in Part XIV of UNCLOS which contains

1 Marta Chantal Ribeiro, 'South Atlantic Perspectives on the Future International Legally Binding Instrument under the LOSC on Conservation and Sustainable Use of BBNJ' (2017) 32 *The International Journal of Marine and Coastal Law* 733, 746.

2 L. Valdés et al (eds), *Global Ocean Science Report: The Current Status of Ocean Science around the World* (Report, IOC-UNESCO, 2017) 24.

3 Harriet Harden-Davies and Paul Snelgrove, 'Science Collaboration for Capacity Building: Advancing Technology Transfer through a Treaty for Biodiversity beyond National Jurisdiction' (2020) 7(40) *Frontiers in Marine Science* 1, 1.

4 Cymie Payne, 'Biodiversity in High Seas Areas: An Integrated Legal Approach', *American Society of International Law* (ASIL Insights, 1 September 2017) <https://www.asil.org/insights/volume/21/issue/9/biodiversity-high-seas-areas-integrated-legal-approach>.

5 *Oceans and the Law of the Sea: Report of the Secretary-General*, UN Doc A/65/69 (29 March 2010) [8].

DOI: 10.4324/b22996-8

the Convention's normative CBTT framework. Part XIV can be described as the 'Sleeping Giant of UNCLOS.' Its provisions have enormous untapped potential but have remained dormant, inactive and underutilised since the adoption of the Convention. The development of an ILBI offers a timely and much-needed wake-up call and provides the opportunity to revitalise and strengthen the existing CBTT formula enshrined in UNCLOS. This chapter identifies key mechanisms to enhance the implementation of existing UNCLOS requirements in an effort to wake the Sleeping Giant from its slumber.

BBNJ negotiators face a challenging task in shaping an ILBI's CBTT provisions.[6] Certain delegates are keen to see Part XIV simply incorporated *mutatis mutandis* into the new instrument.[7] However, as Ribeiro warns, merely revisiting the formula in UNCLOS and underscoring the importance of CBTT will not provide 'the necessary transformation required by developing States.'[8] In other words, existing UNCLOS obligations 'should not be merely repeated but enhanced.'[9] As with the other elements of the package deal, BBNJ negotiators will need to find a 'sweet-spot' for CBTT, 'one that requires enough effort from States to generate real ... benefits but not efforts that are so costly that States choose not to participate in, or implement, the agreement.'[10] After all, the goal is to have an ILBI that is truly universal and inclusive. This chapter offers a potential way forward and could assist BBNJ negotiators in finding the elusive sweet-spot.

7.1 CBTT under UNCLOS

7.1.1 Introducing the Sleeping Giant

CBTT are key concepts in international environmental policy.[11] The following sections introduce these two concepts and examine the untapped potential of Part XIV of UNCLOS. A brief historical analysis of Part XIV is undertaken to

6 CB is often used interchangeably with 'capacity development.' This book uses CB in accordance with the BBNJ package deal.

7 Ronán Long and Mariamalia Rodríguez Chaves, 'Anatomy of a New International Instrument for Marine Biodiversity beyond National Jurisdiction: First Impressions of the Preparatory Process' (2015) 6 *Environmental Liability* 213, 225 referring to Elisa Morgera et al, 'Summary of the First Session of the Preparatory Committee on Marine Biodiversity of Areas beyond National Jurisdiction: 28 March–8 April 2016' *Earth Negotiations Bulletin* (Online Bulletin, 11 April 2016) 15 <https://enb.iisd.org/events/1st-session-bbnj-preparatory-committee/summary-report-28-march-8-april-2016>.

8 Ribeiro (n 1) 746.

9 *Statement by the President of the Conference at the Closing of IGC 1*, UN Doc A/CONF.232/2018/7 (20 September 2018) annex ('Informal Working Group on Capacity-Building and the Transfer of Marine Technology') 7 ('*IGC 1 Closing Statement*').

10 E.M. De Santo et al, 'Protecting Biodiversity in Areas beyond National Jurisdiction: An Earth System Governance Perspective' (2019) 2 *Earth System Governance* 100029, 1–7, 2.

11 Monika Böhm and Ben Collen, 'Toward Equality of Biodiversity Knowledge through Technology Transfer' (2015) 29(5) *Conservation Biology* 1290, 1291.

understand its lack of implementation. This analysis exposes mistakes made during UNCLOS III and serves as a potential warning to BBNJ negotiators to avoid similar pitfalls in the development of an ILBI.

7.1.1.1 Capacity-building (CB)

The CB concept dates back to the 1950s but gained prominence in the 1990s.[12] Capacity and CB are imprecise terms open to different interpretations. Capacity has been defined as 'the ability of people, organisations and society as a whole to manage their affairs successfully.'[13] It is used to describe both a process and an outcome and is dynamic and multidimensional in nature.[14] CB is a spectrum of processes or activities that aim to improve the ability of a person or entity to carry out and achieve stated objectives.[15]

Approaches to CB include technology cooperation, programmes of assistance, collaborative arrangements and partnerships.[16] To build capacity these approaches must address three general levels: (1) the societal (the creation of an enabling environment), (2) the institutional (organisation building and strengthening) and (3) the individual level (human resource development).[17] Together, these levels form 'an integrated system.'[18]

Although CB is not referenced in UNCLOS, the Convention provides a number of CB initiatives. For example, Article 202 requires States to promote programmes of scientific, educational and technical assistance to developing States for the protection and preservation of the marine environment. This assistance includes training scientific and technical personnel, the supply of equipment and facilities and the development of research and monitoring programmes. UNCLOS also encourages international MSR cooperation,[19] including the flow of scientific data and the transfer of knowledge.

12 Rachel Tiller et al, 'Wealth Blindness beyond National Jurisdiction' (2020) 151 *Marine Pollution Bulletin* 110809, 1–8, 6.

13 Organisation for Economic Co-operation and Development (OECD), 'The Challenge of Capacity Development: Working towards Good Practice' Doc DCD/DAC/GOVNET(2005)5/REVI (Capacity Paper, 1 February 2006) 12 <http://gsdrc.org/docs/open/cc110.pdf>.

14 Lisanne Brown, Anne LaFond and Kate Macintyre, 'Measuring Capacity Building' (Report for MEASURE Evaluation, March 2001) <https://issat.dcaf.ch/content/download/29857/419317/file/664_guidelines%20on%20how%20to%20measure%20capacity%20building.pdf>.

15 Deborah Eade, *Capacity-Building: An Approach to People-Centred Development* (Oxfam, 1997) 2.

16 *Oceans and the Law of the Sea: Report of the Secretary-General*, UN Doc A/65/69 (29 March 2010) 10 [25].

17 United Nations Development Programme, *Capacity Development: A UNDP Primer* (Advocacy Primer, 2009) 11 <https://www.adaptation-undp.org/sites/default/files/downloads/cdg_capacity_development_primer.pdf>.

18 Ibid.

19 UNCLOS, arts 143 and 242.

7.1.1.2 Technology transfer (TT)

The Intergovernmental Panel on Climate Change defines TT as 'a broad set of processes covering the flows of know-how, experience and equipment.'[20] An ILBI will focus on the transfer of marine technology. This term is not defined in UNCLOS. The IOC's Criteria and Guidelines on the Transfer of Marine Technology (IOC Guidelines) defines marine technology as information and data; manuals, guidelines, criteria, standards and reference materials; sampling, methodology and laboratory equipment; observation facilities; computers and software, as well as expertise, knowledge, skills, know-how and analytical methods related to MSR and observation.[21] This broad definition captures 'the multidisciplinary nature' of BBNJ research and encompasses the full 'range of scientific and technological tools that could be required both at sea and onshore.'[22] The IOC Guidelines could therefore assist in defining CBTT terms under an ILBI.[23]

BBNJ delegates generally agree that an ILBI should include a non-exhaustive list of CBTT activities.[24] The Revised Draft Negotiating Text contains an extensive list set out in Appendix 6 of this book. As technology is in a constant state of evolution,[25] the list under an ILBI should be reviewed, assessed and adjusted periodically by a COP 'to reflect technological progress and innovation and to respond and adapt to the evolving needs of States and regions.'[26]

UNCLOS deals generally with TT in Part XIV.[27] Article 266 sets out three overriding obligations for States, namely:

(i) *To cooperate in order to actively promote* the development and transfer of marine science and technology on fair and reasonable terms and conditions, either directly or through international organisations;

20 B. Metz et al, *Methodological and Technological Issues in Technology Transfer: A Special Report of the Intergovernmental Panel on Climate Change* (Cambridge University Press, 2000) 3.

21 Intergovernmental Oceanographic Commission (IOC), 'IOC Criteria and Guidelines on the Transfer of Marine Technology,' Doc IOC/INF-1203 (2005) ('IOC Guidelines').

22 Harriet Harden-Davies, 'Capacity Building and Technology Transfer for Marine Biodiversity in Areas beyond National Jurisdiction' (2017) 111 *American Society of International Law Proceedings of the ASIL Annual Meeting* 243, 243–244.

23 Biliana Cicin-Sain et al, 'Capacity Development as a Key Aspect of a New International Agreement on Marine Biodiversity beyond National Jurisdiction (BBNJ)' (Policy Brief, August 2018) 3.

24 *IGC 1 Closing Statement* (n 9) 6.

25 Kristin Bartenstein, 'XIV: Development and Transfer of Marine Technology' in Alexander Proelss (ed), *United Nations Convention on the Law of the Sea: A Commentary* (C.H. Beck, 2017) 1781.

26 *Revised Draft Text of an Agreement under UNCLOS on the Conservation and Sustainable Use of Marine Biological Diversity of Areas beyond National Jurisdiction*, UN Doc A/CONF.232/2020/3, art 46(3) ('*Revised Draft Negotiating Text*').

27 UNCLOS deals with TT in four other places—see, generally, R.R. Churchill and A.V. Lowe, *The Law of the Sea* (Manchester University Press, 3rd ed, 1999) 417.

(ii) *To promote* the development of the scientific and technological capacity of States (particularly developing States) in respect to the exploration, exploitation, conservation and management of resources, the protection and preservation of the marine environment, MSR and other activities compatible with the Convention;
(iii) *To endeavour to foster* favourable economic and legal conditions for TT for the benefit of all parties concerned on an equitable basis.

To fulfil these obligations, States are required to promote the objectives in Article 268, namely (1) acquiring, evaluating and disseminating marine technological knowledge and facilitating access to information and data; (2) developing marine technology; (3) developing technological infrastructure to facilitate TT; (4) developing human resources; and (5) international cooperative efforts at regional, sub-regional and bilateral levels. The means envisaged for achieving these objectives are set out in Articles 269 and 275–277 of UNCLOS and include the establishment of programmes of technical cooperation, conferences and seminars, scientist exchange, joint ventures and the establishment of scientific and technological research centres.[28] Part XIV thereby provides practical guidance on how to achieve the development of marine technology and its transfer.[29] Moreover, Part XIV recognises that TT is 'inextricably linked' to CB and MSR cooperation.[30]

From the above analysis, it is clear that UNCLOS contains a 'strong conceptual treaty basis' for CBTT.[31] However, Part XIV has 'long been lamented as one of the most under-implemented areas of UNCLOS.'[32] To understand its lack of implementation, it is necessary to examine the ideological context in which Part XIV was negotiated.[33]

7.1.1.3 The making of a dormant regime

UNCLOS III took place at a time when developing States sought economic autonomy in the form of a New International Economic Order (NIEO).[34] As the technological gap between North and South was seen as 'a major factor in

28 Ibid, 417–418.
29 Bartenstein (n 25) 1784.
30 Harriet R. Harden-Davies and Kristina M. Gjerde, 'Building Scientific and Technological Capacity: A Role for Benefit-Sharing in the Conservation and Sustainable Use of Marine Biodiversity beyond National Jurisdiction' (2019) 33(1) *Ocean Yearbook Online* 377, 391.
31 Ronán Long, 'Marine Science Capacity Building and Technology Transfer: Rights and Duties Go Hand in Hand under the 1982 UNCLOS' in Myron H. Nordquist et al (eds), *Law, Science and Ocean Management* (Martinus Nijhoff, 2007) 308.
32 Harden-Davies and Snelgrove (n 3) 2.
33 Ariel W. Gonzalez, 'Cutting a Gordian Knot?: Towards a Practical and Realistic Scheme for the Transfer of Marine Technology' in Myron H. Nordquist et al (ed), *Law, Science and Ocean Management* (Martinus Nijhoff, 2007) 348.
34 Churchill and Lowe (n 27) 3.

economic and political disparity,'[35] a main objective of the NIEO was TT and 'the acceleration and dissemination of scientific knowledge.'[36] Newly independent developing countries claimed that 'the developed world had a moral duty to assist them in bridging the economic development gap by transferring technologies to them on concessional and preferential terms.'[37] The goal was to 'equip all countries with a sound technological base to enable them to participate fully in the global economy and to respond to the basic needs of their populations.'[38] To achieve this, the NIEO doctrine rendered TT 'mandatory upon developed States as a general mechanism of solidarity.'[39]

UNCLOS III provided a perfect setting to assert NIEO demands.[40] Developing States sought an ambitious TT framework, particularly for seabed mining technologies. At the time, only a handful of developed States had the capability of developing and applying the technology required to explore and exploit the deep-seabed.[41] Developing nations were naturally concerned that industrialised countries would use their technological advantage to control the Area and its potentially lucrative mineral resources.[42] Inspired by the NIEO, the regime for the Area attempted to impose a mandatory TT scheme in Annex III of UNCLOS,[43] and granted extensive duties and responsibilities to the ISA 'to ensure that technology and knowledge' used in the Area was 'made available to developing countries upon request.'[44] Developing States also sought strongly worded TT commitments in Part XIV. For example, earlier drafts of Article 266 contained much stronger language, requiring States to facilitate TT, rather than simply requiring them to *cooperate in promoting* it.[45]

However, Article 266, along with other Part XIV provisions, were significantly watered down during UNCLOS III in an effort to appease the interests of a key bloc of developed States. This bloc took issue with the NIEO ideology,

35 Douglas Yarn, 'The Transfer of Technology and UNCLOS III' (1984) 14(1) *Georgia Journal of International and Comparative Law* 121, 127.
36 M.C.W. Pinto, 'Legal Aspects of North/South Transfer of Marine Technology' (1990) 2 *Sri Lanka Journal of International Law* 139, 166.
37 G. Verhoosel, 'Beyond the Unsustainable Rhetoric of Sustainable Development: Transferring Environmentally Sound Technologies' (1998) 11(1) *Georgetown International Environmental Law Review* 49, 50.
38 Oxford University Press, *Max Planck Encyclopedia of Public International Law* vol IX (at June 2014) Michael Waibel and Michael Alford, 'Technology Transfer' [3].
39 Verhoosel (n 37) 52.
40 Colin M. Alberts, 'Technology Transfer and its Role in International Environmental Law: A Structural Dilemma' (1992) 6 *Harvard Journal of Law & Technology* 63, 70.
41 Peter Tobias Stoll, 'The Entry into Force of the Convention on the Law of the Sea: A Redistribution of Competences in Relation to the Management of the International Commons? The Transfer of Technology under the Implementation Agreement' (1995) 55(2) *Zeitschrift Für Ausländisches Öffentliches Recht Und Völkerrecht* 391, 399.
42 Yarn (n 35) 129.
43 UNCLOS, annex III, art 5. This provision was later replaced by Section 5 of the Annex to Part XI Agreement.
44 Bartenstein (n 25) 1767.
45 Ibid.

particularly its claim that technology formed 'part of a universal human heritage.'[46] If this was the case, then all countries would 'have a natural right to free access to technology for improving standards of living for their people.'[47] Developed States never accepted this argument as it was seen to completely ignore 'the costs and incentives that underlie the creation of technologies.'[48] Instead, developed States argued that TT was to occur through business-to-business transactions and they sought the protection of IPRs.[49] The US, in particular, opposed any attempt to deprive their multinational corporations of 'the competitive advantage' they had gained from substantial R&D investment.[50] Attempts made during UNCLOS III to control TT proved unpalatable to developed States. They rejected the Area's mandatory TT scheme and approached the general provisions in Part XIV with caution. The reluctance of developed States to commit to strongly worded obligations 'eventually translated into a framework with only hortatory effect.'[51]

Part XIV obligations are pactum de contrahendo or best effort obligations.[52] As Bartenstein explains, the verb 'shall' which is 'usually indicative of imperative duties and obligations,' is juxtaposed with vague commitments such as *cooperation* (Article 266), *promotion of objectives* (Article 268) and *endeavouring to take action* (Article 269).[53] These provisions are not formulated as strict legal obligations but 'merely dictate a certain standard of behaviour.'[54] They are more reflective of policy goals,[55] with considerable latitude granted to States regarding their implementation.[56] Moreover, even though Part XIV identifies measures to achieve TT, its obligations do not detail how this is to work in practice.[57] Taking the above into account, it is not surprising that Part XIV has gone largely unheeded.[58]

7.1.1.4 A disjunctive and fragmented framework

Aside from UNCLOS and its Implementing Agreements, the importance of CBTT has also been underscored in global and regional instruments relevant to ABNJ, including the CBD, the Intergovernmental Science-Policy Platform

46 Yarn (n 35) 128.
47 Ibid, 128–129.
48 Ibid, 129.
49 Verhoosel (n 37) 50.
50 Jon M. Van Dyke and David L. Teichmann, 'Transfer of Seabed Mining Technology: A Stumbling Block to US Ratification of the Law of the Sea Convention' (1984) 13(4) *Ocean Development and International Law* 427, 427.
51 Bartenstein (n 25) 1765.
52 Ibid, 1769. Ibid.
53 Ibid.
54 Alberts (n 40) 72.
55 Myron H. Nordquist, *United Nations Convention on the Law of the Sea, 1982: A Commentary* (Martinus Nijhoff, 1995) 668.
56 Bartenstein (n 25) 1777.
57 Elisa Morgera and Mara Ntona, 'Seize the Moment: Towards Fairer Capacity Building and Marine Technology Transfer' (Briefing Paper, IIED, August 2018) <https://pubs.iied.org/pdfs/17479IIED.pdf>.
58 Bartenstein (n 25) 1765.

on Biodiversity and Ecosystem Services, the Small Island Development States Accelerated Modalities of Action Pathway and the UNFCCC. Soft law documents such as the 1992 Rio Declaration, the 2002 Johannesburg Declaration and the 2030 Agenda for Sustainable Development are also relevant. While it is beyond the scope of this chapter to assess these instruments, it is important to recognise that there is an existing and 'impressive architecture' for CBTT already in place.[59] However, like Part XIV of UNCLOS, gaps and ambiguities weaken this architecture.[60]

To date, CBTT efforts in ABNJ have been mainly sectoral. The FAO has undertaken work in facilitating the transfer of fisheries technologies to developing States, the IMO provides technical assistance in shipping safety and the IOC assists in TT through its research, information exchange and training programmes.[61] As there is no global mechanism to oversee these various initiatives, the UNGA has repeatedly called for coordination between CBTT activities 'to ensure a targeted approach and to prevent fragmentation or duplication of effort.'[62] BBNJ negotiators therefore need to find a way of bringing existing CBTT efforts together, without undermining them. Section 7.3 of this chapter identifies mechanisms that could enhance existing UNCLOS requirements and improve cross-sectoral CBTT under an ILBI. Before undertaking that analysis, it is necessary to examine the potential role of CBTT in the new instrument.

7.2 The potential role of CBTT under an ILBI

7.2.1 Giant by name, giant by nature

Section 7.1 of this chapter established Part XIV as 'The Sleeping Giant of UNCLOS' based on its dormant, inactive and underutilised provisions. This analogy is also appropriate for describing its intended role in the UNCLOS framework. International MSR cooperation and TT were seen as 'prerequisites to reaping the full benefits' of UNCLOS and were considered critical to its overall success.[63] The same can now be said for the ILBI, with CBTT deserving a higher status than a fourth order element of the BBNJ package deal. Even though this topic has been recognised as a critical cross-cutting element in the BBNJ

59 Cicin-Sain et al (n 23) 7.

60 Harriet R. Harden-Davies, 'Research for Regions: Strengthening Marine Technology Transfer for Pacific Island Countries and Biodiversity beyond National Jurisdiction' (2017) 32(4) *The International Journal of Marine and Coastal Law* 797, 797.

61 Churchill and Lowe (n 27) 418.

62 *Report on the Work of the United Nations Open-Ended Informal Consultative Process on Oceans and the Law of the Sea at its Eleventh Meeting (UNICPOLOS)*, UN Doc A/65/164 (23 July 2010) 13 [52] ('*Report of UNICPOLOS*'); *Options for a Facilitation Mechanism that Promotes the Development, Transfer and Dissemination of Clean and Environmentally Sound Technologies: Report of the Secretary-General*, UN Doc A/67/348 (4 September 2012) 11 [27].

63 Long (n 31) 309.

negotiations,[64] CBTT should be considered a sine qua non of the ILBI. If the topic is not afforded this higher status, CBTT provisions risk being watered down and their importance downplayed in the BBNJ process. This is already evident in a recent survey by Blasiak et al. This survey found that among the package deal elements, CBTT ranked low in priority for BBNJ delegates, a trend evident for both OECD and G77/China groups, as well as Small Island Developing States (SIDS) and least developed countries (LDCs).[65] In fact, CBTT was not the primary focus of any delegates surveyed.[66]

To establish its sine qua non status, the following sections show how CBTT is indispensable to the implementation of the other package deal elements and to the overall objectives of an ILBI. As the Fourth Industrial Revolution gathers pace, the following sections also investigate the potential role of technology in the BBNJ process, particularly the way digital, biological and physical innovations could assist in the implementation of package deal elements.

7.2.1.1 MGRs and benefit-sharing

MGRs are currently the top priority for SIDS and LDCs in the BBNJ negotiations.[67] The gap between North and South is particularly wide in respect to MGR research.[68] Sophisticated and expensive technologies are required to reach deep-seabed environments and sample organisms, including specialised research vessels, in situ sampling tools, molecular biology techniques and technologies associated with the commercialisation process.[69] Developing States generally lack access to these technologies and the human and financial wherewithal required to research and utilise MGRs of ABNJ. Access to relevant information and data also tends to be expensive and limited to academic and scientific institutions in developed countries.[70] During BBNJ negotiations, developing States have promoted CBTT as a means for bridging this gap.[71] The G77/China bloc argue

64 Glen Wright et al, 'The Long & Winding Road: Negotiating a Treaty for the Conservation and Sustainable Use of Marine Biodiversity in Areas beyond National Jurisdiction' (Study No. 8/2018, IDDRI, August 2018) 60.
65 Robert Blasiak et al, 'Negotiating the Use of Biodiversity in Marine Areas beyond National Jurisdiction' (2016) 3 *Frontiers in Marine Science* 1–10, 6.
66 Ibid.
67 Ibid.
68 Wright et al (n 64) 36.
69 Marcel Jaspars and Abbe E.L. Brown, 'Benefit Sharing: Combining Intellectual Property, Trade Secrets, Science and an Ecosystem-Focused Approach' in Myron H. Nordquist and Ronán Long (eds), *Marine Biodiversity of Areas beyond National Jurisdiction* (Brill/Nijhoff, 2021) 99; Salvatore Arico and Charlotte Salpin, 'Bioprospecting of Genetic Resources in the Deep Seabed: Scientific, Legal and Policy Aspects' (UNU-IAS, 2005) 53.
70 Cicin-Sain et al (n 23) 3.
71 Elisabeth Druel et al, 'A Long & Winding Road: International Discussions on the Governance of Marine Biodiversity in Areas beyond National Jurisdiction' (Study No. 07/13, IDDRI, September 2013) 18.

that an ABS regime should not only entail the establishment of a benefit-sharing mechanism, but also the enhancement of CBTT in order to facilitate access to MGRs.[72] To acquire the necessary capacity and technology to benefit fully from MGRs, developing States will require 'access to the knowledge pool' as well as the 'ability to learn, master and adapt relevant technologies.'[73] Thus, CBTT will need to underpin an ABS regime of an ILBI.

This book proposes an ABS model built on compromise, one that attempts to strike a balance between different competing interests.[74] In designing an ABS model, BBNJ negotiators should focus on building scientific and technological capacity. To provide greater access to the MGR knowledge pool, researchers and bioprospectors should be required to share samples and raw data in open-source databases, biorepositories or biobanks.[75] Information sharing could also extend to manuals and guidelines for the collection, storage and curation of biological samples.[76] Non-monetary benefits under an ILBI could include scientific and technical forms of CB at the societal, institutional and individual level. This could include access to ex-situ samples and data, the publication and sharing of scientific knowledge, collaboration in MSR and TT, such as research infrastructure, equipment and training.[77]

Another way an ABS regime could build upon Part XIV provisions is through the establishment of a clearing-house mechanism which could facilitate access to scientific information (i.e. biological inventories and taxonomic studies) as well as education and training in genetic data analysis. The IOC could play a significant role in the establishment of a clearing-house mechanism under an ILBI as it already promotes best practice in terms of sharing samples and research and aims to strengthen MSR cooperation and training in developing countries.[78]

72 Wright et al (n 64) 50 referring to The Group of 77, 'Statement on Behalf of the Group of 77 and China by Mr Farid Dahmane, Permanent Mission of Algeria to the UN, at the Ad Hoc Open-Ended Informal Working Group to Study Issues Relating to the Conservation and Sustainable Use of Marine Biological Diversity beyond Areas of National Jurisdiction' (New York, 7 May 2012) <http://www.g77.org/statement/getstatement.php?id=120507a>.

73 *Oceans and the Law of the Sea: Report of the Secretary-General*, UN Doc A/62/66/Add.2 (10 September 2007) 64 [245].

74 See Chapter 4, Section 4.5.3.

75 IUCN, 'Submission by IUCN Following the Second Session of the Preparatory Committee on the Development of an International Legally Binding Instrument under the United Nations Convention on the Law of the Sea on the Conservation and Sustainable Use of Marine Biological Diversity of Areas Beyond National Jurisdiction' (5 December 2016) 19 <https://www.un.org/depts/los/biodiversity/prepcom_files/rolling_comp/IUCN.pdf>.

76 Harriet Harden-Davies, 'Deep-Sea Genetic Resources: New Frontiers for Science and Stewardship in Areas beyond National Jurisdiction' (2016) 137 *Deep-Sea Research II* 504, 510.

77 Jessica Battle and Duncan Currie, 'Some Critical Issues to Be Resolved on Marine Genetic Resources in the Context of the Marine Biological Diversity Preparatory Committee Discussions' (Discussion Paper, WWF International, March 2016) 6.

78 European Union, 'Development of an International Legally-Binding Instrument under UNCLOS on the Conservation and Sustainable Use of Marine Biological Diversity of

7.2.1.2 ABMTs including MPAs

We now turn to ABMTs, including MPAs. The identification, approval and designation of MPAs in ABNJ will not be a simple or inexpensive exercise. Developing States will require technical, scientific and funding support for the identification of priority protection areas and the development and review of proposals and management plans.[79] One area that requires particular attention is the ability to monitor, control and enforce high seas MPAs. As the benefits of protected areas can only be realised through effective monitoring and enforcement, technological innovations could greatly assist developing States.

Traditionally, efforts to prevent illegal fishing and other prohibited activities in MPAs have relied upon aircraft and patrol vessels.[80] This often proves expensive for even the wealthiest of nations, and ABNJ are too vast for this type of surveillance to be effective in and of itself. The protection of MPAs under an ILBI will require new approaches and 21st-century technology.[81] For example, 'The Eyes in the Sky' satellite-based project was recently launched in conjunction with the UK's designation of a 834,334 square kilometre MPA in South Pacific waters surrounding the Pitcairn Islands.[82] This marked 'the first time any government has combined the creation of a fully protected marine reserve with a detailed plan for surveillance and enforcement using state-of-the-art technology.'[83] The Eyes in the Sky forms part of a larger project called 'Eyes on the Seas' which has been in operation since 2015 and is a joint initiative by The Pew Charitable Trusts and Satellite Applications Catapult, a UK-based satellite company.[84] The Eyes on the Seas project effectively merges four sources of technology to police an MPA and detect suspicious activity.[85] The platform combines:

(i) Data from on-board Automatic Identification and Vessel Monitoring Systems;
(ii) Satellite imagery, including radar, optical and thermal imaging;

Areas beyond National Jurisdiction (BBNJ Process), Written Submission of the EU and Its Member States: Capacity-Building and Transfer of Marine Technology (31 January 2017) <https://www.un.org/depts/los/biodiversity/prepcom_files/rolling_comp/EU_Capacity-Building_and_Transfer_of_Marine_Technology.pdf > ('Written Submission of the EU and Member States to PrepCom: Capacity-Building and the Transfer of Marine Technology').

79 Cicin-Sain et al (n 23) 1.

80 The Pew Charitable Trusts, 'Project Eyes on the Seas' (Brief, March 2015) <https://www.pewtrusts.org/-/media/assets/2015/03/eyes-on-the-seas-brief_web.pdf>.

81 Ibid.

82 Allie Wilkinson, 'U.K. Wants Eyes in the Sky to Keep Watch on Its Record Marine Reserve' *Science* (Online Magazine, 19 March 2015) <https://www.sciencemag.org/news/2015/03/uk-wants-eyes-sky-keep-watch-its-record-marine-reserve>.

83 Ibid.

84 'Building the Future of MPA Enforcement: Project Eyes on the Seas and Other High-Tech Surveillance Programs' *MPA News* (Web Page, April–May 2016) <https://mpanews.openchannels.org/news/mpa-news/building-future-mpa-enforcement-project-eyes-seas-and-other-high-tech-surveillance> ('*MPA News*').

85 Ibid.

(iii) Data from RFMO/As on vessel histories, fishing and marine reserve boundaries;
(iv) Automation, including alerts to users when anomalies are detected such as a vessel entering an MPA.[86]

As the Eyes on the Seas system has the capacity to cross-reference and aggregate these multiple data layers in real time, it is able to detect movement that indicates a vessel might be fishing or has entered a marine reserve or other restricted area.[87] Analysts based in the UK (in the Satellite Applications Catapult operations room) investigate the issue by reviewing the vessel's history to determine whether it has been blacklisted by an RFMO/A or has been associated with illegal fishing.[88] Analysts are then able to notify the relevant government and provide them with evidence for enforcement or other appropriate action.[89]

Based on the first 12 months of implementation in the Pitcairn Islands, the Eyes on the Seas project has proven to be an effective 'means of surveillance for a large and isolated area'[90] and may be suitable for monitoring and enforcing MPAs under an ILBI. Most significantly, for the purposes of this chapter, the Eyes on the Seas system has been designed to be a cost-effective monitoring and enforcement tool.[91] This mechanism can be used by resource-poor governments and agencies that may not have the 'financial ability to commercially access and use such technology.'[92] Thus, while 'a brave new tech-based world is emerging' for MPA enforcement, there is no intention, at this stage, to leave developing States behind.[93] The pioneers of Eyes on the Seas are currently working with stakeholders to 'develop an equitable cost-model that would allow all nations' to use this technology.[94] This project provides an example of how a cooperative partnership between government and industry could assist in improving the monitoring and surveillance capabilities of developing States to sustainably manage ABNJ.[95]

7.2.1.3 EIA

The use and management of ABNJ have 'been defined by a profound scarcity of information.'[96] This has limited our 'understanding of ocean processes and

86 Elizabeth M. De Santo, 'Implementation Challenges of Area-Based Management Tools (ABMTs) for Biodiversity beyond National Jurisdiction (BBNJ)' (2018) 97 *Marine Policy* 34, 41.
87 The Pew Charitable Trusts (n 80).
88 Ibid.
89 Ibid.
90 *MPA News* (n 84).
91 The Pew Charitable Trusts (n 80).
92 *MPA News* (n 84).
93 Ibid.
94 The Pew Charitable Trusts (n 80).
95 Daniel C. Dunn et al, 'Empowering High Seas Governance with Satellite Vessel Tracking Data' (2018) 19 *Fish & Fisheries* 729, 729.
96 World Economic Forum, 'Harnessing the Fourth Industrial Revolution for the Earth' (Fourth Industrial Revolution for the Earth Series, November 2017) 5 <http://www3.weforum.org/docs/WEF_Harnessing_4IR_Oceans.pdf>.

conditions, resource use and impacts.'[97] EIA will take on a special role under an ILBI, providing invaluable information and data on the potential impact of anthropogenic pressures on BBNJ. Recent advancements in technology and an 'emerging digital ocean'[98] could assist States in the conduct and evaluation of EIA in ABNJ.

The digital ocean provides an array of new data sources including aquatic telemetry,[99] genetic and acoustic sampling as well as advanced digital sensors carried by satellites, ocean-going drones, buoys, boats and fishing nets.[100] These digital sensors can monitor environmental measures including water temperature, salinity and nutrient levels.[101] The analysis of sonar and video data attached to traditional sampling gear could also 'enhance the capacity for modelling environmental impacts' and collect critical ecosystem information.[102] An example is the recent in situ observations from video and still imagery using manned and unmanned submersibles in the Clarion Clipperton Zone.[103] These observations have resulted in the discovery of new habitats and 'yielded valuable biogeographic information.'[104] These diverse streams of data could assist decision-makers in identifying priority protection areas and in evaluating the effects of activities on BBNJ as part of the EIA process.

Unfortunately, the 'manifold capabilities of the digital ocean'[105] remain largely out-of-reach for developing States due to capacity and technology deficits. During IGC 1, many delegates argued that an ILBI should take into account the special needs of developing States in designing an EIA framework.[106] BBNJ negotiators will need to ensure that developing States obtain the adequate support, infrastructure and knowledge to carry out EIA in compliance with ILBI requirements. For example, a mechanism will be required to ensure that developing States have the capacity to comprehend the content of an EIA and its implications.[107] In addition, financial and technical support for the development and review of EIA will be necessary; this could include a voluntary peer review mechanism or 'twinning' amongst States Parties as well as the opportunity to submit joint EIA where appropriate.[108] An overarching global network and centralised database could

97 Ibid.
98 Ibid.
99 See, e.g. Tammy E. Davies et al, 'Tracking Data and the Conservation of the High Seas: Opportunities and Challenges' (2021) 58(12) *Journal of Applied Ecology* 2703–2710.
100 Ibid.
101 Ibid, 11.
102 Pierre Girard and Thomas Du Payrat, 'An Inventory of New Technologies in Fisheries' (Issues Brief, OECD, 2017) 20.
103 Stefanie Kaiser, Craig R. Smith and Pedro Martinez Arbizu, 'Editorial: Biodiversity of the Clarion Clipperton Fracture Zone' (2017) 47(2) *Marine Biodiversity* 259, 262.
104 Ibid.
105 World Economic Forum (n 96) 9.
106 *IGC 1 Closing Statement* (n 9) 8.
107 *Chair's Streamlined Non-Paper on Elements of a Draft Text of an International Legally-Binding Instrument under UNCLOS*, (2007) 36 [199] ('*Chair's Streamlined Non-Paper*').
108 Ibid, 36 [198].

bring together the various sources of data emerging from the digital ocean and promote a transparent environment for data sharing.[109] As the interpretation and translation of data into useful information require technical tools and knowledge, CBTT must also underpin this element of the BBNJ package deal.

7.2.2 Overall objectives of an ILBI

Based on the above it is clear that the acquisition, exchange and application of scientific knowledge and technologies will be required across all elements of the BBNJ package deal, from the provision of baseline data for EIA, to the designation and monitoring of MPAs, as well as the access to and utilisation of MGRs.[110] Without effective CBTT, the other substantive elements of an ILBI will not be realised.[111] Naturally, the implementation of an ILBI will not depend on any single technological innovation, rather, a whole ecosystem of technologies need to be included in the BBNJ toolbox to ensure the long-term conservation and sustainable use of BBNJ.

Aside from its importance to the other three issues of the package deal, CBTT is also integral to the overall objectives of an ILBI. The success of an ILBI will depend, in part, on science and technology to access BBNJ, to analyse it and to implement conservation measures to protect it.[112] Therefore, it is imperative for BBNJ negotiators to reinforce the need for CBTT and to strengthen relevant UNCLOS provisions by fostering 'a new paradigm of technology transfer and innovation based on knowledge exchange, open data and scientific capacity development.'[113] In other words, the success of an ILBI depends on finding innovative ways to wake the 'Sleeping Giant of UNCLOS.'

7.3 Mechanisms to wake the Sleeping Giant of UNCLOS

7.3.1 A guide to strengthen existing UNCLOS requirements

Given the indispensability of CBTT to an ILBI, it will not be enough simply to incorporate Part XIV *mutatis mutandis* into the new instrument. Instead, new mechanisms need to be developed. Given the extreme caution exhibited by developed States to Part XIV provisions during UNCLOS III, BBNJ negotiators will need to tread very carefully when attempting to impose new CBTT measures. One of the thorniest issues is whether these measures should be mandatory or voluntary. So far, the solutions brought to the BBNJ negotiations reflect two opposing views. On one hand, developed States maintain that sharing should

109 Ibid, 35 [195].
110 Harden-Davies (n 22) 243.
111 Cicin-Sain et al (n 23) VII.
112 Stephen Minas, 'Marine Technology Transfer under a BBNJ Treaty: A Case for Transnational Network Cooperation' (2018) 112 *AJIL Unbound* 144, 144.
113 Harden-Davies (n 60) 822.

always be on a voluntary basis and on mutually agreed terms. On the other hand, developing States wish to see mandatory obligations imposed and argue that the duty to provide scientific and technical assistance should be 'at no cost or low cost' and on preferential terms.[114] In another case of history repeating itself, BBNJ negotiators are faced with the same questions that plagued UNCLOS III negotiators, namely—'what should be provided, who should provide it, and to whom it should be provided.'[115] Delegations remain divided on these issues, which pose a significant obstacle to consensus-building.[116] In order to reach a balanced outcome, this work argues that the following mechanisms need to be incorporated into an ILBI and underpinned by a renewed sense of, and duty, to cooperate.

7.3.2 Formalising a clearing-house mechanism

A main flaw of Part XIV is that its obligations 'are expressed in general terms and leave out details of how CBTT can work in practice.'[117] The establishment of a clearing-house mechanism under an ILBI could provide an invaluable practical tool. An open access web-based clearing-house could be tasked with the following functions:

- Providing a repository database for the storage, dissemination and sharing of knowledge, data and information relevant to BBNJ;[118]
- Promoting and facilitating access to technologies including expertise and know-how;[119]
- Providing a platform to register capacity needs to facilitate dialogue between those able to provide CBTT and those requiring it;[120]
- Raising awareness on projects, programmes, workshops, seminars and training courses;
- Building a human and technological network to provide on-going technical support from experts and providing a forum for practitioners working on similar issues.[121]

Under the IOC Guidelines, the IOC is mandated to establish a clearing-house mechanism for TT to provide Member States with 'direct and rapid access to

114 Ribeiro (n 1) 746.
115 Rachel Tiller et al, 'The Once and Future Treaty: Towards a New Regime for Biodiversity in Areas beyond National Jurisdiction' (2019) 99 *Marine Policy* 239, 240.
116 Ibid.
117 Morgera and Ntona (n 57).
118 Cicin-Sain et al (n 23) 13.
119 Written Submission of EU and its Member States to PrepCom: Capacity-Building and the Transfer of Marine Technology (n 78) 4 [13(c)].
120 Cicin-Sain et al (n 23) 35.
121 Ibid, 31.

relevant sources of information, practical experience and scientific and technical expertise.'[122] The IOC Guidelines also provide a technical assistance scheme. States submit a 'Transfer of Marine Technology Application' and the IOC is to 'respond by facilitating contact with technology "donors" or by providing technical assistance more directly.'[123] Initially, the IOC Guidelines were considered a key milestone as they presented an opportunity to operationalise Part XIV of UNCLOS.[124] However, implementation of the IOC Guidelines has fallen short. A dedicated clearing-house mechanism has not been established, 'due primarily to resource constraints and lack of requests from developing nations.'[125] In 2017, in an interesting turn of events, the IOC Assembly decided to establish the Group of Experts on Capacity Development, which is mandated to 'advise the [IOC] Assembly on, and start implementation of, the Transfer of Marine Technology Clearing House Mechanism' in accordance with the IOC Guidelines.[126] The EU has suggested the IOC be tasked with the development of a clearing-house mechanism under an ILBI or at least have a coordinating role.[127] This suggestion has merit as the IOC is the only IGO with a specific mandate in MSR and CB.[128] Its mandate also spans all ocean basins, including ABNJ, 'which qualifies the Commission on the ground of geographic competency.'[129]

While BBNJ delegates broadly agree on the importance of a clearing-house mechanism, disagreements remain on its format, content and functions.[130] The G77/China bloc, CARICOM, Pacific SIDs and Like-Minded Latin American Countries seek a detailed list of functions for a clearing-house, like the one

122 Written Submission of the EU and Member States to PrepCom: Capacity-Building and the Transfer of Marine Technology (n 78) 5 [16].
123 Minas (n 112) 146.
124 Gonzalez (n 33) 345.
125 IOC, *Ad Hoc Report of the IOC of UNESCO to the 4th Session of the Preparatory Committee on Marine Biological Diversity of Areas beyond National Jurisdiction,* (Information Document, IOC/INF-1347, 17 June 2017) 15 ('*IOC Ad Hoc Report*').
126 IOC, *Decisions of the Twenty-Ninth Session of the IOC Assembly*, Doc IOC-XXIX/3s/Decisions (12 July 2017) Decision IOC-XXIX/10.1 ('*IOC Groups of Experts on Capacity Development*') 23.
127 Elisa Morgera et al, 'Summary of the First Session of the Intergovernmental Conference on an International Legally Binding Instrument under the UN Convention on the Law of the Sea on the Conservation and Sustainable Use of Marine Biodiversity of Areas beyond National Jurisdiction 4–17 September 2018' *Earth Negotiations Bulletin* (Online Bulletin, 20 September 2018) 13 ('Summary of IGC 1') <https://enb.iisd.org/events/1st-session-intergovernmental-conference-igc-international-legally-binding-instrument-12>.
128 David Leary, 'Agreeing to Disagree on What We Have or Have Not Agreed on: The Current State of Play of the BBNJ Negotiations on the Status of Marine Genetic Resources in Areas beyond National Jurisdiction' (2019) 99 *Marine Policy* 21, 23.
129 IOC, *IOC Potential Contribution to a New International Instrument under UNCLOS on the Conservation and Sustainable Use of Marine Biological Diversity of Areas beyond National Jurisdiction* (Information Document, IOC/INF-1338, 17 May 2016) 1 ('*IOC Potential Contribution*').
130 Cicin-Sain et al (n 23) 27.

contained in Article 51(4) of the Revised Draft Negotiating Text.[131] Some delegates take issue with this list and the one that appeared in the President's Aid to Negotiations. The list in the President's Aid to Negotiations appears to grant a wide range of powers to the clearing-house mechanism including the ability to develop protocols, codes of conduct and guidelines for environmental protection.[132] Japan argues that a clearing-house should not carry out rule-making functions, and Singapore has stressed that the development of protocols and codes of conduct is not the function of a knowledge repository.[133] Some delegates would prefer the modalities of the clearing-house to be elaborated upon by a COP at a later stage.[134] The sentiment that a clearing-house mechanism should simply act as a knowledge repository poses a greater issue. In order to enhance, stimulate and strengthen the existing UNCLOS formula, it will be crucial for a clearing-house to perform functions above and beyond that of a knowledge repository. For example, it will need to promote and facilitate TT. BBNJ negotiators could draw inspiration from innovative mechanisms found under existing environmental treaties.[135] A leading example is the Climate Technology Centre and Network (CTCN) created by the COP to the UNFCCC.[136]

The CTCN relies upon consortium partners (a small group of organisations with sectoral and regional expertise) and network members with expertise in climate technology to respond to technical assistance requests.[137] Minas argues that a network mechanism for TT, incorporating CTCN features, could effectively take on a 'match-making' role under an ILBI, 'connecting requesting States with expert network members to provide tailored advice on marine technology.'[138]

In a recent IOC survey, a majority of countries indicated a preference for a 'Hub and Spoke' network model for a clearing-house mechanism under an ILBI.[139] Essentially, this would comprise a central hub (overseen by the Secretariat alone or in combination with another organisation, such as the IOC) linked to regional and national nodes with the possibility of establishing thematic portals.[140] Other relevant nodes might include regional clearing-houses, as well as

131 Tallash Kantai et al, 'Summary of the Second Session of the Intergovernmental Conference on the Conservation and Sustainable Use of Marine Biodiversity of Areas beyond National Jurisdiction: 25 March–5 April 2019' *Earth Negotiations Bulletin* (Online Bulletin, 8 April 2019) 12 ('Summary of IGC 2') <https://enb.iisd.org/events/2nd-session-intergovernmental-conference-igc-conservation-and-sustainable-use-marine/summary>.

132 *President's Aid to Negotiations*, UN Doc A/CONF.232/2019/1 (3 December 2018) 20.

133 Summary of IGC 2 (n 131) 12.

134 *IGC 1 Closing Statement* (n 9) 7.

135 Minas (n 112) 147.

136 *Report of the Conference of the Parties*, UN Doc FCCC/CP/2010/7/Add.1 (15 March 2011) (Decision 1/CP.16, para. 117).

137 Minas (n 112) 147.

138 Ibid, 148.

139 Ariel Troisi, 'Introduction to Facilitating Capacity Development, Transfer of Marine Technology and Ocean Science in BBNJ' (Conference Paper, BBNJ IGC-2 Side Event, 27 March 2019).

140 Ibid.

academia, research institutions, industry, NGOs and other entities that could contribute BBNJ-relevant information.[141] As BBNJ research is located in different institutions and databases around the world, a hub and spoke network model may assist in facilitating cross-sectoral CB by providing a link to existing databases, repositories, gene banks and other platforms used to exchange information. The clearing-house website could also provide an interoperable search function providing one-stop access to all affiliated nodes.[142]

7.3.3 Enhancing the data-sharing infrastructure

The enhancement of data sharing could also assist in achieving the objectives of Part XIV of UNCLOS. BBNJ negotiators should focus on ensuring equitable access to data through the use of a global online data-sharing platform or meta-database, linked to a clearing-house mechanism. The IOC's OBIS is a leading example. OBIS provides an online, user-friendly system for accessing data on marine life.[143] It provides open access to over '47 million observations of 116,000 marine species, integrated from more than 2,000 databases, representing 600 institutions connected through 20 national, regional and thematic nodes.'[144] This includes the 'Deep-Sea OBIS node,' hosted by the OBIS Secretariat and managed by the Senckenberg Research Institute and Natural History Museum.[145] This node 'aims to provide a single integrated access point' to data on 'deep-sea organisms and their ecosystem properties, including habitat and environmental characteristics.'[146] OBIS could offer an invaluable 'support mechanism for BBNJ governance' by providing scientific analysis in support of a number of international processes in ABNJ.[147] However, the Deep-Sea OBIS node requires further development, and this can only be achieved through cooperation and collaboration among the wider MSR community.[148]

Based on the mechanisms identified thus far, it is clear that BBNJ issues touch on several areas of IOC competence.[149] While calls have been made for the IOC to

141 Cicin-Sain et al (n 23) 33.

142 Ibid, 31.

143 Daphnis De Pooter et al, 'Toward a New Data Standard for Combined Marine Biological and Environmental Datasets: Expanding OBIS beyond Species Occurrences' (2017) 5(5) *Biodiversity Data Journal* 1, 3.

144 Ibid.

145 Kristina M. Gjerde, 'The UN Decade for Ocean Science and the Role of IOC in Facilitating and Coordinating International Cooperation in Marine Scientific Research' (Conference Paper, BBNJ IGC-2 Side Event, 27 March 2019).

146 'Deep-Sea OBIS Node' *Global Biodiversity Information Facility* (Web Page) <https://www.gbif.org/publisher/f0d23bad-fee1-435d-bdb6-d26a600cad62>.

147 IOC, 'Transfer of Marine Technology: Knowledge Sharing and Capacity Development for Sustainable Ocean and Coastal Management' (Brochure, IOC/BRO/2014/3, 2015) 7 <https://unesdoc.unesco.org/ark:/48223/pf0000232586?locale=en>.

148 Gjerde (n 145).

149 *IOC Potential Contribution* (n 129) 1.

play a key role under an ILBI, this decision is ultimately one for BBNJ delegates. Arguably, not recognising IOC's competencies and strengths could undermine the organisation and its CBTT programmes and initiatives.

7.3.4 An innovative funding model

A lack of financial resources is another impediment to CBTT. UNCLOS does not have a standing financial mechanism.[150] Instead, it relies mainly on contributions to 'voluntary trust funds and to the Assistance Fund, which have not provided sufficient funding for the implementation of the Convention.'[151] In order for an ILBI to be effective, CBTT will require adequate funding. This is essential to ensure that all States can participate in and assume their responsibilities under the instrument. As Cameroon cautions, 'without dedicated funding, many developing States will not be able to participate' in BBNJ conservation.[152] While funding has been acknowledged as a key component of an ILBI, delegations disagree on the nature and sources of these funds, as well as the mechanisms that should be used to generate them.[153]

Developed States, including the US and Australia, wish to see the establishment of a voluntary funding stream and have rejected language that would impose mandatory funding or the development of operational, endowment, contingency or rehabilitation/liability funds.[154] Developing States stress that voluntary funding streams throughout the UN system are inadequate, inaccessible, unsustainable and unpredictable.[155] Kenya argues that adhering to a voluntary model in an ILBI would be akin to 'shooting ourselves in the foot.'[156] A voluntary funding model would not provide the necessary transformation required by developing States. In an attempt at compromise, BBNJ negotiators should consider an innovative hybrid model for funding, one that combines both voluntary and mandatory mechanisms and relies on a range of different financing types.

Mandatory contributions could include payments made at different stages of the R&D chain of MGRs; premiums paid during the EIA approval process as

150 *Report on the Work of the UNICPOLOS at Its Eleventh Meeting*, UN Doc A/65/164 (23 July 2010) 12 [50].

151 Voluntary trust funds relating to the CLCS, the Informal Consultative Process on Oceans and Law of the Sea and the BBNJ conference. The Assistance Fund under UNFSA is to provide financial assistance to developing States Parties to assist them in the implementation of the Agreement. However, the Assistance Fund is currently depleted as it relies on voluntary contributions—see, generally, Cicin-Sain et al (n 23) 41–44.

152 UN, 'As Intergovernmental Negotiations on New Ocean Treaty Continue, Delegates' Divergent Views Emerge on Funding, Review Processes, Subsidiary Bodies' (Meetings Coverage, SEA/2100, 3 April 2019) ('UN Meetings Coverage – Divergent Views Emerge on Funding').

153 Ibid.

154 Ibid.

155 Summary of IGC 2 (n 131) 12.

156 UN Meetings Coverage – Divergent Views Emerge on Funding (n 152).

well as visitor entry fees to MPAs.[157] These payments could be made to an ILBI Contribution Fund and used to support the implementation of other elements of the package deal including CBTT. In terms of voluntary contributions, these could come from a range of sources including States Parties, international financial institutions, donor agencies, IGOs, NGOs and the private sector, as well as philanthropic sources.

Clearly, to be successful an ILBI will require a financial mechanism to facilitate funding. A number of options are open to BBNJ negotiators. First, the management of finances could be left in the hands of the Secretariat of an ILBI. Second, a separate financial mechanism could be established. This could be an entirely new entity or an existing body, such as the Global Environment Facility, which serves as a financial mechanism to five conventions, including the CBD and UNFCCC.[158] Interestingly, the UNFCCC has designated a new entity (the Green Climate Fund) and an existing entity (the Global Environment Facility) to act as the financial mechanism for the Convention.[159] In addition, the UNFCCC has several special funds, including the Least Developed Countries Fund.[160] In a recent review of financial resources available to conventions, the UNFCCC came out on top having 'raised the largest amount of financing.'[161] Unsurprisingly, conventions relying on voluntary contributions raised the least amount of funding.[162] This may prompt BBNJ negotiators to adopt a financial mechanism in line with the UNFCCC. Irrespective of the model chosen, it is clear that without financial assistance, it will not be possible for developing States to comply with the ILBI. As the Federated States of Micronesia poignantly stated, 'there must be some kind of money or nothing is going to happen.'[163]

7.3.5 A monitoring, review and follow-up mechanism

Part XIV of UNCLOS also lacks a mechanism for measuring the success of CBTT efforts. In fact, UNCLOS does not possess much in the way of institutions to supervise its implementation. UNCLOS established three separate bodies,

157 Cicin-Sain et al (n 23) 40.

158 Ibid. At IGC 4, the UK expressed support for the GEF as the financial mechanism under an ILBI, because it could provide support for implementation prior to the first COP – see Tallash Kantai and Paola Bettelli, 'Summary of the Fourth Session of the Intergovernmental Conference on an International Legally Binding Instrument under the UN Convention on the Law of the Sea on the Conservation and Sustainable Use of Marine Biodiversity of Areas beyond National Jurisdiction: 7-18 March 2022' *Earth Negotiations Bulletin* (Online Bulletin, 21 March 2022) 19 <https://enb.iisd.org/sites/default/files/2022-03/enb25225e.pdf>.

159 Ibid.

160 Ibid.

161 Ibid, XI.

162 Ibid.

163 Tiller et al (n 115) 240 referring to submission by the Federated States of Micronesia at IGC 1.

the Commission on the Limits of the Continental Shelf, ITLOS and the ISA; however, each one has relatively limited functions. The Meeting to the State Parties to UNCLOS only deals with procedural matters and does not function like the COP of other Multilateral Environmental Agreements such as the Paris Agreement or CBD. The Division for Ocean Affairs and the Law of the Sea of the Office of Legal Affairs serves as a Secretariat of UNCLOS and has three core functions: (1) the provision of advice, assistance and research on the implementation of UNCLOS; (2) monitoring and research activities and maintaining a comprehensive information system; and (3) providing training, fellowship and technical assistance.[164] Under the existing UNCLOS framework, there is no central organisation for implementing CBTT provisions. Thus, the law of the sea essentially remains a decentralised system.[165]

Article 47 of the Revised Draft Negotiating Text provides for CBTT activities to be monitored and reviewed periodically, in order to review the needs and priorities of developing States and to make recommendations on how CBTT could be enhanced under the instrument. A decision will need to be made on whether a subsidiary body should be established to oversee the delivery and effectiveness of CBTT. Some delegates are keen to see an entity, such as a scientific or technical committee or advisory body, entrusted with the monitoring and review functions under an ILBI.[166] CARICOM argues for a review conference or Meeting of States Parties to be convened on a regular basis to assess needs and to fill in any gaps.[167] States Parties could also be required to submit annual reports. However, in imposing reporting requirements, due regard should be given to the capacity and resource constraints of developing States.[168] Reporting procedures should therefore be 'simple, targeted and operate as expeditiously as possible.'[169]

7.3.6 A renewed sense of, and duty, to cooperate

This chapter has identified four mechanisms that could breathe life into the dormant regime of Part XIV of UNCLOS. While BBNJ negotiators should consider

164 'Division for Ocean Affairs and the Law of the Sea, Its Functions and Activities' *United Nations* (Web Page, 14 October 2016) <https://www.un.org/Depts/los/doalos_activities/about_doalos.htm>.

165 Yoshifumi Tanaka, 'Zonal and Integrated Management Approaches to Ocean Governance: Reflections on a Dual Approach in International Law of the Sea' (2004) 19(4) *The International Journal of Marine and Coastal Law* 483, 506.

166 *IGC 1 Closing Statement* (n 9) 7–8.

167 Summary of IGC 1 (n 127) 14.

168 See, e.g. Alliance of Small Island States (AOSIS), 'Submission on Capacity Building and Transfer of Technology at the Second Session of the Preparatory Committee on the Development of an International Legally Binding Instrument under the United Nations Convention on the Law of the Sea on the Conservation and Sustainable Use of Marine Biological Diversity' (5 December 2016) 4<https://www.un.org/depts/los/biodiversity/prepcom_files/rolling_comp/AOSIS-capacity_building_and_transfer_of_technology.pdf>.

169 Ibid.

the inclusion of these mechanisms in an ILBI, in order for them to be truly effective, they will need to be underpinned by a meaningful duty to cooperate. The obligation to cooperate is considered the cornerstone of Part XIV,[170] as it is referenced either directly or indirectly in almost all of its provisions.[171] However, the nature and content of the obligation to cooperate are not spelled out in Part XIV and remain unclear.[172] An ILBI should define and operationalise this duty in order to enhance and strengthen existing UNCLOS requirements.

In accordance with Part XIV, an ILBI could impose an obligation on States Parties to facilitate cooperation in CBTT to assist developing States to achieve the objectives of the instrument. In terms of operationalising this obligation, an ILBI should promote and facilitate various forms of international cooperation, including engagement in North-South, South-South and triangular cooperation, collaborative initiatives among governments and regional and sectoral organisations and the development of joint research projects, including public-private partnerships.[173] Cooperation could also include sharing technical facilities such as research vessels and new automated devices and technologies discussed in Section 7.2 of this chapter.[174]

Cross-sectoral CBTT 'should be primary aspects of cooperative efforts.'[175] An ILBI should aim to facilitate cooperation and coordination between the numerous frameworks, organisations and sectoral bodies that currently undertake CBTT initiatives in ABNJ. BBNJ negotiators could draw inspiration from the FAO's 'ABNJ Capacity Project.' This project aims to promote effective global and regional linkages through information exchange by organising 'cross-sectoral, multi-stakeholder workshops' and utilising an ABNJ information web-portal.[176] This framework could be built upon under an ILBI and overseen by the IOC. With additional support, the IOC could play a significant role in facilitating cooperation 'by bringing different sectors together and providing a forum where joint implementation of intersectoral and international programmes can be agreed upon' concerning BBNJ.[177]

170 Pinto (n 36) 170.
171 Irini Papanicolopulu, 'Section 4 Cooperation among International Organizations' in Alexander Proelss (ed), *United Nations Convention on the Law of the Sea: A Commentary* (C.H. Beck, 2017) 1808, 1811.
172 Ibid.
173 *Chair's Streamlined Non-Paper* (n 107) 41 [220]; Petro Tolochko and Alice B.M. Vadrot, 'The Usual Suspects? Distribution of Collaboration Capital in Marine Biodiversity Research' (2021) 124 *Marine Policy* 104318, 1–15, 1.
174 Gunnar Kullenberg, 'Capacity Building in Marine Research and Ocean Observations: A Perspective on Why and How' (1998) 22(3) *Marine Policy* 185, 195.
175 *Oceans and the Law of the Sea: Report of the Secretary-General*, UN Doc A/64/66/Add.2 (19 October 2009) 54 [205].
176 Miriam Balgos et al, 'Workshop on Capacity Development to Improve the Management of Marine Areas beyond National Jurisdiction (ABNJ): Needs, Experiences, Options and Opportunities' (Workshop Report, FAO, 2017) 10.
177 Kullenberg (n 174) 195.

7.4 Conclusion

As we embark on this great collective journey, we pledge

that no one will be left behind.[178]

The conservation and sustainable use of BBNJ presents a collective challenge to the international community. Like UNCLOS, an ILBI must aim for universal participation not only in formal adherence to the new instrument but also to its full and effective implementation. It falls to BBNJ negotiators to ensure that all States, especially developing countries, are able to participate in and assume their responsibilities and obligations under the instrument.[179] This can only be achieved through meaningful CBTT, which is a sine qua non of an ILBI, crucial to the successful implementation of the other elements of the BBNJ package deal and 'indispensable for realising the overall objectives of marine environmental protection and sustainable development'[180] in ABNJ.

Part XIV of UNCLOS provides a conceptual framework for CBTT. However, this chapter has established Part XIV as the 'Sleeping Giant of UNCLOS.' Its provisions have enormous untapped potential but suffer 'from the gravest implementation gap.'[181] An historical analysis of Part XIV shows that its provisions 'represent the deep division between North and South'[182] that permeated UNCLOS III negotiations. As originally drafted, the regime represented developing countries' efforts to incorporate NIEO ideals into UNCLOS in an attempt 'to shift the balance of economic and industrial power from the North to the South.'[183] Yet, the persistent opposition by developed States during UNCLOS III resulted in a regime with only hortatory effect.

This chapter has identified a number of mechanisms BBNJ negotiators could use in an effort to enhance, stimulate and strengthen existing UNCLOS requirements in Part XIV. In order for these mechanisms to be effective they will need to be underpinned by a meaningful duty to cooperate. These mechanisms

178 *Transforming Our World: The 2030 Agenda for Sustainable Development*, UN Doc A/RES/70/1 (25 September 2015) preamble.

179 Cicin-Sain et al (n 23) 1.

180 People's Republic of China, 'Written Submission of the Government of the People's Republic of China on Elements of a Draft Text of an International Legally Binding Instrument under the United Nations Convention on the Law of the Sea on the Conservation and Sustainable Use of Marine Biological Diversity of Areas Beyond National Jurisdiction' (20 April 2017) 11 [27] <https://www.un.org/depts/los/biodiversity/prepcom_files/streamlined/China.pdf>.

181 Kristine Dalaker Kraabel, 'The BBNJ PrepCom and Institutional Arrangements: The Hype about the Hybrid Approach' in Myron H. Nordquist, John Norton Moore and Ronán J. Long (eds), *The Marine Environment and United Nations Sustainable Development Goal 14: Life below Water* (Brill Nijhoff, 2018) 153.

182 Alberts (n 40) 72.

183 A. Marvasti, 'An Assessment of the International Technology Transfer Systems and the New Law of the Sea' (1998) 39 *Ocean & Coastal Management* 197, 198.

could wake the 'Sleeping Giant of UNCLOS' and provide the necessary transformation required by developing States to assist in building a practical and tangible regime for CBTT under an ILBI.

References

Agreement Relating to the Implementation of Part XI of the United Nations Convention on the Law of the Sea of 10 December 1984, Opened for Signature 16 November 1994 (1994) 33 *ILM* 1309 (entered into force 28 July 1996) (Part XI Implementing Agreement).

Alberts, Colin M, 'Technology Transfer and its Role in International Environmental Law: A Structural Dilemma' (1992) 6 (Fall Issue) *Harvard Journal of Law & Technology* 63–84.

Alliance of Small Island States (AOSIS), 'Submission on Capacity Building and Transfer of Technology at the Second Session of the Preparatory Committee on the Development of an International Legally Binding Instrument under the United Nations Convention on the Law of the Sea on the Conservation and Sustainable Use of Marine Biological Diversity' (5 December 2016) 4 <https://www.un.org/depts/los/biodiversity/prepcom_files/rolling_comp/AOSIS-capacity_building_and_transfer_of_technology.pdf> accessed 31 March 2022.

Arico, Salvatore and Charlotte Salpin, *Bioprospecting of Genetic Resources in the Deep Seabed: Scientific, Legal and Policy Aspects* (UNU-IAS, 2005).

Balgos, Miriam, Biliana Cicin-Sain, Meredith Kurz and Ujwala Ramakrishna, 'Workshop on Capacity Development to Improve the Management of Marine Areas Beyond National Jurisdiction (ABNJ): Needs, Experiences, Options and Opportunities' (*Workshop Report*, FAO, 2017) <http://www.fao.org/3/a-i7970e.pdf> accessed 31 March 2022.

Bartenstein, Kristin, 'XIV: Development and Transfer of Marine Technology' in Alexander Proelss (ed), *United Nations Convention on the Law of the Sea A Commentary* (C.H. Beck, 2017) 1764.

Battle, Jessica and Duncan Currie, 'Some Critical Issues to be Resolved on Marine Genetic Resources in the Context of the Marine Biological Diversity Preparatory Committee Discussions' (Discussion Paper, WWF International, March 2016).

Blasiak, Robert, Jeremy Pittman, Nobuyuki Yagi and Hiroaki Sugino, 'Negotiating the Use of Biodiversity in Marine Areas beyond National Jurisdiction' (2016) 3 *Frontiers in Marine Science* 1–10. DOI: 10.3389/fmars.2016.00224.

Böhm, Monika and Ben Collen, 'Toward Equality of Biodiversity Knowledge through Technology Transfer' (2015) 29(5) *Conservation Biology* 1290–1302. DOI: 10.1111/cobi.12529.

Brown, Lisanne, Anne LaFond and Kate Macintyre, 'Measuring Capacity Building' (Report for MEASURE Evaluation, March 2001) <https://issat.dcaf.ch/content/download/29857/419317/file/664_guidelines%20on%20how%20to%20measure%20capacity%20building.pdf> accessed 31 March 2022.

'Building the Future of MPA Enforcement: Project Eyes on the Seas and Other High-Tech Surveillance Programs' *MPA News* (Web Site, April–May 2016) <https://mpanews.openchannels.org/news/mpa-news/building-future-mpa-enforcement-project-eyes-seas-and-other-high-tech-surveillance> accessed 31 March 2022.

Chair's Streamlined non-paper on Elements of a Draft Text of an International Legally Binding Instrument under the United Nations Convention on the Law of the Sea on the Conservation and Sustainable Use of Marine Biological Diversity of Areas Beyond National Jurisdiction Fourth Session of the PrepCom (10–21 July 2017) <https://www.un.org/depts/los/biodiversity/prepcom_files/Chairs_streamlined_non-paper_to_delegations.pdf> accessed 31 March 2022.

Churchill, R.R, and A.V. Lowe, *The Law of the Sea* (Manchester University Press, 3rd ed, 1999).

Cicin-Sain, Biliana, Marjo Vierros, Miriam Balgos, Alexis Maxwell, Meredith Kurz, Tina Farmer, Atsushi Sunami, Miko Maekawa, Iwao Fujii, Awni Benham, Julian Barbiere, Salvatore Aricò, Kirsten Isensee, Ward Appeltans, Harriet Harden-Davies, Aimee Gonzales, Stephen Adrian Ross, Alfonso Ascencio Herrera, Chapi Mwango, Annekah Mason, Ronán Long, Larry Hildebrand, Philippe Vallette, Joseph Appiott, Yugraj Yadava, Kouete Koffi Afachawo, Odanwu Chizoba Margaret, Abdul Rahman Bin Abdul Wahab, Andre Polejack, Lizanne Aching, Jenny Bowie-Wilches, Transform Aqorau, Rudolf Hermes, Dominique Benzaken, Laleta Davis-Mattis, Nguyen Chu Hoi, Abou Bamba, Rose Lesley Kautoke and Bojotlhe Butale, 'Capacity Development as a Key Aspect of a New International Agreement on Marine Biodiversity Beyond National Jurisdiction (BBNJ)' (Policy Brief, August 2018) <http://www.fao.org/fileadmin/user_upload/common_oceans/docs/policy-brief-on-bbnj-capacity-development-aug-2018.pdf> accessed 31 March 2022.

Craik, Neil, 'The Duty to Cooperate in the Customary Law of Environmental Impact Assessment' (2020) 69(1) *International & Comparative Law Quarterly* 239, 248–249. DOI: 10.1017/S0020589319000459.

Davies, Tammy E, Ana P.B. Carneiro, Bruno Campos, Carolina Hazin, Daniel C. Dunn, Kristina M. Gjerde, David E. Johnson, Maria P. Dias, 'Tracking Data and the Conservation of the High Seas: Opportunities and Challenges' (2021) 58(12) *Journal of Applied Ecology* 2703–2710. DOI: https://doi.org/10.1111/1365-2664.14032.

De Pooter, Daphnis, Ward Appeltans, Nicolas Bailly, Sky Bristol, Klaas Deneudt, Menashe Eliezer, Ei Fujioka, Alessandra Giorgetti, Philip Goldstein, Mirtha Lewis, Marina Lipizer, Kevin Mackay, Maria Marin, Gwenaelle Moncoiffe, Stamatina Nikolopoulou, Pieter Provoost, Shannon Rauch, Andres Roubicek, Carlos Torres, Anton van de Putte, Leen Vandepitte, Bart Vanhoorne, Matteo Vinci, Nina Wambiji, David Watts, Eduardo Klein Sala and Francisco Hernandez, 'Toward a New Data Standard for Combined Marine Biological and Environmental Datasets: Expanding OBIS Beyond Species Occurrences' (2017) 5(5) *Biodiversity Data Journal* e10989: 1–37. DOI: 10.3897/BDJ.5.e10989.

De Santo, Elizabeth M, 'Implementation Challenges of Area-based Management Tools (ABMTs) for Biodiversity Beyond National Jurisdiction (BBNJ)' (2018) 97 *Marine Policy* 34–43. DOI: 10.1016/j.marpol.2018.08.034.

De Santo, E.M, A. Asgeirsdóttir, A. Barros-Platiau, F. Biermann, J. Dryzek, L.R. Goncalves, R.E. Kim, E. Mendenhall, R. Mitchell, E. Nyman, M. Scobie, K. Sun, R. Tiller, D.G. Webster and O. Young, 'Protecting Biodiversity in Areas Beyond National Jurisdiction: An Earth System Governance Perspective' (2019) 2 *Earth System Governance* 100029: 1–7. DOI: 10.1016/j.esg.2019.100029.

'Deep-sea OBIS Node' Global Biodiversity Information Facility (Web Page) <https://www.gbif.org/publisher/f0d23bad-fee1-435d-bdb6-d26a600cad62> accessed 31 March 2022.

Delimitation of the Maritime Boundary in the Gulf of Maine Area (Canada/United States) (Provisional Measures) (1984) *ICJ Rep* 292.

Division for Ocean Affairs and the Law of the Sea, 'Its Functions and Activities' *Oceans and Law of the Sea United Nations* (Web Page, 14 October 2016) <https://www.un.org/Depts/los/doalos_activities/about_doalos.htm> accessed 31 March 2022.

Druel, Elisabeth, Julien Rochette, Raphaël Billé, Claudio Chiarolla, 'A Long and Winding Road - International Discussions on the Governance of Marine Biodiversity in Areas Beyond National Jurisdiction' (Study No. 7/2013, IDDRI, September 2013).

Dunn, Daniel C, Caroline Jablonicky, Guillermo O. Crespo, Douglas J. McCauley, David A. Kroodsma, Kristina Boerder, Kristina M. Gjerde and Patrick N. Halpin, 'Empowering High Seas Governance with Satellite Vessel Tracking Data' (2018) 19 *Fish & Fisheries* 729–739. DOI: 10.1111/faf.12285.

Eade, Deborah, *Capacity-Building: An Approach to People-Centred Development* (Oxfam, 1997).

European Union, 'Development of an International Legally-Binding Instrument under UNCLOS on the Conservation and Sustainable Use of Marine Biological Diversity of Areas beyond National Jurisdiction (BBNJ Process), Written Submission of the EU and Its Member States: Capacity-Building and Transfer of Marine Technology' (31 January 2017) <https://www.un.org/depts/los/biodiversity/prepcom_files/rolling_comp/EU_Capacity-Building_and_Transfer_of_Marine_Technology.pdf> accessed 31 March 2022 ('Written Submission of the EU and Member States to PrepCom: Capacity-Building and the Transfer of Marine Technology').

Girard, Pierre and Thomas Du Payrat, 'An Inventory of New Technologies in Fisheries' (Issues Brief, OECD, 2017).

Gjerde, Kristina M, 'The UN Decade for Ocean Science and the Role of IOC in Facilitating and Coordinating International Cooperation in Marine Scientific Research' (Conference Paper, BBNJ IGC-2 Side Event, 27 March 2019).

Gonzalez, Ariel W, 'Cutting a Gordian Knot?: Towards a Practical and Realistic Scheme for the Transfer of Marine Technology' in Myron H. Nordquist et al. (ed), *Law, Science and Ocean Management* (Martinus Nijhoff, 2007) 348. DOI: https://doi.org/10.1163/ej.9789004162556.i-850.100.

Harden-Davies, Harriet, 'Deep-sea Genetic Resources: New Frontiers for Science and Stewardship in Areas Beyond National Jurisdiction' (2016) 137 *Deep-sea Research II* 504–513. DOI: 10.1016/j.dsr2.2016.05.005.

Harden-Davies, Harriet, 'Capacity Building and Technology Transfer for Marine Biodiversity in Areas Beyond National Jurisdiction' (2017a) 111 *American Society of International Law* Proceedings of the ASIL Annual Meeting 243–245. DOI: 10.1017/amp.2017.75.

Harden-Davies, Harriet, 'Research for Regions: Strengthening Marine Technology Transfer for Pacific Island Countries and Biodiversity Beyond National Jurisdiction' (2017b) 32(4) *The International Journal of Marine and Coastal Law* 797–822. DOI: 10.1163/15718085-13204023.

Harden-Davies, Harriet and Paul Snelgrove, 'Science Collaboration for Capacity Building: Advancing Technology Transfer Through a Treaty for Biodiversity Beyond National Jurisdiction' (2020) 7 *Frontiers in Marine Science* 1–14. DOI: 10.3389/fmars.2020.00040.

Harden-Davies, Harriet R. and Kristina M. Gjerde, 'Building Scientific and Technological Capacity: A Role for Benefit-Sharing in the Conservation and Sustainable Use of Marine Biodiversity Beyond National Jurisdiction' (2019) 33(1) *Ocean Yearbook Online* 377–400. DOI: 10.1163/9789004395633_015.

IOC, *IOC Criteria and Guidelines on the Transfer of Marine Technology*, Doc IOC/INF-1203 (IOC, 2005).

IOC, 'Transfer of Marine Technology: Knowledge Sharing and Capacity Development for Sustainable Ocean and Coastal Management' (Brochure, IOC/BRO/2014/3, 2015) <https://unesdoc.unesco.org/ark:/48223/pf0000232586?locale=en> accessed 31 March 2022.

IOC, 'Potential Contribution to a New International Instrument under UNCLOS on the Conservation and Sustainable Use of Marine Biological Diversity of Areas Beyond National Jurisdiction' (Information Document, IOC/INF-1338, 17 May 2016).

IOC, *Ad Hoc Report of the IOC of UNESCO to the 4th Session of the Preparatory Committee on Marine Biological Diversity of Areas Beyond National Jurisdiction* (Information Document, IOC/INF-1347, 17 June 2017a) <https://unesdoc.unesco.org/ark:/48223/pf0000256190> accessed 31 March 2022.

IOC, *Decisions of the Twenty-Ninth Session of the Assembly*, IOC Doc. IOC-XXIX/3s/Decisions (IOC, 12 July 2017b) 10.1 para.(v).

IUCN, 'Submission by IUCN Following the Second Session of the Preparatory Committee on the Development of an International Legally Binding Instrument under the United Nations Convention on the Law of the Sea on the Conservation and Sustainable Use of Marine Biological Diversity of Areas Beyond National Jurisdiction' (5 December 2016) ('Written submission of IUCN to PrepCom') <https://www.un.org/depts/los/biodiversity/prepcom_files/rolling_comp/IUCN.pdf> accessed 31 March 2022.

Jaspars, Marcel and Abbe E.L. Brown, 'Benefit Sharing: Combining Intellectual Property, Trade Secrets, Science and an Ecosystem-Focused Approach' in Myron H. Nordquist and Ronán Long (eds) *Marine Biodiversity of Areas Beyond National Jurisdiction* (Brill/Nijhoff, 2021) 97–130. DOI: https://doi.org/10.1163/9789004422438_007.

Kaiser, Stefanie, Craig R. Smith and Pedro Martinez Arbizu, 'Editorial: Biodiversity of the Clarion-Clipperton Fracture Zone' (2017) 47 *Marine Biodiversity* 259–264. DOI: 10.1007/s12526-017-0733-0.

Kantai, Tallash, Asheline Appleton, Priscila Pereira de Andrade, Bernard Soubry and Asterios Tsioumanis, 'Summary of the Second Session of the Intergovernmental Conference on the Conservation and Sustainable Use of Marine Biodiversity of Areas Beyond National Jurisdiction: 25 March–5 April 2019' *Earth Negotiations Bulletin* (Online Bulletin, 8 April 2019) <https://enb.iisd.org/download/pdf/enb25195e.pdf> accessed 31 March 2022.

Kantai, Tallash and Paola Bettelli, 'Summary of the Fourth Session of the Intergovernmental Conference on an International Legally Binding Instrument under the UN Convention on the Law of the Sea on the Conservation and Sustainable Use of Marine Biodiversity of Areas beyond National Jurisdiction: 7-18 March 2022' *Earth Negotiations Bulletin* (Online Bulletin, 21 March 2022) 19 <https://enb.iisd.org/sites/default/files/2022-03/enb25225e.pdf>.

Kraabel, Kristine Dalaker, 'The BBNJ PrepCom and Institutional Arrangements: The Hype about the Hybrid Approach' in Myron H. Nordquist, John Morton

Moore and Ronán Long (eds), *The Marine Environment and United Nations Sustainable Development Goal 14* (Brill, 2019) 137. DOI: https://doi.org/10.1163/9789004366619_012.

Kullenberg, Gunnar, 'Capacity Building in Marine Research and Ocean Observations: A Perspective on Why and How' (1998) 22(3) *Marine Policy* 185–195. DOI: 10.1016/S0308-597X(98)00005-0.

Lac Lanoux Arbitration 24 *ILR* (1957) 119.

Leary, David, 'Agreeing to Disagree on What We Have or Have not Agreed on: The Current State of Play of the BBNJ Negotiations on the Status of Marine Genetic Resources in Areas Beyond National Jurisdiction' (2019) 99 *Marine Policy* 21–29. DOI: 10.1016/j.marpol.2018.10.031.

Long, Ronán, 'Marine Science Capacity Building and Technology Transfer: Rights and Duties Go Hand in Hand under the 1982 UNCLOS' in Myron H. Nordquist et al. (eds), *Law, Science and Ocean Management* (Martinus Nijhoff, 2007) 308. DOI: https://doi.org/10.1163/ej.9789004162556.i-850.80.

Long, Ronán and Mariamalia Rodríguez Chaves, 'Anatomy of a New International Instrument for Marine Biodiversity Beyond National Jurisdiction First Impressions of the Preparatory Process' (2015) 6 *Environmental Liability* 213.

Marvasti, A, 'An Assessment of the International Technology Transfer Systems and the New Law of the Sea' (1998) 39 *Ocean & Coastal Management* 197–210. DOI: 10.1016/S0964-5691(98)00025-8.

Metz, Bert, John K. Turkson, Ogunlade R. Davidson, Jan-Willem Martens, Sascha N.M. van Rooijen and Laura Van Wie McGrory, *Methodological and Technological Issues in Technology Transfer: A Special Report of the Intergovernmental Panel on Climate Change* (Cambridge University Press, 2000).

Minas, Stephen, 'Marine Technology Transfer under a BBNJ Treaty: A Case for Transnational Network Cooperation' (2018) 112 *AJIL Unbound* 144–149. DOI: 10.1017/aju.2018.46.

Morgera, Elisa and Mara Ntona, 'Seize the Moment: Towards Fairer Capacity Building and Marine Technology Transfer' (Briefing Paper, IIED, August 2018) <https://pubs.iied.org/pdfs/17479IIED.pdf> accessed 31 March 2022.

Morgera, Elisa, Daniela Diz, Tallash Kantai and Asterios Tsioumanis, 'Summary of the First Session of the Preparatory Committee on Marine Biodiversity of Areas Beyond National Jurisdiction: 28 March–8 April 2016' *Earth Negotiations Bulletin* (Online Bulletin, 11 April 2016) <https://enb.iisd.org/download/pdf/enb25106e.pdf> accessed 31 March 2022.

Morgera, Elisa, Asheline Appleton, Daniela Diz and Asterios Tsioumanis, 'Summary of the First Session of the Intergovernmental Conference on an International Legally Binding Instrument under the UN Convention on the Law of the Sea on the Conservation and Sustainable Use of Marine Biodiversity of Areas Beyond National Jurisdiction 4–17 September 2018' *Earth Negotiations Bulletin* (Online Bulletin, 20 September 2018) <https://enb.iisd.org/download/pdf/enb25179e.pdf> accessed 31 March 2022.

Nordquist, Myron H. (ed), *United Nations Convention on the Law of the Sea 1982: A Commentary* (Martinus Nijhoff Publishers, 1985).

Nordquist, Myron H, John Norton Moore and Ronán J. Long (eds), *The Marine Environment and United Nations Sustainable Development Goal 14: Life Below Water* (Brill Nijhoff, 2018).

Organisation for Economic Co-operation and Development (OECD), 'The Challenge of Capacity Development: Working Towards Good Practice' Doc DCD/DAC/GOVNET(2005)5/REVI (1 February 2006) <http://gsdrc.org/docs/open/cc110.pdf> accessed 31 March 2022.

Papanicolopulu, Irini, 'Section 4 Cooperation among international organizations' in Alexander Proelss (ed), *United Nations Convention on the Law of the Sea A Commentary* (C.H. Beck, 2017) 1808.

Payne, Cymie, 'Biodiversity in High Seas Areas: An Integrated Legal Approach', *American Society of International Law* (ASIL Insights, 1 September 2017) <https://www.asil.org/insights/volume/21/issue/9/biodiversity-high-seas-areas-integrated-legal-approach> accessed 31 March 2022.

People's Republic of China, 'Written Submission of the Government of the People's Republic of China on Elements of a Draft Text of an International Legally Binding Instrument under the United Nations Convention on the Law of the Sea on the Conservation and Sustainable Use of Marine Biological Diversity of Areas Beyond National Jurisdiction' (20 April 2017) 11 [27] <https://www.un.org/depts/los/biodiversity/prepcom_files/streamlined/China.pdf> accessed 31 March 2022.

Pinto, M.C.W, 'Legal Aspects of North/South Transfer of Marine Technology' (1990) 2 *Sri Lanka Journal of International Law* 139–182.

President's Aid to Negotiations, UN Doc A/CONF.232/2019/1 (3 December 2018).

Report on the Work of the United Nations Open-ended Informal Consultative Process on Oceans and the Law of the Sea at Its Eleventh Meeting (UNICPOLOS), UN Doc A/65/164 (23 July 2010).

Revised Draft Text of an Agreement Under the United Nations Convention on the Law of the Sea on the Conservation and Sustainable Use of Marine Biological Diversity of Areas Beyond National Jurisdiction, UN Doc A/CONF.232/2020/3 (18 November 2019) <https://undocs.org/pdf?symbol=en/a/conf.232/2020/3> accessed 31 March 2022.

Ribeiro, Marta Chantal, 'South Atlantic Perspectives on the Future International Legally Binding Instrument under the LOSC on Conservation and Sustainable Use of BBNJ' (2017) 32 *The International Journal of Marine and Coastal Law* 733–764. DOI: 10.1163/15718085-13204017.

Statement by the President of the Conference at the Closing of the First Session of the Intergovernmental Conference on an International Legally Binding Instrument under the United Nations Convention on the Law of the Sea on the Conservation and Sustainable Use of Marine Biological Diversity of Areas Beyond National Jurisdiction, UN Doc A/CONF.232/2018/7 (20 September 2018) <https://documents-dds-ny.un.org/doc/UNDOC/GEN/N18/294/09/PDF/N1829409.pdf?OpenElement> accessed 31 March 2022.

Stoll, Peter Tobias, 'The Entry into Force of the Convention on the Law of the Sea: A Redistribution of Competences in Relation to the Management of the International Commons? The Transfer of Technology Under the Implementation Agreement' (1995) 55(2) *Zeitschrift Für Ausländisches Öffentliches Recht Und Völkerrecht* 391–420.

Tanaka, Yoshifumi, 'Zonal and Integrated Management Approaches to Ocean Governance: Reflections on a Dual Approach in International Law of the

Sea' (2004) 19 *International Journal of Marine and Coastal Law* 483–514. 10.1163/1571808053310143.

The Group of 77, 'Statement on Behalf of the Group of 77 and China by Mr Farid Dahmane, Permanent Mission of Algeria to the United Nations, at the Ad Hoc Open-ended Informal Working Group to Study Issues Relating to the Conservation and Sustainable Use of Marine Biological Diversity Beyond Areas of National Jurisdiction' (New York, 7 May 2012) <http://www.g77.org/statement/getstatement.php?id=120507a> accessed 31 March 2022.

The Pew Charitable Trusts, 'Project Eyes on the Seas' (Brief, March 2015) <https://www.pewtrusts.org/-/media/assets/2015/03/eyes-on-the-seas-brief_web.pdf> accessed 31 March 2022.

Tiller, Rachel, Elizabeth De Santo, Elizabeth Mendenhall and Elizabeth Nyman, 'The Once and Future Treaty: Towards a New Regime for Biodiversity in Areas Beyond National Jurisdiction' (2019) 99 *Marine Policy* 239–242. DOI: 10.1016/j.marpol.2018.10.046.

Tiller, Rachel, Elizabeth De Santo, Elizabeth Mendenhall, Elizabeth Nyman and Ian Ralby, 'Wealth Blindness Beyond National Jurisdiction' (2020) 151 *Marine Pollution Bulletin* 110809: 1–8. DOI: 10.1016/j.marpolbul.2019.110809.

Tolochko, Petro, and Alice B.M. Vadrot, 'The Usual Suspects? Distribution of Collaboration Capital in Marine Biodiversity Research' (2021) 124 *Marine Policy* 104318: 1–15. DOI: 10.1016/j.marpol.2020.104318.

Troisi, Ariel, 'Introduction to facilitating Capacity Development, Transfer of Marine Technology and Ocean Science in BBNJ' (Conference Paper, BBNJ IGC-2 Side Event, 27 March 2019).

UN, 'As Intergovernmental Negotiations on New Ocean Treaty Continue, Delegates' Divergent Views Emerge on Funding, Review Processes, Subsidiary Bodies' (Meetings Coverage, SEA/2100, 3 April 2019).

UNDP, 'Capacity Development: A UNDP Primer' (Advocacy Primer, 2009) <https://www.adaptation-undp.org/sites/default/files/downloads/cdg_capacity_development_primer.pdf> accessed 31 March 2022.

UNFCCC, *Report of the Conference of the Parties*, UN Doc FCCC/CP/2010/7/Add.1 (15 March 2011) (Decision 1/CP.16, para. 117).

United Nations Convention on the Law of the Sea, opened for signature 10 December 1982 (1982) 1833 *UNTS* 397 (entered into force 16 November 1994) (UNCLOS).

United Nations Declaration on Environment and Development, UN Doc. A/CONF.151/5/Rev.1 (Rio Declaration, 1992).

United Nations General Assembly, *Oceans and the Law of the Sea-Report of the Secretary-General,* UN Doc A/62/66/Add.2 (10 September 2007).

United Nations General Assembly, *Oceans and the Law of the Sea-Report of the Secretary-General,* UN Doc A/64/66/Add.2 (19 October 2009).

United Nations General Assembly, *Oceans and the Law of the Sea-Report of the Secretary-General,* UN Doc A/65/69 (29 March 2010).

United Nations General Assembly, *Options for a Facilitation Mechanism that Promotes the Development, Transfer and Dissemination of Clean and Environmentally Sound Technologies-Report of the Secretary-General,* UN Doc A/67/348 (4 September 2012).

United Nations General Assembly, *Transforming our World: The 2030 Agenda for Sustainable Development,* UN Doc. A/RES/70/1 (25 September 2015).

Valdés, L (ed), *Global Ocean Science Report: The Current Status of Ocean Science Around the World* (Report, IOC-UNESCO, 2017).

Van Dyke, Jon M. and David L. Teichmann, 'Transfer of Seabed Mining Technology: A Stumbling Block to US Ratification of the Law of the Sea Convention' (1984) 13(4) *Ocean Development and International Law* 427–455. DOI: 10.1080/00908328409545736.

Verhoosel, G, 'Beyond the Unsustainable Rhetoric of Sustainable Development: Transferring Environmentally Sound Technologies' (1998) 11(1) *Georgetown International Environmental Law Review* 49–76.

Waibel, Michael and Michael Alford, 'Technology Transfer' in *Max Planck Encyclopedia of Public International Law vol IX* (Oxford University Press, at June 2014).

Wilkinson, Allie, 'U.K. Wants Eyes in the Sky to Keep Watch on Its Record Marine Reserve' (2015) *Science* 19 March 2015 <https://www.sciencemag.org/news/2015/03/uk-wants-eyes-sky-keep-watch-its-record-marine-reserve> accessed 31 March 2022.

World Economic Forum, 'Harnessing the Fourth Industrial Revolution for the Earth' (Fourth Industrial Revolution for the Earth Series, November 2017) <http://www3.weforum.org/docs/WEF_Harnessing_4IR_Oceans.pdf> accessed 31 March 2022.

Wright, Glen, Julien Rochette, Kristina Gjerde and Isabel Seeger, *The Long & Winding Road: Negotiating a Treaty for the Conservation and Sustainable Use of Marine Biodiversity in Areas Beyond National Jurisdiction* (Study No. 8/2018, IDDRI, August 2018).

Yarn, Douglas, 'The Transfer of Technology and UNCLOS III' (1984) 14(1) *Georgia Journal of International and Comparative Law* 121–153.

8 A bridge to the future protection of BBNJ

Introduction

> *Protecting the biodiversity of the high seas by bringing good governance and law to the whole ocean is the single most important thing we can do to turn the tide for the blue heart of our planet.*[1]

For most of human history, the ocean was considered so 'bountiful and resilient that it was impossible to deplete or disrupt it.'[2] This overarching narrative was based on the false premise that 'the ocean is so vast, it is simply too big to fail.'[3] But it is failing. The world's oceans are heading towards an ecological and societal tipping point.[4] ABNJ face a multitude of anthropogenic pressures that have intensified over recent decades. Impacts from the traditional maritime uses of fishing and shipping are being felt in ever deeper and more distant waters, and there is growing interest in new and emerging activities, with untold consequences for marine life. The existing international law framework for ABNJ is inadequate for ensuring the long-term conservation and sustainable use of BBNJ. The development of an ILBI presents an opportunity to improve upon the status quo of ocean governance in ABNJ. In concluding this book, it must be asked what the future holds in store for the BBNJ process and more specifically,

1 Matt McGrath, 'UN Treaty Would Protect High Seas from Over Exploitation', *BBC News* (Web Page, 4 September 2018) quoting Professor Alex Rogers <https://www.bbc.com/news/science-environment-45397674>.

2 Jane Lubchenco and Steven D. Gaines, 'A New Narrative for the Ocean' (2019) 364(6444) *Science* 911.

3 Ibid.

4 Ove Hoegh-Guldberg et al, *Indispensable Ocean: Aligning Ocean Health and Human Well-Being* (Guidance from the Blue Ribbon Panel to the Global Partnership for Oceans No 82651, 2013) 25 quoting Dawn J. Wright, Chief Scientist, Esri and Professor of Geography and Oceanography, Oregon State University, United States <http://documents1.worldbank.org/curated/en/111381468155703584/pdf/826510WP0Indis00Box379862B00PUBLIC0.pdf>.

DOI: 10.4324/b22996-9

whether the negotiations are on track to finalising an 'effective, practicable and future proof'[5] instrument. To answer this question, it is important to consider the progress made to date, the current state of play and the future prospects of the BBNJ negotiation process.

8.1 Significant milestones

Over the last 15 years, a number of significant achievements have been made in the BBNJ negotiation process. Most notably, at the final BBNJ Working Group in 2015, delegations took the historic step of recommending to the UNGA that an ILBI should be developed to protect BBNJ.[6] This was the culmination of nine years of substantive and, at times, intense debate on the scope, parameters and feasibility of such an instrument. The recommendations of the Working Group were subsequently approved in UNGA Resolution 69/292.[7] This landmark resolution represented, on the world stage, an acknowledgement of the dire challenges facing BBNJ and the urgent need for action. Although BBNJ-related issues had been on the international agenda for decades, the decision taken by the UNGA to commence a negotiation process validated the need for a comprehensive international framework to address the conservation and sustainable use of BBNJ. This decision was further endorsed on 24 December 2017, when the UNGA, in Resolution 72/249, decided to convene an IGC.[8] Despite undergoing a complex drafting stage, this resolution was ultimately co-sponsored by 141 States and adopted by consensus.[9] Arguably, these achievements have been spurred by a new spirit of shared responsibility for the common areas of the ocean.

8.1.1 A flourishing cooperative spirit

The State Parties to UNCLOS were prompted by the desire to settle, in a spirit of mutual understanding and cooperation, all issues relating to the law of the sea.[10] Continuing in this tradition, one of the other significant achievements of

5 *Statement by the President of the Conference at the Closing of IGC 3*, UN Doc A/CONF.232/2019/10 (13 September 2019) 1 ('*IGC 3 Closing Statement*').

6 *Letter Dated 13 February 2015 from the Co-Chairs of the Ad Hoc Open-Ended Informal Working Group to the President of the General Assembly*, UN Doc A/69/780, United Nations General Assembly, 69th sess, Item 74(a) (13 February 2015).

7 *Development of an International Legally Binding Instrument under UNCLOS on the Conservation and Sustainable Use of Marine Biological Diversity of Areas beyond National Jurisdiction*, GA Res 69/292, UN Doc A/RES/69/292 (6 July 2015, adopted 19 June 2015) ('UNGA Res 69/292').

8 *International Legally Binding Instrument under UNCLOS on the Conservation and Sustainable Use of Marine Biological Diversity of Areas beyond National Jurisdiction*, GA Res 72/249, UN Doc A/RES/72/249 (19 January 2018, adopted on 24 December 2017) ('UNGA Res 72/249') para 1.

9 Glen Wright et al, 'The Long and Winding Road: Negotiating a Treaty for the Conservation and Sustainable Use of Marine Biodiversity in Areas beyond National Jurisdiction' (Study No 08/18, Institute for Sustainable Development and International Relations, August 2018) 45.

10 UNCLOS, preamble.

the BBNJ process has been the fostering of a renewed sense of cooperation in addressing ocean-related issues. This has been evident since the first meeting of the BBNJ Working Group in 2006. According to the *Earth Negotiations Bulletin*, the 'spirit of cooperation' at this initial meeting was 'palpable' and reflected not only a shared understanding of the complexity of BBNJ issues, but a willingness to address them on an international scale.[11] Over 250 participants attended this meeting, representing governments, UN agencies, industries, IGOs and NGOs.[12] Based on the number of attendees, it was clear that the international community understood that the challenges confronting BBNJ transcend the boundaries of a single state and require collective action and cooperation in response.[13]

The level of engagement by all delegations has remained relatively consistent throughout the BBNJ negotiations. In an effort to provide an open, inclusive and transparent process,[14] PrepCom and IGC meetings have been open to all UN members, members of the specialised agencies and parties to UNCLOS.[15] Relevant organisations, funds and programmes of the UN system, interested global and regional IGOs and other international bodies have also been able to participate as observers.[16] To secure the widest level of participation, UNGA Resolution 69/292 established a special voluntary trust fund to assist developing countries to attend BBNJ meetings.[17]

Notwithstanding a number of teething problems, the spirit of good will and cooperation has continued to flourish throughout the BBNJ process, with the IGC President, Rena Lee, regularly thanking delegations for their continued 'passion, dedication, cooperation and willingness to listen and talk to one another.'[18] This cooperative spirit has arguably led to other significant milestones, including reaching a consensus on a package deal of issues.

8.1.2 Agreement on a package deal

At the 2011 meeting of the BBNJ Working Group, delegations agreed for all future discussions to be structured around a package deal of issues. The desire to agree on a package deal mirrored UNCLOS III negotiations. At UNCLOS III,

11 Karen Alvarenga et al, 'Summary of the Working Group on Marine Biodiversity beyond Areas of National Jurisdiction: 13–17 February 2006' *Earth Negotiations Bulletin* (Online Bulletin, 20 February 2006) 9 <https://enb.iisd.org/download/pdf/enb2525e.pdf>.

12 Ibid.

13 Dinah Shelton, 'Common Concern of Humanity' (2009) 39(2) *Environmental Policy and Law* 83, 83.

14 Tallash Kantai et al, 'Summary of the Third Session of the Intergovernmental Conference on the Conservation and Sustainable Use of Marine Biodiversity of Areas beyond National Jurisdiction: 19–30 August 2019' *Earth Negotiations Bulletin* (Online Bulletin, 2 September 2019) 10 ('Summary of IGC 3') <https://enb.iisd.org/download/pdf/enb25218e.pdf>.

15 UNGA Resolution 69/292 (n 7) para 1(a); UNGA Resolution 72/249 (n 8) para 8.

16 UNGA Resolution 69/292 (n 7) para 1(a); UNGA Resolution 72/249 (n 8) para 12.

17 UNGA Resolution 69/292 (n 7) para 5.

18 *IGC 3 Closing Statement* (n 5) 3.

participating States recognised that UNCLOS should not be treated like 'a basket of fruit from which one can pick only those one fancies.'[19] Instead, UNCLOS was to represent 'a complex and indivisible package of closely interrelated compromise solutions to all major problems of the law of the sea.'[20] A package deal approach was therefore seen as a 'means to substantially address a complex set of issues that had proven to be difficult to solve unless tying them together.'[21] Today, the same reasoning must be applied in the BBNJ context. Given the highly interconnected nature of the marine environment, BBNJ-related issues are mutually entangled and influence one another.[22]

The adoption of a package deal also accords with the UNCLOS Preamble, which recognises that 'the problems of ocean space are closely interrelated and need to be considered as a whole.' These words indicate powerfully the need to take a holistic approach to ocean governance and are no less relevant today than they were in 1982.[23] As a new challenge facing the law of the sea, the conservation and sustainable use of BBNJ needs to be dealt with in a holistic fashion and not in a piecemeal way.

The package deal concept is also an effective negotiating technique as it works on the premise that 'nothing is agreed until everything is agreed.'[24] As States displayed substantially divergent attitudes to multiple issues during the first three meetings of the BBNJ Working Group, it was agreed that a package deal approach could assist in finding trade-offs and reciprocal support between different areas of bargaining. While the final shape of an ILBI remains unclear, there is no doubt that if the package deal negotiations can be concluded it 'will represent a milestone development in the history of the law of the sea.'[25] It was

19 Hugo Caminos and Michael R. Molitor, 'Progressive Development of International Law and the Package Deal' (1985) 79 *American Journal of International Law* 871, 877 quoting the Deputy Foreign Minister Gouzhenko of the Soviet Union Verbatim records of the 191st plenary meeting (1982), 17 Third United Nations Conference on the Law of the Sea, Official Records 106–107.

20 Ibid.

21 Fernanda Millicay, 'Marine Genetic Resources of Areas beyond National Jurisdiction and Intellectual Property Rights' in Tomas Heidar (ed), *New Knowledge and Changing Circumstances in the Law of the Sea* (Brill Nijhoff, 2020) 65, 65.

22 R. Long and Z. Sun (eds), 'Biodiversity beyond National Jurisdiction: Towards the Development of a Balanced, Effective and Universal International Agreement' (Workshop and Side Events Report, World Maritime University Workshop, 7 February 2019) 74; Pascale Ricard, 'Marine Biodiversity beyond National Jurisdiction: The Launch of an Intergovernmental Conference for the Adoption of a Legally Binding Instrument under the UNCLOS' (2018) 19 (4) *Maritime Safety and Security Law Journal* 84, 93.

23 Richard Barnes, David Freestone and David M. Ong, 'The Law of the Sea: Progress and Prospects' in Richard Barnes, David Freestone and David M. Ong (eds), *The Law of the Sea Progress and Prospects* (Oxford University Press, 2006) 3.

24 G.M. Danilenko, *Law-Making in the International Community* (Martinus Nijhoff Publishers, 1993).

25 David Leary, 'Agreeing to Disagree on What We Have or Have Not Agreed on: The Current State of Play of the BBNJ Negotiations on the Status of Marine Genetic Resources in Areas beyond National Jurisdiction' (2019) *Marine Policy* 21, 28.

clear from IGC 3 discussions that the use of a draft negotiating text could greatly assist in accelerating this process.

8.1.3 The production of a draft negotiating text

In stark contrast to the first two IGC meetings, IGC 3 negotiations focused on a draft text produced by the IGC President on 17 May 2019, featuring 70 draft articles and 2 draft annexes.[26] The draft text was praised by nearly all delegations as it substantially changed 'the tenor, pace and detail of interventions' at IGC 3.[27] Significantly, it enabled delegations to move away from a conceptual approach to a textual basis to constructively explore 'space for compromise.'[28] This inspired many delegations to circulate text-based proposals throughout the course of the meeting (in the form of 'Conference Room Papers').[29]

Additionally, in order to create 'a lower-stakes atmosphere,'[30] IGC 3 adopted a new working format involving a combination of plenary sessions, informal working groups and informal-informals.[31] As the informal-informals were not web-cast or open to the press, and attendance by NGOs and IGOs was limited to ten seats, delegations were able to engage in frank discussion. Delegations left IGC 3 feeling 'quite positive' with many noting that this conference had allowed them to gain a better understanding of each other's positions.[32] In turn, progress, although minimal, was made on the package deal.

Regarding MGRs, it was agreed that an ILBI should include benefit-sharing modalities, but there was no consensus on what they should be.[33] There was also general convergence on the geographical and temporal scope of the ILBI.[34] For

26 *Draft Text of an Agreement under UNCLOS on the Conservation and Sustainable Use of Marine Biological Diversity of Areas beyond National Jurisdiction*, UN Doc A/CONF.232/2019/6 (17 May 2019).

27 Elizabeth M. De Santo et al, 'Stuck in the Middle with You (and Not Much Time Left): The Third Intergovernmental Conference on Biodiversity beyond National Jurisdiction' (2020) 117 *Marine Policy* 103957, 1–9, 2.

28 Elisa Morgera et al, 'Summary of the First Session of the Intergovernmental Conference on an International Legally Binding Instrument under the UN Convention on the Law of the Sea on the Conservation and Sustainable Use of Marine Biodiversity of Areas beyond National Jurisdiction 4–17 September 2018' *Earth Negotiations Bulletin* (Online Bulletin, 20 September 2018) 17 <https://enb.iisd.org/events/1st-session-intergovernmental-conference-igc-international-legally-binding-instrument-under>.

29 Summary of IGC 3 (n 14) 19.

30 De Santo et al (n 27) 2.

31 Tallash Kantai et al, 'Third Session of the Intergovernmental Conference (IGC) on the Conservation and Sustainable Use of Marine Biodiversity of Areas beyond National Jurisdiction: 19–30 August 2019' *Earth Negotiations Bulletin* (Online Bulletin, 19 August 2019) 1 <https://enb.iisd.org/download/pdf/enb25208e.pdf>.

32 Summary of IGC 3 (n 14) 22.

33 Fran Humphries and Harriet Harden-Davies, 'Practical Policy Solutions for the Final Stage of BBNJ Treaty Negotiations' (2020) 122 *Marine Policy* 104214, 1–7, 2.

34 Summary of IGC 3 (n 14) 22.

example, delegates agreed that MGR provisions should only apply after entry into force of the instrument, rather than retrospectively.[35] On ABMTs, delegates converged on the need to provide an open, inclusive and transparent consultation and assessment process.[36] Moreover, delegates generally agreed on the need to identify priority areas for protection based on the best available science, traditional knowledge of indigenous peoples and local communities and the application of the precautionary principle/approach and an ecosystem approach.[37] In respect to EIA, text-based discussions helped to develop a clear understanding of the various options for each step of the assessment process, and there was broad support for a provision on the obligation to conduct EIA.[38] Discussions on CBTT also showed progress, particularly concerning the potential role of a COP in respect to developing guidelines and undertaking monitoring and review functions.[39] Delegates also generally agreed that a clearing-house mechanism would provide a 'vital information-exchange platform.'[40]

Despite progress made at IGC 3, the level of disagreement between States remained very high and a finished product seemed a long way down the track. The COVID-19 pandemic impacted the work of the IGC, and it remains unclear what lasting effect this will have for on-going BBNJ negotiations. IGC 4 was postponed twice due to the pandemic. While some delegates 'were grateful for the unplanned hiatus,'[41] others were keen to return to the negotiating table and build on the momentum generated at IGC 3. The cloud of the pandemic hung over IGC 4, with NGOs and civil society effectively side-lined during the first week of discussions due to COVID-19 restrictions. Despite there being a collaborative and constructive spirit to propel the BBNJ process forward, leading into IGC 5, a number of sticking points remain on each issue of the package deal.

8.2 The current state of play

MGRs continue to be the most contentious area. This is due, in large part, to the on-going ideological debate between the G77/China coalition and a group

35 Ibid.

36 Ibid.

37 Humphries and Harden-Davies (n 33) 3.

38 *IGC 3 Closing Statement* (n 5) 13.

39 Ina Tessnow-von Wysocki, 'Slow Progress in the Third BBNJ Meeting: Negotiations are Moving—but Sideways' (Maripoldata, 6 September 2019) <https://www.maripoldata.eu/slow-progress-in-the-third-bbnj-meeting-negotiations-are-moving-but-sideways/>.

40 Summary of IGC 3 (n 14) 22.

41 Tallash Kantai and Paola Bettelli, 'Summary of the Fourth Session of the Intergovernmental Conference on an International Legally Binding Instrument under the UN Convention on the Law of the Sea on the Conservation and Sustainable Use of Marine Biodiversity of Areas beyond National Jurisdiction: 7-18 March 2022' *Earth Negotiations Bulletin* (Online Bulletin, 21 March 2022) 1 ('Summary of IGC 4') <https://enb.iisd.org/sites/default/files/2022-03/enb25225e.pdf>.

of developed States, including the US, Japan, South Korea and Russia.[42] So far, these two camps have maintained their 'traditional trench warfare positions,'[43] even though the draft text does not explicitly refer to the CHM or freedom of the seas concepts. In their opening statement at IGC 3, the G77/China bloc asserted that the conservation and sustainable use of BBNJ, including MGRs, 'can only be achieved when guided by the bedrock principle of CHM.'[44] This sentiment was again underlined at the conclusion of IGC 4.[45] In contrast, a group of developed States, whose nationals, corporations and flag vessels are most likely to engage in MGR collection and utilisation, continue to rely on the Grotian doctrine to oppose additional burdens being placed on these activities.[46] Russia, for example, argues for the 'strongest and most explicit version of the freedom of the seas' by contending that an ILBI should not regulate access to MGRs.[47] Others relied on the Grotian tradition to argue that as the 'in situ collection of MGRs rarely has a commercial purpose,' this is better understood as marine scientific research, which is already recognised as a high seas freedom under UNCLOS.[48] The vexed relationship between CHM and freedom of the seas was also evident in benefit-sharing discussions. For example, the US and South Korea prefer voluntary, non-monetary benefit-sharing, while the G77/China bloc, CARICOM and the African Group insist on mandatory sharing of monetary and non-monetary benefits.[49]

Based on IGC discussions, it is clear that the legacy of Grotius' *Mare Liberum* continues to influence and condition the position maritime States take on issues concerning international waters, including BBNJ. The fact that maritime States continue to use the freedom of the seas concept to prop up and support their position on BBNJ issues confirms its continuing vitality in the development of the law of the sea. For this group, the Grotian doctrine still serves as 'rhetorical reinforcement for the point of departure'[50] when deliberating on matters of ocean governance. Consequently, maritime States remain extremely cautious of

42 De Santo et al (n 27) 4.

43 David Leary and S. Kim Juniper, 'Addressing the Marine Genetic Resources Issue: Is the Debate Heading in the Wrong Direction?' in Clive Schofield, Seokwoo Lee and Moon-Sang Kwon (eds), *The Limits of Maritime Jurisdiction* (Koninklijke Brill, 2014) 769, 785.

44 Group of 77, 'Statement on Behalf of the Group of 77 and China by H.E. Ambassador Feda Abdelhady-Nasser, State of Palestine, Chair of the Group of 77, at the Opening of the Third Session of the Intergovernmental Conference on an International Legally Binding Instrument under UNCLOS on the Conservation and Sustainable Use of Marine Biological Diversity of Areas beyond National Jurisdiction' (19 August 2019) <http://statements.unmeetings.org/media2/21996878/palestine-obo-g77-and-china.pdf>.

45 See, comments by the G77/China bloc, the African Group and Botswana on behalf of the Landlocked Developing Countries in 'Summary of IGC 4' (n 41) 18.

46 De Santo et al (n 27) 4.

47 Ibid.

48 Ibid; Summary of IGC 4 (n 41) 4 .

49 Ibid.

50 W.E. Butler, 'Grotius and the Law of the Sea' in Hedley Bull, Benedict Kingsbury and Adam Roberts (eds), *Hugo Grotius and International Relations* (Clarendon, 1992) 210, 220.

any attempt to further erode or tamper with traditional high seas freedoms.[51] Geopolitical uncertainty in the wake of COVID-19 may cause this group of States to cling ever harder to the Grotian tradition, particularly if their economic interests come under threat.

However, as was the case with UNCLOS, the successful conclusion of an ILBI will depend on winning the support of this powerful bloc of States. Accordingly, this book has presented options for the main substantive components of an ILBI to be underpinned by a set of micro and macro compromises carefully designed to appeal to the interests of maritime States while at the same time promoting the protection of BBNJ. The potential areas of compromise advocated for in this book are an attempt to avoid the BBNJ negotiations from getting bogged down in long-standing debates, which may impose inherent limitations on the adoption of an effective ILBI and ultimately spell failure for the BBNJ process.

Turning to the other elements of the package deal, States continue to struggle to define ABMTs and 'how they relate to one another.'[52] For example, a real sticking point concerns the distinction between 'establishing' versus 'designating' MPAs. While this appears to be a matter of semantics, it continues to hold up progress and reinforces the need for internationally agreed definitions of key terms in an ILBI.[53] Delegations also remain divided on the criteria to use for designating ABMTs and whether there should be different processes for different tools.[54] The adjacency issue continues to spark disagreement along with the question of how to designate ABMTs and MPAs without undermining existing arrangements (where they exist).[55] On EIAs, there are two main areas of disagreement. The first concerns the degree to which the EIA process should be internationalised under an ILBI. At IGC 4, one delegate stated that 'we have to recognise that a certain degree of internationalisation is required, since the BBNJ instrument, itself, is an international agreement.'[56] The second area of disagreement relates to whether the stages of an EIA should be outlined in the instrument or set out in supplementary guidelines. States also remain split on the threshold or criteria to use to trigger an assessment, with delegates divided between an 'activity-oriented' and an 'impact-oriented' approach.[57] The topic of CBTT continues to re-open the familiar divisions between North and South that characterised UNCLOS III. Delegations, in the traditional categories of developed versus developing States, have become firmly entrenched on either side of the monetary versus non-monetary and mandatory versus voluntary debate.[58] Thus, CBTT obligations,

51 For example, at IGC 4, one delegate quipped that 'access to the high seas cannot be prohibited' – see Summary of IGC 4 (n 41) 20.
52 De Santo et al (n 27)
53 Summary of IGC 4 (n 41) 6.
54 *IGC 3 Closing Statement* (n 5) 9.
55 Summary of IGC 4 (n 41) 7.
56 Ibid, 20.
57 Humphries and Harden-Davies (n 33) 4.
58 De Santo et al (n 27) 7.

namely, 'what should be provided, who should provide it, and to whom it should be provided,' still present a significant hurdle to consensus building.[59]

Taking into account the level of divergence that remains between States on key issues in the BBNJ process, it is safe to say that the international community will have its hands full over the next few years developing an ILBI. While it is hoped that an ILBI will provide the necessary tools and mechanisms to protect, conserve and sustainably use BBNJ, it will ultimately come down to the political will of States and finding a workable balance between competing interests. If one word was selected to characterise UNCLOS III it would have to be 'balance.' UNCLOS is considered a landmark multilateral environmental agreement because of its package deal which carefully and delicately balanced the rights and jurisdiction of coastal States with the objectives and desires for freedom of navigation of maritime States. To devise an effective and universally acceptable instrument, BBNJ negotiators must follow in the tradition of attempting to find an equilibrium between the simultaneous pursuit of a common concern (the protection of BBNJ) and conflicting interests, and in this respect, the development of an ILBI is a case of history repeating itself.

8.3 Bridging the divide—potential compromise solutions

This book has formulated a blueprint of potential compromise solutions BBNJ negotiators could consider in attempting to find an equilibrium between the competing interests at play.

In respect to MGRs, Chapter 4 of this book suggests that the CCH concept could bridge the gap between the competing principles of freedom of the seas and CHM and provide a rationale legal foundation for the conservation and sustainable use of BBNJ, including the ABS of MGRs. Chapter 4 also lays out a golden middle way for the three pillars of an ABS regime. In terms of access, this book argues that an open access approach could appeal to maritime States and alleviate concerns of further erosion of the Grotian doctrine. An open access approach should be underpinned by key compromises, including the provision of advance notice and benefit-sharing obligations. As maritime States, the R&D sector and the deep-sea MSR community are unlikely to agree to an overly stringent approach to benefit-sharing and a light approach will not address the equity concerns of developing States, this book proposes a benefit-sharing model built on compromise. Under this model, access could trigger certain benefit-sharing obligations including the sharing of MGRs to a common domain, which, in turn, could promote sustainable use and encourage research and innovation.[60] A com-

59 Summary of IGC 4 (n 41) 21; Rachel Tiller et al, 'The Once and Future Treaty: Towards a New Regime for Biodiversity in Areas beyond National Jurisdiction' (2019) 99 *Marine Policy* 239, 240.

60 Morten Walløe Tvedt and Ane E. Jørem, 'Bioprospecting in the High Seas: Regulatory Options for Benefit Sharing' (2013) 16(3–4) *The Journal of World Intellectual Property* 150, 160.

mon domain approach could also be coupled with an embargo option to sustain the biodiscovery pipeline. Turning to the last pillar of an ABS regime, monitoring and compliance, this book promotes the establishment of a new body to oversee a compliance system centred around reporting obligations. A new body is more likely to appeal to maritime States, as this bloc is reluctant to agree to any extension to the ISA's mandate given its close affiliation with the CHM principle.[61]

Chapter 5 of this book identified and investigated a number of compromise solutions that could assist in bridging the divide between high seas freedoms and the establishment of MPAs. First, in order to alleviate the strategic concerns of maritime States, this book argues for the IMO to have a heightened role under an ILBI in respect to the designation of MPAs, to guarantee the input of specialised technical expertise and to ensure that a balance is maintained between BBNJ protection and the preservation of high seas navigational freedoms. Second, in order to reassure fishing States that ILBI negotiations will not be used as a backdoor way of reopening fisheries discussions, it is contended that the purpose and legal effect of an ILBI as an 'implementing agreement' to UNCLOS should be continually reinforced in BBNJ discussions. Third, in an attempt to resolve the geopolitical issues associated with the interplay between an ILBI and existing arrangements, this book suggests that the term 'undermine' should be interpreted in line with UNFSA and taken to mean 'undermine the effectiveness or reduce the effectiveness.'[62] Thus, measures adopted under an ILBI that strengthen and elaborate upon existing obligations or promote the capacity, cooperation and coherence of existing bodies should be understood as enhancing the effectiveness of the current international law framework, not reducing it. Lastly, while it is evident that the adjacency issue is likely to stoke fears of creeping coastal State jurisdiction, this must be balanced against the fact that MPAs are most successful when they involve all relevant stakeholders in their development and implementation. An ILBI should therefore provide an obligation to consult adjacent coastal States and take their interests into account when a high seas MPA is to be established in proximity to a coastal State.[63]

Turning to the third element of the BBNJ package deal, Chapter 6 sets out a number of compromise solutions to overcome sticking points relating to EIAs. For example, as delegations continue to disagree on the extent to which the EIA process should be internationalised under an ILBI, this book proposes a multi-layered management approach, in an attempt to break the deadlock on this issue. Under this approach, States could govern the EIA process for activities that are likely to have a minor or transitory impact, with a compliance committee

61 See Chapter 2, Section 2.3.3.

62 Glen Wright et al, 'High Seas Fisheries: What Role for a New International Instrument?' (Study No. 03/16, IDDRI, August 2016) 10.

63 Alex Oude Elferink, 'Coastal States and MPAs in ABNJ: Ensuring Consistency with the LOSC' in David Freestone (ed), *Conserving Biodiversity in Areas beyond National Jurisdiction* (Brill Nijhoff, 2019) 83.

providing limited oversight to ensure consistency in approach.[64] However, a scientific and technical body should be charged with overseeing the EIA process for activities likely to have more than a minor or transitory impact or that are likely to occur in a sensitive or vulnerable marine area. This body could provide advice to the relevant decision-making body on whether and how the proposed activity should proceed. In this way, a multi-layered management approach could provide an appropriate compromise solution, one that ensures protection by introducing a certain degree of international scrutiny and oversight to the EIA process.

Chapter 7 of this book identifies a number of mechanisms BBNJ negotiators could use in an effort to enhance, stimulate and strengthen existing UNCLOS requirements for CBTT in Part XIV of UNCLOS. These mechanisms include (1) formalising a clearing-house mechanism; (2) enhancing the data-sharing infrastructure; (3) establishing an innovative funding model; and (4) developing an effective monitoring, review and follow-up procedure. In order for these mechanisms to be effective, this book contends that they will need to be underpinned by a meaningful duty to cooperate. While the duty to cooperate in Article 197 of UNCLOS has been recognised as forming part of customary international law, the nature and content of the obligation to cooperate are not spelled out in Part XIV and remain unclear.[65] The development of an ILBI therefore presents an opportunity to define, codify and operationalise this duty in order to enhance and strengthen existing UNCLOS requirements relating to CBTT.

8.4 Looking over the horizon—the future prospects of an ILBI

Looking to the future, it is uncertain what long-term effect the COVID-19 pandemic will have on the BBNJ negotiation process. While it resulted in negotiations moving mostly online, it set negotiations back months or even years and arguably the significant gap between IGC meetings contributed to the failure to reach a final agreement by the conclusion of IGC 4. As this book has taken the step of investigating and proposing potential areas of compromise, this work could take on an even greater relevance in a post-pandemic BBNJ context as governments seek to steer negotiations back on track. This book has been researched and written as a comprehensive guide that may be of use to BBNJ negotiators as they embark on the next round of negotiations to devise an instrument that will adequately reflect contemporary maritime realities as well as those anticipated in the future. It may also be of assistance to policymakers and their legal advisors within governments who will have the burden of implementing the provisions of

64 Emily Barritt and Jorge E. Viñuales, 'Legal Scan: A Conservation Agenda for Biodiversity beyond National Jurisdiction' (Cambridge Centre for Environment, Energy and Natural Resource Governance, University of Cambridge, May 2016) 84.

65 Irini Papanicolopulu, 'Section 4 Cooperation among International Organizations' in Alexander Proelss (ed), *United Nations Convention on the Law of the Sea: A Commentary* (C.H. Beck, 2017) 1808, 1811.

an ILBI, and for them a comprehensive understanding of the BBNJ process will be a valuable tool in this task.

While the focus of this book has been predominately on the four thematic clusters of the package deal, important cross-cutting issues have also been discussed, including the potential role of modern governance principles and approaches as well as institutional arrangements. Due to the manifold and complex challenges that confront BBNJ, it is currently one of the most interesting and challenging areas of growth in the law of the sea and is sure to prove a fertile ground for further research in the future. A number of areas warrant further exploration including the question of how an ILBI could contribute to making ABNJ more resilient to anthropogenic stressors, particularly climate change-related impacts.

The 2019 Intergovernmental Science-Policy Platform on Biodiversity and Ecosystem Services (IPBES) biodiversity assessment report identified climate change as one of five direct drivers of change in nature.[66] The report notes that climate change is already impacting marine biodiversity at both the ecosystem and genetic levels.[67] Ocean warming, acidification and deoxygenation and the changes associated with them 'may threaten the biodiversity, productivity, and resilience of the ocean globally' and could undermine conservation efforts in ABNJ.[68] Popova et al argue that a conservation regime for ABNJ requires 'climate-proofing' as areas deemed important for protection now may change in the future due to climate-driven impacts.[69] Thus, BBNJ negotiators may need to consider approaches that 'go beyond currently proposed adaptive management.'[70] Yadav and Gjerde have suggested using seven key principles in ABNJ management to enhance the resilience of the oceans to climate change impacts.[71] These seven principles include: (1) maintaining diversity and redundancy, (2) managing connectivity, (3) managing slow variables and feedbacks, (4) fostering complex adaptive systems thinking, (5) encouraging learning, (6) broadening participation and (7) promoting polycentric governance.[72] While spatial constraints have prevented a thorough examination of these principles in this book, the adoption

66 E.S. Brondizio et al (eds), 'Global Assessment Report on Biodiversity and Ecosystem Services of the Intergovernmental Science-Policy Platform on Biodiversity and Ecosystem Services' (IPBES Secretariat, 2019).

67 IPBES, 'Nature's Dangerous Decline "Unprecedented" Species Extinction Rates 'Accelerating' (Media Release, 2019) <https://ipbes.net/news/Media-Release-Global-Assessment>.

68 Siddharth Skekhar Yadav and Kristina Maria Gjerde, 'The Ocean, Climate Change and Resilience: Making Ocean Areas beyond National Jurisdiction More Resilient to Climate Change and Other Anthropogenic Activities' (2020) 122 *Marine Policy* 104184, 1–9, 2.

69 Ekaterina Popova et al, 'Ecological Connectivity between the Areas beyond National Jurisdiction and Coastal Waters: Safeguarding Interests of Coastal Communities in Developing Countries' (2019) 104 *Marine Policy* 90, 98.

70 Ibid.

71 Yadav and Gjerde (n 68) 3.

72 These principles were originally presented in R. Biggs, M. Schluter and M.L. Schoon (eds), *Principles for Building Resilience: Sustaining Ecosystem Services in Socio-Ecological Systems* (Cambridge University Press, 2015).

of a resilience approach in an ILBI could assist in identifying priority areas for the establishment of ABMTs and help marine ecosystems to cope with current and future environmental threats.

Another issue that is receiving growing attention is the settlement of disputes under an ILBI. While delegations generally agree that any disputes concerning the interpretation or application of the ILBI should be settled by peaceful means, they have been unable to agree on an appropriate dispute settlement mechanism.[73] Some delegates argue that the provisions set out in Part XV of UNCLOS should apply *mutatis mutandis* to any dispute between States Parties, others suggest giving relevant jurisdiction to ITLOS, and a number favour States Parties being given the choice to select the appropriate mechanism.[74] While it is open to debate which mechanism will be more effective or successful in the BBNJ context, Shi has proposed four criteria to use in assessing potential mechanisms.[75] These criteria are (1) incorporating the principle of State consent in international law, (2) ensuring cost-effectiveness in addressing disputes, (3) not undermining relevant existing instruments, frameworks and bodies and (4) maintaining the balance of interests between States.[76]

Shi's final criterion correlates with an overarching theme in this book, namely, that just like UNCLOS, the key to achieving an effective ILBI will be finding (and maintaining) a delicate balance between the competing interests of different States. As Oxman notes 'international law at any given time represents an equilibrium between opposing pressures.'[77] If the wish of the international community is to establish an ILBI of a universally acceptable character, the instrument will need to be the product of trade-offs and concessions.[78] To quote the President of UNCLOS III (1973–1980) Hamilton Shirley Amerasinghe, 'there will need to be a considerable mutual accommodation and a determined political will to subordinate national interests to the transcendental'[79] objective of protecting BBNJ for present and future generations. While this book has focused on the proposal of a series of macro and micro compromise solutions for the package deal, the same reasoning should be applied to other BBNJ issues, including the settlement of disputes. This issue and others are sure to keep legal commentators and academics busy for a number of years as the international community begins to turn the page on a new chapter in ocean governance.

73 Humphries and Harden-Davies (n 33) 5.

74 Summary of IGC 3 (n 14) 19.

75 Yubing Shi, 'Settlement of Disputes in a BBNJ Agreement: Options and Analysis' (2020) 122 *Marine Policy* 104156, 1–10.

76 Ibid, 4–6.

77 Bernard H. Oxman, 'The Territorial Temptation: A Siren Song at Sea' (2006) 100(4) *The American Journal of International Law* 830, 850.

78 Leary (n 25) 28.

79 Statement by H. Shirley Amerasinghe, 'The Third United Nations Conference on the Law of the Sea' in Myron H. Nordquist (ed), *United Nations Convention on the Law of the Sea 1982: A Commentary* (Martinus Nijhoff Publishers, 1985) 1.

Of course, writing a new chapter for the law of the sea was never going to be an easy task. In the current political and economic climate, there is little appetite to negotiate new treaties. Regrettably, many efforts to solve environmental issues at the international level meet with limited success or even outright failure.[80] Like all diplomatic negotiations, the main challenge is not only bringing all relevant States to the negotiating table but finding innovative ways to keep them there. In concluding this book, it is clear that the development of an ILBI will rest on four important factors: (1) compromise, (2) strategic retreat, (3) political will and (4) bridge-building to arrive at decisions acceptable to all stakeholders.[81] While one must be cautious about speculating too far on what future negotiations may bring,[82] this book provides a timely contribution to efforts within the UNGA by providing insight into the trade-offs that will need to be made to devise a constructive and effective approach to the conservation and sustainable use of BBNJ and proposing a course of action the international community could follow in order to find a pragmatic way forward. Overall, this book has offered a blueprint for an ILBI, one that lays the foundations for building a bridge of compromise over the troubled waters of ABNJ.

References

Alvarenga, Karen, Kati Kulovesi, Elisa Morgera and Cecilia Vaverka, 'Summary of the Working Group on Marine Biodiversity Beyond Areas of National Jurisdiction: 13–17 February 2006' *Earth Negotiations Bulletin* (Online Bulletin, 20 February 2006) <https://enb.iisd.org/download/pdf/enb2525e.pdf> accessed 31 March 2022.

Amerasinghe, H. Shirley, 'The Third United Nations Conference on the Law of the Sea' in Myron H. Nordquist (ed), *United Nations Convention on the Law of the Sea 1982: A Commentary* (Martinus Nijhoff Publishers, 1985).

Barnes, Richard, 'The Proposed LOSC Implementation Agreement on Areas Beyond National Jurisdiction and Its Impact on International Fisheries Law' (2016) 31(4) *The International Journal of Marine and Coastal Law* 583–619. DOI: 10.1163/15718085-12341411.

Barnes, Richard, David Freestone and David M. Ong, 'The Law of the Sea: Progress and Prospects' in Richard Barnes, David Freestone and David M. Ong (eds), *The Law of the Sea Progress and Prospects* (Oxford University Press, 2006) 1. DOI: 10.1093/acprof:oso/9780199299614.003.0001.

80 Oran R. Young and Olav Schram Stokke, 'Why Is It Hard to Solve Environmental Problems? The Perils of Institutional Reductionism and Institutional Overload' (2020) 20 *International Environmental Agreements* 5–19, 5.

81 Eden Charles, 'Foreword' in Glen Wright et al (eds), 'The Long & Winding Road: Negotiating a Treaty for the Conservation and Sustainable Use of Marine Biodiversity in Areas beyond National Jurisdiction' (Study No. 8/2018, IDDRI, August 2018) 5.

82 Richard Barnes, 'The Proposed LOSC Implementation Agreement on Areas beyond National Jurisdiction and Its Impact on International Fisheries Law' (2016) 31(4) *The International Journal of Marine and Coastal Law* 583, 585.

Barritt, Emily and Jorge E. Viñuales, *Legal Scan: A Conservation Agenda for Biodiversity Beyond National Jurisdiction* (Cambridge Centre for Environment, Energy and Natural Resource Governance, University of Cambridge, May 2016).

Biggs, R, M. Schlüter and M.L. Schoon (eds), *Principles for Building Resilience: Sustaining Ecosystem Services in Socio-Ecological Systems* (Cambridge University Press, 2015). DOI: https://doi.org/10.1017/CBO9781316014240.

Brondizio, E.S, J. Settele, S. Díaz and H.T. Ngo, *Global Assessment Report on Biodiversity and Ecosystem Services of the Intergovernmental Science-Policy Platform on Biodiversity and Ecosystem Services* (IPBES Secretariat, 2019).

Butler, W.E, 'Grotius and the Law of the Sea' in Hedley Bull, Benedict Kingsbury and Adam Roberts (eds), *Hugo Grotius and International Relations* (Clarendon, 1992) 209. DOI: 10.1093/0198277717.003.0006.

Caminos, Hugo and Michael R. Molitor, 'Progressive Development of International Law and the Package Deal' (1985) 79 *American Journal of International Law* 871–890. DOI: 10.2307/2201830.

Charles, Eden, 'Foreword' in Glen Wright et al, *The Long & Winding Road: Negotiating a Treaty for the Conservation and Sustainable Use of Marine Biodiversity in Areas Beyond National Jurisdiction* (Study No. 8/2018, IDDRI, August 2018).

Danilenko, G.M, *Law-Making in the International Community* (Martinus Nijhoff Publishers, 1993).

De Santo, Elizabeth M, Elizabeth Mendenhall, Elizabeth Nyman and Rachel Tiller, 'Stuck in the Middle with You (and Not Much Time Left): The Third Intergovernmental Conference on Biodiversity Beyond National Jurisdiction' (2020) 117 *Marine Policy* 103957: 1–9. DOI: 10.1016/j.marpol.2020.103957.

Development of an International Legally Binding Instrument Under the United Nations Convention on the Law of the Sea on the Conservation and Sustainable Use of Marine Biological Diversity of Areas Beyond National Jurisdiction, GA Res 69/292, UN Doc A/RES/69/292 (6 July 2015, adopted 19 June 2015).

Draft Text of an Agreement Under the United Nations Convention on the Law of the Sea on the Conservation and Sustainable Use of Marine Biological Diversity of Areas Beyond National Jurisdiction, UN Doc A/CONF.232/2019/6 (17 May 2019) <https://documents-dds-ny.un.org/doc/UNDOC/GEN/N19/146/28/PDF/N1914628.pdf?OpenElement> accessed 31 March 2022.

Group of 77, 'Statement on Behalf of the Group of 77 and China by H.E. Ambassador Feda Abdelhady-Nasser, State of Palestine, at the Opening of the Third Session of the Intergovernmental Conference on an International Legally Binding Instrument under UNCLOS on the Conservation and Sustainable Use of Marine Biological Diversity of Areas Beyond National Jurisdiction' (New York, 19 August 2019) <http://statements.unmeetings.org/media2/21996878/palestine-obo-g77-and-china.pdf> accessed 31 March 2022.

Hoegh-Guldberg Ove, Transform Aqorau, Ragnar Arnason, Thiraphong Chansiri, Nelson Del Rio, Henry Demone, Sylvia Earle, Mary H. Feeley, Dimitri Gutierrez, Ray Hilborn, Naoko Ishii, Chris Lischewski, Jane Lubenchenco, Kim Anh Nguyen, David Obura, H.E. Rolph Payet, Tuiloma Neroni Slade, John Tanzer, Johán H. Williams, Dawn J. Wright and Jintao Xu, *Indispensable Ocean: Aligning Ocean Health and Human Well-being* (Guidance from the Blue Ribbon Panel to the Global Partnership for Oceans No 82651, 2013) <http://documents1.worldbank

.org/curated/en/111381468155703584/pdf/826510WP0Indis00Box3798 62B00PUBLIC0.pdf> accessed 31 March 2022.

Humphries, Fran and Harriet Harden-Davies, 'Practical Policy Solutions for the Final Stage of BBNJ Treaty Negotiations' (2020) 122 *Marine Policy* 104214: 1-7. DOI: 10.1016/j.marpol.2020.104214.

International Legally Binding Instrument under the United Nations Convention on the Law of the Sea on the Conservation and Sustainable Use of Marine Biological Diversity of Areas Beyond National Jurisdiction, GA Res 72/249, UN Doc A/RES/72/249 (19 January 2018, adopted on 24 December 2017).

IPBES, 'Nature's Dangerous Decline "Unprecedented" Species Extinction Rates "Accelerating" (Media Release, 2019) <https://ipbes.net/news/Media-Release-Global-Assessment> accessed 31 March 2022.

Kantai, Tallash, Jennifer Bansard, Tasha Goldberg, Katarina Hovden and Asterios Tsioumanis, 'Third Session of the Intergovernmental Conference (IGC) on the Conservation and Sustainable Use of Marine Biodiversity of Areas Beyond National Jurisdiction: 19–30 August 2019' *Earth Negotiations Bulletin* (Online Bulletin, 19 August 2019a) 1 <https://enb.iisd.org/download/pdf/enb25208e.pdf> accessed 31 March 2022.

Kantai, Tallash, Jennifer Bansard, Tasha Goldberg, Katarina Hovden and Asterios Tsioumanis, 'Summary of the Third Session of the Intergovernmental Conference on the Conservation and Sustainable Use of Marine Biodiversity of Areas Beyond National Jurisdiction: 19–30 August 2019' *Earth Negotiations Bulletin* (Online Bulletin, 2 September 2019b) <https://enb.iisd.org/download/pdf/enb25218e.pdf> accessed 31 March 2022.

Kantai, Tallash and Paola Bettelli, 'Summary of the Fourth Session of the Intergovernmental Conference on an International Legally Binding Instrument under the UN Convention on the Law of the Sea on the Conservation and Sustainable Use of Marine Biodiversity of Areas beyond National Jurisdiction: 7-18 March 2022' *Earth Negotiations Bulletin* (Online Bulletin, 21 March 2022) ('Summary of IGC 4'). <https://enb.iisd.org/sites/default/files/2022-03/enb25225e.pdf> accessed 31 March 2022.

Leary, David, 'Agreeing to Disagree on What We Have or Have Not Agreed on: The Current State of Play of the BBNJ Negotiations on the Status of Marine Genetic Resources in Areas Beyond National Jurisdiction' (2019) 99 *Marine Policy* 21–29. DOI: 10.1016/j.marpol.2018.10.031.

Leary, David and S. Kim Juniper, 'Addressing the Marine Genetic Resources Issue: Is the Debate Heading in the Wrong Direction?' in Clive Schofield, Seokwoo Lee and Moon-Sang Kwon (eds), *The Limits of Maritime Jurisdiction* (Koninklijke Brill, 2014) 769.

Letter Dated 13 February 2015 from the Co-Chairs of the Ad Hoc Open-ended Informal Working Group to the President of the General Assembly, UN Doc A/69/780, United Nations General Assembly, 69th Sess, Item 74(a) (13 February 2015) <https://documents-dds-ny.un.org/doc/UNDOC/GEN/N15/041/82/PDF/N1504182.pdf?OpenElement> accessed 31 March 2022.

Long, R. and Z. Sun (eds) 'Biodiversity Beyond National Jurisdiction: Towards the Development of a Balanced, Effective and Universal International Agreement' (*Workshop and Side Events Report, World Maritime University Workshop*, 7 February 2019).

Lubchenco, Jane and Steven D. Gaines, 'A New Narrative for the Ocean' (2019) 364 (6444) *Science* 911. DOI: 10.1126/science.aay2241.

McGrath, Matt, 'UN Treaty Would Protect High Seas from Over Exploitation' *BBC News* (Web Page, 4 September 2018) quoting Professor Alex Rogers <https://www.bbc.com/news/science-environment-45397674> accessed 31 March 2022.

Millicay, Fernanda, 'Marine Genetic Resources of Areas Beyond National Jurisdiction and Intellectual Property Rights' in Tomas Heidar (ed) *New Knowledge and Changing Circumstances in the Law of the Sea* (Brill Nijhoff, 2020) 65. DOI: https://doi.org/10.1163/9789004437753_006.

Morgera, Elisa, Asheline Appleton, Daniela Diz and Asterios Tsioumanis, 'Summary of the First Session of the Intergovernmental Conference on an International Legally Binding Instrument under the UN Convention on the Law of the Sea on the Conservation and Sustainable Use of Marine Biodiversity of Areas Beyond National Jurisdiction 4–17 September 2018' *Earth Negotiations Bulletin* (online, 20 September 2018) <https://enb.iisd.org/download/pdf/enb25179e.pdf> accessed 31 March 2022.

Oude Elferink, Alex, 'Coastal States and MPAs in ABNJ: Ensuring Consistency with the LOSC' in David Freestone (ed), *Conserving Biodiversity in Areas Beyond National Jurisdiction* (Brill Nijhoff, 2019) 56. DOI: https://doi.org/10.1163/9789004391703_004.

Oxman, Bernard H, 'The Territorial Temptation: A Siren Song at Sea' (2006) 100(4) *The American Journal of International Law* 830–851. DOI: 10.1017/S0002930000031912.

Papanicolopulu, Irini, 'Section 4 Cooperation Among International Organizations' in Alexander Proelss (ed), *United Nations Convention on the Law of the Sea A Commentary* (C.H. Beck, 2017) 1808.

Popova, Ekaterina, David Vousden, Warwick H.H. Sauer, Essam Y. Mohammed, Valerie Allain, Nicola Downey-Breedt, Ruth Fletcher, Kristina M. Gjerde, Patrick N. Halpin, Stephen Kelly, David Obura, Gretta Pecl, Michael Roberts, Dionysios E. Raitsos, Melita Samoilys, Ussif Rashid Sumaila, Sean Tracey and Andrew Yool, 'Ecological Connectivity between Areas Beyond National Jurisdiction and Coastal Waters: Safeguarding Interests of Coastal Communities in Developing Countries' (2019) 104 *Marine Policy* 90–102. DOI: 10.1016/j.marpol.2019.02.050.

Ricard, Pascale, 'Marine Biodiversity Beyond National Jurisdiction: The Launch of an Intergovernmental Conference for the Adoption of a Legally Binding Instrument under the UNCLOS' (2018) 19(4) *Maritime Safety and Security Law Journal* 84–102.

Shelton, Dinah, 'Common Concern of Humanity' (2009) 39(2) *Environmental Policy and Law* 83–86.

Shi, Yubing, 'Settlement of Disputes in a BBNJ Agreement: Options and Analysis' (2020) 122 *Marine Policy* 104156: 1–10. DOI: 10.1016/j.marpol.2020.104156.

Statement by the President of the Conference at the Closing of the Third Session of the Intergovernmental Conference on an International Legally Binding Instrument under the United Nations Convention on the Law of the Sea on the Conservation and Sustainable Use of Marine Biological Diversity of Areas Beyond National Jurisdiction, UN Doc A/CONF.232/2019/10 (13 September 2019) <https://documents-dds-ny.un.org/doc/UNDOC/GEN/N19/281/55/PDF/N1928155.pdf?OpenElement> accessed 31 March 2022.

Tiller, Rachel, Elizabeth De Santo, Elizabeth Mendenhall and Elizabeth Nyman, 'The Once and Future Treaty: Towards a New Regime for Biodiversity in Areas Beyond National Jurisdiction' (2019) 99 *Marine Policy* 239–242. DOI: 10.1016/j.marpol.2018.10.046.

Tvedt, Morten Walløe and Ane E. Jørem, 'Bioprospecting in the High Seas: Regulatory Options for Benefit Sharing' (2013) 16(3–4) *The Journal of World Intellectual Property* 150–167. DOI: 10.1002/jwip.12010.

United Nations Convention on the Law of the Sea, opened for signature 10 December 1982 (1982) 1833 *UNTS* 397 (entered into force 16 November 1994) (UNCLOS).

Wright, Glen, Julien Rochette, Lucie Blom, Duncan Currie, Carole Durussel, Kristina Gjerde and Sebastien Unger, 'High Seas Fisheries: What Role for a New International Instrument?' (Study No. 03/16, IDDRI, August 2016).

Wright, Glen, Julien Rochette, Kristina Gjerde and Isabel Seeger, 'The Long & Winding Road: Negotiating a Treaty for the Conservation and Sustainable Use of Marine Biodiversity in Areas Beyond National Jurisdiction' (Study No. 8/2018, IDDRI, August 2018).

Wysocki, Ina Tessnow-von, 'Slow Progress in the Third BBNJ Meeting: Negotiations are Moving-but Sideways' (Maripoldata, 6 September 2019) <https://www.maripoldata.eu/slow-progress-in-the-third-bbnj-meeting-negotiations-are-moving-but-sideways/> accessed 31 March 2022.

Yadav, Siddharth Skekhar and Kristina Maria Gjerde, 'The Ocean, Climate Change and Resilience: Making Ocean Areas Beyond National Jurisdiction more Resilient to Climate Change and Other Anthropogenic Activities' (2020) 122 *Marine Policy* 104184: 1–9. DOI: 10.1016/j.marpol.2020.104184.

Young, Oran R. and Olav Schram Stokke, 'Why Is It Hard to Solve Environmental Problems? The Perils of Institutional Reductionism and Institutional Overload' (2020) 20 *International Environmental Agreements* 5–19. DOI: 10.1007/s10784-020-09468-6.

Appendix 1 Section B of the PrepCom Report—areas of divergence

- The common heritage of mankind and the freedom of the high seas;
- With regard to MGRs, including the question of the sharing of benefits, further discussions required on whether the ILBI should regulate access to MGRs; the nature of these resources; what benefits should be shared; whether to address intellectual property rights and whether to provide for the monitoring of the utilisation of MGRs of ABNJ;
- With regard to ABMTs, including MPAs, further discussions required in respect to the most appropriate decision-making and institutional set up;
- With regard to EIAs, further discussions required regarding the degree to which the process should be conducted by States or be 'internationalised' as well as on whether an ILBI should address strategic environmental impact assessments;
- With regard to capacity-building and the transfer of marine technology, further discussions required on the terms and conditions for the transfer of marine technology;
- Further discussions required on institutional arrangements and the relationship between the institutions established under an ILBI and relevant global, regional and sectoral bodies. A related issue that would also require further attention is how to address monitoring, review and compliance;
- With respect to funding, further discussions are required on the scope of the financial resources required and whether a financial mechanism should be established.

DOI: 10.4324/b22996-10

Appendix 2 Comparison of proposed statements of principles for ABNJ

	Freestone	*IUCN*	*Oude Elferink*
Protection and preservation of the marine environment	✓	✓	✓
Conservation of high seas living marine resources and biodiversity	✓		
Conditional freedom of activity on the high seas	✓	✓	
Cooperation	✓	✓	✓
Sustainable and equitable use	✓	✓	✓
Precautionary approach	✓	✓	✓
Ecosystem approach	✓	✓	✓
Transparency and open decision-making processes	✓	✓	✓
Use of best available science	✓		
Responsibility of States to control the actions of the nationals and consequences for breach of international legal obligations	✓		
Public availability of information		✓	✓
Science-based approach to management		✓	✓
Responsibility of States as stewards of the global marine environment		✓	✓
Respect for the law of the sea, particularly UNCLOS and related instruments			✓
Integrated approach			✓

DOI: 10.4324/b22996-11

Appendix 3 Nagoya Protocol on Access to Genetic Resources and the Fair and Equitable Sharing of Benefits arising from their Utilization to the Convention on Biological Diversity, Annex 'Monetary and Non-Monetary Benefits'

Monetary benefits may include, but not be limited to:

(a) Access fees/fee per sample collected or otherwise acquired;
(b) Up-front payments;
(c) Milestone payments;
(d) Payment of royalties;
(e) Licence fees in case of commercialisation;
(f) Special fees to be paid to trust funds supporting conservation and sustainable use of biodiversity;
(g) Salaries and preferential terms where mutually agreed;
(h) Research funding;
(i) Joint ventures;
(j) Joint ownership of relevant intellectual property rights.

Non-monetary benefits may include, but not be limited to:

(a) Sharing of research and development results;
(b) Collaboration, cooperation and contribution in scientific research and development programmes, particularly biotechnological research activities, where possible in the Party providing genetic resources;
(c) Participation in product development;
(d) Collaboration, cooperation and contribution in education and training;
(e) Admittance to *ex situ* facilities of genetic resources and to databases;
(f) Transfer to the provider of the genetic resources of knowledge and technology under fair and most favourable terms, including on concessional and preferential terms where agreed, in particular, knowledge and technology that make use of genetic resources, including biotechnology, or that are relevant to the conservation and sustainable utilisation of biological diversity;
(g) Strengthening capacities for technology transfer;
(h) Institutional capacity-building;

DOI: 10.4324/b22996-12

(i) Human and material resources to strengthen the capacities for the administration and enforcement of access regulations;
(j) Training related to genetic resources with the full participation of countries providing genetic resources, and where possible, in such countries;
(k) Access to scientific information relevant to conservation and sustainable use of biological diversity, including biological inventories and taxonomic studies;
(l) Contributions to the local economy;
(m) Research directed towards priority needs, such as health and food security, taking into account domestic uses of genetic resources in the Party providing genetic resources;
(n) Institutional and professional relationships that can arise from an access and benefit-sharing agreement and subsequent collaborative activities;
(o) Food and livelihood security benefits;
(p) Social recognition;
(q) Joint ownership of relevant intellectual property rights.

Appendix 4 Minimum dataset of information for collectors

- Details about the collector (MSR group or commercial bioprospector);
- The geographical area(s) of sampling (the water column, seabed or both);
- The period of sampling including the start date and duration;
- A description of the research project including access procedure(s) (i.e. use of destructive devices, drilling or other disturbance such as light);
- A description of the targeted resource if possible (type and quantity sought);
- Whether the activity will occur in or around VMEs or EBSAs (i.e. will sampling target fragile ecosystems or species that are rare or sensitive to interference?);
- An evaluation of potential impacts on BBNJ.

DOI: 10.4324/b22996-13

Appendix 5 Comparison of existing criteria to identify priority protection areas

Characteristic	*FAO criteria for VMEs*	*IMO criteria for PSSAs*	*CBD criteria for EBSAs*	*Criteria in PrepCom Report*	*Criteria in Revised Draft Negotiating Text*
Uniqueness and/or rarity	✓	✓	✓	✓	✓
Functional significance of habitat/critical habitat	✓	✓			
Fragility	✓	✓	✓		✓
Life-history traits of component species	✓		✓	✓	✓
Structural complexity	✓				
Dependency		✓		✓	✓
Representativeness		✓		✓	✓
Diversity		✓	✓	✓	✓
Productivity		✓	✓	✓	✓
Spawning or breeding grounds		✓			
Naturalness		✓	✓	✓	✓
Integrity		✓			
Biogeographic importance		✓			
Importance for threatened, endangered or declining species/or habitats			✓	✓	✓
Vulnerability, fragility, sensitivity and slow recovery			✓	✓	✓
Connectivity				✓	✓
Ecological processes				✓	✓
Economic and social factors				✓	✓
Special importance of the species found therein					✓
Cultural factors					✓
Cumulative and transboundary impacts					✓
Adequacy and viability					✓
Replication					✓
Feasibility					✓

DOI: 10.4324/b22996-14

Appendix 6 Article 46 of the Revised Draft Negotiating Text List of CBTT activities

- The sharing of relevant data, information, knowledge and research;
- Information dissemination and awareness-raising;
- The development and strengthening of relevant infrastructure (i.e. equipment);
- The development and strengthening of institutional capacity and national regulatory frameworks or mechanisms;
- The development and strengthening of human resources and technical expertise through research collaboration, technical support, education and training;
- The development and sharing of manuals, guidelines and standards;
- The development of technical, scientific and research programmes, including biotechnological research activities.

DOI: 10.4324/b22996-15

Index

Printed in the United States
by Baker & Taylor Publisher Services